"What a great gift from John and Kyle. Thes[e]
often are left unmined. May they teach us a[...]

John Ortberg, senior pastor of Menlo Church, a[...] [...] *[...] More if You Were More*
Like Me

"In popular Christian culture where contemplation often is dismissed as Buddhist or
New Age, this collection of essays convincingly argues, biblically and historically,
that Spirit-initiated abiding in and communing with the divine presence powerfully
enriches love for God. Here is an *apologia* for a core Christian habit that is crucial
for the good of the soul and the church."

Bruce Demarest, senior professor of Christian formation, Denver Seminary

"We have been waiting a long time for this book . . . a couple of centuries, perhaps.
We've been reading the early Fathers and the Catholic mystics, but few have put into
our hands the rich resources from the evangelical tradition that might help us pray
contemplatively. So with all due respect, let us read . . . and let us pray."

Julie Canlis, adjunct professor of graduate studies in theology, Whitworth University

"This book is an important contribution in a time when there is growing evangelical
interest in contemplative spirituality. For the skeptical, this work addresses many of
the common concerns. For the curious, this is an excellent introduction to the major
themes and unique voices of contemplative spirituality. For all, this is a deep dive
into a broad and rich Christian tradition in which you'll discover hidden treasures
you didn't know were available to you—right here in your very own theological
home. I'm grateful to Strobel and Coe."

Chuck DeGroat, professor of pastoral care and Christian spirituality, senior fellow,
Newbigin House of Studies

"I often get fairly nervous about the trendiness in contemporary spirituality. Therefore,
I am pleased by this new volume which provides some needed context for the historic and contemporary discussion about contemplation in the Christian life. Evangelicals sometimes have strong opinions about contemplation—whether positive or
negative. But sadly, those opinions are too often ignorant of historic Christian practices and relevant theological debates. Thankfully, this volume is aware of the
promises and perils of contemplation and contemplative prayer; consequently, these
authors can help inform our discussion and even our practices. You likely won't
agree with everything here, but you will learn and be challenged."

Kelly M. Kapic, professor of theological studies, Covenant College, author of *Embodied Hope*

"We have needed this resource for quite some time—a thorough consideration of the
character of Christian contemplation that is biblical, historical, theological, comparative, and practical. And thanks to the editorial work of Coe and Strobel we have
it—an invaluable guide to the state of the current evangelical conversation regarding
this essential dimension of the Christian life."

Gordon T. Smith, president and professor of systematic and spiritual theology at Ambrose
University, author of *Called to Be Saints* and *Evangelical, Sacramental, and Pentecostal*

"A collection of essays is tricky business, often some are good and others are poor. Things get even trickier when the topic is somewhat controversial, as contemplation tends to be among evangelicals. Happily, John Coe and Kyle Strobel have done excellent work in *Embracing Contemplation*. The essays are uniformly excellent and present a cogent argument for understanding and practicing a spiritual discipline that has helped believers for hundreds of years. Thanks for a job well done."

Chris Hall, president of Renovaré

"This is a rich collection of essays about the contemplative life. All serious Christians need this wonderful resource."

James M. Houston, emeritus professor of spiritual theology, founding principal of Regent College, Vancouver, Canada

"I am so excited about this work, particularly the aim of it—to generate the right sort of conversation about contemplation, a topic central to any fulsome perspective on Christian spirituality. And what a life-giving conversation it is! Aided by rich historical, biblical, and theological inquiries and followed by constructive proposals, this work clearly demonstrates the fact that contemplation is fundamental to a maturing Christian life. Thanks be to God!"

Ruth Haley Barton, founder of the Transforming Center, author of *Invitation to Solitude and Silence, Sacred Rhythms,* and *Invitation to Retreat*

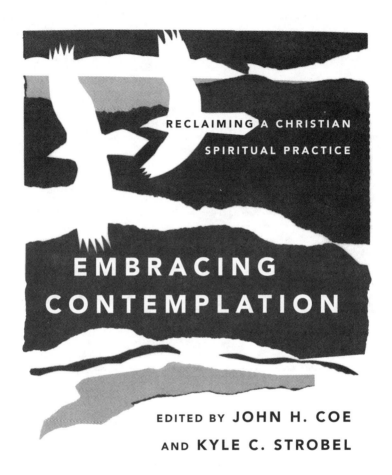

RECLAIMING A CHRISTIAN
SPIRITUAL PRACTICE

EMBRACING
CONTEMPLATION

EDITED BY JOHN H. COE
AND KYLE C. STROBEL

IVP Academic

An imprint of InterVarsity Press
Downers Grove, Illinois

InterVarsity Press
P.O. Box 1400, Downers Grove, IL 60515-1426
ivpress.com
email@ivpress.com

InterVarsity Press® is the book-publishing division of InterVarsity Christian Fellowship/USA®, a
movement of students and faculty active on campus at hundreds of universities, colleges, and schools
of nursing in the United States of America, and a member movement of the International Fellowship of
Evangelical Students. For information about local and regional activities, visit intervarsity.org.

Scripture quotations, unless otherwise noted, are from The Holy Bible, English Standard Version,
copyright © 2001 by Crossway Bibles, a division of Good News Publishers. Used by permission. All rights reserved.

The following are reproduced by permission of the Journal of Spiritual Formation and Soul Care: "'To Gaze on the
Beauty of the Lord': The Evangelical Resistance and Retrieval of Contemplation" by Tom Schwanda; "In Your Light
They Shall See Light: A Theological Prolegomena for Contemplation" by Kyle Strobel; "Contemplation and
Contemplative Prayer" by James C. Wilhoit; "Is Thoughtless Prayer Really Christian? A Biblical/Evangelical
Response to Evagrius of Pontus" by Evan B. Howard; and "The Controversy Over Contemplation
and Contemplative Prayer: A Historical, Theological, and Biblical Resolution" by John Coe.

Permission has been granted by both Hans Boersma and Eerdmans Publishing Company to republish an essay
from his book The Beatific Vision: Christocentricity in the Christian Tradition (Eerdmans, 2018), published here
as "The Beatific Vision: Contemplating Christ as the Future Present."

Chapter 11 is adapted from "Centering Prayer" by James Wilhoit in Life in the Spirit: Spiritual Formation in
Theological Perspective, ed. Jeffrey P. Greenman and George Kalantzis. Copyright © 2010 by Jeffrey P. Greenman
and George Kalantzis. Used by permission of InterVarsity Press, P.O. Box 1400, Downers Grove, IL 60515,
www.ivpress.com. An earlier version was published in the Journal of Spiritual Formation and Soul Care.

Cover design: Cindy Kiple
Interior design: Daniel van Loon
Images: Ravens, Wallington, John (Contemporary Artist) / Private Collection / Bridgeman Images

ISBN 978-0-8308-5230-7 (print)
ISBN 978-0-8308-7368-5 (digital)

Printed in the United States of America ∞

InterVarsity Press is committed to ecological stewardship and to the conservation of natural resources
in all our operations. This book was printed using sustainably sourced paper.

Library of Congress Cataloging-in-Publication Data
Names: Coe, John H., editor.
Title: Embracing contemplation : reclaiming a Christian spiritual practice /
  edited by John H. Coe and Kyle C. Strobel.
Description: Downers Grove : InterVarsity Press, 2019. | Includes index. |
  Identifiers: LCCN 2018050677 (print) | LCCN 2018054284 (ebook) | ISBN
  9780830873685 (eBook) | ISBN 9780830852307 (pbk. : alk. paper)
Subjects: LCSH: Contemplation. | Spiritual formation. | Spiritual
  life—Christianity. | Evangelicalism.
Classification: LCC BV5091.C7 (ebook) | LCC BV5091.C7 E43 2019 (print) | DDC
  248.3/4—dc23
LC record available at https://lccn.loc.gov/2018050677

P   25   24   23   22   21   20   19   18   17   16   15   14   13   12   11   10   9   8   7   6   5   4   3   2   1

Y   38   37   36   35   34   33   32   31   30   29   28   27   26   25   24   23   22   21   20   19

CONTENTS

ACKNOWLEDGMENTS   *ix*

INTRODUCTION Retrieving the Heart of the Christian Faith
—*John H. Coe and Kyle C. Strobel*   *1*

PART 1 HISTORICAL INQUIRIES

1 The Controversy Over Contemplation and Contemplative Prayer:
A Historical, Theological, and Biblical Resolution—*John H. Coe*   *19*

2 Is Thoughtless Prayer Really Christian? A Biblical/Evangelical
Response to Evagrius of Pontus—*Evan B. Howard*   *37*

3 Medieval Ressourcement—*Greg Peters*   *56*

4 Sabbatical Contemplation? Retrieving a Strand in
Reformed Theology—*Ashley Cocksworth*   *74*

5 "To Gaze on the Beauty of the Lord": The Evangelical
Resistance and Retrieval of Contemplation—*Tom Schwanda*   *95*

6 Christian Contemplation and the Cross: The Pathway
to Life—*Diane Chandler*   *118*

PART 2 CONSTRUCTIVE PROPOSALS

7 Biblical Spirituality and Contemplative Spirituality—*Steven L. Porter*   *139*

8 Contemplation by Son and Spirit: Reforming the
Ascent of the Soul to God—*Kyle C. Strobel*   *166*

9 Gospel-Centered Contemplation? A Proposal—*Ryan A. Brandt*   *185*

10 The Beatific Vision: Contemplating Christ as the
Future Present—*Hans Boersma*   *203*

11 Contemplative and Centering Prayer—*James Wilhoit*   *224*

12 Contemplative Prayer in the Evangelical and
Pentecostal Traditions: A Comparative Study—*Simon Chan*   *241*

13 A Distinctively Christian Contemplation:
A Comparison with Other Religions—*Glen G. Scorgie*   *259*

CONCLUSION Recovering Contemplation
—*John H. Coe and Kyle C. Strobel*   *283*

CONTRIBUTORS   *287*

INDEXES—General *289*—Scripture *291*

ACKNOWLEDGMENTS

THE ORIGINAL IDEA FOR THIS VOLUME was birthed out of a discussion on contemplation and contemplative prayer from the 65th Annual Meeting of the Evangelical Theological Society in Baltimore in 2013. Out of that initial engagement of the question, five essays were published in the *Journal of Spiritual Formation and Soul Care* 7, no. 1 (spring 2014). The contributors of those essays adapted and/or developed their work for this volume. Thank you to the *Journal of Spiritual Formation and Soul Care* for allowing us to republish the following essays: "'To Gaze on the Beauty of the Lord': The Evangelical Resistance and Retrieval of Contemplation" by Tom Schwanda; "In Your Light They Shall See Light: A Theological Prolegomena for Contemplation" by Kyle Strobel; "Contemplation and Contemplative Prayer" by James C. Wilhoit; "Is Thoughtless Prayer Really Christian? A Biblical/Evangelical Response to Evagrius of Pontus" by Evan B. Howard; and "The Controversy Over Contemplation and Contemplative Prayer: A Historical, Theological, and Biblical Resolution" by John Coe. Furthermore, permission has been granted by both Hans Boersma and Eerdmans Publishing Company to republish an essay from his book *The Beatific Vision: Christocentricity in the Christian Tradition* (Eerdmans, 2018), published here as "The Beatific Vision: Contemplating Christ as the Future Present."

We would like to thank Biola University and Talbot School of Theology for creating the context to wrestle through the Christian spiritual tradition in distinctively evangelical ways, and for their continued support of the Institute of Spiritual Formation. Our colleagues as well as students here at the institute have been a blessing and encouragement to us, and we cannot imagine a better context to attend to these questions and practices. In fact, there is little doubt in our minds that our students will move this discussion and life of contemplation beyond where we are able to go.

Special thanks goes to those who assisted in the production of this volume. Several students helped in various ways on the manuscript, with editing and formatting, and we are grateful for their service to us in that way, in particular Alex Middleton, Garrett Shipley, and Scuter Koo. We would also like to thank InterVarsity Press and our editor David McNutt for their excitement about this project and their continued support of us throughout. To all of the contributors who were willing to write for this volume, thank you for your work here. Our hope is that it is a blessing to those who read it, that it leads to a deeper conversation on the nature of both contemplation and prayer, and that it ends in our adoring and loving God himself.

INTRODUCTION

Retrieving the Heart of the Christian Faith

JOHN H. COE AND KYLE C. STROBEL

[The] great part of that work of a Christian ought to be contemplation.

JONATHAN EDWARDS

THERE HAS BEEN A GROWING INTEREST in spiritual formation over the past several decades. The spiritual formation discussion has never become a unified movement, nor does it entail a singular set of beliefs, regardless of what some critics might claim. Rather, it would be more accurate to claim that a conversation has arisen concerning what a distinctively evangelical view of the Christian life might entail. This has led to many different focal points, from spiritual disciplines to the spiritual tradition, from sanctification to piety, to an explicit excavation of evangelicalism's own spiritual history.[1] At its best, the spiritual formation conversation seeks to attend deeply to Scripture, the spiritual and theological traditions broadly, and the Protestant tradition more narrowly, to provide a robustly spiritual theology for the sake of faithfulness in the church today. At its worst, the spiritual formation conversation has often failed to take theology seriously, focusing simply on disciplines or spiritual practices that it fails to understand or that don't make sense according to the theological imperatives of Protestantism.

This volume seeks to play to the best of the spiritual formation conversation, not by providing the final word on the topic of contemplation, but

---

[1] For the most recent and substantial treatment of this, see D. Bruce Hindmarsh, *The Spirit of Early Evangelicalism: True Religion in a Modern World* (Oxford: Oxford University Press, 2018).

by helping to generate the right sort of conversation. Contemplation has always been a central topic of Christian spirituality broadly and Protestant spirituality more specifically. Furthermore, contemplation has often been assumed as a key aspect of spiritual formation, but it hasn't really been assessed to the degree necessary in our own contemporary discussions. Instead of providing a single view, arguing for a theoretical and practical approach to contemplation and/or contemplative prayer (more on this term later), the goal of this volume is to bring together authors across the Protestant spectrum whose essays will prod and guide the reader to think and attend more deeply to the contemplative dimension of the Christian faith. While the contributors of this volume may differ on various matters, such as the nature and validity of contemplative prayer, and forms of it like centering prayer, as well as what it entails to read the spiritual tradition in a distinctively *evangelical* sort of way, we believe it is important to pull from various voices to foster a broader conversation. The differing viewpoints of the authors, therefore, are meant to encourage a deeper and more theologically robust conversation about contemplation and prayer for spiritual formation in the evangelical church today. But this immediately raises a question: What is a distinctively evangelical understanding of contemplation?

A DISTINCTIVELY EVANGELICAL UNDERSTANDING OF CONTEMPLATION

Richard Lovelace, in his work *Dynamics of Spiritual Life*, coined the term "the sanctification gap" to speak to modern evangelicalism's neglect of their own spiritual tradition. In his words, "There seemed to be a sanctification gap among Evangelicals, a peculiar conspiracy somehow to mislay the Protestant tradition of spiritual growth and concentrate on frantic witnessing activity, sermons on John 3:16 and theological arguments over eschatological subtleties."[2] While the concentrations may have changed, Lovelace's critique remains as accurate now as it did nearly four decades ago. Even with the revival of interest in spiritual formation, a term used to name the nature, processes, and directives of redeemed Christian existence, there has not always been a recovery of a distinctively evangelical understanding of

---

[2]Richard F. Lovelace, *Dynamics of Spiritual Life: An Evangelical Theology of Renewal* (Downers Grove, IL: InterVarsity Press, 1979), 232.

formation. To put it differently, and perhaps more helpfully, there remains a gap in contemporary evangelicalism between our expectations in the Christian life and engagement with the in-depth spiritual theology that our forebears managed to articulate. While this is true across the various topics and issues in spiritual formation, maybe nowhere else is this gap so wide as with contemplation.

Take, for example, the work of Richard Baxter. Richard Baxter was a seventeenth-century Puritan pastor best known for two of his works now considered spiritual classics: *The Reformed Pastor* and *The Saints' Everlasting Rest*. Lesser known is Baxter's immense manual on the Christian care of souls called *A Christian Directory*. The work spans a million and a quarter words and is heralded by Tim Keller as "the greatest manual on biblical counseling ever produced" and by John MacArthur as "a purely Biblical treatment of the spiritual ills and cures of men." In the foreword to a modern republication, J. I. Packer claims that *A Christian Directory* "is the fullest, most thorough, and in this writer's judgment, most profound treatment of Christian spirituality and standards that has ever been attempted by an English-speaking Evangelical author."[3] It would be difficult to find a more apt figure to represent Protestant spirituality (from within a distinctively Reformed and Puritan vein) than Baxter, endorsed by evangelical thinkers not linked to the contemporary retrieval of evangelical spiritual formation. It is helpful, in light of that, to pause and reflect briefly on Baxter's own development of contemplation.

In *A Christian Directory*, Baxter asks the question: "What is a contemplative life? and what is an active, obediential life?"[4] By engaging the topic in this fashion, Baxter reveals that he has attended to how Roman Catholics articulate the two major vocations of Christian existence, often modeled after Mary and Martha, deemed the contemplative life and the active life respectively. Like Puritan and Protestant spirituality generally, Baxter was well-read in Roman Catholic sources, and it seems that a Jesuit spiritual classic, *The First Booke of the Christian Exercise, Appertayning to Resolution by Robert Parsons*, played a key role in his conversion.[5] But following his

---

[3]J. I. Packer, "Introducing 'A Christian Directory,'" in Richard Baxter, *A Christian Directory* (Morgan, PA: Soli Deo Gloria Publications, 2000).

[4]Baxter, *A Christian Directory*, 259.

[5]See Robert McNulty, "The Protestant Version of Robert Parson's *The First Booke of the Christian Exercise*," *The Huntington Library Quarterly* 22, no. 4 (1959): 271-300.

Protestant and Reformed inclinations, Baxter refused to simply appropriate Catholic spirituality wholesale, adapting it critically through a Protestant theological apparatus. Nonetheless, he discovered distinctions from the tradition that some today might consider Roman Catholic that are actually part of the Christian reservoir of thought that Protestants have always mined for their own use. Baxter refused to believe that Protestants don't have equal right to the tradition as their Roman Catholic counterparts. Instead, they choose to follow Paul's example, who rejected choosing one authority over the other, eventually telling the Corinthians, "For all things are yours, whether Paul or Apollos or Cephas or the world or life or death or the present or the future—all are yours, and you are Christ's, and Christ is God's" (1 Cor 3:21-23). Utilizing this distinction to think about the mixture of contemplative and active dimensions of Christian existence, Baxter starts by saying,

> Every active Christian is bound to somewhat of contemplation; and all contemplative persons are bound to obedience to God, and to so much of action as may answer their abilities and opportunities. But yet some are much more called to the one, and some to the other; and we denominate from that which is most eminent and chief. We call that a contemplative life, when a man's state and calling alloweth and requireth him to make the exercises of his mind on things sublime and holy, and the affecting of his heart with them to be his principal business, which taketh up the most of his time. And we call that an active, obediential life, when a man's state and calling requireth him to spend the chief part of his time in some external labour or vocation, tending to the good of ourselves and others.[6]

By setting up the discussion this way, Baxter assumes that all Christians are called to some form of the mixed life—the active and the contemplative—but that the degree to which one focuses on one over the other is a question of one's state and one's calling.[7] In his continued development, Baxter also claims that "it is lawful, and a duty, and a great mercy to some, to live almost

---

[6]Baxter, *A Christian Directory*, 259.

[7]Interestingly, Baxter also claims that there is a state he calls "a passive, obediential life," which entails "a life in which their obedient bearing of the cross, and patient suffering, and submission to the chastising or trying will of God, is the most eminent and principal service they can do him," and that this is "above contemplation or action." Ibid. However Baxter understands this state, this is an interesting, and distinctively evangelical, way to consider the various vocations.

wholly, yea altogether, in contemplation and prayer, and such holy exercises."[8] Of the various examples he gives, one is the student studying for ministry, suggesting that seminary education should have both the contemplative and active in mind in the curriculum.[9] So, for Baxter, "Every christian must use so much contemplation, as is necessary to the loving of God above all, and to the worshipping of him in spirit and in truth," but the "calling of a minister of the gospel, is so perfectly mixed of contemplation and action, (though action denominate it, as being the end and chief,) yet he must be excellent in both."[10] Baxter goes on to worry about the minister who fails to be "excellent in contemplation," a shortcoming that will thwart the calling of the congregation to "draw near" to God.

Richard Baxter is not an anomaly in the background of evangelical spirituality but represents the standard narrative in his own unique way. This is why the claim that contemplation or spiritual formation is Roman Catholic is simply uninformed and akin to claiming that prayer must be Roman Catholic as well. The sanctification gap, as noted by Lovelace, has caused many to suppose that the spiritual formation movement is ushering in new ideas or simply Roman Catholic or New Age mysticism. (Tom Schwanda navigates these critiques in his chapter in this volume.) Rather, the spiritual formation conversation is seeking to do the kind of work that folks like Baxter, Jonathan Edwards, and John Wesley were up to, not simply repeating what they said, but taking up the robust spiritual theology they modeled. The overall goal is not reclaiming historical theology for its own sake but constructively retrieving their theological instincts, impulses, and guidance for the sake of rich, in-depth, and profound care of souls. Toward that end, we turn now to key features of the discussion concerning contemplation and contemplative prayer before turning to an overview of the volume as a whole. Because the term *contemplation* is often misunderstood or unhelpfully linked primarily to other religious groups, this introduction will establish a preliminary understanding of contemplation that will be fleshed out with greater complexity in the chapters. The goal is not to say everything that needs to be said at the outset, but to provide a first-things account of

---

[8] Ibid.
[9] Ibid., 260.
[10] Ibid.

the basic features of contemplation that will be nuanced, built on, and advanced in differing directions throughout this volume.

CONTEMPLATION AND CONTEMPLATIVE PRAYER

One of the goals of this volume is to offer current thinking across evangelicalism on the nature of contemplation. For the sake of clarity, and because this volume does not provide a unified view on the topic, it proves helpful to introduce some key questions here. One key issue concerns the distinction between natural and supernatural contemplation, and how we should distinguish between our ability to contemplate things in our world compared to the things "above," as Paul names the heavenly realm in Colossians 3. Natural contemplation is something all human persons do (we all contemplate what we find beautiful and good), and something we are called to do by Paul in his letter to the Philippians: "Finally, brothers, whatever is true, whatever is honorable, whatever is just, whatever is pure, whatever is lovely, whatever is commendable, if there is any excellence, if there is anything worthy of praise, think about these things" (Phil 4:8). While Paul is calling us to contemplate specific things, it is axiomatic to say that all persons contemplate what they consider good. In our flesh, the good we contemplate is often sinful, and so Paul calls us to contemplate the good and the true, which should, it would seem, lead us to contemplate God, who is truth and goodness itself.

While natural contemplation seems relatively clear, it is less so when we turn our attention to the contemplation of God, not because contemplation is a species of prayer for the spiritual elite or because contemplation itself is difficult to understand, but because it does not primarily rest on our ability (as does natural contemplation). If we come to consider supernatural contemplation as simply natural contemplation turned upward, then the focus would primarily rest on our own technique and ability, and we might make the error of believing that the contemplation of God was something we could generate. Rather, the contemplation of God is made available to the believer in the Spirit. As the Spirit descends to the depths of the believer, groaning with "groanings too deep for words" in intercession (Rom 8:26), the Spirit is revealing the love and presence of God to the soul (Rom 5:5). Contemplation is a call to attend to the presence of God that has been made available in Christ by the Spirit. This means that while we can talk about techniques in contemplation, these are simply practices we can employ to seek to be present to God, who is always present to his children. As techniques of contemplation, they generate neither a state nor a condition, nor are they meant to somehow control the Spirit's activity; rather, techniques are meant to ready and open the heart to God.

Along these lines, it is helpful to consider Paul's prayer in Ephesians 3:14-21. Here, Paul prays that we would be strengthened with power by the Spirit in our inner person, that Christ would dwell in our hearts through faith, that we would be rooted in love, to know the immensity of this love, and that we would be filled with the fullness of God. The focus in this passage is on the work God has done in Christ and how that is being applied to the believer in the Spirit, and how, by faith, the believer is strengthened in their inner life, rooted in love, and pressed into the "love of Christ that surpasses knowledge" to be filled to all the "fullness of God" (Eph 3:19). The believer is not generating anything here, but takes on a receptive posture of openness to the work God has done and is doing in the depth of one's soul. Notice, furthermore, that there is not a specific act of prayer attached to Paul's longing. The focus is not on technique, although that will have to be discussed, but is on receiving the presence and love of God in Christ by the Spirit.

Following Paul's discussion in Ephesians, we can address, in broad strokes, the first things that should be said about an evangelical understanding of contemplation, and how that might be formed into an account of contemplative prayer (if this is something we think we should do). If we consider, at the most base level, that contemplation names our being open to God who is always with us, then contemplation and contemplative prayer are the simplest experiences in the Christian life; they simply name our openness to the presence of God in the Spirit. This inclination is that God's love calls us to open to him—to be rooted and grounded in his love—so that we can be more open to his life penetrating our own. Far from being an elitist or sophisticated spirituality, contemplation is the essence of simplicity and is open to all. This is the very opposite of the contemporary criticism from Christians who argue that contemplation is some kind of New Age action in which we seek to create or conjure religious experience. It is the very opposite; we merely obey by opening to Christ's inner presence and love in the Spirit. Furthermore, following Baxter, the contemplative life is not one form or style of Christian existence, nor is contemplation a kind of spiritual attitude or set of disciplines that characterize a kind of spiritual life (although it will order these). Rather, the Christian life is the result of the work of the indwelling Spirit who sanctifies, makes righteous, saves, redeems, and transforms the believer into the image of Christ, and his love is the primary power of transformation in the Christian life. Following this reality, the contemplative orientation of Christian existence simply names the center of Christian realism—that God is with us in the Spirit and that we are truly with God in Christ. Our calling is to embrace this reality and be open to the work God is already doing on our behalf and the truth of who we already are in Christ Jesus.

In this sense, contemplation and the contemplative life of prayer, at bottom, are merely synonyms for "walking in the Spirit" as Paul mentions in Galatians 5. We walked in the flesh in our former life, training all our capacities in the weakness of human autonomy from God (flesh). Now, since we already "live by the Spirit," we are to learn to walk in all those capacities with the Spirit (Gal 5:25). So in my thoughts, my fears, my angers, my playing golf, my work, my writing, and so on, I am to relearn how to walk, no longer alone, but with the Spirit—to open to his love and presence in all I am, experience, and do. To walk in the Spirit is to retrain my capacities within the presence of God in Christ by the Spirit. This is not another spiritual discipline or type of spirituality, but is a fundamental feature of our new life in the Spirit. To contemplate is simply to walk with, and be with, God in all I do; this is not simply an intellectual endeavor, as if the intellect could be bracketed off of our personhood to engage in spiritual things without our affect. Rather, following the likes of Jonathan Edwards and the Puritans in general we need religious affection in our walking with God. God is not calling his people to an abstract knowledge of himself, but to an affectionate knowledge of who he is. This affection is the fruit of his love and presence, and is available to us only in Christ Jesus. This affectionate knowledge names the reality of the whole person available and open to God for his work of transformation, trusting that God is at work on the whole of our personality, intellect, and emotional lives.

Therefore, the core of the Christian life is contemplation: the human counterpart to God's self-giving grace that is an openness to God's work in the Spirit, binding us to the life of Christ, that forms our fundamental posture of presenting ourselves to God. This contemplative feature of Christian existence forms all Christian faithfulness and, therefore, helps establish the contours of a life of prayer, which is nothing else than a life lived with God or, in Paul's words, a life of praying without ceasing (1 Thess 5:17). We recognize that *contemplative prayer* is something of a confusing term. The ancient church, as far as we can tell, did not use this terminology in the way moderns have grown accustomed to. Contemplation and the contemplative dimension of redeemed existence was assumed, but this was not necessarily understood as a kind of prayer, as much as the culmination of our praying or a culmination of living with God and walking with the Spirit. It may have been the telos of prayer, but the act of contemplation was not understood as prayer. In a similar way that a distinction has been drawn between meditation and prayer, or even meditation and contemplation, there was a distinction between contemplation and prayer as such. In our day, the opposite is assumed in many circles. Therefore, instead of taking contemplative prayer as an obvious given, the focus of this book is on contemplation, and out of that we seek to point forward to ways that contemplation might inform prayer, taking on, as we will see in the conclusion, the distinctively relational features of evangelical theology and spirituality.

This first-things overview of contemplation sets up the material that will now be advanced and dissected in differing ways, seeking to answer questions like: What might a distinctively evangelical notion of contemplation entail? Does contemplation form specific kinds of prayer, and if so, how? Can we speak meaningfully about the experience of contemplation, and should we seek to give a kind of phenomenology of contemplation? What does it mean to say that our contemplation "worked" or "didn't work," and how do we attend to faithfulness in our openness to the Lord? These questions, and many others, will serve to drive this conversation and those that flow from this volume, recognizing that while contemplation itself is a simple reality, that does not mean its depths are equally simple. Different contributors will name, at times, conflicting instincts for how contemplation could form our understanding of prayer. Even the language used to talk about this will vary, with some talking about silent prayer, centering prayer, or contemplative prayer; but it is important that contemplation is addressed in its own right with prayer as a subsequent and related practice of our life with God, and out of that biblical and theological structure, a development of contemplative prayer can be addressed. To use an image that might help explain the simplicity-complexity structure of this volume, we should remember that the notion of sight is quite simple. It is easy to speak about what it means to see. But once we talk about how we can see, and the difficulties that come with our seeing, the discussion gets increasingly complex. Similarly, now we see through a mirror dimly (1 Cor 13:12), and this volume seeks to give voice to the complexity of that reality.

OVERVIEW OF VOLUME

As noted, the goal of this volume is not to bring together a group of evangelicals who are necessarily in agreement concerning contemplation or contemplative prayer, but to canvas key thinkers across evangelicalism to address these topics. In short, the goal is to start a conversation that is not currently being had. There are, no doubt, evangelicals naively accepting any form of contemplation and contemplative prayer on offer by the world, just as there are, no doubt, evangelicals who are rejecting these out of hand because they naively assume any possible contemplation is worldly. What has yet to be seen is a robust discussion of contemplation and contemplative prayer in a distinctively evangelical way. This volume seeks to fill that gap. What follows is an overview of how each chapter fits together under two broad sections: "Historical Inquiries" and "Constructive Proposals." These sections were added after the chapters were written in an attempt to provide some organization to the flow of material, so they should not be taken too strictly (as if they provided direction to the material content of the chapters). Each author has an eye on the tradition and an eye on constructively engaging it. We will conclude with a short reflection at the end of the volume on where this conversation should go and what avenues seem most fruitful to pursue.

Part 1: Historical inquiries. In our first essay, John Coe addresses one of the core issues of Christian contemplation and how it differs from other forms of contemplation (in particular, New Age, Neoplatonic, or Eastern panentheistic forms). Any notion of contemplation relying on these philosophical constructs will be sub-Christian. To develop his argument, Coe attends to the early church's Nicene articulation of creation *ex nihilo* and their articulation of a robust Creator-creature distinction intended to undermine those philosophical frameworks that argued for some kind of kinship between God and persons so that by some flight of the mind one could contemplate the mind of God. Nicene theology denied the creature as having a kinship with God and therefore affirmed that Christian contemplation must have an entirely different structure—a distinctively theological structure (something developed in different ways throughout this volume). Christian contemplation, therefore, cannot rest on natural ability or technique to reach the divine, but must be funded by God's self-revelation, and therefore is a response to God's self-giving in Word and Spirit to the believer in love. Thus, according to Coe, the controversy over Christian contemplation and the providing of the Christian theological grounding and understanding of it had already been settled by the church nearly seventeen hundred years ago.

Coe's chapter gives a helpful foundation for the historical, theological, and biblical issues that will inevitably arise in discussions of contemplation. Following his analysis, Evan B. Howard narrates the thought of one of the most influential spiritual writers of desert spirituality, Evagrius of Pontus. By doing so, Howard gets to one of the prevailing focal points of what is often called contemplative prayer, which is the wordless quality of this form of praying. This wordless prayer unveils one approach to how prayer and contemplation can connect. For Evagrius, prayer should move to a wordless state of contemplation, and therefore his ideal can be talked about as a form of contemplative prayer (leaving aside, for the time being, whether that language is useful). Focus on the removal of distracting thoughts has a long history in Christian spirituality, and this struggle with thoughts, more specifically disordered thoughts, becomes a focal point of Evagrius's method. After narrating the movement of Evagrius's theology of prayer, Howard turns to evaluation. The question, Is this actually Christian? drives Howard's response, providing what might be called a critical appropriation of key features of Evagrius's thought while pushing against some of its more radical features.

Following Howard's discussion of early Christian desert spirituality, Greg Peters turns to medieval spirituality to excavate potential resources for our own spiritual practice. Peters begins his essay with a helpful orientation to some of the key biblical passages that supported contemplation in that era. While some of the specific passages might not resonate with modern readers, Peters's identification of these texts provides an important orientation to how medieval spirituality understood its biblical precedents. Peters continues with an exposition of key figures in the medieval spiritual tradition, moving from Richard of St. Victor to Thomas Aquinas and then to Bernard of Clairvaux, leading to a focus on love as the end of contemplation (because love, in fact, is God himself). This medieval articulation of contemplation sets up Ashley Cocksworth's chapter, which develops a strand of contemplation from within Reformed theology. This may seem far removed from the medieval era, but Reformed spirituality is heavily funded by both Augustine and Bernard of Clairvaux, even if it is caught up into a different theological and ecclesial framework. Cocksworth's goal is to recover a focus on Sabbath from the Reformed tradition—John Calvin in particular—in a way that could help us reconsider the realities of contemplation and contemplative prayer. By attending to the contemplative dimension of Calvin's spirituality, his focus on the mediation of Christ, and the nature of Christian Sabbath, Cocksworth unearths helpful resources to consider contemplation from within the Protestant theological heritage.

Continuing Cocksworth's focus on the Protestant spiritual tradition, Tom Schwanda introduces the reader to criticisms of contemplation and spiritual formation that have arisen in popular-level online discourse. Unraveling these criticisms, and showing how they are not based on actual views held by evangelicals, Schwanda continues by giving four features of what might be called classical evangelical statements of contemplation. Turning to figures from both Reformed and Wesleyan camps, Schwanda outlines the views of Jonathan Edwards, Susanna Anthony, Sarah Jones, and Francis Asbury on the nature and task of contemplation, revealing a deep vein of contemplation in the very foundation of evangelical spirituality.

The last chapter in this section provides something of a helpful overview and synthesis of much of what is addressed thus far. In this essay, Diane

Chandler brings to the conversation a much-needed focus on the cross as the centerpiece for any understanding of a distinctively Christian contemplation. After moving through numerous historical figures on contemplation, Chandler focuses her own retrieval on the cross, using the cross to link together evangelical soteriology and ecclesiological practices. Chandler concludes with another sweeping overview of key figures of the tradition and the centrality of the cross in their spirituality generally and their understanding of contemplation more specifically. Chandler concludes with practical guidance on adopting this form of contemplation into one's spiritual life.

Part 2: Constructive proposals. As noted above, these two sections are not to bifurcate historical and constructive proposals, as if contributors had to choose one over the other. Rather, each essay focuses on a specific aspect of contemplation and utilizes various resources for making their argument. That said, this section focuses less on historical inquiries and argumentation toward more constructive proposals. The first chapter, by Steven L. Porter, is an exposition of biblical spirituality that undergirds a contemplative dimension to Christian existence. To do so, Porter develops four key principles to the agapeic reality of God, as pointed to in Scripture, and how the Christian is called to partake in this reality. Far from producing a focus on abstract contemplation of the idea of God, this biblical dimension of contemplation is a focus on personal communion with the God of love. This points to various forms that prayer might take, but Porter worries that contemplative prayer, as it is often understood, is too narrow to capture the biblical vision of Christian prayerfulness.

Following Porter's development of the biblical material on contemplation, Kyle Strobel narrates what a distinctively theological account of contemplation may entail. To do so, Strobel articulates the ground and possibility of contemplation by focusing on God's self-giving in Son and Spirit. Focusing on the Son as the great high priest, Strobel offers a view of contemplation as a partaking in the gaze of the Son on the Father and the Father on the Son that anticipates the beatific vision of eternity. Strobel then applies his account to an approach to silent prayer, mooring silence within the intercessory prayers of the Son and Spirit and the believer's faith in their intercession. Following in the same vein as Strobel, Ryan Brandt offers a gospel-centered approach to contemplation by focusing on God's own contemplative life, union with Christ, and the believer's experience of love. One of the fruits of this account is a focus on the interpretive task of the Christian and how contemplation speaks into a distinctively Christian reading of the biblical text. Brandt goes on to ground the eschatological reality of contemplation in the future beatific vision of God.

While both Strobel and Brandt usher in the beatific vision as a key aspect of mooring contemplation theologically, Hans Boersma focuses on this feature specifically. Starting with the Gospel of John, and then moving to the New Testament more broadly, Boersma develops a biblical doctrine of the beatific vision, while interweaving a broad range of historical figures reflecting on both the biblical texts and theological development of the doctrine. Using the beatific vision as the fulfillment of the anticipations we receive in this age, Boersma continues by utilizing the thought of Irenaeus. In particular, Boersma focuses on Irenaeus's notion of the pedagogical process by which God matures his people, a process of increasing sight. After addressing three theophanies depicting God as a tutor in sight, Boersma concludes with a reflection on the nature of contemplation.

After three straight chapters attempting to provide the theological framework of contemplation, we turn to James Wilhoit's exposition of centering prayer. Centering prayer is a technique often found in Roman Catholic spiritual writers, most specifically Thomas Keating. Wilhoit walks the reader through Keating's approach to the technique of centering prayer before turning to its theological foundations. Wilhoit continues to develop his account by turning to the topic of mindfulness, addressing biblical material to articulate an account of biblical mindfulness, then turning to the uniqueness of centering prayer in the spiritual tradition. Wilhoit concludes his essay by engaging evangelical criticisms of centering prayer. This essay includes the volume's most explicit focus on a form of contemplative prayer, and it shows how this particular form of prayer is of a piece with the theological foundations undergirding it. Wilhoit's essay is thus a helpful case study in how a theological construct gives rise to a spiritual practice, which may prove helpful as evangelicals consider the previous chapters' theological development and differing constructs that might arise from them.

The final two chapters broaden the conversation. The first, by Simon Chan, addresses contemplative prayer in the evangelical and Pentecostal traditions. Chan provides a helpful overview of evangelical spirituality before turning to Pentecostal spirituality and its distinctive focus on glossolalia. Linking glossolalia to categories more familiar in the history of Christian spirituality, Chan links discussions not often connected, providing points of contact for Pentecostal spirituality and experience with both evangelical spirituality and the spiritual tradition more broadly. Widening the discussion even more, Glen G. Scorgie addresses Christian contemplation in relation to other religions' contemplative traditions. Scorgie rightly notes that it is important to enter into comparison with other religious practices, not for the purpose of adjusting our own practices (as if Christianity lacked the internal resources to consider its own spirituality), but to attend to the differences. Israel continually practiced things their foreign neighbors did, at the very call of God, and yet there was always a distinct difference that uniquely formed the purpose, telos, or nature of the Jewish appropriation. Similarly, as will be seen throughout this book, it is these distinctives that make Christian contemplation, in part, so interesting. After engaging in a broad sweep of comparative analyses with other religious traditions, Scorgie focuses in on the distinctively Christian features of Christian contemplation.

The volume concludes with a short reflection on the book as a whole, pulling together several key threads and pointing forward to ways that this discussion could and should be advanced in different areas. The field of evangelical spirituality has been missing a broad and deep discussion of contemplation, attending to the historical, theological, and comparative features necessary to do so well. This book seeks to address that lacuna, but it does not try to do everything. In the conclusion we will note points of tension among contributors and possibilities for continued development along different trajectories. In the end, the goal will be to build on and advance this discussion into areas of spiritual theology in which our forebears were so robustly interested: What does it mean when all I experience is myself and my sin? Where is God when I can barely get myself to pray? Why doesn't God reveal himself more profoundly to me? These must be addressed by a robust account of spiritual theology.

PART 1

HISTORICAL INQUIRIES

THE CONTROVERSY OVER CONTEMPLATION AND CONTEMPLATIVE PRAYER

A Historical, Theological, and Biblical Resolution

JOHN H. COE

THE TOPIC AND PRACTICE OF CONTEMPLATION and contemplative prayer in contemporary Christian spirituality has become controversial to a number of very sincere believers. One example is Ray Yungen's *A Time of Departing*, in which he believes that contemplative prayer is fundamentally linked to worldviews foreign to Christianity. As he states, "Contemplative prayer and panentheism go together like a hand in a glove—to promote one is to promote both. They are inseparable."[1] I will not give a complete response to all the issues raised by Yungen or other critics of Christian approaches to contemplative prayer and contemplation. However, I would like to address two of the central concerns that have been raised, namely, that contemplation and contemplative prayer are fundamentally non-Christian in their worldview orientation and that they cannot be grounded theologically, biblically, or in historic orthodox (in the best sense of that word) Christianity.

I hope to make clear the distinction between a truly biblical, Christian approach to contemplative prayer in contrast to a distorted, truncated view evident in New Age or Eastern pantheism or panentheism, particularly as they are reflected back into ancient Platonic, Neoplatonic, and Origenic

---

[1]Ray Yungen, *A Time of Departing* (Silverton, OR: Lighthouse Trails Publishing, 2002), 72.

views of contemplation.[2] This will include, first, how the Nicene theology of creation *ex nihilo* provided the history of Christian theology with the proper theological corrective to many false views of contemplation and contemplative prayer derived from a faulty view of God, reality, and the human soul. Second, I will argue that a truly Christian approach to contemplative prayer can be made consistent and grounded in revelation, original sin, and a new covenant understanding of the cross and the Spirit. Finally, I will argue that the Scriptures actually teach a form of contemplation and contemplative prayer.

A SUB-CHRISTIAN VERSION OF CONTEMPLATION BASED ON A FALSE VIEW OF GOD, REALITY, AND THE HUMAN SOUL

Many sub-Christian versions of contemplation and contemplative prayer are based on some notion of *pantheism* and *panentheism*. Though there are many forms of these worldviews, let us understand pantheism simply as the belief that God is identical with the world so that all is God and God is all, and let us understand panentheism as the belief that all things are imbued with God's being in the sense that all things are in God or that God is unfolding himself through all things. These worldview ideas evident in New Age and Eastern religion are, in part, contemporary revivals of the proto-Gnostic, Neoplatonic, or Origenic heresies or heterodoxies of the first four centuries CE. They all share in common some sense that the fundamental ontological split of reality is between Spirit and matter—the latter often being either illusory or having less being than the realm of Spirit. How this relates to contemplation or contemplative prayer on this worldview can be captured in figure 1.

It is particularly important to notice in figure 1 that, according to Origen, following Plato and Plotinus, and consistent with popular New Age approaches to religion, the fundamental way to ontologically break up the world is between the realm of the Spirit and the realm of the material world. As Andrew Louth says,

---

[2] I do not have space to go into the details of various New Age, Hindu, or Buddhist practices of contemplative prayer, but will only generalize on this in light of the mysticism of the ancient Platonic and Neoplatonic proto-Gnosticism evident in early Christian Origenic spirituality of the third and fourth centuries CE.

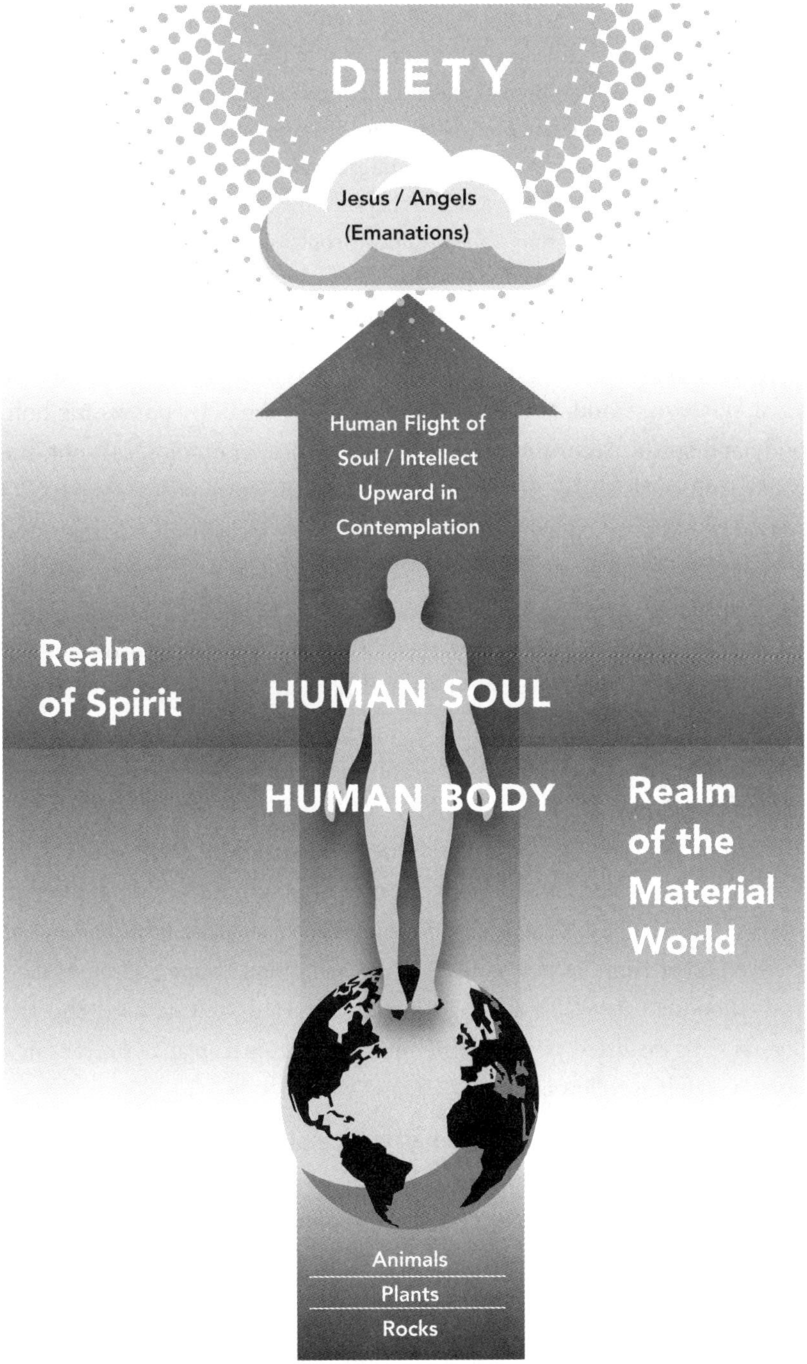

Figure 1. Sub-Christian view of reality

As we have seen, contemplation was a unifying principle in Origen's cosmos. . . . Behind this was the Platonic idea of the soul's kinship with the divine: it was this kinship that made contemplation possible and which was realized in contemplation. . . . . Neither for Plato nor for Origen were souls created: they were pre-existent and immortal. The most fundamental ontological distinction in such a world was between the spiritual and the material. The soul belonged to the former realm in contrast to its body which was material: the soul belonged to the divine, spiritual realm and was only trapped in the material realm by its association with the body.[3]

As a result of this spirit-body split of the universe, there is a fundamental kinship between God, angels, and human souls, the latter possessing both body and spirit. According to this biblically foreign ontological split, the soul in some way shares in or has kinship with the ontology (being) of God so that by effort and grace (the latter included by Origen), the human soul can shed its connection with the body and by mental techniques such as meditation or contemplation know God as he knows himself. This knowledge is accomplished by means of some kind of "flight of the soul upward" as an ascent to know the mind of God.[4] Again, this intellectual assent is made possible due to the belief that the human person shares ontologically in some kind of kinship of spirit with universal Spirit or the being of God.

This biblically foreign metaphysics has, in turn, produced distorted views of contemplation and contemplative prayer. Contemporary and popular versions of Eastern and New Age philosophies have stripped biblical contemplative prayer from its true context of the Christian triune redeemer God and embedded it within a deficient and distorted view of God and the person. This distorted view of contemplation or contemplative prayer often portrays itself as follows:

1. Sub-Christian contemplation or contemplative prayer is an approach to knowing "God" due to the kinship of the human soul and God as a kind of return of the divine spark in humanity to its original divinity

---

[3]Andrew Louth, *The Origins of the Christian Mystical Tradition from Plato to Denys* (Oxford: Clarendon Press, 1981), 76-77.

[4]Louth provides an in-depth discussion of the Platonic and Neoplatonic elements in Origen and Alexandrian mysticism in general in his *Origins*, 52-74.

in some pantheistic or panentheistic manner, thereby obscuring the absolute ontological distinction between the finite created human spirit and the infinite Creator Spirit of God.

2. Sub-Christian contemplation or contemplative prayer is not dependent on God revealing himself but on intellectual techniques and acts of devotion to "reach" or "ascend" to know God.

3. Sub-Christian contemplation or contemplative prayer rejects an orthodox view of original sin as well as the necessary work of Christ on the cross to reconcile humanity to God, but rather affirms that the chasm between God and humanity can be bridged by some kind of human soul effort.

4. Sub-Christian contemplation or contemplative prayer often involves a use of silence and certain divine words or mantras to evacuate consciousness in an attempt to empty the self in order to return to its divine origin.

5. In some cases, sub-Christian contemplation or contemplative prayer aims at altered states of consciousness for the sake of therapeutic euphoria or ecstasy with the divine.

In general, unbiblical and sub-Christian approaches to contemplation or contemplative prayer represent the attempt of human effort and natural fortitude to meet the deep hunger for God apart from the true revelation of God in Christ and the empowering work of his indwelling Spirit.

A HISTORICAL CORRECTION TO CHRISTIAN CONTEMPLATION IN NICENE ORTHODOXY: CREATION *EX NIHILO*, THE NATURE OF SOULS, AND THE KNOWLEDGE OF GOD

In the first place, the orthodox Christian position evident in Nicene theology was a major correction to the Origenic approach to mysticism and contemplation, along with all later attempts to understand contemplation based on the kinship of the human soul with the being of God. As Louth says,

> Athanasius marks an important step forward in the Christian understanding of the soul's way to God. In contrast to earlier forms of mystical theology based upon the Platonist's premises of the soul's natural kinship with God,

> Athanasius posits a great ontological gulf between God and all else—souls included. This gulf can only be crossed by God: man can only know God if God comes to him, comes *down* into the realm of corruption and death that man inhabits. And this he does in the Incarnation. . . . No longer will they [human souls] be drawn upwards to holiness in ever greater likeness to the invisible God.[5]

There is no kinship or soul connection, ontologically speaking, between God and human persons that allows humans to cross over the divide to know the mind and person of God in contemplation or meditative techniques. Athanasius and Nicene theology make it clear: God must reveal himself to humanity to bridge this divide.

In particular, the doctrine of creation *ex nihilo* was not only a watershed correction and clarification of our understanding of Christology and the incarnation but also a correction to a false view of contemplation in Origen. Athanasius and Gregory of Nyssa, perhaps the greatest of the Cappadocian theologians, by affirming creation *ex nihilo*, reject the spirit-matter dualism of all reality and affirm the absolute distinction between the infinite Creator triune God and all other finite created beings, which includes finite matter and finite created spirits (angels and humans). As Louth says,

> Gregory's theology is deeply Nicene and, more precisely, deeply Athanasian. For him, no less than for Athanasius, the soul, along with all other creatures, is created out of nothing. . . . For Gregory the realm of the intelligible is divided into the uncreated and creative on the one hand and, on the other, that which is created—and this is the fundamental divide. Thus, the distinction between the uncreated, intelligible reality to which category belong only the members of the Blessed Trinity, and the created order, cuts across even the Platonic distinction between intelligible and sensible. The gulf between uncreated and created is such for Gregory that there is no possibility of the soul passing across it: there is no ecstasy, in which the soul leaves its nature as created and passes into the uncreated.[6]

Because God creates all reality out of nothing (creation *ex nihilo*), it turns out that no created reality shares in the ontology of God. In particular, the human person, body and soul, are part of the created order and cannot

---

[5]Louth, *Origins*, 99-100 (emphasis original).
[6]Ibid.

bridge the ontological gap in order to know the mind of God. As a result, orthodox Christian teaching has affirmed throughout the ages that we cannot know God as he is in himself (a heresy condemned by the church fathers Chrysostom, Gregory, Basil, and others, later called *ontologism*). There is no ontological kinship between God and humankind that provides immediate epistemological access to knowing God as he is in himself. How then can we know God in light of this great ontological chasm? The answer of the Nicene fathers was that we can know God only as he wills to reveal himself into the created order. This was the genius of the Nicene doctrine of creation *ex nihilo* as it affected the doctrine of knowing God and contemplation. This was a turning point in the history of Christian theology and its view of Christian contemplation. Figure 2 captures this Nicene movement away from the Platonic/Neoplatonic view of reality to the absolute ontological distance between the Creator and the creature and its relation to understanding Christian contemplation.

Notice in figure 2 that in contrast to the Origenic view of the world, Nicene theology begins with creation *ex nihilo*, which insists that the fundamental way to ontologically divide the universe is by the uncreated Creator God and the created universe. In this case, human souls share no natural or essential kinship with God. In fact, contrary to the Neoplatonic vision, human souls share more ontological kinship with human bodies, plants, and rocks than with the essence of God, though we are relationally made in the image of God. In that case, contemplation is not fundamentally an intellectual assent made possible by human effort.

If God is to be known, it must be by his initiative to break into the finite, created realm to reveal himself. This is precisely what God did in the incarnation and in sending the indwelling Holy Spirit, two realities and doctrines central to Nicene theology and theological reflection thereafter.

> His [Gregory of Nyssa's] awareness of the unbridgeable gulf between the uncreated and the created implied by the radical doctrine of *creation ex nihilo* gives to his mysticism its peculiar character and leads him to focus all the more clearly on the very heart of mysticism: an experience of immediacy with God Himself in love. His understanding of this doctrine of creation out of nothing means that there is no point of contact between the soul and God, and so God is totally unknowable to the soul, and the soul can have

TRIUNE GOD

The Uncreated, Creator and Infinite Order of Things

Self-Disclosing Revelation of God in Christ and the Holy Spirit into the Finite Realm by the Incarnation and Indwelling Spirit as Understood by Scripture

The Created Finite Order of Things

Incarnated Christ

Angels / Demons

Human persons: body and soul (believers indwelt by HS)

Animals

Plants

Rocks

Figure 2. The Nicene view of reality

no experience of God *except in so far as God makes such experience possible.* It is the unknowability of God which leads to Gregory's insistence that it is only in virtue of the Incarnation, *only because God has manifested Himself—and His love—among us, that we can know Him at all.*[7]

Because God exists in the infinite order of things, he is unknowable to the mind of the creature unless he reveals himself. Nicene theology affirmed that contemplation and personal knowledge of God is possible only due to divine revelation whereby God reveals himself in love to the believer based on the incarnation and, subsequent, the indwelling Holy Spirit. Consequently, for the Nicene theologians and later theological reflection in the Western church, contemplation and contemplative prayer are less an intellectual or epistemic ascent into the mind of God. Rather, they are more a relational journey and experience of love inwardly in the human soul as a response to the self-revelation of God by the incarnate Christ and indwelling Holy Spirit. In that sense, we do not know God as he knows himself, but only as he reveals himself in love to us. Being made in God's image does provide our souls the capacity to experience the revelation of God's love by his relational presence in union with our human spirit. However, they do not share the same ontology so that we can by mental ascent or intellectual (in)sight behold God as something akin to ourselves. This becomes the dominant theological corrective to Origenic spirituality. In a real sense, the contemporary controversy over Christian contemplation and the providing of the Christian theological grounding and understanding of it had, to a great degree, already been settled by the church nearly seventeen hundred years ago.

A NEW COVENANT THEOLOGICAL GROUNDING OF CHRISTIAN CONTEMPLATION IN REVELATION, THE CROSS, AND THE HOLY SPIRIT

In contrast to the popular versions of Origenic spirituality and its New Age and Eastern cousins, this Nicene approach to Christian contemplation and contemplative prayer[8] are also grounded in the new covenant view of

---

[7] Ibid., 81 (emphasis added).

[8] Throughout this chapter I am using *contemplation* and *contemplative prayer* somewhat synonymously. Though some might want to make a distinction between the two, for simplicity's sake I will conflate them and argue that these both refer to a kind of openness toward the indwelling presence of God, as I will discuss below.

revelation, the cross, and the Holy Spirit. Thus the knowledge of God involved in various Christian spiritual practices related to contemplation and contemplative prayer is not the result of human effort but is grounded in the work of God on behalf of the believer. That is, knowledge of God is grounded in the following central truths of the faith:

1. Knowledge of God cannot be attained by human effort alone but is grounded solely on God's sovereign choice to *reveal himself* in creation (Rom 1:18-23), Word (2 Tim 3:16; Heb 4:12), his works and incarnation (Heb 1:1-2), and the indwelling Spirit (Rom 8:15-17; 1 Cor 2:14-16).

2. *Personal* knowledge of God cannot be attained by human effort or spiritual activities on their own due to the pervasive and radical effects of original sin but is made possible in the atoning, finished work of Christ on the cross (Rom 3:12; 5:18-21; 6:23), which reconciles the believer to God, making relationship with and knowledge of God possible once again.

3. *Personal* knowledge of God cannot be attained by human effort or spiritual activities on their own but is grounded in the regenerating and ongoing illuminating and vivifying ministry of the indwelling Holy Spirit, who connects us back with God (Rom 8:15-17; 1 Cor 2:14-16; Titus 3:15).

Because God dwells in the infinite order of things and we in the finite, humans and angels alike cannot know God unless God reveals himself. Moreover, due to original sin, God must not only reveal himself if we are to know him but also act on our behalf in redemption, otherwise no human would even respond to the given revelation (Eph 2:1-12). This is entirely in contrast to any contemporary gnostic or New Age heresy declaring the basic potential goodness of the human spirit when detached from the body (Rom 3:12). And finally, this personal knowledge of God is not based solely on our effort in prayer but on the work of the indwelling Christ and Spirit revealing the love of God and filling us with their presence (Eph 3:16-19).

Contemplation and contemplative prayer grounded in Christ: Colossians as a Pauline model / response to the proto-Gnostic heresy. This skeletal discussion of non-Christian forms of contemplative prayer and the biblical-theological response is exemplified, in part, in Paul's response to the Colossian heresy. Putting together the pieces of this heresy gives us the following picture.[9] A false teaching had come into the church at Colossae that affirmed some kind of Jewish ritual-mysticism combined with a Greek/Hellenistic proto-Gnostic belief of mystical experiences, magic, and rigorous ascetic behavior, resulting in the basic message that there was something deeper in the Christian life than just faith in Christ. According to this heterodoxy, God alone dwells in the fullness of deity; however, by means of religious devotion, ascetic behavior, and self-denial there are various emissaries (sent ones) of God, including perhaps Christ and angels, of which and through which we can enjoy mystical experiences relevant to the deity (Col 3:18-23).

Paul responds to this Jewish/proto-Gnostic mysticism by both denouncing what is false and unnecessary, and affirming what we already have by faith in Christ. The following represent his overall response in Colossians:

1. This Jewish/proto-Gnostic mysticism is a mere false philosophy and tradition of humanity, and does not find its source in a revelation of God (Col 2:8).

2. This Jewish/proto-Gnostic mysticism is built on the "elementary principles of the world" (NASB; *stoicheia tou kosmou*)—the ABCs or the basic moral principles that have structured humanity, morality, society, and religion and have demonic spirit forces behind them—to which we have died in Christ (Col 2:8, 20).

   This Jewish/proto-Gnostic mysticism fails to recognize that in Christ is the fullness of deity (Col 1:19) and, more to the point, that believers have been joined to Christ by faith so that they have the fullness of deity within them—"and you have been filled in him"[10] (*kai este en autō peplērōmenoi*)—so that believers are already filled with the life of God (Col 2:9-10).

3. Our being filled with Christ who has the fullness of deity (Christ in us) is neither accomplished by ascetic practices, nor by practicing

---

[9]For an interesting and thoughtful discussion of Paul's response to the alleged Colossian heresy, see Peter O'Brien, *Colossians, Philemon*, Word Biblical Commentary (Waco, TX: Word Books, 1982), xxx-xli, 101-56.

[10]See translation in ibid., 102.

rituals or self-denial, nor by efforts in attaining religious experience. Rather, our being filled with the life of God is accomplished solely by faith in Christ's work on the cross, which brings us in union with his death and resurrection (Col 2:11-15). Thus believers are not to let false teachers be judges regarding any need to follow certain rituals or any need to seek religious experiences to get more of God (Col 2:16-17).

According to Paul, we already have all we need in Christ and by means of Christ in us. Thus there is no need to get more of God outside of what God has already done for us in Christ and by means of Christ in us.

Consequently, according to Paul, religious experience of God is not based on our meditative efforts to fly into the mind of God or on any other kind of religious experience outside of ourselves. Rather, God has already revealed himself to us by the written Word and the indwelling Word. We do not need mystical experience or ascetic practices in order to be joined with and experience the fullness of God or to seek experiences outside ourselves—we are already joined with him and he is in us—the fullness of deity (Col 2:10; see Col 1:27: "Christ in you, the hope of glory").[11] Of course, this does not mean we automatically experience these realities. Our part is to open to his inner presence, to what he has revealed both in his Word and in his Spirit.

Contemplation and contemplative prayer are grounded in the Word and Spirit and is a response to the Spirit. Consequently, in the history of the church and the testimony of Scripture, the Christian practices of meditation and contemplative prayer by which the believer may come to know God more deeply are grounded in the biblical notion of revelation in Word and Spirit. In the first place, meditation is typically understood as a deep cogitation of the Word and work of God whereby the Spirit employs truth and love to transform the heart of the person (Ps 1:2; 119:11, 16).

Most relevant to the present study, while contemplation or contemplative prayer is grounded in the Word and work of Christ and the Spirit, it most specifically can be understood as an opening of the believer's heart to attend

---

[11]In Colossians there is no mention of the Holy Spirit where we might expect it, as in Ephesians, for it is the indwelling Christ that is the focus there. We don't need to go beyond Christ—he has the fullness of deity so that we don't need emissaries to help us find God or visions or theophanic emanations of angel experiences (Col 2:8-23). The fullness of deity is within us—there is no need for religious experience outside of Christ in us. Paul's message to the Colossians is that we have all we need in Christ (Col 2:2-3).

to the person and ministry of the indwelling Holy Spirit (the indwelling Christ). Or perhaps another way of putting the same, contemplation can be understood as allowing oneself to be influenced by the Holy Spirit, who is always attending to our soul. Interestingly, Paul's command in Colossians to let the Word of Christ dwell in our hearts, resulting in speaking to one another in sung prayers (psalms), is correlated in Ephesians with being filled with or allowing the Holy Spirit to fill or control us. Notice the passive voice of the imperative in which we are not the agent of filling ourselves with the Spirit but we are commanded (the imperatival force) to allow ourselves to be filled or influenced by the Spirit (the passive voice). This meta-command of allowing oneself to be filled with the Spirit is supposed to color all other commands, has a family resemblance to the meta-command to walk in the Spirit, and suggests to the believer that we are to attend not only to Christ but also to the Holy Spirit, who reveals God to us.

We can thus understand Christian contemplation or contemplative prayer as follows: Contemplation (contemplative prayer) is the act and experience whereby our human spirit opens to and attends to the indwelling Spirit of Christ, who is continually revealing himself to us and bearing witness to our spirit that we are children of God, loved by God in Christ, but in such a way that this opening of our spirit is in fact due to the movement of God's Spirit by which we even cry out to God—"Abba, Father"—in the first place.

In that sense, Christian contemplation and contemplative prayer are less our work of fortitude and more God's moving in our heart to respond to God's revealing presence and work. We are neither active nor passive in this process but interactive, as Dallas Willard used to say of the Christian life in general.[12] In Thomas Aquinas's words, he is the cause or first mover in our heart to even respond to God.[13]

What that experience will be like is not something we can control; it is up to the Holy Spirit to do what he wills. The Spirit's work may be consoling or it may be self-revealing and purgative. We don't measure or discern the presence of the Spirit by how it feels to us. The Spirit has his purposes and

---

[12]See, e.g., Richard J. Foster and Dallas Willard, "Christian Discipline as a Means to Grace: A Conversation between Richard J. Foster and Dallas Willard," *Conversations Journal* 4, no. 1 (2006): http://dallaswillardcenter.com/wp-content/uploads/2014/05/Christiandisciplinesasameanstograce.pdf.

[13]Thomas Aquinas, *Summa Theologica* 2a2ae, q. 6 a. 1 (*Summa Theologica*, ed. Thomas Gildby, trans. Blackfriars [London: Eyre and Spottiswoode, 1972], 31:165-67).

may reveal to the believer deeply consoling realities of his love, presence, and acceptance—all of which might feel quite pleasant to the believer. But the Spirit might also wish to reveal in love more harrowing truths about our sin, our falseness, and our unhealthy attachments. We might feel this experience as less spiritual and more psychological, that is, more about the truth of our sinfulness and neediness. But the point for the maturing believer in contemplation will not be how it feels but only what is revealed in the Spirit's presence. This is much like the maturing husband who is less interested in how it feels to be with his wife but more interested in the wife herself and what is being revealed regardless of whether it feels consoling or not. Much more can be said on this subject of religious experience and consolation, but this would take us into a full-blown spiritual theology and phenomenology of contemplation, which might be the topic for a further volume.

Consequently, the believer in contemplation or contemplative prayer is merely opening his or her heart and will and responding to the indwelling Spirit, who is (1) continuously strengthening the believer in the inner person, dwelling in our hearts through faith and loving the believer in the depths of the heart based on the finished work of Christ (Eph 3:16-19); (2) continuously leading and bearing witness to the believer's heart that one is a son of God by which one cries out "Abba, Father" (Rom 8:14-15); and (3) continuously interceding for the believer (and transforming us) to be perfected into the image of Christ (Rom 8:26-29; Gal 5:16-25; Col 1:28-29). These marvelous realities are always going on in the soul despite our present experience of them or how we feel.

A BIBLICAL APPROACH TO CONTEMPLATION
AND CONTEMPLATIVE PRAYER

As I have argued, true, biblical contemplative prayer is simply an appropriate obedience or response to the indwelling Spirit, which is reflected in Paul's prayers for us to open more deeply to and attend to the person and work of the Spirit. This is exemplified in the following prayers of Paul:

> For this reason I bow my knees before the Father, from whom every family in
> heaven and on earth is named, that according to the riches of his glory he may
> grant you to be strengthened with power through his Spirit in your inner

being, so that Christ may dwell in your hearts through faith—that you, being rooted and grounded in love, may have strength to comprehend with all the saints what is the breadth and length and height and depth, and to know the love of Christ that surpasses knowledge, that you may be filled with all the fullness of God. (Eph 3:14-19)

And again,

That the God of our Lord Jesus Christ, the Father of glory, may give you the Spirit of wisdom and of revelation in the knowledge of him, having the eyes of your hearts enlightened, that you may know what is the hope to which he has called you, what are the riches of his glorious inheritance in the saints, and what is the immeasurable greatness of his power toward us who believe. (Eph 1:17-19)

These prayers are at the heart of Paul's new covenant spirituality of what it is to be in Christ and to open to the reality of Christ in us. The historical practice of Christian contemplation and contemplative prayer merely mirrors these biblical texts and prayers of Paul on our behalf. Thus contemplation or contemplative prayer is merely obedience to Paul's injunction to attend to the presence and reality of the indwelling Spirit of Christ and his work in the inner person. There could be nothing simpler than and more biblical than this. It is one of the relational aspects of the Christian faith that evangelicalism has always insisted on.

Consequently, Christian contemplation and contemplative prayer appear merely to be an attempt to obey the prayers of Paul in Ephesians through the practice of opening the heart to one's experience inwardly in order to discern the reality of the Spirit's work in the believer's soul or inner person. They are practical ways for the believer to attend to, cooperate with, and participate in the work of the Spirit, who is attempting to bring about the following realities in our lives (Phil 2:12-13):

1. That we be strengthened with power in the inner person (Eph 3:16)

2. That Christ may dwell in our hearts through faith (Eph 3:16)

3. That we be rooted and grounded in love (Eph 3:17)

4. That we come to know the extent of the love of God (Eph 3:18-19)

5. That we be filled with all the fullness of God (Eph 3:19)

6. That we be given a spirit of wisdom and revelation in the knowledge of God (Eph 1:17)

7. That we have the eyes of our heart enlightened to know our hope, the riches of his glory, and the greatness of God's power toward us (Eph 1:18-19)

These are not merely truths or things we know by the Scripture, but fundamentally things to be known in experience, which we are invited to receive from the indwelling Spirit. And contrary to pagan contemplative prayer, biblical practice of contemplative prayer does not make these realities happen; it only puts the human will in a position to experience or discern the reality of what the Spirit has already made available to the inner person on the basis of the finished work of Christ on the cross.

Finally, notice that the fruits of contemplative prayer in opening the heart to the presence and work of God is also reflected in those psalms that encourage the believer to "taste and see that the LORD is good" (Ps 34:8), "Delight yourself in the LORD" (Ps 37:4), and "Rest in the Lord and wait patiently" (Ps 37:7 KJV). Contemplative prayer is an expression of the heart that hungers for the living God:

> As a deer pants for the flowing streams,
>   so pants my soul for you, O God.
> My soul thirsts for God,
>   for the living God. (Ps 42:1-2)

Contemplation or contemplative prayer is simply the believer's heart adoring and loving the true triune God who now has made his abode in that human heart (Jer 31:31-35; Jn 17:20-21).

CONCLUSION

In general, then, biblical Christian contemplation or contemplative prayer is clearly contrary to its pagan, distorted counterpart in the following ways:

1. Christian contemplation or contemplative prayer is not a return to a person's own original divinity (pantheism or panentheism) but is the process by which the believer's spirit experiences more deeply the ministry of the Holy Spirit on the basis of Christ's redemptive work, as one is more and more filled with all the fullness of God

(Eph 3:19; 5:18). This never obscures the absolute ontological distinction between the finite human spirit and the Spirit of God. Rather, this is the heart of a true Christian mysticism that is more relational in orientation and rejects pagan mysticism that is primarily ontological in nature.

2. Christian contemplation or contemplative prayer is entirely dependent on God revealing himself in order to strengthen the believer, love the believer, and so on. We pray, but it is up to God to provide what he wishes for our good (Phil 2:12-13).

3. Christian contemplation or contemplative prayer is grounded in an orthodox view of original sin requiring the work of Christ in the new covenant to reconcile humanity to God. Apart from this, the human spirit cannot experience the Spirit of God (Eph 2:5).

4. Christian contemplative prayer may involve a use of silence or Scripture, not as a way to empty the self of itself in some return to its own fanaticized divinity but rather to empty the heart of unnecessary distractions and expectations in an attempt to open the human spirit to the person and work of the Holy Spirit (Eph 1:17-19), who dwells within and in relational union with our spirit.

5. Christian contemplation or contemplative prayer does not aim at producing altered states of consciousness for the sake of therapeutic euphoria or ecstasy with the divine. Rather, it puts the human will in a place to be open to the presence, work, and will of the Spirit of God as a response to the command to be filled with or influenced by the Spirit (the force of the passive voice in Eph 5:18), regardless of the resulting feeling (consolation or dryness). God is present regardless of how we feel, so that faith (trust) and not feelings becomes our access to letting the Spirit affect us as well as our way of discerning the presence of God.[14]

6. Christian contemplation or contemplative prayer is not the result of a technique or something engineered by our doing spiritual disciplines.

---

[14]There is much more to say here on the psychology of feelings and faith in relationship to knowledge of God in contemplation. There is much confusion on this deep matter. Nothing short of a full-blown spiritual theology of contemplation is needed to tease out the interaction between the human spirit and God's Spirit in knowing God, which may be the subject of a further volume on contemplation by the authors.

Rather, it is from beginning to end a work of the Spirit of God on the human spirit by which we even cry out to God as Father in the first place (Rom 8:15) and by which we in fullness and maturity come to know the love of God by being rooted and grounded in the love of the indwelling Christ in our spirit (Eph 3:17-19). The implication of this new covenant spirituality is that we participate and interact with God, but it is he who initiates and generates religious presence, prayer, maturity, and sanctification.

In summary, the Christian, biblical approach to contemplation and contemplative prayer primarily highlights the human spirit in response to the person and sanctifying work of the indwelling Spirit on the basis of the revelation of God in Christ, which alone meets the deepest human hunger for reality and the living God. This is what we were made for, and this is where we are going.

IS THOUGHTLESS PRAYER REALLY CHRISTIAN?

A Biblical/Evangelical Response to Evagrius of Pontus

EVAN B. HOWARD

I CONFESS THAT I HAVE ENVIED C3PO. There is a scene in a *Star Wars* movie where C3PO, a highly intelligent and comical robot, looks over to his owner and says, "Sir, if you'll not be needing me, I'll close down for awhile." Then he switches a button and bingo, all his thinking is gone. In all honesty there are times when I would like my experience of prayer to be like that. Sometimes my mind is so full of ideas and questions and plans and deadlines that I would love just to sit with God, switch a button somewhere, and be done with all the chatter in my head.

I know I am not alone. I have met with Christian leaders who after years of manipulating words and concepts and experiences to navigate their relationship with God find themselves increasingly comfortable with silence. Perhaps unanswered prayers or big questions just accumulate to the point where it is not worth trying to put together the words any more. Or perhaps we have now seen God, and trite words or shallow concepts cannot begin to express the pure holiness of God. For whatever reason, some Christians pray in a manner that does not use words, or even particular thoughts or feelings.

Other Christians express concern with this kind of prayer. Some suggest that biblical prayer speaks with words and is not a matter of silence. Some are concerned that the practices of what is often called contemplative prayer is an invention of early monks whose innovations were unfaithful to the life and message of Jesus and the original apostles.[1]

Consequently, it behooves us to carefully examine the practice and viewpoints of these early monks and to offer a biblical and evangelical evaluation. This present essay aims to do just that particularly in dialogue with one of the most influential early monks of Christian history: Evagrius of Pontus (346–399 CE). It is common knowledge among patristic scholars that Evagrius was the most prolific writer, and perhaps the earliest system-atizer, of desert spirituality. Augustine Casiday opens his introduction to a translation of Evagrius's works by saying simply, "Evagrius was, and still is, the teacher of prayer par excellence for the Greek Christian tradition."[2] Evagrius articulated a paradigm of spiritual life that was to serve as a foun-dation for such spiritual theologians as Maximus the Confessor in the East and John Cassian in the West. More to our purpose here, various notions of word/thought-lessness are central to Evagrius's understanding of Christian prayer. In this essay, then, I will present a brief summary of Evagrius's life, monastic practice, and teaching on prayer, drawing special attention to those places in his works where he speaks about the avoidance of thoughts in prayer. Having summarized the approach of Evagrius, I will then offer a few reflections by way of evaluation and application for our practice of prayer today.

THE LIFE OF EVAGRIUS

Evagrius was the son of a country bishop in what is now Turkey.[3] A preco-cious child, Evagrius was mentored by Basil the Great and Gregory of

---

[1] For a sample of this kind of critique, see Christian Research Network, "Contemplative Prayer," accessed October 24, 2013, http://christianresearchnetwork.org/topic/contemplative-prayer/.

[2] A. M. Casiday, "Why Evagrius Matters," in *Evagrius Ponticus*, trans. A. M. Casiday, The Early Church Fathers (London: Routledge, 2006), 3.

[3] Evagrius's disciple Palladius recorded the most complete biographical sketch of Evagrius we possess. See Palladius, *The Lausiac History*, trans. Robert T. Meyer, Ancient Christian Writers 34 (New York: Paulist Press, 1964), 110-14. For summaries of the life of Evagrius see John Eudes Bamberger, trans., *Evagrius Ponticus: The Praktikos and Chapters on Prayer*, Cistercian Studies Series 4 (Kalamazoo, MI: Cistercian Publications, 1981), xxxv-xlviii, and Augustine Casiday, *Reconstructing the Theology of Evagrius Ponticus: Beyond Heresy* (Cambridge: Cambridge University Press, 2013), 1-72. I have recorded an audio account of the life of Evagrius that was originally presented at a Renovaré Conversation in 2012 and is currently available at The Spirituality Shoppe, http://spiritualityshoppe.org/old-monastic-wisdom-for-new-monastic-people/.

Nazianzus.[4] He rose in the ranks of the academic elites and in time his spiritual life grew careless. After a near-affair with a married noblewoman, Evagrius was warned by God in a dream to flee the city and attend to his soul. He traveled to the Holy Land and was welcomed by Melania and by Rufinus, translator of the works of Origen. Again he grew comfortable and neglected his soul. He suffered a fever and was only healed when he resolved to make things right with God. Again he relocated, this time settling (around 383) among the monastic communities of Lower Egypt. He learned from some of the most well-respected desert elders of that time. Indeed he became one of them: his circle of colleagues was known as "The Group of Ammonius and Evagrius." Evagrius made his living by copying manuscripts in his cell, one of the first monks to pursue this form of livelihood. In time he wrote his own works, pioneering the genre of "centuries": a way of collecting proverbial sentences in groups of about a hundred. He died in Egypt in 399, just in time to miss the condemnation of some of his ideas under the label of "Origenism."[5] Evagrius was the first to record sayings of the desert elders. And as I mentioned above, he was also the first to systematize a desert-inspired theology of the spiritual life and prayer.

EVAGRIUS'S MONASTIC PRACTICE

Evagrius was above all a monastic theologian. Thus, in order to better understand Evagrius's thought about prayer, it is necessary to sense something of Evagrius's daily life and rhythms as a monk.[6] The chief elements of this

---

[4]For an example of Evagrius's early defense of the trinitarian faith, see his letter *On the Faith* previously attributed to Basil, but now confirmed to be the work of Evagrius. In Casiday, *Evagrius Ponticus*, 45-58.

[5]On the Origenist and related anthropomorphite controversies, see, for example, Elizabeth A. Clark, *The Origenist Controversy: The Cultural Construction of an Early Christian Debate* (Princeton, NJ: Princeton University Press, 1992); Paul Patterson, *Visions of Christ: The Anthropomorphite Controversy of 399 CE* (Tübingen: Mohr Siebeck, 2012). I am indebted to Tomader Kamel Awadallah for her partnership in exploring these debates.

[6]Evagrian scholarship is paying increasing attention to interpreting Evagrius in light of his monastic practice. See, for example, Columba Stewart, "Imageless Prayer and the Theological Vision of Evagrius Ponticus," *Journal of Early Christian Studies* 9, no. 2 (summer 2001): 173-204, in light of his "The Practices of Monastic Prayer: Origins, Evolution, and Tensions" (paper presented at "Living for Eternity: The White Monastery and Its Neighborhood," a symposium at the University of Minnesota, Minneapolis, March 6–9, 2003), http://egypt.umn.edu/Egypt/1 -pb%20pdfs/stewart.pdf; and Luke Dysinger, *Psalmody and Prayer in the Writings of Evagrius Ponticus* (Oxford: Oxford University Press, 2005).

rhythm were Scripture reading, manual labor, and prayer, with occasional interruptions by a visitor. Columba Stewart summarizes their form of prayer: "The form was simple, consisting of the recitation of memorized biblical texts with periodic pauses for vocal and possibly silent prayer, accompanied by ritual gestures and changes of posture."[7] A prayer could refer to one cycle of this form or to a moment of rising or prostrating interspersed between times of reading and meditation. Monks sometimes listed the number of times this cycle was performed: Evagrius prayed perhaps one hundred times each day, rising perhaps every ten minutes to offer prayer to God.[8]

Two important conclusions can be drawn from this brief sketch of monastic rhythm. First, whatever wordless or thought-less prayers might be suggested in Evagrius's writings, we can be confident that in practice he was absolutely saturated with the reading of and meditation on the words of Scripture. A second conclusion is that when Evagrius speaks of a "time of prayer" he does not necessarily refer to an extended period of personal devotion. More likely this phrase describes "the 'refreshing' interval which followed each chanted psalm or reading at the daily canonical prayers."[9] We shall explore the significance of these two conclusions below.

EVAGRIUS'S MYSTICAL THEOLOGICAL SYSTEM
AND LANGUAGE FOR PRAYER

Evagrius was both a mystic and a theologian. His mysticism grew from his monastic practice of prayer. In his theological system he developed the thought of Origen. Furthermore, Evagrius was a consistent thinker: his understanding of prayer was of a piece with his larger theological framework. Consequently, just as it is important to understand Evagrius's monastic practice, so also it is valuable to grasp Evagrius's view of the transformative path leading to ever-increasing union with God.[10]

---

[7]Stewart, "Practices of Monastic Prayer," 98.

[8]See Palladius, *Lausiac History* 38.10; Dysinger, *Psalmody and Prayer*, 51; Stewart, "Imageless Prayer," 185.

[9]Dysinger, *Psalmody and Prayer*, 196. See also, for example, Evagrius, *Praktikos* 23, 25; *Gnostikos* 45; *Skemmata*, 4; *De oratione* 68-69; *Ad monachos* 15.

[10]For Evagrius's theological system, see, for example, William Harmless, *Desert Christians: An Introduction to the Literature of Early Monasticism* (Oxford: Oxford University Press, 2004), 345-71; Casiday, *Reconstructing*, 73-250.

Evagrius describes this path in language tailored to his particular audience, monks in training. We may summarize his approach to this path as follows: After a monk settles down into a place of stillness there are two primary stages of growth. The first is a season of ascetical practice, called *praktikos*, during which the monk's primary focus is on the removal of sinful passions. The second is a season of mystical knowledge called *gnostikos*, during which the emphasis shifts toward the contemplation of various objects: nature, spiritual realities, leading finally to the knowledge of the trinitarian God.

Evagrius speaks of prayer with the same range of terms and concepts that we do today, reflecting the breadth and richness of his own monastic practice. He speaks of ordinary petitionary prayer and gatherings for prayer. He speaks of meditation on Scripture.[11] And yet, while he comprehends prayer in all its variety and fullness, he ultimately points his disciples toward "pure" prayer or the higher forms and experiences of prayer.

The journey of the spiritual life is frequently complicated, Evagrius reminds his readers, by various obstructions lying along the path. Many of these obstacles appear in the form of thoughts, and consequently an important part of Evagrian spirituality is the removal of these obstacles, these thoughts, from the way of prayer. For, as William Harmless writes of Evagrius in his *Desert Christians*, "Evagrius suggests that prayer is, in the end, wordless . . . to move beyond words into wordless contemplation. Prayer in its higher form meant not simply moving beyond words; it meant 'the stripping away of thoughts.'"[12] This stripping away of thoughts takes a different shape at each stage of spiritual development. I will summarize this process of ever-nuanced removal of thoughts in the section that follows. Then, once we have traveled his path to pure prayer, we will be better able to consider his—and our own—approach to thought-less, contemplative prayer today.

Beginners: Ordinary avoidance of distractions. As mentioned above, Evagrius's monk passes through various stages of maturing. The preliminary stage is a stage of settling in to "the way of stillness": through the abandonment

---

[11]Evagrius, *Kephalia Gnostica* 4.76; *De oratione* 5-6, 31-33, 37; *Foundations of the Monastic Life* 9, 11; *Skemmata* 27-30.

[12]Harmless, *Desert Christians*, 352.

of possessions and family, and through fasting, manual labor, and prayer. The young monk in this season aims to clear away the clutter that has surrounded him (or her—Evagrius also wrote instructions for women) and to establish a new pattern of life focused entirely on the pursuit of God. This monk is to pray "with fear and trembling, with effort, with vigilance and wakefulness."[13] The point is for newcomers to exercise intention to establish themselves in whole-hearted devotion to God. Thoughts of the comforts and vanity of one's previous life are to be set aside. Instead of preoccupying one's thoughts with memories from the past, the monk is to contemplate the future, giving "heed to the day of your death." Evagrius gives explicit instructions in his *Foundations of the Monastic Life* regarding how the young monk is to imagine their death and judgment, describing how they are to "call to mind" both heaven and hell.[14]

As the monk begins to settle into a new way of life, they must learn to dismiss not only thoughts of home but also ordinary distractions. In his treatise *On Prayer*, Evagrius offers some basic guidance: "Stand resolute, fully intent on your prayer. Pay no heed to the concerns and thoughts that might arise the while. They do nothing better than disturb and upset you so as to dissolve the fixity of your purpose. . . . Strive to render your mind deaf and dumb at the time of prayer and then you will be able to pray."[15]

Maturing Christians: Removal of sinful thoughts. The shift from needing to eliminate thoughts of home and the simple distractions of life to addressing temptations or irritations indicates a transition to the stage of *praktikos*, wherein the monk learns to address their own habits from within. When Evagrius's disciples moved into the stage of ascetical practice it was then time to recognize—and to remove—those thoughts rising in their minds as a result of sinful passions. Disordered thoughts were bound to get in the way of relationship with God. Evagrius identified eight basic categories of these thoughts,

---

[13]Evagrius, *Foundations* 11. Here and elsewhere through this chapter, all quotations of *Foundations* are from the translation of Robert E. Sinkewicz, in *Evagrius of Pontus: The Greek Ascetic Corpus*, Oxford Early Christian Studies (Oxford: Oxford University Press, 2003).

[14]Evagrius, *Foundations* 9. See also Benedicta Ward, trans., *The Sayings of the Desert Fathers: The Alphabetical Collection*, Cistercian Studies 59 (Kalamazoo, MI: Cistercian Publications, 1975), "Evagrius," 4, 64.

[15]Evagrius, *De oratione* 9-12. Here and elsewhere through this chapter, all quotations of *De oratione* are from the translation of John Eudes Bamberger, *Evagrius Ponticus: The Praktikos and Chapters on Prayer*, Cistercian Studies 4 (Kalamazoo, MI: Cistercian Publications, 1981).

which he labeled *logismoi*. He states, "There are eight general and basic categories of thoughts. . . . First is that of gluttony, then impurity, avarice, sadness, anger, acedia, vainglory, and last of all pride."[16] Our job as maturing Christians is to learn to recognize these thoughts—and particularly those toward which we might be more predisposed—and then to rid ourselves of them.

At this point in the monk's education in prayer the aim is not necessarily to remove all thoughts, but rather, to quote Evagrius, "those which assail it from *thymos* [anger or disordered irascibility] and *epithymia* [lust or disordered affectivity] and those which are against nature."[17] Evagrius was deeply concerned with the influence of the sinful passions in our lives and their ability to prevent us from reaching the goal of pure prayer. Consequently, as soon as we are able we must devote careful attention and serious effort to the removal of vice-driven thoughts from our prayer (and our life), and conversely we must strive to acquire both the holy apathy (*a-patheia*—without passions) and Christian love, which enable us to perceive and pursue our trinitarian God.

More mature Christians: Elimination of image and representation. But Evagrius does not want his disciples to stop there. As the stage of ascetical practice develops into a season of mystical knowledge, Evagrius insists that it is necessary to clear away still other forms of thought that stand in the way of perceiving and relating to God. Over time we become overly attached to particular ways of imagining or experiencing God. In these times it is wise to combat our narrow God-images with the idol-smashing practice of watchfulness. Evagrius advises his followers: "When you are praying do not fancy the Divinity like some image formed within yourself. Avoid also allowing your spirit to be impressed with the seal of some particular shape, but rather, free from all matter, draw near the immaterial Being and you will attain to understanding."[18] Evagrius lived in a world largely populated by

---

[16]Evagrius, *Praktikos* 6; an early version of what we now call the "seven deadly sins." All quotations of the *Praktikos* are from the translation of Bamberger, *The Praktikos and Chapters on Prayer*.

[17]Evagrius, *Kephalia Gnostica* 6.83. Here and elsewhere through this chapter, all quotations of the *Gnostika* and the *Kephalia Gnostika* are from the translation of Luke Dysinger found at www .ldysinger.com/Evagrius/02_Gno-Keph/00a_start.htm. See also *De oratione* 53. For more on the epistemology that influences Evagrius here, see, for example, Stewart, "Imageless Prayer," 187-91; Robert E. Sinkewicz, introduction to *On Thoughts (Peri Logismon)*, in *Evagrius of Pontus: The Greek Ascetic Corpus*, trans. Robert E. Sinkewicz, Oxford Early Christian Studies (Oxford: Oxford University Press, 2003), 136-53; Dysinger, *Psalmody and Prayer*, 35-38.

[18]Evagrius, *De oratione* 66.

pagans who conceived the gods with crude anthropomorphic images. Evagrius wanted none of this for his Christian followers, for the Christian God transcended mere imaginary forms. Even if God seems to appear to us, we must not permit ourselves to be deceived by the thought that God is somehow localized or something quantitative, for, Evagrius states, "God is without quantity and without all outward form."[19] Thoughts born of the material world—and even human thoughts about God—can draw the mind of the mature Christian away from the immaterial God. For prayer to be pure, our mind must also be pure, because the God we pray to is pure.[20] To borrow the language of Carmelite mysticism, Evagrius is here advocating a kind of "acquired contemplation": training the mind to withdraw from thoughts of God that are inadequate to the Object of faith for the sake of a prayer that reflects both the purest sincerity of our hearts and the inexpressible majesty of God.[21]

Prayer as a gift and a state. Whereas at times Evagrius speaks as if pure prayer were an acquired contemplation—the fruit of the practices of virtue and watchfulness—at other times he emphasizes that pure prayer is a gift of the grace of God (an infused contemplation). "If you wish to pray then it is God whom you need. He it is who gives prayer to the man who prays," Evagrius affirms. "The Holy Spirit takes compassion on our weakness, and though we are impure he often comes to visit us. If he should find our spirit praying to him out of love for the truth he then descends upon it and dispels the whole army of thoughts and reasonings that beset it."[22] As Gabriel Bunge states, "In its highest form as 'spiritual prayer' prayer is no longer the work of man but the gift of God, made possible only by the visitation and personal presence of the Spirit and the Son. It is they alone who liberate the 'spiritual prayer' in the human person."[23]

---

[19]Evagrius, *De oratione* 67.

[20]See, for example, Evagrius, *De oratione*. 56-57, 72; *Skemmata* 20-23.

[21]See, for example, Evagrius, *Peri Logismoi* 40. It is especially important to see how chap. 40 is nested within the development of chaps. 39-43. See also *De oratione* 69-70; Stewart, "Imageless Prayer," 190; Sinkewicz, *Evagrius of Pontus*, 147, 152-53. On the distinctions between *acquired* and *infused* contemplation, see, for example, Adolphe Tanquerey, *The Spiritual Life: A Treatise on Ascetical and Mystical Theology*, trans. Herman Branderis (Tournai, Belgium: Desclée, 1923), 637-50.

[22]Evagrius, *De oratione* 58, 62.

[23]Gabriel Bunge, "The 'Spiritual Prayer': On the Trinitarian Mysticism of Evagrius of Pontus," *Monastic Studies* 17 (1987): 198, 202; and Dysinger, *Prayer and Psalmody*, 172.

When prayer has reached its final development, it is best not to describe prayer as an act but more accurately as a state. Thus Evagrius reflects that "prayer is the state of mind that comes to be from the single-light of the Holy Trinity."[24] Evagrius portrays this state of prayer as a "place of God" much as Mount Sinai was the place where Moses met face to face with the Lord, or with the image of "sapphire light" taken from Ezekiel.[25] It is a state where the one in prayer discovers his or her own true state in coming face to face with God in his pure state.[26] William Harmless summarizes,

> At a deeper level, Evagrius implies that prayer is not just an activity of the mind; it is a state of mind, a *katastasis*. That means that prayer is not so much something one *does* as something one *is*. . . . Evagrius does not think of this higher form of prayer as ecstatic—at least not in the strict sense. Ecstasy (*ekstasis*) literally means to "stand outside" oneself. For Evagrius, prayer is not *ekstasis*, not leaving oneself; it is a *katastasis*, a coming to one's true state.[27]

We have now followed Evagrius down the path of prayer. From the simple removal of ordinary distractions, through resistance to thoughts arising from sinful passions and the elimination of shallow representations present in the human mind, until in the end we find ourselves bathing in the dazzling light of the Trinity itself, we have encountered one form of the removal of thoughts from our practice of prayer after another. The question we must ask ourselves, now that we have gained some comprehension of Evagrius, is: Is it Christian? Does this practice of the elimination of thoughts cohere with a biblical view of relationship with God? Or to ask in a different way, can we as evangelicals affirm or condone such a practice?

A BIBLICAL AND EVANGELICAL RESPONSE

As should be obvious, a Christian reply to Evagrius must respond to his recommendations in the context of each stage of development. Thus, with regard to beginning and maturing nuns/monks, I can only affirm Evagrius's

---

[24]Evagrius, *Skemmata* 22. Here and elsewhere through this chapter, all quotations of the Skemmata are from the translation of William Harmless and Raymond R. Fitzgerald in their article "The Sapphire Light of the Mind: The *Skemmata* of Evagrius Ponticus," *Theological Studies* 62 (2001): 521-29. See also Harmless and Fitzgerald, "Sapphire Light," 517-19.

[25]On these themes, see Stewart, "Imageless Prayer," 195-98; Dysinger, *Psalmody and Prayer*, 166-71; Evagrius, *De oratione* 56-57.

[26]See especially Evagrius, *Skemmata* 2, 4; *Peri Logismoi* 39.

[27]Harmless, *Desert Christians*, 352.

advice that authentic Christian commitment is best fostered when freed from obsessing thoughts of return to one's old way of life. Similarly, when one's attention is obscured by a swirling fog of preoccupations, we can reasonably guess that prayer will be impaired. It is hard to "draw near with a true heart" (Heb 10:22) when we are overly distracted. It is obvious, furthermore, that our prayer does not benefit by preserving thoughts that arise from sinful passions. Indeed, we are commanded in Scripture to rid ourselves of these (e.g., Gal 5:19-21; Eph 4:17–5:4). Consequently, while we cannot demand that all Christians eliminate every distraction or sinful thought from interfering with their prayers, it seems perfectly appropriate to expect the maturing Christian to make efforts to curb such patterns and thereby pray lifting up increasingly "holy hands" (1 Tim 2:8).

When we assess Evagrius's advice to more mature Christians, however, a few concerns arise. In order to communicate a biblical/evangelical response to these concerns it will be necessary first to say something about God, about silence, and about prayer. Having reviewed what we know (and what we don't know) from Scripture on these points, we will then be in a place to consider reasonable recommendations for the practice of wordless (and even thought-less) prayer today.

The transcendent greatness of God. What kinds of prayer are most fitting for the God of the Christian faith? This is the question that drives Evagrius's advice not only to mature Christians, but to all Christians. To the beginner it is wise to reflect on the judicial aspect of God's character. Likewise, it is wise to remember God as Savior. But these words, these ideas, for Evagrius, only point to God. They do not define God in himself. The words and metaphors are valuable for a beginner who is being weaned from paganism to the specifically biblical and Christian God. But for the more mature it is often wiser to leave these images and metaphors behind, for ultimately God is an "immaterial Being," "without quantity or outward form." Thus, for Evagrius, a tight hold on the words, concepts, and images we use to interact with God may only serve (for the mature Christian) to misdirect prayer from its rightful Object.[28]

Evagrius here is only echoing a theme found throughout Christian Scripture and tradition. God is by definition transcendent. The God to

---

[28]See, for example, Evagrius, *Gnostikos* 27; *Kephalia Gnostika* 2.21.

whom we pray is not only *Deus revelatus* but also *Deus absconditus*, not only a God who self-reveals, but also a God who hides.[29] Elihu queries Job, "Can you find out the deep things of God?" (Job 11:7). Isaiah declares that the Lord's understanding "is unsearchable" (Is 40:28). Paul explores the doctrine of God's sovereignty in Romans only to conclude by proclaiming, "Oh, the depth of the riches and wisdom and knowledge of God! How unsearchable are his judgments and how inscrutable his ways!" (Rom 11:33; see also 1 Cor 2:16; Is 40:13).[30] True, God is the one who is revealed. Thus, we can and must speak. But God is also the One who transcends. Of this God, nothing can be said.[31]

Silence. This brings us to the next point: silence. What does silence mean in the Scriptures or in early Christian tradition? How does (or how should) silence function for the people of God? Is there a relationship between silence and prayer? These are important questions, for Scripture must serve as "our basis for our understanding the concepts of silence and solitude and how they relate to spirituality,"[32] particularly as we develop an evangelical response to Evagrius.

The notion of silence in Scripture encompasses a number of terms and even distinct concepts.[33] There is the virtue of the quietness of life (1 Thess 4:11; 1 Tim 2:2). There is the place of silence in death (Ps 94:17) and the silence of God who fails to respond to prayer (Ps 88). Jesus is silent before his accusers as a suffering servant (Jn 19:8-9; see Is 53:7). More relevant to our purposes, however, are the themes of trust and reverence.

A number of passages speak of silence or stillness, expressing a sense of calm trust in the sovereign hand of God. The psalmist affirms, "For God alone my soul waits in silence" (Ps 62:1, 5 NRSV). In Psalm 46:10 the psalmist

---

[29]On this theme in Christian doctrine, see, for example, Donald Bloesch, *Christian Foundations,* vol. 3, *God the Almighty: Power, Wisdom, Holiness, Love* (Downers Grove, IL: InterVarsity Press, 1995), 49, 59-65.

[30]See also *Gregory of Nyssa: The Life of Moses,* trans. Abraham J. Malherbe and Everett Ferguson, Classics of Western Spirituality (New York: Paulist Press, 1978), 2.163.

[31]I have addressed the relationship between the character of God and our spirituality more fully in *The Brazos Introduction to Christian Spirituality* (Grand Rapids: Brazos, 2008), 113-44.

[32]Robert L. Plummer, "Are the Spiritual Disciplines of 'Silence and Solitude' really Biblical?," *Journal of Spiritual Formation and Soul Care* 2, no. 1 (2009): 109.

[33]On this see, for example, Paolo Torresan, "Silence in the Bible," *Jewish Bible Quarterly* 31, no. 3 (2003): 153-60; Göran Eidevall, "Sounds of Silence in Biblical Hebrew: A Lexical Study," *Vetus Testamentum* 62 (2012): 159-74; Diarmaid MacCulloch, *Silence: A Christian History* (New York: Viking, 2013), 11-52.

proclaims the invitation of God: "Be still, and know that I am God." These
are psalms of trust and hope. While these psalms do not describe a particular
discipline of devotion, they do promote a mood of devotion, a mood of
setting aside anxious thoughts to rest in trustful stillness within the care
of the Almighty. And, as psalms, they were written in the context of the
practice of personal and corporate worship (see also Ps 4:4; 37:7; Lam 3:26).
Perhaps we step closer to a description of a practice of silence with Psalm 131.
Again, a psalm of hope (Ps 131:3), this psalm expresses the same confident
resignation to the care of God. "I have calmed and quieted my soul" (Ps
131:2). What is unique about this psalm is that it gives no context. It is a
simple psalm of ascent, written to express and to foster the worship of the
people of God as they approach their God. It describes patterns of thoughts:
more correctly, thoughts removed. The psalmist has eliminated
thoughts arising from pride or haughtiness or even inappropriate concerns
(Ps 131:1). In place of these unwanted thoughts the psalmist fosters a quiet
faith, symbolized by a silent rest in God's parental care (Ps 131:2).

The Scriptures also mention a silence that communicates a sense of reverence before the supremely holy God. In Habakkuk 2:20 we read,

> But the LORD is in his holy temple;
>   let all the earth keep silence before him.

Similarly in Zechariah 2:13 we hear the command to "Be silent, all flesh,
before the LORD, for he has roused himself from his holy dwelling." In Habakkuk the immediate context concerns idolatry. Whereas God mocks
("Alas!") those who speak to a wooden idol that itself cannot speak
(Hab 2:18-19), those who approach the LORD are commanded to keep silent.
Words are inappropriate before the Almighty.[34] In Zechariah, the context is
the impending deliverance of God (Zech 2:6-12). After all Israel had been
through, consideration of the restoration of God's people could only be made
in silence. The matter was too great for words (see also Amos 5:13; Zeph 1:7).
Perhaps even more significant is the account in Revelation 8:1, where, after
the seventh seal is opened, "There was silence in heaven for about half an
hour." While loud praise is the dominant response to God throughout the

---

[34]The very name of God (YHWH) is meant to be unpronounced, a continual reminder that the
Creator is ultimately named not in words, but in silence.

Apocalypse, we find here that at times silence—and even extended silence—is a perfectly appropriate response to the supreme holiness of God.[35] The point here is that, as with scriptural descriptions of trusting silence, these passages of reverent silence, while not providing guidelines for a normative spiritual discipline of silence, offer relevant images of appropriate wordlessness before the transcendent and holy Lord. Indeed, it is this theme of reverent silence that is particularly developed immediately following the New Testament period in such figures as Ignatius of Antioch and Clement of Alexandria (with whose writings Evagrius was well acquainted).[36]

Prayer. Having offered some comments with regard to our understanding of both God and silence, I now venture a few thoughts on prayer.[37] First, prayer is described in Scripture as both request and as a general term identifying various kinds of communication with God. Paul, for example, can speak of the Christian community offering up "supplications, prayers, intercessions, and thanksgivings" (1 Tim 2:1), which he later summarizes with the word "pray" a few verses later (1 Tim 2:8). Similarly both the Psalms and the Lord's Prayer itself model a range of communication with God.

Second, we know little about the specific practices of the people of Scripture. We don't know how much speech and how much silence were involved when Jesus spent the whole night praying (Lk 6:12). We read that Jesus prayed for one hour in Gethsemane, and yet only two sentences are recorded (Mk 14:35-37). We don't know what was going on during Peter's

---

[35] See Peter Wick, "There Was Silence in Heaven (Revelation 8:1): An Annotation to Israel Knohl's 'Between Voice and Silence,'" *Journal of Biblical Literature* 117, no. 3 (1998): 512-14; David E. Aune, *Revelation 6–16*, Word Biblical Commentary 52B (Dallas: Word, 1998), 508 (1 Kings 19:11-12 is also relevant).

[36] On Ignatius of Antioch see his *Letter to the Magnesians* 8.2, in which he interprets the incarnation of the Son Jesus from the one God as the Word proceeding from silence. On Clement see Raoul Mortley, "The Theme of Silence in Clement of Alexandria," *Journal of Theological Studies* 24, no. 1 (1973): 197-202.

[37] On prayer in the Scriptures, see, along with the treatments in the dictionaries, Patrick D. Miller, *They Cried to the Lord: The Form and Theology of Biblical Prayer* (Minneapolis: Fortress, 1994); Robert J. Karris, *Prayer and the New Testament: Jesus and His Communities at Worship*, Companions to the New Testament (New York: Herder and Herder, 2000). More generally see, for example, Hans Urs von Balthasar, *Prayer*, trans. Graham Harrison (San Francisco: Ignatius, 1986); Donald Bloesch, *The Struggle of Prayer* (San Francisco: Harper and Row, 1980); James Houston, *The Transforming Friendship: A Guide to Prayer* (Oxford: Lion, 1989); and Richard Foster, *Prayer: Finding the Heart's True Home* (San Francisco: HarperSanFrancisco, 1992). For my own treatment of prayer in the Christian tradition, see Howard, *Brazos Introduction*, 299-335.

prayer when he received the vision of the sheet (Acts 10:9-12) or when Paul was caught up into the third heaven and "heard inexpressible things" (2 Cor 12:2-4 NIV). We know clearly that Christians prayed. Nevertheless, we can only see faint glimpses of the actual habitual prayer disciplines of the earliest Christians.

Finally, it is fair to say that the place of silence in spiritual practices is neither emphasized nor condemned in the Scriptures. We find silence mentioned in a few places, as I have described above. I might also mention the "groanings too deep for words" through which the Spirit ministers in prayer (Rom 8:26). Yet, as with forms of small group fellowship or evangelism technique, Scripture does not provide us with universally normative patterns of devotional practice. So, do we "prohibit what the Scripture does not promote," or do we "permit what the Scripture does not prohibit?" An old question indeed.

A few recommendations. With no biblical mandate either to prescribe or to prohibit a practice of silent prayer, the wisest course of action is to respectfully consider the relevant material in both Scripture and tradition (Evagrius, in this case) and to offer recommendations that promote the authentic development of a sincere and "true" Christian religion.[38]

1. It seems good and natural that we would—and even should—foster different experiences of prayer appropriate to different stages of our maturity in Christ. It seems false, however, that we should demand or even expect our maturity to be tightly linked to any particular practice or experience.

Evagrius's approach to thought-less prayer is, as we have seen, inextricably linked to his understanding of the stages of spiritual formation. While he would encourage a beginner to imagine God's presence in the final resurrection, such imaginings are, for the more mature, to be left behind. What do we say to this?

Certainly we must acknowledge that Christians mature in stages, and that these stages are somewhat recognizable (see 1 Cor 3:1-2; Eph 4:14-16; Heb 5:12-13).[39] Though the Bible does not develop this in detail, it seems

---

[38]On the evangelical notion of "true religion," see Evan B. Howard, "Evangelical Spirituality," in *Four Views of Christian Spirituality*, ed. Bruce Demarest (Grand Rapids: Zondervan, 2012), 165-68.

[39]For a more developed account of the stages of Christian transformation, see Howard, *Brazos Introduction*, 247-54.

reasonable to assume that our experience of prayer will change over time. Consider how our communication develops within human relationships. I have noticed, in the decades of my own marriage, that there is now less chatter and more space for a pleasant wordless silence between my spouse and me. Couldn't the same be true for our relationship with God, particularly for those who have spent significant investment in developing intimate communication?[40] Maturity of life and freedom for consecrated devotion will, I believe, facilitate changes in the way we pray, even facilitating greater space for silence.[41]

Nonetheless, we must reject any insistence on particular experiences or practices. Though Paul clearly permits speaking in tongues, for example, he soundly reproves those who would insist on their use or who might identify themselves, through the use of tongues, in any sense as superior Christians. The point is not to impose some practice as a normative sign of maturity, but rather to nurture a sincere love of God. Thus I must reject any insistence that the removal of all images become a normative and universal requirement for all Christians. While there are advantages to different kinds of thought-removal at different stages, silence can also be mis-practiced: to the harm of both the individual praying and the community of faith.

2. It seems good and natural that we would—and even should—permit a communicative presence with God that takes place without particular words, images, or even thoughts, as part of sincere, whole-hearted devotion to God. It seems false, however, that we would reduce the fullness of Christian devotion to a single form or pattern of experience.

Here, rather than speaking of spiritual development, I wish to make a similar point regarding the breadth of Christian spirituality in general. First, our prayer life is broad because human experience is broad. Jesus declared that the greatest commandment is to "love the Lord your God with all your heart and with all your soul and with all your strength and with all your mind" (Lk 10:27). Jesus' point here was not to delineate precise faculties, but

---

[40]For example, 1 Tim 5:5 describes widows who continue "in supplications and prayers night and day." I see this as an early example of Christian monastic practice and assume that these widows will, simply because of the context of their life and work, learn to experience prayer with a richness unavailable to others.

[41]Richard Foster states of contemplative prayer by a "word of warning": "contemplative prayer is not for the novice." Foster, Prayer, 156.

rather simply to advocate a whole-hearted devotion to God.[42] It seems fair to assume that loving God with our whole mind might involve a variety of prayer experiences.

Our experience of prayer is broad also because God is broad. Evagrius is clear about his doctrine of God: "God is without quantity and without all outward form." Evagrius is no pagan and makes no room for idolatry—whether represented by statues or by mental imagery. And at one level I must agree. While I urge that our prayer, like that of the early nuns and monks, be saturated in the words and images of Scripture, I also deeply acknowledge that to know God's love is to know a love that "surpasses knowledge" (Eph 3:19). I suspect we all carry around little mental idols with us: expectations about God that fall short of God's true nature, images of God that reflect our own culture more than the fullness of God. And sometimes the Holy Spirit invites us to let these little mental idols go. In the midst of our requests or our praise, we simply run out of words. We lie in the presence of God with our remnants of tongues-speaking. We stand before God with our fragments of liturgy. We let ourselves go in silence to the One who is beyond all our petty words and images and feelings.

Yet for this very reason I find Evagrius's *nous*-centered approach to prayer perhaps too narrow. It is unsatisfactory for me to settle the medieval debate between Franciscans and Dominicans (between will and intellect) simply on one side or the other. God is the one who fills and overfills all our layers and categories of feeling, thought, and action. Morton Kelsey finds a privileged sanctuary for God in the imaginative unconscious.[43] Thomas Keating encourages us to leave all thought behind as we remain before God with pure intention.[44] Evagrius identifies contemplation with a pure intellectual union with God. I would argue that each of these expressions of human diversity manifests some hues of color in the white light of God's fullness. I think there is an important difference between "we may benefit

---

[42]For a psychological perspective on this breadth, see for example, Andrew B. Newberg and Mark Robert Waldman, *How God Changes Your Brain: Breakthrough Findings from a Leading Neuroscientist* (New York: Ballantine, 2009).

[43]See Morton Kelsey, *Encounter with God: A Theology of Christian Experience* (New York: Paulist Press, 1988); Kelsey, *The Other Side of Silence: Meditation for the Twenty-First Century*, rev. ed. (Mahwah, NJ: Paulist Press, 1997).

[44]For example, Thomas Keating, *Open Mind, Open Heart: The Contemplative Dimension of the Gospel* (New York: Continuum, 1994).

from periods of thought-less/imageless prayer" and "we must aim toward thought-less/imageless prayer."[45]

3. It seems good and natural that we would want to avoid undue distractions in our times of prayer, even the subtle distractions of our own ways of perceiving and relating to God. It seems uncharitable, unnatural, and even false, however, that we would expect an extraordinary degree of recollection or mental purity as a prerequisite for authentic or mature encounter with Christ.

My final response to Evagrius regards neither our formation in prayer, nor the breadth of our experience in prayer, but rather to the simple act of prayer itself.

One thing we know is that the devil seeks to lead us off the path of union with and conformity to Christ. The devil is like a roaring lion (1 Pet 5:8), at times disguised as an angel of light (2 Cor 11:14). It is only logical to assume that our enemy would introduce all manner of thoughts and feelings in order to keep us from authentic prayer. Thus Evagrius rightly asserts: "The devil so passionately envies the man who prays that he employs every device to frustrate that purpose."[46] Furthermore, it is only logical to assume, given the fact that Christians are both saved and sinners, that our habits of prayer are influenced in various degrees by our own sinful passions. Consequently, the more we shed our lies and dysfunctional feelings during prayer, the more we are able to be truly present to God and open to the presence of the Holy Spirit. And the more we mature, the subtler are these thoughts to which we must attend.

But are we then to make some particular standard of recollection in prayer a norm for all believers—or at least for all the highly regarded believers? I think not. What about Christians who have attention deficit disorder or some other kindred condition? This, to me, is not the gospel of Jesus, who welcomed the least who came to him in faith. We must recognize first that intimate relationship is quite compatible with a fair amount of distraction and even dysfunction. Dominican author Simon Tugwell offers

---

[45]This distinction is at the heart of the "Origenist controversy," which ultimately led to the condemnation of some of Evagrius's works. On this controversy, see Elizabeth A. Clark, *The Origenist Controversy: The Cultural Construction of an Early Debate* (Princeton, NJ: Princeton University Press, 1992).

[46]Evagrius, *De oratione* 46.

a helpful comparison between human communication and prayer in this regard:

> When we talk to one another, there may be a hundred and one things popping in and out of our minds that have nothing whatsoever to do with our conversation, but they do not in any serious way impede communication. It is only in extreme cases that we get so distracted that conversation becomes impossible. . . . It is far better to make do with that very ordinary modicum of concentration that allows us to carry on conversations in spite of the hubbub in the background.[47]

We must remember that our practice of prayer is not merely a matter of our own ability to remove distraction, vice, and inappropriate thoughts, but is also, and more importantly, an interaction with the actively present Holy Spirit of Christ. We need not despair when we don't know how to pray, because "the Spirit himself intercedes for us with groanings too deep for words" (Rom 8:26). Prayer is ultimately more about God's grace than about our performance. Karl Barth is right, I think, when he says: "Perhaps we doubt the sincerity of our prayer and the worth of our request. But one thing is beyond doubt: it is the answer that God gives. Our prayers are weak and poor. Nevertheless, what matters is not that our prayers be forceful, but that God listens to them. That is why we pray."[48] Evagrius understood this, as we have heard already, saying that "he [the Holy Spirit] who has compassion on the ignorant will come to visit even such an insignificant person as yourself. That is when you will receive the most glorious gift of prayer."[49] Both Evagrius and evangelicalism recognize a place for both divine and human initiative in the life of prayer. However, whereas evangelicalism—ever eager to make the gospel available to the least—places greater weight on the work of the Spirit, Evagrius—ever the monastic coach—places greater weight on the performance of the one praying. I suspect that each of us has our own strengths and weaknesses.

---

[47]Simon Tugwell, *Prayer in Practice* (Springfield, IL: Templegate, 1974), 18-19. For Tugwell's own evaluation of Evagrius, see his *Ways of Imperfection: An Exploration of Christian Spirituality* (Springfield, IL: Templegate, 1985), 25-36.

[48]Karl Barth, *Prayer*, ed. Don Saliers, 50th anniversary ed. (Louisville: Westminster John Knox, 2002), 13.

[49]Evagrius, *De oratione* 69.

CONCLUSION

So what do we say about thought-less prayer? What does it mean for an individual—or for a community of faith—to approach the revealed yet infinite Trinity? I suggest, with reference both to Evagrius and to the spirit of evangelicalism, that we promote or prohibit various forms of thoughtlessness in a spirit of Christian wisdom. This wisdom must be rooted in the fundamental themes of Scripture and the practice of frequent reflection on Scripture. It must be guided by attention to the unique character of those praying. This wisdom should be sensitive to the dynamics of the work of Christ's Spirit. And finally it must be devoted to the aims of whole-gospel living to the glory of the unsearchable God.

MEDIEVAL RESSOURCEMENT

GREG PETERS

BY THE LATE MIDDLE AGES (i.e., from about 1200) there was a tendency among the era's philosophers and theologians to strive for specificity in their writing and in expressing, with great (sometimes excruciating) detail, the essence of the Christian faith. This is evidenced clearly in the theological *summae* produced by such intellectual lights as Peter of Spain (d. 1277), William of Ockham (d. 1347), and especially Thomas Aquinas (d. 1274). To illustrate the depths of these theological texts, one only needs to peruse the contents of Thomas's *Summa theologica* (*ST*). For example, in part III, question 80 of the *ST*, Thomas turns his attention to questions about eucharistic reception. In the third article he asks whether the just person alone may eat Christ sacramentally. That is, do the bread and wine remain the transubstantiated body and blood if they are eaten by unjust persons (i.e., open, unrepentant sinners)? He responds by saying, yes, unjust persons still receive the bread and wine as the body and blood because, though unjust, they know it to be the transubstantiated body and blood. However, an unbeliever, an animal (!), or someone who does not know the elements to be the Eucharist (e.g., a person thinks that the host is not consecrated) will not be eating Christ sacramentally. The bread and the wine are still the transubstantiated body and blood of Jesus, but to these persons (and animals) they will simply be consuming bread and wine; that is, they are not eating Christ sacramentally.

Now, what is different, perhaps even strange to twenty-first-century believers, about this discussion is the need to include a mention of animals eating consecrated eucharistic elements. Despite the fact that the Middle

Ages likely had a harder time keeping mice out of the tabernacle for the reserved host, there is also just the sheer expansiveness of theological *summae*.
Despite the fact that Thomas was addressing what was then a practical
matter, he was also addressing it because his *Summa* was extensive enough
to allow him to address it as a matter of course. This is perhaps strange to us
today, but it was run-of-the-mill theologizing to a high medieval theologian
like Thomas.

Such neat compartmentalizing is not really in vogue these days, though
analytic theologians lean in this direction. More popular are the narratival
and dramatic approaches of George Lindbeck, Hans Frei, Stanley Hauerwas,
and Kevin Vanhoozer, for example. Nonetheless, both medieval and modern
theologians have to deal with (or, at least, should deal with) the concept of
contemplation, which, by its very nature, appears not to be easily catego-
rized. It is a more slippery category, especially in the medieval era. And
slippery not because it lacks content or is too ephemeral but slippery because it is experiential and existential. In contemplation the most hidden
mysteries of God reveal themselves to (sometimes) unsuspecting recipients.[1]
Despite this more personal, less categorical nature of contemplation, it was
still treated in *summae* and works dedicated to discussions of the spiritual
life. Thus, in this chapter I will investigate the nature of contemplation as
understood in the medieval church using select theological and spiritual texts.

For medieval theologians and practitioners, contemplation was a reality
given license by the Bible itself and in at least two ways. First, the Old Testament narrative concerning Rachel and Leah was consistently interpreted
throughout the Middle Ages as a text describing the relationship of the active
and contemplative life, as was the New Testament story of Mary and Martha.
In Genesis 28–29 we are told that Jacob, Isaac's son, is sent to his uncle Laban
in order to find a wife from among Laban's daughters. In obedience Jacob
went to Laban, but while on the way he experienced a dream, in which "there
was a ladder set up on the earth, and the top of it reached to heaven. And
behold, the angels of God were ascending and descending on it! And behold,
the Lord stood above it and said, 'I am the LORD.'" (Gen 28:12-13). After being

---

[1]The recipients are not unsuspecting because they are not eager to participate in contemplation.
On the contrary, many monastic orders in the Middle Ages spent the bulk of their time in activity that prepared them for contemplation or even, they would say, *in* contemplation. Yet the most
profound contemplative moments often came unexpectedly, of which more will be said below.

promised by the Lord that he would receive the land on which he was standing, that his offspring would be numerous, and that God would be with them, Jacob awoke and proclaimed, "Surely the LORD is in this place, and I did not know it. . . . How awesome is this place! This is none other than the house of God, and this is the gate of heaven" (Gen 28:16-17). To memorialize this event Jacob erected a pillar and named the place Bethel ("the house of God"), then continued on his journey. Arriving in his uncle's land, Jacob meets Rachel, Laban's younger daughter, who comes to water the flocks. Jacob hurriedly rolled the stone away from the well for Rachel and then "kissed Rachel and wept aloud" (Gen 29:11). A month later Laban asks Jacob, "what shall your wages be" for serving me? The text says,

> Now Laban had two daughters. The name of the older was Leah, and the name of the younger was Rachel. Leah's eyes were weak, but Rachel was beautiful in form and appearance. Jacob loved Rachel. And he said, "I will serve you seven years for your younger daughter Rachel." Laban said, "It is better that I give her to you than that I should give her to any other man; stay with me." So Jacob served seven years for Rachel, and they seemed to him but a few days because of the love he had for her. (Gen 29:16-20)

So Jacob faithfully served Laban, and at the conclusion of the seventh year he asked Laban to honor the agreement. Deciding that his oldest daughter should not go unmarried while his youngest daughter married, Laban tricked Jacob into consummating marriage with Leah instead of Rachel for, according to Laban, "'It is not so done in our country, to give the younger before the firstborn. Complete the week of this one, and we will give you the other also in return for serving me another seven years.' Jacob did so, and completed her week. Then Laban gave him his daughter Rachel to be his wife" (Gen 29:26-28).

For reasons not entirely obvious, this passage began to be interpreted figuratively as a commentary on the nature of the active versus the contemplative life.[2] For Gregory the Great (d. 604) "Rachel means 'seen beginning,'

---

[2]See Giles Constable, "The Interpretation of Mary and Martha," in *Three Studies in Medieval Religious and Social Thought* (Cambridge: Cambridge University Press, 1995), 3-141. It is important to note that the story of Jacob's vision in Gen 28 is often interpreted by early and medieval Christian exegetes as an example of contemplation, therefore the continuation of the narrative in Gen 29 must, in their minds, illuminate the distinctions between the active and contemplative life.

Leah 'laborer.' What else," he asks, "can Rachel signify but the contemplative life, or Leah but the active?"[3] Thus one must engage in the active life first (i.e., Leah) before moving on to the contemplative life (i.e., Rachel). Again, in the words of Gregory the Great: "After embracing Leah, therefore, Jacob finally gets Rachel, because every perfect person is first united with the fruitfulness of the active life and later embraces the repose of contemplation."[4] Gregory continues by showing that the same is true of the story of Mary and Martha in Luke 10:[5] "What is meant by Mary, who sits and listens to the Lord's words, but the contemplative life? What does Martha, who is occupied with external service, signify but the active life. . . . Great indeed is the value of active life, but contemplation is better, so Mary's role is said never to be taken away."[6] Again, without debating the exegetical merits of this figurative interpretation, what Gregory illustrates for us is that medieval theologians viewed the contemplative life as biblical.[7] Contemplation is not a human construct but a theological, spiritual reality.

Second, this biblical understanding is reinforced by a medieval reading of 2 Corinthians 12:1-4:

> I must go on boasting. Though there is nothing to be gained by it, I will go on to visions and revelations of the Lord. I know a man in Christ who fourteen years ago was caught up to the third heaven—whether in the body or out of the body I do not know, God knows. And I know that this man was caught up into paradise—whether in the body or out of the body I do not know, God knows—and he heard things that cannot be told, which man may not utter.

Medieval theologians took this passage to be speaking unequivocally of a mystical rapture that happened to the apostle Paul and that he was describing the heights of contemplation that can be achieved in this life. In the

---

[3]Gregory the Great, *Moralia in Iob* 6.37.61; Brian Kerns, trans., *Gregory the Great: Moral Reflections on the Book of Job* (Collegeville, MN: Cistercian Publications, 2015), 2:87.

[4]Gregory the Great, *Moralia in Iob* 6.37.61; Kerns, trans., 2:87.

[5]Lk 10:38-42: "Now as they went on their way, Jesus entered a village. And a woman named Martha welcomed him into her house. And she had a sister called Mary, who sat at the Lord's feet and listened to his teaching. But Martha was distracted with much serving. And she went up to him and said, 'Lord, do you not care that my sister has left me to serve alone? Tell her then to help me.' But the Lord answered her, 'Martha, Martha, you are anxious and troubled about many things, but one thing is necessary. Mary has chosen the good portion, which will not be taken away from her.'"

[6]Gregory the Great, *Moralia in Iob* 6.37.61; Kerns, trans., 2:87.

[7]See also Thomas Aquinas, *ST* IIa-IIae, q. 179, a. 1-2.

words of Thomas Aquinas: "Consequently the highest degree of contemplation in the present life is that which Paul had in rapture, whereby he was in a middle state between the present life and the life to come."[8] Though other authors could be cited to drive the point home, these examples should suffice to demonstrate that for medieval theologians contemplation was biblical and, therefore, something to be practiced, even sought after and institutionalized in monasticism.

Since contemplation was biblical it was going to be practiced and talked about. But what, exactly, is it that was being practiced and talked about? If Jacob's vision with the Lord at Bethel and Paul's ascent to the third heaven were emblematic of contemplation, then what was it? Because Gregory the Great's thought is so central to this question throughout the Middle Ages, I will begin with him. In his *Homilies on Ezekiel* Gregory wrote that "the contemplative life is to hold fast with the whole mind, at least to the charity of God, our neighbor but to abstain from external action; to cleave to the sole desire for the Creator."[9] This, of course, is a fairly straightforward definition inasmuch as it is merely a repetition of the Great Commandment (e.g., Mt 22:36-40) coupled with an admonition to desire God the Creator. By the thirteenth century, however, this definition has been enlarged and became much more multifaceted. To illustrate this I will focus on two influential theologians: Richard of St. Victor (d. 1173) and Thomas Aquinas.

Richard of St. Victor, a regular canon at the abbey of St. Victor in Paris, wrote a number of spiritual texts of which *The Mystical Ark* (or *Benjamin Major*) is one. In this work Richard defines contemplation as "the free, more penetrating gaze of a mind, suspended with wonder concerning manifestations of wisdom" or, in agreement with "a distinguished theologian of our time," as "a penetrating and free gaze of a soul extended everywhere in perceiving things."[10] Note that the objects of contemplation are things, for

---

[8]Thomas Aquinas, *ST* IIa-IIae, q. 180, art. 5; Fathers of the English Dominican Province, trans., *St. Thomas Aquinas, Summa Theologica* (Notre Dame, IN: Christian Classics, 1981), 4:1929.

[9]Gregory the Great, *Homilies on the Book of the Prophet Ezekiel* 2.2.8; Theodosia Tomkinson, trans., *Homilies on the Book of the Prophet Ezekiel by Saint Gregory the Great* (Etna, CA: Center for Traditionalist Orthodox Studies, 2008), 285. See also Thomas Aquinas in *ST* IIa-IIae, q. 180, a. 1, *sed contra*.

[10]Richard of St. Victor, *The Mystical Ark* 1.4; Grover A. Zinn, trans., *Richard of St. Victor: The Twelve Patriarchs, The Mystical Ark, Book Three of the Trinity*, Classics of Western Spirituality (New York: Paulist Press, 1979), 157.

"contemplation is always concerned with things [*res*]."[11] This contemplation must be free and penetrating, attempting to gaze on the wise things of God in the world but to do so through things. What are these "things"? Richard enumerates six of them: four are engaged with lower things, and two are engaged with uncreated/divine things. In short, the lowest two forms are engaged with visible, corporeal things; the middle two forms are engaged with invisible, corporeal things; and the highest two forms are engaged with invisible, uncreated things.[12]

"The first kind of contemplation is in consideration of and wonder at corporeal things with respect to all those things which enter the soul by means of the five bodily senses," writes Richard.[13] This is the lowest level of contemplation and is, for most people, the beginning of the contemplative journey since it fixes the believer's gaze on the creation and hence on the Creator.[14] That is, humans are given five senses and, as created things themselves, placed in the middle of other created things. Using these five senses they are then able to begin a journey to God by contemplating that which they can taste, touch, smell, see, and hear. In Richard's reckoning this is a consideration of created things in matter, form, and nature. The second kind of contemplation, then, is related to the first: a consideration of and wonder at the rational principle of created things. According to Richard, "If the first kind of contemplation is rightly understood to take place by considering the actual appearance of corporeal things, it follows, I think, that the second kind of contemplation ought to be understood to take place by examining the rational principle of these same things."[15] In a sense, this "rational principle" is a consideration of how things are made, how well-ordered they are, and how they are wisely disposed. The first kind of contemplation is pursued by imagination and the second by reasoning.

The next two forms of contemplation are concerned with invisible, corporeal things. These two forms occur whenever "we grasp the quality of

---

[11]Richard of St. Victor, *The Mystical Ark* 1.3; Zinn, trans., 157.

[12]Richard of St. Victor, *The Mystical Ark* 1.7.

[13]Richard of St. Victor, *The Mystical Ark* 2.1; Zinn, trans., 174.

[14]This understanding of initial contemplation as a consideration and wonder at corporeal things is not original to Richard and can be found as early as the fourth century in the writings of Evagrius of Pontus (d. 399). See, for example, Augustine Casiday, *Reconstructing the Theology of Evagrius Ponticus: Beyond Heresy* (Cambridge: Cambridge University Press, 2013).

[15]Richard of St. Victor, *The Mystical Ark* 2.7; Zinn, trans., 183.

invisible things by means of the similitude of visible things, and whenever we know the visible things of God by means of visible things of the world."[16] In the words of the apostle Paul: "His invisible attributes, namely, his eternal power and divine nature, have been clearly perceived, ever since the creation of the world, in the things that have been made" (Rom 1:20). Here the person in contemplation begins to use those things contemplated in the first two kinds to move beyond the senses. And this, believes Richard, is what makes a person spiritual: here "a person begins to exist as a living creature, and he learns to be made a spiritual being, because now he should begin to bring together spiritual things and to be formed in the novitiate of his senses, as he endeavors more and more each day to taste those things which are above."[17] This view, of course, relies on the distinction between that which is material and that which is immaterial. Richard believes that materiality conveys spiritual meaning; that the senses can rise above what they are sensing and begin to make assumptions about what is insensible. The foundation for this, in Richard's thought, is that the Scriptures do something similar: "Concerning divine instructions, it should be noted that we ought to understand some things simply and seek nothing in them according to the mystical sense, while some things ought to be employed according to the literal sense, and yet are capable of representing something according to the mystical sense."[18] The contemplation of visible things in similitude leads to two kinds of contemplation: one concerning invisible goods (the third kind of contemplation) and one concerning invisible substances, such as angelic or human spirits (the fourth kind of contemplation).[19]

The highest forms of contemplation are engaged with invisible, uncreated things, of which there are two kinds: things that are above reason but not beyond reason (the fifth kind of contemplation) and things that are both above reason and beyond reason (the sixth kind of contemplation).[20] Due to the suprarational nature of these things, they are only believed by faith though they come to be established as true things "by miracles . . .

---

[16]Richard of St. Victor, *The Mystical Ark* 2.12; Zinn, trans., 190.

[17]Richard of St. Victor, *The Mystical Ark* 2.13; Zinn, trans., 191-92.

[18]Richard of St. Victor, *The Mystical Ark* 2.14; Zinn, trans., 194.

[19]Richard of St. Victor, *The Mystical Ark* 2.16.

[20]Richard of St. Victor, *The Mystical Ark* 4.3.

by authorities . . . [and] by showings."[21] Thus, "there is more need for miracles than examples, more authorities than arguments, more showing than
reasoning."[22] Richard is quick to establish that these mysteries are not above
divine reason but above human reason. Nonetheless, that does not mean
that human reason is unimportant in these highest forms of contemplation
but that human reason is yoked to faith in order to experience these forms
of contemplation, for "human reason does nothing at all in the investigation,
discussion and assertion of these things unless it is supported with a mixture
of faith."[23] The difference between these two forms of contemplation is
rooted in the nature of understanding similitudes. For Richard, in the fifth
kind of contemplation, reason still makes use of similitudes, but in the sixth
kind the things contemplated exceed the nature of all similitude. In short, in
the fifth kind, the contemplator can say, "God is like the angels in this
way. . . ." Whereas in the sixth kind, the contemplator would have to say,
"God is unlike anything that I can imagine and reason."[24] That a person could
ever reach the fifth and sixth kinds of contemplation are the result of grace
working in them, and any experience of the sixth kind of contemplation
comes by way of a divine showing (*divinae revelationes*). Thus, spiritual
persons should be ready and prepared at all times for the sixth kind of contemplation: "We surely ought to spread the wings of our heart by longing
and wait for the time of divine showing at every hour—nay, rather at
every moment."[25]

Thomas Aquinas, a member of the Order of Preachers (or Dominicans),
spent the bulk of his life writing and teaching in Paris, Cologne, Orvieto,
Rome, and Naples. In his magnum opus, the *Summa theologica*, Thomas
dedicates eight articles to the contemplative life. He first asks whether contemplation concerns the affections or only the intellect. He concludes that

---

[21]These "showings" would be the moments of divine ecstasy, granted by God, experienced by some
Christians, such as that detailed by Mechthild of Magdeburg in her *The Flowing Light of the
Godhead*. These "showings" were never considered normative but are recorded throughout
Christian history. See, for example, Elizabeth Alvilda Petroff, ed., *Medieval Women's Visionary
Literature* (Oxford: Oxford University Press, 1986).

[22]Richard of St. Victor, *The Mystical Ark* 4.3; Zinn, trans., 262.

[23]Richard of St. Victor, *The Mystical Ark* 4.3; Zinn, trans., 263.

[24]This distinction forms the basis of the cataphatic and apophatic ways of doing theology, preva-
lent in mystical and spiritual texts. See Andrew Louth, *The Origins of the Christian Mystical
Tradition: From Plato to Denys*, 2nd ed. (Oxford: Oxford University Press, 2007).

[25]Richard of St. Victor, *The Mystical Ark* 4.10; Zinn, trans., 273.

contemplation concerns both the intellect and the affective or appetitive power. The essence of the action of contemplation pertains to the intellect, but the motive cause (i.e., what motivates the contemplative) resides in the will and the appetitive power moves the will, which moves the contemplator "to observe things either with the senses or with the intellect."[26] Furthermore, following Gregory the Great, Thomas says that the contemplative life ends in delight (*delectationem*), and delight is seated in the affective power. Thus contemplation concerns the affections. The end of this contemplation, writes Thomas, is a consideration of truth. That is, those who engage in contemplation are not just cultivating the moral virtues (prudence, temperance, courage, and justice) but seeking and coming to divine truth. But how does one reach this level of contemplating divine truth?

Like Richard, Thomas posits many acts that lead ultimately to contemplating divine truth: "Since, however, God's effects show us the way to the contemplation of God Himself . . . it follows that the contemplation of the divine effects also belongs to the contemplative life, inasmuch as man is guided thereby to the knowledge of God."[27] Though Thomas does not list six kinds of contemplation, his progression follows, in broad outlines, that of Richard, whom he quotes frequently.[28] Thomas thinks of contemplation as the "final act" but concedes that there are other acts leading to this final act. In his own words, "four things pertain, in a certain order, to the contemplative life; first, the moral virtues; secondly, other acts exclusive of contemplation; thirdly, contemplation of the divine effects; fourthly, the complement of all which is the contemplation of the divine truth itself."[29] So the moral virtues prepare one for contemplation by purifying the heart, by disposing the contemplator to reach the contemplation of divine truth. They are the first step in the ascent to divine contemplation and, therefore, justify the active life of striving to become morally virtuous.

---

[26]Thomas Aquinas, *ST* IIa-IIae, q. 180, art. 1; Fathers of the English Dominican Province, trans., 4:1925.

[27]Thomas Aquinas, *ST* IIa-IIae, q. 180, art. 4; Fathers of the English Dominican Province, trans., 4:1928.

[28]In fact, Richard's sixfold form of contemplation is summarized by Thomas in *ST* IIa-IIae, q. 180, art. 4, obj. 3, and in his reply to obj. 3.

[29]Thomas Aquinas, *ST* IIa-IIae, q. 180, art. 4; Fathers of the English Dominican Province, trans., 4:1928.

Next, the contemplative engages in "other acts" (*alii actus*). What are these other acts? "Some pertain to the reception of principles . . . others are concerned with deducing from the principles, the truth."[30] In short, these correspond to Richard's first four kinds of contemplation. Like Richard, Thomas believes that "it is through sensible objects that we come to the knowledge of intelligible things."[31] Therefore, the reception of principles would be gained by the senses, beholding sensible objects, and it would be immaterial, spiritual beings that would be deduced from these principles. The contemplator would employ her faculties of cogitation, imagination, reason, and meditation-consideration to ascend to contemplation proper. At some point she would move from these "other acts" to contemplating the divine effects, preparing her for the contemplation of divine truth. She would do this by withdrawing her soul from external objects, and then she would lay aside all other intellectual discourses and fix her "soul's gaze . . . on the contemplation of the intelligible truth," uniformly concentrating herself on the contemplation of "one simple truth." Then, and only then, can the contemplator be "made uniform unitedly" (*sicut uniformis facta, unite*) so as to be conducted, à la the angels, to delight in God, "the good and the beautiful."[32]

As he concludes, Thomas turns his attention to one final but important question: Is the contemplative life continuous? He answers that it is continuous in the sense that in its nature it is incorruptible and unchangeable and in relationship to humankind it is continuous because it concerns the intellect, which continues as a faculty of the incorruptible soul. Nonetheless, "No action can last long at its highest pitch," and the "highest point of contemplation is to reach the uniformity of Divine contemplation." Thus contemplation at its highest pitch is not continuous, but "it can be of long duration as regards the other contemplative acts."[33] Yet what does this mean to the one who is engaged in contemplation? What does this moment of

---

[30]Thomas Aquinas, *ST* IIa-IIae, q. 180, art. 3; Fathers of the English Dominican Province, trans., 4:1926.

[31]Thomas Aquinas, *ST* IIa-IIae, q. 180, art. 6; Fathers of the English Dominican Province, trans., 4:1930.

[32]Thomas Aquinas, *ST* IIa-IIae, q. 180, art. 6; Fathers of the English Dominican Province, trans., 4:1930.

[33]Thomas Aquinas, *ST* IIa-IIae, q. 180, art. 7, *ad* 2; Fathers of the English Dominican Province, trans., 4:1933.

uniformity with God look like in this life? Perhaps no better answer was given to these questions than that provided by Bernard of Clairvaux (d. 1153).

Bernard, a Cistercian monk and abbot, lived a century before Richard and Thomas, but thanks in large part to his influence, the twelfth century was an era of deep spiritual renaissance.[34] Between 1149 and 1153 Bernard worked on a text that would bear the title *On Consideration*. In this work, written to offer advice to Pope Eugenius V (a fellow Cistercian monk), Bernard says that consideration is not the same as contemplation. Contemplation "can be defined as the true and sure intuition of the mind concerning something, or the apprehension of truth without doubt. Consideration, on the other hand, can be defined as thought searching for truth, or the searching of a mind to discover truth."[35] Applying Bernard's understanding to Richardian thought, the first four (perhaps five) forms of contemplation would be consideration, whereas the last (or last two) forms would be contemplation proper. What Bernard is doing is making room for Eugenius, now that he is the pope, to still be pursuing the monastic life of contemplation despite his busyness and the fact that he will spend a large part of his time engaged in worldly activities. Bernard goes so far as to say that "you are taken from the embrace of your Rachel [i.e., the contemplative life] against your will."[36] So, despite the demanding role of being pope, Eugenius must continue to take seriously his life of piety and engage in consideration of four things in particular: "yourself, what is below you, around you and above you."[37]

First, consideration begins with self-knowledge so that one may know not only what is good in them but also one's deficiencies. Though concepts of self-knowledge were not unknown in antiquity,[38] the practice of self-examination was more widespread in twelfth-century Europe than at any

---

[34]Giles Constable, "Renewal and Reform in Religious Life: Concepts and Realities," in *Renaissance and Renewal in the Twelfth Century*, ed. Robert L. Benson and Giles Constable (Toronto: University of Toronto Press, 1991), 37-67.

[35]Bernard of Clairvaux, *On Consideration* 2.2.5; John D. Anderson and Elizabeth T. Kenna, trans., *Five Books on Consideration: Advice to a Pope* (Kalamazoo, MI: Cistercian Publications, 1976), 52.

[36]Bernard of Clairvaux, *On Consideration* 1.1.1; Anderson and Kenna, trans., 26.

[37]Bernard of Clairvaux, *On Consideration* 2.2.5; Anderson and Kenna, trans., 52. For other authors who have used this quadripartite division, see Anderson and Kenna, trans., *Five Books on Consideration*, 185-86.

[38]See, for example, Augustine of Hippo (d. 430): "let me confess what I know of myself. Let me confess too what I do not know of myself. For what I know of myself I know because you grant me light, and what I do not know of myself, I do not know until such time as my darkness

time since the fifth century.[39] This self-knowledge, continues Bernard, is threefold: what you are, who you are, and what sort of person you are. That is, in the case of Eugenius, he knows that he is a Cistercian monk, the pope, and a man of virtue. For others it might be that she knows herself as a Christian, a mother, and a woman of virtue. Second, one must consider what is below him. One must be aware of the passions and vices that trouble the soul. Further, one must be aware of the unconverted and those espousing heresy in order to preach the gospel and correct. Third, in the case of Eugenius, he needs to consider who is around him, such as other clergy and the kind of people he chooses to work in the papal curia. This involves not only knowing them but also serving them as a shepherd and being an example to them.

Last, one needs to consider those things that are above him. Bernard begins with an acknowledgment: "The former books, although they are entitled 'On Consideration,' nevertheless contain many things which pertain to action, for they teach or advise some things which must not only be considered but acted upon. However, the book at hand will deal with consideration alone, for those things which are above you . . . require not action, but examination."[40] Bernard writes that there are three kinds of consideration: practical, scientific, and speculative. He says that "consideration is practical when it uses the senses and sense objects in an orderly and unified manner to win God's favor. Consideration is scientific when it prudently and diligently scrutinizes and ponders everything to discover God. Consideration is speculative when it recollects itself and, insofar as it is aided by God, frees itself for the contemplation of God."[41] It is here that *On Consideration* becomes a more traditional treatment of contemplation.[42] Elsewhere, however, Bernard uses a different approach to talk about contemplation.

In the Middle Ages theologians such as Peter Lombard, Bernard, and Dante Alighieri wrote not only that God is love but, explicitly among the

---

becomes 'like noonday' before your face" (Henry Chadwick, trans., *Saint Augustine: Confessions* [Oxford: Oxford University Press, 1991], 182-83).

[39]For example, in his *Mirror of Charity* Aelred of Rievaulx (d. 1167) asks, "How great is man's knowledge when he does not even grasp himself?" (Elizabeth Connor, trans., *Aelred of Rievaulx: The Mirror of Charity* [Kalamazoo, MI: Cistercian Publications, 1990], 95).

[40]Bernard of Clairvaux, *On Consideration* 5.1.1; Anderson and Kenna, trans., 139.

[41]Bernard of Clairvaux, *On Consideration* 5.2.4; Anderson and Kenna, trans., 142-43.

[42]See Peter Tyler, "Triple Way," in *The New Westminster Dictionary of Christian Spirituality*, ed. Philip Sheldrake (Louisville: Westminster John Knox, 2005), 626.

persons of the Trinity, that the Holy Spirit is love. That is, love is not merely an emotion or the desire we may have to possess what is beautiful (à la Plato) or merely wishing good things for someone for that person's sake (à la Aristotle) but a person. And in this case, love is a divine person. In saying this they were going back at least to the fifth century with Augustine of Hippo, who wrote that the "Holy Spirit is not just the Father's alone nor the Son's alone, but the Spirit of them both, and thus he suggests to us the common charity by which the Father and the Son love each other."[43] In his *Sentences*, the twelfth-century theologian Peter Lombard (d. 1160) writes that "the Holy Spirit is the love or charity or affection of the Father and the Son."[44] The Lombard concedes that "in the Trinity, love is sometimes ascribed to the substance, which is common to the three persons and is entire in each of them, and sometimes especially to the person of the Holy Spirit."[45] In the end he sides with the view that "it is by the Holy Spirit that the Son is loved by the Father and the Father by the Son."[46] And, to lend support to his position, Peter quotes from Augustine, saying, "And so there are three and no more: the one loving the other who is from him, and the one loving the other from whom he is, and the love itself."[47]

Likewise, the Italian poet and theologian Dante Alighieri (d. 1321) says something similar when he writes that God the Father is the "inexpressible and primal Power" in the Trinity "looking on his begotten Son with Love."[48] Thus the Father is Power, the Son is the Begotten One, and the Holy Spirit is Love.[49] Here we see that Dante, like Peter Lombard, views the Holy Spirit as the love that exists between the Father and the Son.

But Bernard is the quintessential writer on love in the High and late Middle Ages because of his popular *On Loving God.* In this work Bernard establishes a taxonomy in which to think of the spiritual life in terms of love.

---

[43] Augustine of Hippo, *On the Trinity* 15.5.27; Edmund Hill, trans., *Saint Augustine: The Trinity* (New York: New City Press, 1991), 418.

[44] Peter Lombard, *The Sentences*, 1.10.1.2; Giulio Silano, trans., *Peter Lombard: The Sentences*, vol. 1, *The Mystery of the Trinity* (Toronto: Pontifical Institute for Medieval Studies, 2010), 58.

[45] Peter Lombard, *The Sentences* 1.10.1.4; Silano, trans., 59.

[46] Peter Lombard, *The Sentences* 1.10.2.5; Silano, trans., 61.

[47] Peter Lombard, *The Sentences* 1.10.2.5; Silano, trans., 61; quoting Augustine of Hippo, *On the Trinity* 11.5.7.

[48] Dante, *Paradise* 10.1-2; Anthony Esolen, trans., *Dante: Paradise* (New York: Modern Library, 2004), 99.

[49] See also Dante, *Paradise*, 13.52-57 and 79-81.

His guiding question is this: "What, I ask, should be the aim or degree of our love?"[50] Bernard knows that the aim of our love is God, for God "is the efficient and final cause of our love. He offers the opportunity, creates the affection, and consummates the desire."[51] So the Christian should love God not because he gets something out of loving God but because God alone is worthy of our love. Moreover, it is God himself who makes it possible for us to love because he is the efficient and final cause of our love, which is a slight variation on the Christian spiritual tradition's understanding of *exitus* and *reditus*: exit and return. All things come from God himself as Creator and Savior, while at the same time all that exits is made to return. Creation returns in its praise of God, and humans return in union with God in eternal blessedness. Again, God gives us the love by which we love him, for he is the cause and aim of our love.

This love is natural; it is truly human: "Love is not imposed by a precept; it is planted in nature. . . . In this way, man who is animal and carnal, and knows how to love only himself, yet starts loving God for his own benefit, because he learns from frequent experience that he can do everything that is good for him in God and that without God he can do nothing good."[52] Because love is natural a person will automatically love something first, and that something, says Bernard, is oneself. A person loves herself for her own sake, and this is the first degree of love. This is an egotistical love, self-centered, not directed toward others; a result of humankind's fallenness. And, of course, our love is meant to be directed to others (God and neighbors), so in order to do that we need to move beyond this first degree of love. Bernard would insist that to fulfill God's commandment to love one another, we "must have regard to God."[53] Thus the Christian is not meant to remain at this lowest degree but to progress to the second degree described by Bernard thus:

> Man, therefore, loves God, but for his own advantage and not yet for God's sake. Nevertheless, it is a matter of prudence to know what you can do by

[50]Bernard of Clairvaux, *De diligendo Deo* 6.16; Bernard of Clairvaux, *On Loving God*, trans. Robert Walton (Kalamazoo, MI: Cistercian Publications, 1973), 19.

[51]Bernard of Clairvaux, *De diligendo Deo* 7.22; Bernard of Clairvaux, *On Loving God*, 24.

[52]Bernard of Clairvaux, *De diligendo Deo* 8.23, 25; Bernard of Clairvaux, *On Loving God*, 25 and 27.

[53]Bernard of Clairvaux, *De diligendo Deo* 8.25; Bernard of Clairvaux, *On Loving God*, 27.

yourself and what you can do with God's help to keep from offending him who keeps you free from sin. If man's tribulations, however, grow in frequency and as a result he frequently turns to God and is frequently freed by God, must he not end, even though he had a heart of stone in a breast of iron, by realizing that it is God's grace which frees him and comes to love God not for his own advantage but for the sake of God?[54]

Here a person loves God but only because he gets something out of his love for God. This love is better than the egotistical first degree of love, but it is still a far cry from the proper way that a believer is to love God. Therefore, a believer must continue to climb the ladder of love, with God's assistance, reaching the third degree in which

He loves God truthfully and so loves what is God's. He loves purely and he does not find it hard to obey a pure commandment, purifying his heart, as it is written, in the obedience of love. He loves with justice and freely embraces the just commandment. This love is pleasing because it is free. It is chaste because it does not consist of spoken words but of deed and truth. It is just because it renders what it receives. . . . He so loves who says: "Confess to the Lord for he is good." Who confesses to the Lord, not because he is good to him but because the Lord is good, truly loves God for God's sake and not for his own benefit. . . . This is the third degree of love: in it God is already loved for his own sake.[55]

Notice that it is at this step that the Christian begins to look beyond oneself. She is able to love purely and is able to obey the commandments of God because they are no longer just commandments to be obeyed but they are loving admonitions from him who is Love. Loving in this way purifies the heart and freely issues forth in words and actions. Egotism has given way to altruism. Because she receives love, the Christian is able to give love to others.

Note the important transition between the second and third degree of love, in Bernard's reckoning. The lover has moved out of herself and into a love for God because of who God is, not for what he does for her. A shift has occurred from the self to God, from humanity to divinity. The directionality of one's gaze at the third step goes from horizontal to vertical, from inward to outward. To summarize Augustine, we must move *intra se* (within

---

[54]Bernard of Clairvaux, *De diligendo Deo* 9.26; Bernard of Clairvaux, *On Loving God*, 27-28.
[55]Bernard of Clairvaux, *De diligendo Deo* 8.26; Bernard of Clairvaux, *On Loving God*, 28-29.

ourselves) before we can move *extra se* (outside ourselves). But even here, when we love God for his own sake, we still have not yet moved to the highest degree of love, and this appears odd in Bernard's taxonomy. Certainly loving God for his own sake is the highest degree of love? God is, well, God, and therefore he is worthy of all worship. He is the greatest Good, and that alone should be the sole motivation for us to love God for his own sake.

Yet Bernard's psychology, so heavily indebted to Augustine, posits a yet higher degree of love: when a person loves himself for the sake of God. The abbot of Clairvaux writes that the person moving from the third degree to the fourth degree "no longer loves himself, except for God" because he is "inebriated with divine love" (*divino debriatus amore animus*). Bernard describes the state in this way: "To lose yourself, as if you no longer existed, to cease completely to experience yourself, to reduce yourself to nothing is not a human sentiment but a divine experience."[56]

To accomplish this "it is therefore necessary for our souls to reach a similar state in which, just as God willed everything to exist for himself, so we wish that neither ourselves nor other beings to have been nor to be except for his will alone; not for our pleasure." Ultimately "it is in a spiritual and immortal body, calm and pleasant, subject to the spirit in everything, that the soul hopes to attain the fourth degree of love, or rather to be possessed by it; for it is in God's hands to give it to whom he wishes, it is not obtained by human efforts. I mean he will easily reach the highest degree of love when he will no longer be held back by any desire of the flesh."[57] For Bernard, "It is deifying [*deificari est*] to go through such an experience."[58] And like Augustine, Dante, and Peter Lombard, Bernard understands that this love, this kind of charity, is God himself: "Charity which somehow holds and brings together the Trinity in the bond of peace."[59]

Though not as obviously about contemplation at first glance as *On Consideration*, *On Loving God* is possibly the greatest medieval work on contemplation, and no one knew this as well as Dante, who uses Bernard in *Paradiso* to guide him to the most profound and intimate contemplation of God.[60]

---

[56]Bernard of Clairvaux, *De diligendo Deo* 10.27; Bernard of Clairvaux, *On Loving God*, 29.

[57]Bernard of Clairvaux, *De diligendo Deo* 8.28-29; Bernard of Clairvaux, *On Loving God*, 30-31.

[58]Bernard of Clairvaux, *De diligendo Deo* 8.28; Bernard of Clairvaux, *On Loving God*, 30.

[59]Bernard of Clairvaux, *De diligendo Deo* 12.35; Bernard of Clairvaux, *On Loving God*, 37.

[60]See Dante, *Paradise* 31.58–33.145.

Dante chooses Bernard because the Cistercian had not only written about such contemplation but also because he himself had experienced it. Bernard confesses in *On Loving God* that God grants the fourth degree of love to whomever he wishes but claims to be skeptical that anyone actually attains it: "I doubt if he ever attains the fourth degree during this life. . . . Let those who have had the experience make a statement; to me, I confess, it seems impossible."[61] Yet Dante says that Bernard, "in our world, by contemplating, tasted Heaven's peace."[62] Bernard himself admits that though the fullness of contemplating God is eschatological, there are those in this life who experience it, albeit in passing.[63] In the end Bernard is talking about something that is experienced, not simply theologized about; though his theology of contemplation is systematized, it is the result of experience.

And this is what should be taken away from medieval conceptions of contemplation—that contemplation is something that is not abstractly theological but theological because it is experiential. There are many treatises in the Middle Ages that purport to record ecstatic contemplative moments. These works are often difficult to interpret because they are the reports of someone's (subjective) experience. This does not mean that they should all be given credibility simply because they are experiential, nor does it mean that they should be rejected out of hand because they are experiential. Rather, they should be treated with caution, keeping in mind that medieval persons (including theologians) viewed contemplation as biblical and, therefore, something that will happen to some people, even if those contemplative visions are fleeting.

Moreover, these medieval authors describe a healthy balance between materiality and immateriality. Matter is not bad but is, in fact, essential in contemplative ascent to God and truth. Many Christian believers today live uncomfortably between materiality and immateriality, between the supposedly already and not-yet. In medieval contemplative theology, matter is not something to be bemoaned or regretted; rather, it is to be used as an aid

---

[61]Bernard of Clairvaux, *De diligendo Deo* 15.39; Bernard of Clairvaux, *On Loving God*, 41.

[62]Dante, *Paradise*, Canto 31.110-11; Esolen, trans., 337. See also the *Amplexus Bernardi* (Embrace of Bernard) tradition in James France, *Medieval Images of Saint Bernard of Clairvaux* (Kalamazoo, MI: Cistercian Publications, 2007), 179-203. This tradition is understood to be an artistic (and literary) presentation of Bernard attaining the fourth degree of love.

[63]See Bernard of Clairvaux, *De diligendo Deo* 10.27.

in one's contemplation. In fact, it is the proper way to be contemplative. God, as Creator, has made all things good (see Gen 1:31). Therefore, to use these good things intentionally as aids to contemplation is not only right theologically but also sound practice. It does not redeem creation but makes use of creation's very goodness; it recognizes creation's divine origin. Thus Christians today would do well to contemplate God's creation not because creation care is in vogue but because it is the way to experience in this life those things that are immaterial.

Finally, contemplation is not something subjective or ethereal. Rather, it is living fully into Jesus' commandment that we love God with all our heart and with all our soul and with all our mind and that we love our neighbor as ourselves. In Bernardine terms, contemplation is nothing other than an act of loving. Though we begin by loving ourselves, we must move beyond ourselves to love others and in loving others to loving God. To be contemplative is to love well. But even if we approach contemplation in a more Richardian or Thomistic manner (where the goal is to be in communion with God, who is truth himself) we are still striving for something divine: truth. In the words of John, "the true worshipers will worship the Father in spirit and truth" (Jn 4:23). And given that truth inheres in the things that surround us (both material things that we can sense and immaterial things that we cannot sense), then we come to truth by contemplating those very things. Thus contemplation is not an option for Christian believers but a commandment.

SABBATICAL CONTEMPLATION?

Retrieving a Strand in Reformed Theology

ASHLEY COCKSWORTH

INTRODUCTION

The essays assembled in this book aim to rethink what it might mean to speak of contemplation from within the particular context of evangelical theology. That there is need for this kind of work is itself suggestive that contemplation is not always understood to be fundamental to the identity of contemporary evangelicalism. The contemplative strands of the Christian tradition of spirituality, as John Coe has demonstrated in his contribution, might even be seen to rub against some of evangelicalism's core commitments. Although tracing the complex set of interlocking factors that contribute to why contemplation is too infrequently considered as part and parcel of evangelical spirituality is not the primary task of this chapter, it is worth exploring just one of the significant barriers that needs to be overcome if contemplative prayer is to be reclaimed.

Built into the logic of Protestantism is something of a hermeneutics of suspicion. The magisterial reformers distrusted systems of thought that they judged to be alien to the biblical worldview and, therefore, to obscure the truth of the gospel of Jesus Christ. They called for a repositioning of Christianity according to "the plain meaning of Scripture"—*sola Scriptura*. This hermeneutic of suspicion provided much of the impetus for the initial round of Protestant reformations, in which evangelicalism, as we know it today, finds its historical footing. The culmination of this strand of Protestant identity can be detected in the writings of Adolf von Harnack, the great nineteenth-century German theologian. Harnack's historical project intensified the

Protestant quest for purity and its bid to reclaim the true "essence" of Christianity in its attempt to peel away the many layers of philosophical baggage that he thought had distorted the purity of the gospel.[1] More specifically, Harnack traced the influence of Hellenistic philosophy on the development of early Christian doctrine and found that the early church—in its doctrine and practice—had fallen from the essence of Christianity into the murky world of a particular brand of Greek philosophical abstraction. Harnack believed that Christianity's earliest theologians had been held captive by this nonbiblical worldview and had progressively Hellenized original Christianity. But once the layers of philosophical distortion have been identified and expunged, the gospel is laid bare and the church finally set free.

Harnack's so-called Hellenization thesis was disseminated far and wide. It reached well into the next century and cast a long shadow over much of twentieth-century Protestantism. Of its endemicity, Karl Barth considered it to be "one of the theological things that sparrows thrill from the rooftops."[2] Harnack's thesis shaped much of Protestant theology's engagement with the historical traditions of spirituality and in particular mysticism and its core practices—such as contemplative prayer.[3] A significant consequence of Christianity styled in this Hellenistic mode was identified by one of Harnack's most important heirs. In his classic study *The Christian Doctrine of Justification and Reconciliation*, Albrecht Ritschl concluded that "wherever mysticism is found, the thought of justification no longer retains its true significance as the key to the whole domain of the Christian life."[4] In other words, mysticism, influenced more by Hellenistic philosophy than Christian theology, is guilty of trespassing on that most hallowed ground of evangelicalism: the justification of the sinner before God depends on Jesus Christ alone—*solo Christo*.

Associated with mysticism is, of course, contemplative prayer. Like mysticism, contemplative prayer was rendered by the Hellenization thesis "other" to genuine Christian theology and practice, belonging instead to the

---

[1]For example, Adolf von Harnack, *What Is Christianity?* (London: Williams & Norgate, 1904).

[2]Karl Barth, *The Theology of John Calvin*, trans. Geoffrey W. Bromiley (Grand Rapids: Eerdmans, 1995), 326.

[3]See Bernard McGinn, *The Presence of God: A History of Western Christian Mysticism*, vol. 1, *The Foundations of Mysticism: Origins to the Fifth Century* (New York: Crossroad, 1992), 266-91.

[4]Albrecht Ritschl, *The Christian Doctrine of Justification and Reconciliation: The Positive Development of the Doctrine* (Edinburgh: T&T Clark, 1902), 113.

alien world of Neoplatonism. It was seen by many therefore to be "funda-mentally non-Christian."[5] As Bernard McGinn explains, "A number of theo-logians have viewed the Greek notion of mystical contemplation as an intrusion into Christianity of at best dubious worth."[6]

It would seem that some version or other of the Hellenization thesis still lurks behind much of evangelicalism's interaction with the contemplative strands of Christian spirituality. In his classic study on evangelical prayer, Donald G. Bloesch, for example, places contemplation in opposition to its more biblical counterpart: "prophetic prayer."[7] Prophetic prayer (that is, "biblical, evangelical prayer") is active, petitionary, and verbal—just as the Bible prescribed. Contemplation, however, is part of "a spiritual orientation quite different from that of biblical, prophetic faith."[8] As opposed to pro-phetic prayer, contemplation is fundamentally, and problematically, passive. We are catching sight here of a fault line that is very often drawn through the tradition of Christian prayer that distinguishes sharply the petitionary (active) from the contemplative (passive). The Protestant work ethic, which also plays into Protestant readings of mysticism, and the suspicion of the nonactive perpetuated further by Max Weber's classic treatise on the subject, made it inevitable that contemplative prayer's perceived passivity would run against the grain of evangelicalism's instinctive gravitation to the *vita activa*.[9]

The potent cocktail of the Protestant work ethic and Harnack's Helleni-zation thesis was as unhelpful as it was pervasive. Its consequence: contem-plative and evangelical streams of spirituality were destined to flow in opposite directions. However, the Hellenization thesis is now showing signs of abatement. George Kalantzis has recently argued that "the hellenization-thesis

---

[5]John Coe also elaborates on this in his contribution to this volume, "The Controversy Over Contemplation and Contemplative Prayer: A Historical, Theological, and Biblical Resolution." Harnack's Hellenization thesis can be seen, for example, to provide the conceptual heavy lifting for open theism's critique and rejection of the God of classical theism, as voiced in the move-ment's flagship manifesto, Clark Pinnock et al., *The Openness of God: A Biblical Challenge to the Traditional Understanding of God* (Downers Grove, IL: InterVarsity Press, 1994).

[6]McGinn, *Foundations of Mysticism*, 6.

[7]Donald G. Bloesch, *The Struggle of Prayer* (London: Harper & Row, 1980); see in particular the chapter "Prayer and Mysticism" for a rehearsal of the Hellenization thesis.

[8]Ibid., 115.

[9]See Max Weber, *The Protestant Ethic and the Spirit of Capitalism* (Oxford: Oxford University Press, 2009).

. . . has outlived its purposes."[10] In place of an inherent suspicion of the past, Kalantzis recommends a hermeneutic drawn from the virtues of "patience and attention."[11] A textually attentive reading of the classical sources of Christian theology reveals that Harnack's thesis was more likely fulfilled in the reverse. What is to be found is "not the hellenization of the gospel but the evangelization of Hellenism."[12]

With this significant obstacle to contemplation weakened, an opportunity presents itself to reconceive evangelicalism's relation to the historical traditions of Christianity afresh. In fact, this work is already underway. Within contemporary evangelicalism there are any number of projects of retrieval that seek in deliberate ways, often with fascinating results, to reconceive how evangelicalism relates to the historical traditions of Christian theology and spirituality.[13]

One way of brokering this chapter's dialogue between evangelicalism and contemplation is to participate in these wider projects of retrieval by looking beyond the bounds of evangelical spirituality and into the historical traditions of Christian spirituality to retrieve a form of contemplative prayer that can move within the grain of the core commitments of evangelicalism.[14] The path I will take, however, does not involve reaching outside of evangelism to exploit these potential points of contact. Instead, I am going to shift the focus onto excavating forgotten strands of the evangelical tradition itself to see what resources evangelicalism has available to cultivate a theology of contemplation on its own grounds. My aim in this chapter is to point the way, therefore, to a practice of contemplative prayer that is indigenously evangelical, robustly biblical, and demonstrably Christocentric.

---

[10]George Kalantzis, "The Radicalness of the Evangelical Faith," in *Evangelicals and the Early Church: Recovery, Reform, Renewal*, ed. George Kalantzis and Andrew Tooley (Eugene, OR: Wipf and Stock, 2011), 242-52 (243).

[11]Ibid., 249.

[12]Kevin J. Vanhoozer and Daniel J. Treier, *Theology and the Mirror of Scripture: A Mere Evangelical Account* (Downers Grove, IL: IVP Academic, 2015), 118.

[13]Among many others, see Daniel H. Williams, *Retrieving the Tradition and Renewing Evangelicalism: A Primer for Suspicious Protestants* (Grand Rapids: Eerdmans, 1999); Kalantzis and Tooley, *Evangelicals and the Early Church*; Kyle Strobel and Jamin D. Goggin, eds., *Reading the Christian Spiritual Classics: A Guide for Evangelicals* (Downers Grove, IL: IVP Academic, 2013); and W. David Buschart and Kent Eilers, *Theology as Retrieval: Receiving the Past, Renewing the Church* (Downers Grove, IL: IVP Academic, 2015).

[14]An example of this kind of work can be found in Dennis E. Tamburello, *Union with Christ: John Calvin and the Mysticism of St Bernard* (Louisville: Westminster John Knox, 1994).

It accesses this homegrown practice of contemplation by developing some important but generally neglected avenues of one of the principal architects of evangelical theology: the sixteenth-century Reformed theologian John Calvin, drawing in particular on his writings on the Sabbath.

This chapter unfolds in three sections. The first stage of my argument requires tracing the contemplative in the formal sections of Calvin's doctrine on prayer as it appears in the definitive edition of the *Institutes*. This sets up the second section's detailed excavation of Calvin's theology of Sabbath in a bid to describe what might be called a sabbatical framework for thinking about contemplation. The final section turns a corner to gesture toward how this framework might shape the actual practice of contemplation.

CALVIN ON PRAYER

There are just shy of one hundred chapters constituting the definitive edition of Calvin's *Institutes of the Christian Religion*. Of those chapters, the longest (chapter 20 of book 3) is on prayer.[15] The fruit of those ninety or so pages is a meditation on the experience of prayer that is spiritually rich, pastorally profound, doctrinally sharp, and largely free from the polemics for which Calvin is often known, bar the rather savage but not unpredictable "rejection of erroneous doctrines of the intercessions of saints" (3.20.21-27). What unfolds over the course of this lengthy engagement with prayer is a vision of Christian existence that is shot through with the benefits of the grace of God received in prayer. And the vision is good, very good. The Christian, who exercises faith most fully in prayer, becomes a partaker of heavenly glory, lifted by the work of the Holy Spirit into seeing the divine through the very eyes of Christ. Calvin quotes words from Ambrose—himself well known for devising a form of "scriptural contemplation"—to that effect. Christ "is our mouth, through which we speak to the Father; he is our eye,

---

[15] All references are to the *Institutes of the Christian Religion*, ed. John T. McNeill, trans. Ford Lewis Battles, Library of Christian Classics (Philadelphia: Westminster, 1960), hereafter in parentheses: book, chapter, and section number. There is more to Calvin's theology of prayer than is to be found in the *Institutes*. Prayer features in his catechetical writing, commentaries, and sermons. For a fuller picture of Calvin's theology of prayer than is possible in this chapter, see I. John Hesselink's introduction in *John Calvin, on Prayer: Conversations with God* (Louisville: Westminster John Knox, 2006), 1-37. For a comparison of the development of Calvin's doctrine of prayer across the various editions of the *Institutes*, see Elsie Anne McKee, "John Calvin's Teaching on the Lord's Prayer," in *The Lord's Prayer: Perspectives for Reclaiming Christian Prayer*, ed. Daniel L. Migliore (Grand Rapids: Eerdmans, 1993), 88-106.

through which we see the Father; he is our right hand, through which we offer ourselves to the Father" (3.20.21).

Like many before him, Calvin includes in his meditation on prayer a verse-by-verse exegesis of the Lord's Prayer (3.20.34-42). Calvin's is breathless and far-reaching. Indeed, the Lord's Prayer might even be seen to set the tone for his overall theology of prayer, which, if the fault line identified above is in any way accurate, is often seen to fall on the more active side of the Christian life. Because the mark of our union with Christ—on which prayer depends—is generally found in the manner of our outward lives, his theology of prayer instinctively drifts on an active trajectory. Our union with Christ remains only a possibility until it is actualized in a certain way, lived out in concrete patterns of action. "When, for example, we pray that 'his name be sanctified' [Mt 6:9; Lk 11:2], we should, so to speak, eagerly hunger and thirst after that sanctification" (3.20.6). It is our action that makes us fully human. Not only is Calvin's theology of prayer active in tone, the practices of prayer he prioritizes also take on a decidedly active flavor.

To be found in chapter twenty is an exploration of the mechanics of petition, the ethical imperative of thanksgiving, and a very careful analysis of the christologically shaped practice of intercession (where Calvin is at his best). The amplification of the active aspects of prayer makes Calvin an unlikely hero for explicating the contemplative. Although the contemplative is not explicitly brought to the surface in chapter twenty of the *Institutes*, at the outset of the chapter Calvin writes that of the rich variety of practices of prayer, at its deepest level prayer is a practice of "pure contemplation of God" (3.20.4). Contemplation functions at a subterranean level in Calvin's understanding of the Christian life. Its logic undergirds and shapes the full "choreography" of prayer as it is concretely practiced in the life of the church—on this, more in the third section.[16] Understood on these terms, a contemplative logic can be detected in the shaping of Calvin's understanding of the practice of theology itself. His theology takes on a "contemplative orientation," bent toward the praise and glorification of God.[17]

---

[16]The term is borrowed from Matthew Myer Boulton, *God Against Religion: Rethinking Christian Theology Through Worship* (Grand Rapids: Eerdmans, 2008).

[17]On this, see Randall Zachman, *John Calvin as Teacher, Pastor, and Theologian: The Shape of His Writings* (Grand Rapids: Baker Academic, 2006), 99.

"GOD BE PRAISED" (4.10.23). So Calvin ends the *Institutes*. These words capture in nuce the prayerful intention of the entire doctrinal project of Calvin's theology. All theology, if it is to count as theological, is doxologically orientated, underwritten by contemplation. For Calvin, as for those writers more deliberately grounded in the contemplative tradition, God is a mystery known only by God, and our knowledge of God is a participation in the knowledge God has of God.[18] The theologian's most effective posture, therefore, is not that of speech but of a contemplative openness to the priority of God's Word.

Calvin unfolded his contemplative orientation for all things on a very grand scale—well beyond the pages of the *Institutes*. It is not only his theological writing that was structured around the doxological practices of praise and thanksgiving but the very city of Geneva. Calvin's vision for Geneva was for a city saturated in prayer. The Christian life in its entirety, Calvin instructs, "ought to be a sort of practice of godliness" (3.19.2). It is well documented that Calvin's reforming project of civic life involved breaking down the walls of the monasteries. Far from destroying monastic sensibility, his aim was to unleash it on the rest of city. As Barth writes of Calvin, in Geneva monasticism "broke out of the cloister and became a universal matter."[19] What was once practiced in the monasteries by some was to be made available for all. All Christians should, Calvin insists, be "completely engaged" in prayer (3.20.50). The Christian life for all Genevans would be punctuated by a rhythm of prayer that ended up looking a lot like "a monastic rule."[20] There would be daily recital of the psalmody (the Genevan Psalter), there would be catechetical instruction (the Geneva Catechism),[21] there would be prayer "when we arise in the morning, before we begin daily work, when we sit down to a meal, when by God's blessing

---

[18]For a discussion of how this plays out in Augustine's contemplative theology, see A. N. Williams, "Contemplation: Knowledge of God in Augustine's De Trinitate," in *Knowing the Triune God: The Work of the Spirit in the Practices of the Church*, ed. James J. Buckley and David S. Yeago (Grand Rapids: Eerdmans, 2001), 121-46.

[19]Barth, *Theology of John Calvin*, 51. See also, Matthew Myer Boulton, *Life in God: John Calvin, Practical Formation, and the Future of Protestant Theology* (Grand Rapids: Eerdmans, 2011), chap. 2.

[20]Herman J. Selderhuis, *John Calvin: A Pilgrim's Life* (Downers Grove: IVP Academic, 2009), 161.

[21]All references are to "The Catechism of the Church of Geneva (1545)," in *Calvin: Theological Treatises*, ed. J. K. S. Reid, Library of Christian Classics (Philadelphia: Westminster, 1960), 88-139—hereafter in parentheses: *Geneva*, followed by page number.

we have eaten, when we are getting ready to retire" (3.20.50). Theology and discipleship alike would take on a contemplative (almost monastic) character, set to the rhythm of prayer.

Calvin and the contemplative traditions are jointly committed, therefore, to what has been called the "integrity" of prayer and theology, spirituality and doctrine.[22] There is a further connection between Calvin and the contemplative tradition to be found in chapter twenty of the *Institutes* that is worth exploring at this point, not least because it has a significant bearing on my discussion of the Sabbath. Throughout his investigation of prayer, time and again Calvin can be found interacting with Paul's theory of prayer, expounded with tantalizing suggestion in Romans 8. Like Paul's, undergirding Calvin's theory of prayer is the notion that "we do not know what to pray for as we ought" (Rom 8:26). Beginning chapter twenty, then, is a rather bleak picture of the state of humanity. "We clearly see how destitute and devoid of all good things man is, and how he lacks all aids to salvation. Therefore, if he seeks resources to succor him in his need, he must go outside of himself and get them elsewhere" (3.20.1). At this point, Calvin is thinking specifically about faith. And in respect of faith, the "elsewhere," Calvin goes on to say, is located in Christ. In good Reformation theology, it is in Jesus Christ that our faith is grounded. Interestingly, this same christological argument is then applied to the "chief exercise of faith" (3.20), which for Calvin is prayer.

Human prayer, which "springs from faith" (3.20.27), depends on a prior movement of grace. Just as faith is not our work but God's work in us by the activity of the Holy Spirit, who unites us with the vicarious faith of Jesus Christ, prayer too is the work of the divine in us. Citing Romans 8, Calvin writes that "in order to minister to this weakness, God gives us the Spirit as our teacher in prayer," "intercedes for us with unspeakable groans," and unites us with the vicarious prayer of the praying Son (3.20.5).

Although Calvin is clear that prayer is the work of the Holy Spirit, he is also clear that the Spirit's work in us, conforming us in the likeness of the Son, is "by no means to hinder or hold back our own effort" (3.20.5). Prayer, for Calvin, is not a finite resource. The more the divine works in us does

---

[22]On this, see Mark A. McIntosh, *Mystical Theology: The Integrity of Theology and Spirituality* (Oxford: Blackwell, 2000).

not, for Calvin, mean the less room there is for us to work. Under the conditions of the "noncompetitive" agential scenario Calvin sets up in his understanding of the divine-human relation,[23] prayer involves a "messy entanglement" of God and humanity—united in the one prayer of the Son without competition or confusion.[24] God "enjoins with his own voice" our voice (3.20.12), and makes it, and us, holy. The Geneva Catechism brilliantly captures Calvin's christologically driven understanding of prayer when it instructs. "He who prays thus conceives his prayers *as from the mouth of Christ himself*, since he knows his own prayer to be assisted and recommended by the intercession of Christ (Rom. 8:34)" (Geneva, 112 [emphasis added]).

Romans 8, frequently cited by Calvin, is also a favorite among the contemplatives. As Sarah Coakley has uncovered, in Romans 8 (as it is received by writers such as Origen, Evagrius, and Athanasius) is to be found a "prayer-based" doctrine of the Trinity that is pneumatologically leading, daringly "incorporative" in terms of its presentation of the divine-human relation, and rooted in a deep sort of contemplative waiting on the divine.[25] Under the conditions of contemplation, the Holy Spirit catches the pray-er up into the divine Sonship, and from there the pray-er is incorporated into the life of the trinitarian divine. In other words, a theology of prayer styled in the Romans 8 tradition is not only pneumatologically leading but also grounded in the theme of union with the Son, which is now widely considered to be one of the abiding themes in Calvin's theology.[26]

That Calvin prioritizes the petitionary in his exposition of prayer and speaks of the "sure hope that our prayer will be answered" (3.20.11) might appear surprising to those familiar with the allegations that Calvin is prone elsewhere in his theology to the systematic separation of the divine from the

---

[23]For an investigation of "noncompetitive" agency from a Reformed perspective, see Kathryn Tanner, *God and Creation in Christian Theology: Tyranny and Empowerment?* (Oxford: Blackwell, 1988).

[24]I'm borrowing the phrase "messy entanglement" from Sarah Coakley, *God, Sexuality and the Self: An Essay "On the Trinity"* (Cambridge: Cambridge University Press, 2012).

[25]Coakley, *God, Sexuality and the Self*, esp. chap. 4.

[26]See, among others, Julie Canlis, *Calvin's Ladder: A Spiritual Theology of Ascent and Ascension* (Grand Rapids: Eerdmans, 2010); Charles Partee, *The Theology of John Calvin* (Louisville: Westminster John Knox, 2008); and J. Todd Billings, *Calvin, Participation, and the Gift: The Activity of Believers in Union with Christ* (Oxford: Oxford University Press, 2007).

human.[27] Calvin's unflinching commitment to the "certainty that prayer is granted" (3.20.12) arises out of this central christological intuition. At the heart of Calvin's theology of prayer is the proposition that we cannot pray as we ought without, that is, a mediated relationship with God. The work of mediation falls not on the saints (as Calvin fiercely argues over some seven subsections) or indeed on the church but exclusively on the person of the one true Mediator: Jesus Christ. "Christ is constituted the only Mediator, by whose intercession the Father is for us rendered gracious and easily entreated" (3.20.19). Any practice of prayer that bypasses the mediation of Christ is "to dishonor Christ and strip him of the title of sole Mediator, which, as it has been given to him by the Father as a unique privilege, ought not to be transferred to another" (3.20.21). Therefore, just as one cannot have faith by one's own action, one cannot pray without the action of the person of the Mediator. "No prayer is pleasing to God unless this Mediator sanctifies it" (3.20.27). It is on this christological basis that Calvin sees God answering prayer: in our prayer God hears God's own voice.

This takes us to the theme of contemplation. If contemplative prayer is to be pleasing to God, it must be grounded—as all prayer must be—in the doctrine of the mediation of Christ. Because the long chapter dedicated to prayer in the *Institutes* lacks sufficient resources to develop the contemplative dimension in Calvin's theology, we are to look elsewhere, to his doctrine of Sabbath.

CONTEMPLATION OF COSMIC PROPORTION

"For the most part, contemporary Christians pay little attention to the Sabbath," argues Walter Brueggemann.[28] This is a view shared by many others, including Karl Barth, Jürgen Moltmann, and Dorothy Bass, who likewise lament the neglect of the Sabbath in the practice and theology of contemporary Christianity.[29] The stakes are high when the Sabbath is overlooked. Getting the Sabbath wrong has implications that reach all the way

---

[27]For an investigation of the critiques and a persuasive rebuttal, see Billings, *Calvin, Participation, and the Gift*, chap. 1.

[28]Walter Brueggemann, *Sabbath as Resistance: Saying No to the Culture of Now* (Louisville: Westminster John Knox, 2014), ix.

[29]Karl Barth, *Church Dogmatics*, ed. Thomas F. Torrance, trans. Geoffrey W. Bromiley (Edinburgh: T&T Clark, 1961), III/4:50; Jürgen Moltmann, *God in Creation: A New Theology of Creation and the Spirit of God* (London: SCM Press, 1985), 276-96; and Dorothy C. Bass, "Keeping Sabbath,"

back to the doctrine of God. In short, to neglect the Sabbath means to get God wrong. According to Moltmann, "God, the active Creator, came to be placed so much in the centre of the picture that the God who rested on the Sabbath came to be overlooked."[30]

The Reformed tradition is richly resourced to redress the neglect of the Sabbath in contemporary theology. Barth, for example, begins his doctrine of creation with a profound meditation on the Sabbath (CD III/1), announces his description of the shape of human freedom before God with a celebration of the Sabbath rest (CD III/4, §53.1), and ends his account of the active life there too (CD III/4, §55.3). "The Sabbath commandment explains all the other commandments," he writes.[31] And in Barth's writings on the Sabbath is to be found a curious, almost throwaway commendation of "what one might call the Sabbath mysticism of Calvin."[32]

The Sabbath features in a number of Calvin's writings. You can find references to the Sabbath in his sermons, in the Geneva Catechism, in his biblical commentaries (on Genesis, Exodus, and Hebrews in particular), and in the *Institutes*. Across these writings, Calvin recognizes that although the coming of Christ means that the Sabbath, belonging as it does to the category of law, has to be reimagined, it is crucial that the Sabbath is not abolished (2.8.28). To observe the Sabbath is what it means to inhabit the image of God. "When he finished the creation of the world in six days, he dedicated the seventh to the contemplation of his works. To incite us more strongly to this, he sets before us his own example. For nothing is more to be desired than that we be formed in his image" (*Geneva*, 112). Just as God contemplated God's completed work of creation on the Sabbath, so should we. Getting the Sabbath wrong means, then, also getting the doctrine of humanity wrong.

For the damage it does to our understandings of God, the self, and indeed the world, Calvin writes that God "enjoined obedience to almost no other commandment as severely as to this" (2.8.29). So important is the Sabbath that the seventh day, as the child says to the minister in the Geneva Catechism, must be practiced "continually" (*Geneva*, 112). The Sabbath "is not

---

in *Practicing Our Faith: A Way of Life for a Searching People*, 2nd ed. (San Francisco: Jossey-Bass, 2010), 75-88.

[30]Moltmann, *God in Creation*, 149.

[31]Barth, *Church Dogmatics*, III/4:53.

[32]Ibid., III/4:59.

confined within a single day but extends through the whole course of our life, until, completely dead to ourselves, we are filled with the life of God" (2.8.31). In other words, the Sabbath gives definition, shape, and meaning to the whole course of human existence.

In the Geneva Catechism, the child is asked for three reasons why the Sabbath is practiced. The first of the three reasons, fleshed out programmatically in the *Institutes*, is the most relevant to the present discussion. The Sabbath, Calvin instructs, is first and foremost about "spiritual rest" in which one sets aside all things to "contemplate his [God's] works" (*Geneva*, 112). One of the lingering suspicions of contemplation, however, is the fear that the time opened up by the Sabbath rest would be wasted in lazy self-contemplation. Resting is a luxury not afforded to us by the busyness of the Christian life. For example, Barth sensed in contemplation the "indolence condemned in Scripture,"[33] which "in the last resort is . . . self-contemplation."[34] But what is to be found in Calvin's theology of contemplation, shaped by the Sabbath, is anything but a preoccupation with inner states of becoming, which is perhaps why Barth found his "Sabbath mysticism" so compelling: Calvin's, in fact, is a theology of contemplation on a cosmic scale.

It is fascinating, as Randall Zachman has brilliantly teased out, that the first place Calvin looks to "contemplate" the works of God is the night sky.[35] God "clothes himself, so to speak, with the image of the world, in which he would present himself for our contemplation."[36] In the stars, the planets, the celestial canopy, Calvin sees the light of divine glory made manifest. To contemplate the works of God, then, is quite simple: "you start at night."[37] To contemplate God means to step outside at night and look upward toward the "beautiful arrangement and wonderful variety" of the "courses and station of the heavenly bodies."[38] Of course, those familiar with Calvin's

---

[33]Ibid., III/4:474.

[34]Ibid., II/1:651.

[35]Randall C. Zachman, *Reconsidering John Calvin* (Cambridge: Cambridge University Press, 2012), chap. 1; and Zachman, "Contemplating the Living Image of God in Creation," in *Calvin Today: Reformed Theology and the Future of the Church*, ed. Michael Welker, Michael Weinrich, and Ulrich Möller (London: T&T Clark, 2013), 33-47.

[36]John Calvin, *Commentaries on the Book of Genesis* (Grand Rapids: Eerdmans, 1948), 60.

[37]Zachman, *Reconsidering John Calvin*, 13.

[38]John Calvin, *The Commentaries of John Calvin on the Book of Psalms* (Edinburgh: Calvin Translation Society, 1845), 1:309 (hereafter *Psalms*).

epistemology will know well that the kind of knowledge that contemplation yields, if it is to count as knowledge of God, needs the most thorough qualification. It is only when seen through the "spectacles of Scripture" (1.6.1), and indeed through the "eyes" of Christ (3.20.21), as Calvin puts it, that the divine glory the stars refract comes into focus. But it might be less well known that Calvin also feeds into his epistemological qualifications the ethical imperative of the Sabbath rest. It is only as one enjoys Sabbath rest—and all that rest entails—that the requisite practices of attention are sharp enough to notice the presence of God in the night's sky. When you take Sabbath rest, for Calvin, you all of a sudden start to notice things that might otherwise have passed you by. It is for that training in practices of attention that Calvin believed God instituted the Sabbath.

What is being offered by Calvin is a practice of contemplation on the largest scale known to him. It is contemplation of cosmic proportion. Citing Psalm 19:1, Calvin says that

> when we behold the heavens, we cannot but be elevated, by the contemplation of them, to Him who is their great Creator; and the beautiful arrangement and wonderful variety which distinguish the courses and station of the heavenly bodies, together with the beauty and splendor which are manifest in them, cannot but furnish us with evident proof of his providence.[39]

The curious appeal to the term *elevation*, and its relation to the metaphor of ascent, will be discussed below. The points to be noted at this juncture are first that, as far as Calvin sees it, on the Sabbath, contemplation and rest claim an ancient privilege over action and work. The Sabbath, which is as old as creation itself, provides the space in the midst of the busyness of life for us to look up at the night sky and be "ravished with wonder at his infinite goodness, wisdom, and power."[40] And second, Calvin is pushing a radically theocentric account of contemplation: it is the contemplation of God. To this end, he recommends being "trained in piety" (by which, he means "to assemble . . . for the hearing of the Word, the breaking of the mystical bread, and for public prayers") to provide corporate accountability against contemplation drifting into idle self-contemplation (2.8.28 and 2.8.32).

---

[39]Psalms, 309.
[40]Psalms, 309.

There is much fruit for theological picking in the way Calvin links contemplation with the Sabbath. Yet it is only "pleasing" to God, as Calvin would say, so long as it is grounded christologically in the doctrine of the mediation of Christ. It is to this loose end that we now turn. Calvin is quite clear that the Sabbath rest is not, strictly speaking, human action. Instead, it is first and foremost God's action: it is God's rest into which we rest. "In short," he writes, "we must rest from all activities of our own contriving so that, having God worked in us [Heb 13:21], we may repose in him [Heb 4:9]" (2.8.29). As we've seen with his doctrine of prayer, there is to be found, then, in his treatment of the Sabbath a doctrine of participation styled in the contemplative logic of Romans 8. We are called to rest "from all our works . . . [so] that the Lord may work in us through the Spirit," Calvin writes (2.8.34). The Holy Spirit incorporates the pray-er into the contemplation of the Son—who for Calvin is the "full light" of God—in order that we might see as the Son sees, contemplate as the Son contemplates, pray "as from the mouth of Christ himself" (*Geneva*, 112).[41] Just as resting on the Sabbath means to be incorporated into the rest of God, so too of contemplation. Contemplation, strictly speaking, means to be incorporated by the mediation of the Son into God's own contemplation. Sure enough, the Geneva Catechism instills in the child the sense that resting contemplatively on the Sabbath means "being grafted into the body of Christ, and made members of his" (*Geneva*, 113). Thus Calvin writes with reference to the mystical union:

> That joining together of Head and members, that indwelling of Christ in our hearts—in short, that mystical union—are accorded by us the highest degree of importance, so that Christ, having been made ours, makes us sharers with him in the gifts with which he has been endowed. We do not, therefore, contemplate him outside ourselves from afar in order that his righteousness may be imputed to us, but [rather] because we put on Christ and are engrafted into his body—in short, because he deigns to make us one with him. (3.11.10)

Earlier I noted Calvin's curious use of the term *elevation*, and it is on this note that we find a further contemplative theme to bring this section to a

---

[41]For Calvin's analysis of Christ as the true light, which interestingly takes place in a chapter on Jesus Christ the Mediator, see *Calvin: Commentaries*, ed. Joseph Haroutunian, Library of Christian Classics (Louisville: Westminster John Knox, 1996), 144. Commenting on Calvin's use of the metaphor of light, Barth writes that "he [Calvin] sees all other lights . . . in the light of this one light." *The Theology of Calvin*, 164.

close. "When we behold the heavens, we cannot but be elevated, by the contemplation of them, to Him who is their great Creator."[42] Calvin is here utilizing (albeit modified according to the evangelical criterion of *solo Christo*) that staple metaphor so widely deployed in the contemplative traditions of spirituality: the metaphor of ascent. In her fine study of the theme, Julie Canlis draws out that the crucial twist Calvin adds to the typology of ascent is that this is "no longer a story of humanity's ascent to God by grace (Aquinas), or of the soul's ascent (Augustine), but of Christ's ascent."[43] For Calvin, the pray-er's ascent is irreducibly bound—grafted—to Christ's. In this sense, Calvin can be seen to actualize the contemplative progression of the soul's graded ascent through particular stages—often cast in terms of the three ways of purgation, illumination, and union. These have no interest to him.[44] "Calvin shrugs off this stylistic device like an old garment and exclusively focuses on the believer's ascent *en Christo*."[45] In addition to the strongly christological character of Calvin's account of "Sabbath mysticism," and on a more fundamental level perhaps, notions of progress make little sense once contemplation (framed sabbatically) is seen to be about God's work in us. Sabbatical contemplation is about gift: the gift of sharing, by way of the Son, in God's own rest. And it is in this sense that contemplation, like other forms of prayer, is made pleasing to God (3.20.27).

THE PRACTICE OF SABBATICAL CONTEMPLATION

In answer to the question, what does all this mean in terms of the actual practice of contemplation? Calvin does not afford a straightforward answer. In fact, he is resolutely coy about prescribing too neatly the shape of sabbatical practices. Although in his engagement with the Sabbath he cites particular things to do (such as "meditating on the works of God," "reading Scripture," and so on) these feel rather generic, neither specifically Reformed nor

---

[42]*Psalms*, 309.

[43]Canlis, *Calvin's Ladder*, 43 (emphasis added).

[44]Brian Brock charts a helpful connection between the Sabbath and the Reformation theology of justification by faith alone: by resting from our work the Sabbath functions as an anti-Pelagian reminder of the priority of divine action and for us to rely on God's work alone. See Brian Brock, *Christian Ethics in a Technological Age* (Grand Rapids: Eerdmans, 2010), 292. As Barth writes, the Sabbath "points him away from everything that he himself can will and achieve and back onto what God is for him and will do for him." *Church Dogmatics*, III/4:53.

[45]Canlis, *Calvin's Ladder*, 49.

intentionally sabbatical. Beyond his concern to protect the territory of the Sabbath from getting cluttered with legalistic detail that gets in the way of sheer delight in God, there are at least two further reasons for Calvin's coyness.

First, sabbatical contemplation cannot readily be limited to a self-contained spiritual practice. Just as the Sabbath cannot be restricted to just one day of the week, as Calvin well stresses, neither can contemplation. In the same way that Calvin tore down the walls of the monastery to allow the monastic mindset to permeate Geneva more widely, he says that the Sabbath must be exercised continually and its contemplative logic permeate and regulate every day of the week. Sabbatical contemplation is not a practice among other practices, then, but is best understood as a way of life—permanently defining, shaping, and underlying all practices of Christian discipleship.

Second, contemplation styled in the logic of the Sabbath can complexify the very way the term spiritual *practice* is used.[46] Sabbatical contemplation isn't really a practice in the sense that it isn't really something that we do. If anything, sabbatical contemplation entails the cessation of doing; or to use traditional language, the practice of sabbatical contemplation paradoxically is about resting from practice. The "believers ought to lay aside their own works," Calvin says, "to allow God to work in them" (2.8.28). Following Calvin, who is here channeling the hallmark of a Reformed theology of the priority of grace, the Sabbath is about a gift. The Sabbath, which is freely given before all human activity even begins, overlays contemplation within an overt theology of grace. And as a grace-drenched and propelled practice, the Reformed tradition offers something to the wider tradition of contemplative spirituality by offsetting the falsely elitist directions in which contemplation has sometimes traveled. Sabbatical contemplation is not the preserve of the spiritual elite. It is given to all precisely as grace and irrespective of human technique, merit, or spiritual stature.

In lieu of prescribing too neatly the kinds of practices that might count as sabbatical contemplation, it is perhaps more revealing to offer some reflections on the effect sabbatical contemplation has on particular practices. If sabbatical contemplation is about the reordering of the entire self before God in light of

---

[46]On this, see Sarah Coakley, "Deepening Practices: Perspectives from Ascetical and Mystical Theology," in *Practicing Theology: Beliefs and Practices in Christian Life*, ed. Miroslav Volf and Dorothy C. Bass (Grand Rapids: Eerdmans, 2001), 78–93.

the freedom of the Sabbath, then the effects of sabbatical contemplation are multiple and far-reaching. There are two particularly relevant practical implications, however, that I'd like to focus on to bring this essay to a conclusion.

I said earlier that one of the curious features of Calvin's theology of contemplation is his focus on the stars and the night sky. To contemplate God, for Calvin, was very simple: you look up. It strikes me that not much of contemporary technological life is spent looking up, as Calvin would have expected. We inhabit a different posture. Much of life is spent looking down; not so much at the "devices and desires of our own hearts," as the Book of Common Prayer has it, as the devices in our hands: at smartphones and tablets. Setting aside time on the Sabbath, as many of those who articulate theological responses to technology have argued, means resting not only from "total work" but also from the devices that distract our eyes from the sky.[47] The Sabbath calls us to total rest, and that means resting from the things that define the rest of the week. In the reposturing of the Sabbath, we are released from the grip of our handheld devices, our false dependency on them, and their gravitational pull downward—which is a peculiarly modern iteration of the *homo incurvatus in se*—in order to be redirected upward, toward the stars. The alternative (contemplative) posture of the Sabbath is heavenward, recovering a position more akin to the ancient "orans": eccentrically heads up, arms stretched, eyes directed to the heavens.[48] To practice a kind of contemplation conceived in the logic of the Sabbath, therefore, involves the reordering of our technological practices on which we are becoming increasingly dependent.

---

[47]See Brock, *Christian Ethics*, esp. chap. 7. Another area of lively engagement with the Sabbath can be found in theological engagements with the theme of work. For an important use of the Sabbath as part of a wider critique of capitalist ideologies of work, see John Hughes, *The End of Work: Theological Critiques of Capitalism* (Oxford: Blackwell, 2007), chap. 1. When seen at the week's end, the Sabbath is in the precarious position of being hijacked by capitalist agendas that would see the Sabbath as a helpful way of ensuring a more productive workforce. Workers would return from the weekend's leisure time feeling refreshed and ready for more work. This is, as Brueggemann argues, "a recognizable echo of the ancient Hebrew slaves, harassed by many supervisors and taskmasters who kept reminding them of the inadequacy of their production." *Sabbath as Resistance*, 12-13. And it is far from what Calvin means by rest. Sabbath rest, as Barth points out, is not at the week's end but begins the week. See *Church Dogmatics*, III/4:71. Resting on the Sabbath relativizes work and it mitigates against its idealization. The Sabbath functions in Barth's theology as a deliberate, iconoclastic ploy to smash the idolatries of work.

[48]On body posture and prayer, see Gabriel Bunge, *Earthen Vessels: The Practice of Personal Prayer According to the Patristic Tradition* (San Francisco: Ignatius, 2002).

But what happens when one is released from the downward drag of handheld devices and is liberated to contemplate the glory of God in the stars but sees nothing? While Calvin could step out into the night to be confronted by the radiant light of the stars and the planets, "we all cannot do this, as Calvin could, because of ambient light."[49] The night sky no longer radiates the celestial light that reflects the glory of God but a light of a different making: a thick layer of smog and orange glow that stands between the contemplative gazer and the works of God as a reminder of the polluting effects of our 24/7 culture of consumerism, neon advertisement, and industry. As Michael Northcott comments,

> Artificial light . . . enables industrial humans to live their lives independently of the rhythms of the earth. It makes possible 24-hour shift working in factories and offices and so subject time to a new industrial urgency in which "time is money." The commodification of time creates the drive for a pattern of work and activity which is unremitting, and which subverts traditional restraints on the exigencies of work, including the Sabbath. Cities lit with electricity increasingly become places, which never sleep, where both work and entertainment proceed through the night. Revelers return bleary eyed to the artificial light of their offices the next day, even as maintenance and shift workers make their way to bed.[50]

The night sky, in short, has become an idol, in the fullest sense of that term. It gets in the way of God.[51] What we are talking about is a modern-day golden calf. The golden veneer of the night sky takes form as the perpetual orange glow that reflects back the ambient light of our always-on culture. "Imagine him [Calvin] in the sixteenth century at night looking up at the sky. It must have felt like the Milky Way was right there for him to touch."[52] For us, that light is at risk of not getting in.

The metaphor of light is a staple in the contemplative traditions of spirituality.[53] Often taken to be a metaphor for the presence of God, the

---

[49]Zachman, *Reconsidering John Calvin*, 15.
[50]Michael S. Northcott, *A Moral Climate: The Ethics of Global Warming* (London: Darton, Longman & Todd, 2007), 189.
[51]For Calvin's treatment of idols, see *Institutes* 1.8.
[52]Zachman, *Reconsidering John Calvin*, 15.
[53]For example: Paul Murray, OP, *In the Grip of Light: The Dark and Bright Journey of Christian Contemplation* (London: Bloomsbury, 2012).

movement of the soul's ascent is frequently described by contemplative writers as a journey from darkness to the brilliant brightness of the divine—a light so bright it is experienced as darkness. Therefore, when the light no longer gets in, the presence of God and our contemplative resting into that illuminating presence is blocked. In this sense, light pollution is a contemplative issue. It stops us from seeing and therefore worshiping God. And precisely as a contemplative issue, it might only be met satisfactorily by a contemplative response.

To the ecological issue of the blocking of the light, therefore, sabbatical contemplation also has something to say. The Sabbath is a time for us to rest—from our constant work, from consumerism, from technology. It is also time for the land to rest. "In the seventh year there shall be a Sabbath of complete rest for the land" (Lev 25:4). On the Sabbath, the land would be left uncultivated; the land would be returned to God one year in seven; and the animals that work the land would rest. Therefore, as Moltmann writes, "the ecological day of rest should be a day without pollution of the environment—a day when we leave our cars at home, so that nature too can celebrate its Sabbath."[54]

Allowing the land to celebrate the Sabbath might help, then, to go some way in allowing the light back in so that once again we are flooded with the illuminating presence of God. But the kind of sabbatical contemplation I'm describing goes even further. If ambient light is to be diagnosed as not only a symptom of idolatry but as an idol itself, then, to adapt an argument Sarah Coakley makes of the idolatry of patriarchy, it is only in the "kneeling work" of contemplation that idols are truly slayed—at their root.[55] More than allowing the land to take sabbatical rest, the Sabbath is about the examination of the very desires that prevent the land from resting in the first place and the offering of those misdirected desires to God to be transformed from within.

My point—illustrated by the examples of technological and ecological practices—is that human desire is redirected as one is engrafted into the sabbatical rest of God. Sabbatical contemplation is not simply a practice in itself but transforms the whole course of human existence. Human desires

---

54Moltmann, *God in Creation*, 296.
55Coakley, *God, Sexuality and the Self*, 327.

are reconstituted according to the rhythm of sabbatical contemplation so that we start to see the world differently; we start to reimagine our use of technology, our use of the land, our relationship to our jobs and careers, and so on, in a different light. Indeed, we start to view the practice of rest differently. Understood from the perspective of the Sabbath, the fissure that separates sharply the active (petitionary) from the passive (contemplation), perpetuated by the likes of Bloesch, is problematized. For in sabbatical contemplation is to be found a peculiarly active sort of passivity: rest. On closer inspection, resting in God is hard work—it requires action, commitment, and even the countercultural reordering our desire and its practical outworkings.

CONCLUSION

By way of a conclusion, having established the link between the Sabbath and contemplation, the methodological move I've been articulating in this chapter can now be brought to completion. In effect, this chapter has utilized aspects of the justly celebrated argument Bernard McGinn made of mysticism and applied it to one of the core practical commitments of mystical theology: contemplation. In the introduction to his multivolume work on mysticism, McGinn argues that "no mystic (at least before the present century) believed in or practiced 'mysticism.' They believed and practiced Christianity . . . that is, religions that contained mystical elements as parts of a wider historical whole."[56] In other words, mysticism is not something that can be easily separated from Christianity and compartmentalized into a fringe strand of spirituality. Instead, it is inherent to Christianity. As with mysticism, so too of contemplation. Although contemplation emerges with varying degrees of intensity (taking, for example, institutional embodiment in monasticism), it is something that ultimately belongs to the shared inheritance of all Christians. It should be seen as part and parcel of what it means to be a creature imaging the Creator and therefore as fundamental to evangelical spirituality as it is to other (more explicitly contemplative) branches of the Christian spiritual tradition. In terms of accessing the contemplative dimension that is inherent within evangelicalism, this chapter has identified a symbiotic relationship between the Sabbath and

---

[56]McGinn, *Foundations of Mysticism*, 266-67.

contemplation. The contemporary neglect of the biblical practice of the Sabbath goes hand in hand with the neglect of the practice of contemplation. The recovery of the Sabbath might, then, not only help to point the way to a recovery of the contemplative dimensions of evangelical spirituality but also help evangelicalism deepen its self-understanding and biblical identity.

But if there's one particular thing to take from Calvin to shape our contemporary practices of contemplation, it is this. At root, Calvin's theology is one long meditation on the absolute priority of God. Before all that we do, before all actions, practices, before all existence stands the God who calls us into being. The Sabbath, which serves to affirm and protect the radical priority of divine grace, reframes contemplation as God's work in us. Calvin's rich protection of the priority of grace offers a reminder, then, that to practice contemplation is to be released from the anxiety of worrying whether I'm doing it right. Sabbatical contemplation is something given by God, and it is ours for the taking. Let us therefore "enter that rest" (Heb 4:3).

"TO GAZE ON THE BEAUTY OF THE LORD"

The Evangelical Resistance and Retrieval of Contemplation

TOM SCHWANDA

CONTEMPLATION IS OFTEN MISUNDERSTOOD and feared by evangelicals today. One can find critics not only from the fringes of the church but also among well-respected evangelical theologians warning against the dangers of anything vaguely related to contemplation. Why has contemplation become the center of such controversy and vitriolic attacks? It is important to examine seriously both the fears and concerns behind these accusations. Further, it is necessary to recognize that contemplation is not a recent innovation of an exclusive group of spiritual elitists or even heretics, nor is it only an exclusive devotional practice of monastic communities. Rather, it is an attitude and awareness that is present throughout Scripture. Therefore, this chapter will examine the critique of contemporary evangelical contemplation and evaluate its historical accuracy. Once the adversaries of contemplation have been reviewed, the historical definitions and biblical nature of contemplation will be addressed. This will provide a foundation to explore the spiritual experiences of four individuals who were all significant leaders within the church. While the issues surrounding contemplation are larger than the evangelical church, I will focus on American evangelicals since the majority of criticisms have emerged within that sector of the church.[1]

---

[1]When exploring Christian spirituality, context is always critical and since the nature of American evangelicalism is unique when compared with its European and non-Western counterparts,

EVANGELICAL RESISTANCE TO CONTEMPLATION

The best-known critic of contemporary contemplation is Lighthouse Trails. This ministry, based in Eureka, Montana, has been actively sounding the alarm for the evangelical church since 2002. Their website explains their origin and motivation:

> As a response to learning that a mystical-type spirituality had entered the Christian church through many avenues, we began Lighthouse Trails. This spirituality, called contemplative spirituality or spiritual formation, was infiltrating youth groups, churches, seminaries, and Bible studies at an alarming rate through the Spiritual Formation movement, the emerging church, the Purpose Driven movement and so forth.[2]

Their narrow boundaries typically equate anything even remotely connected to spiritual formation as contemplative spirituality and therefore dangerous. A quick review of their website indicates an "Academic Hall of Shame" of North American colleges and seminaries that teach one or more courses on spiritual formation.[3] A number of prominent schools were not listed that are well known for their teaching of spiritual formation, so the total should actually be higher.[4] According to Lighthouse Trails, only sixteen schools were judged to be free of any influence of spiritual formation.[5]

Further, Lighthouse Trails defines contemplative spirituality as

> a belief system that uses ancient mystical practices to induce altered states of consciousness (the silence) and is rooted in mysticism and the occult but

---

this essay will focus only on North American sources. For one example of eighteenth-century British evangelical contemplation, see Tom Schwanda "Gazing at the Wounds: The Blood of the Lamb in the Hymns of John Cennick," in *Heart Religion: Evangelical Piety in England and Ireland, 1690–1850,* ed. John Coffey (Oxford: Oxford University Press, 2016), 113-37.

[2] "Who We Are and What We Do," Lighthouse Trails Research Project, accessed on July 2, 2016, www.lighthousetrailsresearch.com/aboutus.htm.

[3] "Christian Colleges that Promote Spiritual Formation," Lighthouse Trails Research Project, accessed on July 2, 2016, www.lighthousetrailsresearch.com/Colleges.htm. The list includes Azusa Pacific, Baylor, Beeson, Bethel, Biola, Calvin College and Calvin Seminary, Cedarville, Cornerstone, Dallas Seminary, Fuller, Gordon-Conwell, Houghton, Indiana Wesleyan, John Brown, Liberty, Mars Hill (WA), Messiah, Moody, Northern Seminary, North Park, Oral Roberts, Regent College, Reformed Theological Seminary, Taylor, Tyndale Seminary (Toronto), Trinity Evangelical Divinity School, Western Seminary (Holland, MI), and Wheaton.

[4] Other schools that have a strong concentration in spiritual formation include Denver Seminary, Southern Baptist Theological Seminary, and Regent University.

[5] "Colleges that Are *Not* Promoting . . . ," Lighthouse Trails Research Project, accessed on July 2, 2016, www.lighthousetrailsresearch.com/collegesgood.htm.

often wrapped in Christian terminology. The premise of contemplative spirituality is pantheistic (God is all) and panentheistic (God is in all). Common terms used for this movement are "spiritual formation," "the silence," "the stillness," "ancient-wisdom," "spiritual disciplines," and many others.[6]

"Dangerous practitioners" of this include Richard Foster, Dallas Willard, Rick Warren, Tim Keller, John Ortberg, Eugene Peterson, Bruce Demarest, Larry Crabb, Beth Moore, Adele Calhoun, and Gary Thomas, to name only a few.[7] Further, Lighthouse Trails enumerates three false premises on which the movement is based: a denial of the sin nature of humanity, a denial of the atonement, and a denial of God's personal nature.[8] All of the above persons would quickly repudiate this threefold attack. Lest I be misunderstood, let me quickly confess the importance of orthodox doctrine and biblical integrity. Clearly there are aberrant theological teachings and spiritual distortions within the evangelical church. Anyone who teaches Christian spirituality or has read a sampling of devotional books realizes that not everything that bears the name "Christian" is a faithful trinitarian witness to the gospel. Careful discernment is certainly important.[9] While this is a complex matter that should not be overly simplified, Lighthouse Trails reveals a historical ignorance of two thousand years of the Christian church. Further, they distort meanings and define terms such as *spiritual formation* or *spiritual disciplines* in ways that are inconsistent with how evangelicals and other Christians employ them.[10] Unsurprisingly, there is a lingering contempt for anything even vaguely related to the Roman

---

[6]"The Spiritual Formation Movement," Lighthouse Trails Research Project, accessed on July 2, 2016, www.lighthousetrailsresearch.com/spiritualformation.htm.

[7]"Topical Research Index," Lighthouse Trails Research Project, accessed on July 2, 2016, www.lighthousetrailsresearch.com/researchtopics.htm.

[8]"'5 Things You Should Know About Contemplative Prayer' Booklet Will Help Share Truth," Lighthouse Trails Research Project, January 21, 2013, www.lighthousetrailsresearch.com/blog/?p=10780.

[9]Bruce Demarest provides a helpful means of discerning orthodox Christian spirituality. Bruce Demarest, *Satisfy Your Soul: Restoring the Heart of Christian Spirituality* (Colorado Springs, CO: NavPress, 1999), 63-90.

[10]Moody Ministries has responded to the attacks of Lighthouse Trails that they support contemplative prayer. Moody's rebuttal demonstrates how Lighthouse Trails distorts the meaning of the vocabulary of spiritual formation and presents a biblical and historical defense for engaging in spiritual formation and the practice of spiritual disciples. "Moody Responds to Lighthouse Trails," Moody Ministries, September 17, 2007, https://web.archive.org/web/20111223140931/http://www.moodyministries.net/crp_NewsDetail.aspx?id=7080.

Catholic Church. Martin Luther, John Calvin, John and Charles Wesley, John Newton, Jonathan Edwards, and Charles Spurgeon, to name only a few, would be shocked by this reductionist rejection of the treasures of the Western Catholic tradition.

More recently, Ken Silva, pastor of the Connecticut River Baptist Church, has attacked anything vaguely associated with contemplation. Silva is concerned by supposed neo-Gnostic influences and strong inroads that Roman Catholic theology and spirituality have had on Richard Foster, Dallas Willard, Rick Warren, and many others. Tim Keller, in particular, has been accused of teaching Roman Catholic and Quaker mysticism.[11] Redeemer Presbyterian Church in New York City, where Keller was until recently the lead pastor, held a three-week adult education class in Spring 2009 titled "The Way of the Monk," which was strongly attacked by Lighthouse Trails.[12] While David Cloud recognizes the validity of biblical contemplation, though not clearly defined,[13] he is distressed that Donald Whitney from the Southern Baptist Theological Seminary "promotes the practice of silence, journaling, and spiritual direction."[14] Bob DeWaay is another opponent who strongly objects to spiritual formation. He says,

> To hear evangelicals like Dallas Willard and Richard Foster tell us that we need practices that were never spelled out in the Bible to become more like Christ or to get closer to God is astonishing. What is more astonishing is that evangelical colleges and seminaries are requiring their students to study practices that are relics of Medieval Rome, not found in the Bible, and closely akin to the practices of many pagan societies.[15]

The common thread uniting all these detractors is a general disdain for anything even remotely comparable to Roman Catholic spiritual

---

[11]"Tim Keller Teaching Roman Catholic and Quaker Mysticism" (video), Apprising Ministries, June 15, 2012, http://apprising.org/2012/06/15/tim-keller-teaching-roman-catholic-and-quaker-mysticism-to-his-rpc-leaders/.

[12]"Another Popular Christian Leader, Tim Keller, Takes Church into Contemplative," Lighthouse Trails Research Project blog, June 28, 2009, www.lighthousetrailsresearch.com/blog/?p=872.

[13]David W. Cloud, *Evangelicals and Contemplative Prayer* (Port Huron, MI: Way of Life Literature, 2012), 75.

[14]Ibid., 67.

[15]Bob DeWaay, "The Dangers of Spiritual Formation and Spiritual Disciplines: A Critique of Dallas Willard and *The Spirit of the Disciplines*," *Critical Issues Commentary*, November/December 2005, http://cicministry.org/commentary/issue91.htm.

practices. What is lacking is any awareness of how Protestants from the sixteenth century onward adapted Roman Catholic practices that they inherited according to their own emerging Protestant sensibilities and theology.[16]

One might be surprised to hear a similar outcry from Donald Bloesch, the well-respected evangelical theologian who died in 2010. His final book, *Spirituality Old and New*, signaled a significant retreat from his earlier supportive affirmation of contemplation and Christian mysticism.[17] Bloesch, who was influenced by Karl Barth, reflects some of the significant fears of his theological mentor.[18] His ultimate concern was that contemplation and mysticism were inconsistent with a biblical spirituality.[19] One of Bloesch's primary apprehensions regarding contemplation was that according to him prayer was primarily offering our petitions to God, not for enjoying God.[20] While Bloesch correctly asserted that "contemplation does not take precedence over service,"[21] it is not clear that he would agree with the converse, that action is not superior to contemplation. Much like Barth, Bloesch was afraid that contemplation would reduce a person's active involvement in service to the kingdom of God and the world.[22] Bloesch even cautioned readers that "Edwards was partly a mystical . . . theologian in contrast to Barth."[23] While Bloesch raised some legitimate concerns that I would quickly affirm, his consistent blurring of categories created a convoluted message. Bruce Demarest's review of this book echoes many of my concerns. Demarest's concluding sentences are worth quoting; "The renowned Reformed scholar, John Murray, put it well: 'There is an intelligent mysticism in the life of faith.' Mystical spirituality in the . . . relational sense is not a

---

[16]See, e.g., Edmund Bunny's bowdlerization of Jesuit Robert Parsons's devotional manual on prayer. Tom Schwanda, *Soul Recreation: The Contemplative-Mystical Piety of Puritanism* (Eugene, OR: Pickwick, 2012), 131. Also Willem Teellinck's adaption of Thomas à Kempis, *Imitation of Christ*. Schwanda, *Soul Recreation*, 131n59.

[17]Compare Donald G. Bloesch, *Spirituality Old and New* (Downers Grove, IL: IVP Academic, 2007), with Bloesch, *The Struggle of Prayer* (Colorado Springs, CO: Helmers & Howard, 1988).

[18]For a summary treatment of Karl Barth's primary objections to contemplation and mysticism, see Schwanda, *Soul Recreation*, 202-15.

[19]Bloesch, *Spirituality Old and New*, 143, 145, cf. 50.

[20]Ibid., 82, 94, 133.

[21]Ibid., 144.

[22]Ibid., 42. 68, 145.

[23]Ibid., 62, cf. 81.

dangerous distortion of Christian life and mission, but is the very essence thereof."[24]

It is significant that Richard Foster, who more than anybody in evangelical spirituality has been attacked for his teaching on contemplation, recognizes the possible distortions and abuse of contemplation. Not surprisingly, his critics ignore this. Foster devotes four pages in one of his works to the "potential perils" of contemplation, reminding readers not to isolate themselves from ordinary life, to beware of excessive asceticism, not to marginalize the intellectual dimension of faith, and not to ignore the necessity of communal life.[25] In an earlier book he cautions that contemplation is not for the beginner. Moreover, Foster counsels that it requires time for the believer to create a proper biblical foundation and learn the principles of discernment.[26]

A DEFINITION OF CONTEMPLATION

Since there is both confusion and distortion by some regarding the meaning of contemplation, it is critical to examine its definition. This pursuit of clarity is further complicated when some authors employ the terms *contemplation* and *meditation* interchangeably. This is not a recent development but is long-standing historical practice.[27] I understand meditation to be the active use of the mind to engage God through reading and praying of Scripture or some other devotional practices. The key is the active and intentional reflection, or *ruminatio*, on whatever we are considering. Contemplation is a loving attentiveness or grateful gazing on God. It is experiential and savoring rather than discursive or mental dissection. It emphasizes the heart more than the head. Given this distinction between the two terms, some might assume that meditation is more active and contemplation is passive. However, that is not accurate. The cultivated attitude of openness to the Holy Spirit and willingness to wait and rest in God's presence required of contemplation

---

[24]Bruce Demarest, review of Donald G. Bloesch, *Spirituality Old and New* in *Journal of Spiritual Formation and Soul Care* 1, no. 1 (2008): 113.

[25]Richard J. Foster, *Streams of Living Water* (San Francisco: HarperSanFrancisco, 1998), 53-56.

[26]Richard J. Foster, *Prayer: Finding the Heart's True Home* (San Francisco: New York: HarperSanFrancisco, 1992), 156-57; cf. Kenneth Boa, *Conformed to the Image: Biblical and Practical Approaches to Spiritual Formation* (Grand Rapids: Zondervan, 2001), 166.

[27]This paragraph is adapted from Schwanda, *Soul Recreation*, 123.

necessitates active concentration and effort. Thomas White, a seventeenth-century English Puritan, drew this distinction using the bridal language of the Song of Songs: "Meditation is like the kindling of fire and contemplation more like the flaming of it when fully kindled. The one is like the spouse seeking Christ, and the other like the spouse's enjoying of Christ."[28]

Isaac Ambrose (1604–1664) a fellow English Puritan who inspired numerous eighteenth-century evangelicals, provides an important window to contemplation when he raises the question, "What, shall he [i.e., Jesus] ascend, and shall not we in our contemplations follow him? Gaze, O my soul, on this wonderful Object, thou need not fear any check [i.e., loss or misfortune] from God or Angel, so that thy contemplation be spiritual and divine."[29] Ambrose highlights a number of key themes of evangelical contemplation: It is directed to Jesus or another person of the Trinity. It involves an attentive beholding or gazing on this object. Additionally, we do not need to fear any objections from God in our practice of contemplation because God welcomes and encourages it. In other words, God is delighted by our delight in him. A century later, Jonathan Edwards understood contemplation in a similar manner. Kyle Strobel summarizes the visual nature of this beholding of God when he writes, "This gazing is the pilgrim-anticipation of the beatific-glory we behold in heaven."[30] This also helpfully introduces the eschatological nature of contemplation. What we experience now in contemplation prepares us for the beatific vision, when we will see God face-to-face in heaven in all his glory. Therefore, our cultivation of contemplation on earth forms us for the habitual gazing on God in heaven.

Richard Foster recognizes the same importance of our beholding of God: "Put simply, the contemplative life is the steady gaze of the soul upon the God who loves us."[31] Elsewhere Foster declares, "Contemplative prayer

---

[28]Thomas White, *Method of Divine Meditation* (London, 1655), 4-5.

[29]Isaac Ambrose, *Looking unto Jesus* (London, 1658), 871-72.

[30]Kyle Strobel, *Formed for the Glory of God: Learning from the Spiritual Practices of Jonathan Edwards* (Downers Grove, IL: InterVarsity Press, 2013), 133.

[31]Foster, *Streams of Living Water*, 49. See Robert E. Webber, *The Divine Embrace: Recovering the Passionate Spiritual Life* (Grand Rapids: Baker Books, 2006), esp. 46, for a similar reference to gazing and contemplation.

is a loving attentiveness to God."[32] While Foster is strongly theocentric in his definitions, James Houston is more explicitly trinitarian in his language: "Our contemplation of God, in Christ, through the Holy Spirit, is the heart of our friendship with him. Indeed, it is the primary reason why we are alive in this world."[33] Houston's development of contemplation clearly articulates that this is not an exclusive experience for a few advanced saints, but rather an invitation Jesus offers to any who follow him as his disciples. Employing Jesus' parable of the vine and branches in John 15, Houston explores the intimacy that is available to those who seek to live more fully in Christ through his emphasis to "be a person-in-Christ" and to "abide in God."[34] This emphasis on friendship and intimacy with God is also evident in James Wilhoit and Evan Howard's recent book *Discovering Lectio Divina*. They maintain, "Contemplation [is] a resting in God and an enjoyment of the pleasure of his company."[35]

However, contemplation is a gift and always dependent on God's grace. There is no technique which guarantees that if a person prays in a certain way it will produce a contemplative experience. Nonetheless, a person can cultivate a greater sensitivity toward contemplation by using various spiritual practices, including meditating on Scripture, varieties of prayer, worship, acts of mercy and Christian service, and so on. Therefore, contemplation is both an attitude and activity of loving, focused attention or grateful gazing on God that provides a means for keeping company with and enjoying Jesus Christ.

A BIBLICAL FOUNDATION FOR CONTEMPLATION

What we have discovered in the various definitions of contemplation is clearly evident from Scripture. Bernard of Clairvaux, the great twelfth-century writer on contemplation, referred to David as the *maximus contemplator*,[36] and with good reason. Psalm 27:4 declares David's desire:

---

[32]Foster, *Prayer*, 158.

[33]James Houston, *The Transforming Friendship: A Guide to Prayer* (Oxford: Lion, 1989), 200.

[34]Ibid., 200-205.

[35]James C. Wilhoit and Evan B. Howard, *Discovering Lectio Divina: Bringing Scripture into Ordinary Life* (Downers Grove, IL: InterVarsity Press, 2012), 114.

[36]Bernard McGinn, *The Presence of God: A History of Western Christian Mysticism*, vol. 2, *The Growth of Mysticism: Gregory the Great Through the Twelfth Century* (New York: Crossroad, 1994), 508n317.

> One thing I ask from the LORD,
>> this only do I seek:
> that I may dwell in the house of the LORD
>> all the days of my life,
> to gaze on the beauty of the LORD
>> and to seek him in his temple.[37]

Or again from David in Psalm 63:1-5:

> You, God, are my God,
>> earnestly I seek you;
> I thirst for you,
>> my whole being longs for you,
> in a dry and parched land
>> where there is no water.
> I have seen you in the sanctuary
>> and beheld your power and your glory.
> Because your love is better than life,
>> my lips will glorify you.
> I will praise you as long as I live,
>> and in your name I will lift up my hands.
> I will be fully satisfied as with the richest of foods;
>> with singing lips my mouth will praise you.

Both of these Davidic psalms communicate the intense longing and fulfilled delight of being in God's presence. Other Old Testament passages that illustrate contemplation are Psalms 42:1-2; 73:25; and 131:2. The theme of resting in God (e.g., Ps 37:7) is also seen by some as an illustration of the attitude and experience of contemplation. Early Christian writers designated Moses (Deut 34:10) and Elijah (1 Kings 19:12-14) among others to depict contemplation. The early church recognized John's Gospel as reflecting the contemplative life. John 14–17, in particular, reveals the oneness and intimacy of love that Jesus shared with God. Further, within that same portion of Scripture, Jesus prays for our own sharing of that intimacy and enjoyment of the divine love (Jn 14:23; 17:21, 24-26). Paul's mystical experience of being taken up into the third heaven (2 Cor 12:1-4) and his frequent reminders of the life we are called to live in union with Christ (e.g., Gal 2:20;

---

[37] All Scripture unless otherwise noted is from TNIV.

Eph 3:17; Col 2:6-7) have been recognized as an affirmation of contemplation. Mary demonstrates the proper attitude in hearing the reports of her son when she "treasured up all these things [i.e., about Jesus] and pondered them in her heart" (Lk 2:19). Additional New Testament passages reflective of the contemplative life are Luke 10:39, 42; Acts 7:54-56; 2 Corinthians 3:18; and Hebrews 12:2.

EVANGELICAL RETRIEVAL OF CONTEMPLATION

From the myriad of potential evangelicals, I have selected four who demonstrate a healthy biblical and theological understanding of contemplation.[38] These persons are all representative, significant leaders in the church and not outliers. My sample includes two men and two women to confirm that gender is not a determinant. There are two Calvinist and two Wesleyan representatives, verifying that a person's theological tradition is not a factor. Additionally, these individuals are from the eighteenth century, to confirm that contemplation is not a recent fad but has been present within evangelicalism from the very outset.

Jonathan Edwards. The New England pastor and theologian Jonathan Edwards (1703–1758) played a remarkable role in the Great Awakening. Both through his preaching and writing he encouraged a more discerning view of God's surprising works. It is unfortunate that for many people their only association with Edwards is his sermon "Sinners in the Hands of an Angry God." Few readers realize that the turbulent response to the first section of Edwards's sermon on judgment prevented him from completing his message and declaring the good news of God's grace and mercy.[39] The best source for exploring Edwards's understanding and experience of contemplation is his *Personal Narrative.*[40] As the following passage confirms, Edwards

---

[38]I am following David Bebbington's lead in defining evangelicalism as a movement that began in the eighteenth century with the evangelical revivals in England and the Great Awakening in the American colonies, which emphasized the necessity of conversion, the cross, the Bible, and activism. David Bebbington, *Evangelicalism in Modern Britain: A History from the 1730s to the 1980s* (London: Routledge, 1989), 5-17. See Michael A. G. Haykin and Kenneth J. Stewart, eds., *The Advent of Evangelicalism: Exploring Historical Continuities* (Nashville: B & H Academic, 2008), which seeks to push back this origin to at least the seventeenth century.

[39]George M. Marsden, *A Short Life of Jonathan Edwards* (Grand Rapids: Eerdmans, 2008), 68.

[40]For helpful summaries of Edwards's understanding and practice of contemplation, see Michael J. McClymond, *Encounters with God: An Approach to the Theology of Jonathan Edwards* (New York: Oxford University Press, 1998), 37-49, and Strobel, *Formed for the Glory of God*, 113-42.

experienced God through creation, echoing Calvin's belief that creation was the "theater of God's glory":[41]

> I often used to sit and view the moon, for a long time; and so in the daytime, spent much time in viewing the clouds and sky, to behold the sweet glory of God in these things: in the meantime, singing forth with a low voice, my contemplations of the Creator and Redeemer. And scarce anything, among all the works of nature, was so sweet to me as thunder and lightning. Formerly, nothing had been so terrible to me. I used to be a person uncommonly terrified with thunder: and it used to strike me with terror, when I saw a thunderstorm rising. But now, on the contrary, it rejoiced me. I felt God at the first appearance of a thunderstorm. And used to take the opportunity at such times, to fix myself to view the clouds, and see the lightnings play, and hear the majestic and awful voice of God's thunder: which often times was exceeding entertaining, leading me to sweet contemplations of my great and glorious God. And while I viewed, used to spend my time, as it always seemed natural to me, to sing or chant forth my meditations; to speak my thoughts in soliloquies, and speak with a singing voice.[42]

Clearly Edwards was fixated on God's transcendent and awesome beauty and the thunderous glory of God and God's mighty acts in creation, though he also mentioned that God's overwhelming nature revealed through creation turned his thoughts to God as his Redeemer. Notice the proper order for Edwards. As Michael McClymond and Gerald McDermott observe, "Edwards's new God concept did not derive from his experience of nature, but rather the reverse. His 'new sense' of God's glory transformed his perception of the natural world."[43] Therefore, it is most appropriate that as he beheld this "sweet glory of God" his heart overflowed with singing and chanting of his praise to God. Edwards also was inspired to speak soliloquies so that he could both deepen his experience of God's presence and further etch it into his memory. One can easily hear the breathtaking sense of delight that Edwards experiences in God through the majestic nature of

---

[41]John Calvin, *Institutes of the Christian Religion*, ed. John T. McNeill, trans. Ford Lewis Battles, Library of Christian Classics (Philadelphia: Westminster, 1960), 1.5.8; 1.6.2.

[42]Jonathan Edwards, *Personal Narrative*, in *Letters and Personal Writings*, vol. 16, *The Works of Jonathan Edwards*, ed. George S. Claghorn (New Haven: Yale University Press, 1998), 794.

[43]Michael J. McClymond and Gerald R. McDermott, *The Theology of Jonathan Edwards* (New York: Oxford University Press, 2012), 73.

creation. Protestant readers can recognize the depth of appreciation of Louis Dupré and James Wiseman, two Roman Catholic scholars of Christian spirituality, when they declare the "personal narrative of his [i.e., Edwards's] own 'awakening' to a life in God's presence provides us with one of the most convincing documents of mystical experience in our entire tradition."[44]

Later in his life Edwards again spoke of God's glory but now directs it more specifically to Jesus Christ:

> Once, as I rid out into the woods for my health, anno 1737 [i.e., thirty-four years old]; and having lit from my horse in a retired place, as my manner commonly has been, to walk for divine contemplation and prayer: I had a view, that for me was extraordinary, of the glory of the Son of God; as mediator between God and man; and his wonderful, great, full, pure and sweet grace and love, and meek and gentle condescension. . . . The person of Christ appeared ineffably excellent, with an excellency great enough to swallow up all thought and conception. Which continued, as near as I can judge, about an hour; which kept me, the bigger part of time, in a flood of tears and weeping aloud.[45]

This passage reveals Edwards's favorite recreation of horseback riding. George Marsden writes, "When the weather permitted, in the afternoons after dinner he [Edwards] would ride two or three miles to a secluded place where he would walk for a while."[46] Clark Gilpin contends that for Edwards solitude was an essential spiritual practice that increased his attentiveness to God because it minimized the "worldly concerns [that] would divert his attention from life's true and single aim, the glory of God."[47] On this

---

[44]Louis Dupré and James A. Wiseman, eds., introduction to "Jonathan Edwards (1703–58)," in *Light from Light: An Anthology of Christian Mysticism*, ed. Louis Dupré and James A. Wiseman, 2nd ed. (Mahwah, NJ: Paulist Press, 2001), 382. Edwards and Evelyn Underhill are the only Protestant writers among the twenty-one authors included.

[45]Edwards, *Personal Narrative*, 801.

[46]George M. Marsden, *Jonathan Edwards: A Life* (New Haven: Yale University Press, 2003), 135.

[47]W. Clark Gilpin, "'Inward. Sweet Delight in God': Solitude in the Career of Jonathan Edwards," *Journal of Religion* 82, no. 4 (2002): 532. This essay provides a helpful commentary on solitude within Edwards's *Personal Narrative*. Marsden comments that solitude was a significant influence on Sarah Pierpont Edwards's contemplative piety as well. Marsden, *Jonathan Edwards*, 240. See also Donald S. Whitney, *Finding God in Solitude: The Personal Piety of Jonathan Edwards (1703–1758) and Its Influence on His Pastoral Ministry* (New York: Peter Lang, 2014), esp. 97-101, 113-16, on the importance of solitude for Edwards.

occasion Edwards's contemplative focus turns to Jesus Christ. He is obviously deeply enamored of the glory and beauty of the Son of God. His practice of contemplative prayer produced a flood of tears as he spoke of being swallowed up and speechless by this divine encounter. While Edwards does not clarify the nature of his tears, it is likely that they were a combination of repentance for his sin amid the excellency of Jesus Christ and the resulting tears of joyful delight and gratitude for "the sweet grace and love" of Christ. This intersects with the research of McClymond that the tears of "spiritual weepers" reveal an intense passion for God's kingdom.[48] This was obviously true for Edwards, who recorded his interest in "the advancement of Christ's kingdom" in the *Personal Narrative*.[49] This is a clear validation that while contemplatives might occasionally withdraw for a period of time to be with God, they do not lose sight of the larger needs of their surrounding world. For those unfamiliar with Edwards, these are not isolated passages that depict his contemplative practices or experiences. In fact, Edwards used the word *contemplation* thirteen times in this brief spiritual memoir.[50] However, one can demonstrate a contemplative attitude and awareness without the specific use of the term, as will be evident with Francis Asbury. Historically, many contemplative writings focus on love, and it is fascinating to listen to the range of adjectives Edwards affectionately employed to expand his experience of Jesus' grace and love. Elsewhere in Edwards's *Personal Narrative* he employed similar language to speak of his meditation on Scripture.[51] Also meditating on heaven produced other contemplative vocabulary and experiences for Edwards.[52]

Susanna Anthony. Unlike the popularity of Edwards, Susanna Anthony (1726–1791) is not as well known.[53] She was raised in a Quaker home but

---

[48]Michael J. McClymond, "The Practice of Holy Tears: Compunction, *Theosis*, and Union with the Dying and Rising Christ" (paper presented at the Annual Meeting of the American Academy of Religion, November 24, 2013).

[49]Edwards, *Personal Narrative*, 797, 800.

[50]McClymond, *Encounters with God*, 45. McClymond asserts, "For him [i.e., Edwards] spirituality *was* contemplation." Ibid., 38 (emphasis original).

[51]Edwards, *Personal Narrative*, 793, cf. 792.

[52]Ibid., 795; see numerous other examples throughout the *Personal Narrative*.

[53]Susanna Anthony has not attracted the attention she deserves. Therefore, rather than select her good friend, Sarah Osborn, who has been more critically studied, I have chosen Anthony, who is frequently included in the scholarship related to Osborn. See, e.g., Catherine A. Brekus, *Sarah Osborn's World: The Rise of Evangelical Christianity in Early America* (New Haven: Yale University

once converted became part of the First Congregational Church of Newport, Rhode Island. At the age of sixteen Anthony joined a women's religious society that met weekly for many years to dedicate themselves to prayer, Bible reading, and spiritual conversation and prayers for ministers and the advancement of Christ's kingdom throughout the world.[54] Because of her frailty, Anthony was unable to engage in normal daily activities. She devoted herself to sewing and needlework and visited the sick when she was able. Anthony's intentionality in cultivating a vital spiritual life inspired her to remain single so as to dedicate herself more fully to prayer.[55]

Samuel Hopkins, a disciple of Jonathan Edwards and Anthony's pastor for the last years of her life, collected and edited her writings as *The Life and Character of Miss Susanna Anthony*.[56] Significantly, Mark Noll includes Anthony's writings among his list of the top one hundred influential writings of eighteenth-century evangelical spirituality.[57] Hopkins summarized his impressions of Susanna's life by affirming the depth of her spirituality and love for God and neighbor, and he testifies that her character was a worthy example of piety for all people to emulate.[58]

Anthony attempted to put words to her experience of God that can only be described as ineffable:

> [July 8, 1750]: O, if I know anything of heaven, this, this is heaven, to be near my God. There is scarcely any thing that doth so revive and sweetly refresh my soul, even when at the lowest ebb, as this. How soon do I feel the warming, quickening influence of such meditation! O, what can heaven afford equal to the fruition of God! I long for heaven, for freedom from sin; and for the blessed society of perfected saints and angels; constant, and abiding joy flows from the thought of enjoying God, as he is in himself, Father, Son, and Spirit my infinitely full and all-sufficient portion. O happy hour! Come, come.

Press, 2013); Charles E. Hambrick-Stowe, "The Spiritual Pilgrimage of Sarah Osborn (1714–1796)," *Church History* 61, no. 4 (1992): 408-21.

[54]Brekus, *Sarah Osborn's World*, 123, 128, 175.

[55]Ibid., 123.

[56]Susanna Anthony, *The Life and Character of Miss Susanna Anthony*, ed. Samuel Hopkins (Worcester, MA, 1799).

[57]Mark A. Noll, *The Rise of Evangelicalism: The Age of Edwards, Whitefield and the Wesleys* (Downers Grove, IL: IVP Academic, 2003), 295.

[58]Anthony, *Life and Character*, 162-68.

O come, and dawn on my languishing spirit. O come! I would fly to meet the transporting moment. But language fails. My soul swells with the thought, too big to be uttered. I must cease to attempt to express my longing, and lose my soul in contemplation.[59]

This account vividly reflects the heavenly meditation of Psalm 73:25, 28:

> Whom have I in heaven but you? . . .
> But as for me, it is good to be near God.

Not only did Anthony record her deep desire for God in heaven, but she also attempted to capture her triune experience of intimacy, fruition, and enjoyment of God. As she sought to find words to express herself, she realized that the indescribable nature of this wonder and delight left her speechless to utter the fullness of her contemplative experience. Significantly she also drew on the common vocabulary of contemplation that spoke of the warmth of God and the transporting nature of the occasion. Catherine Brekus reports that when Samuel Hopkins edited Sarah Osborn's memoirs, he deleted the more erotic bridal language of Song of Songs.[60] Osborn was Anthony's closest friend and engaged in an active correspondence over forty years. If Hopkins removed the bridal language from Osborn, it is highly plausible that he did the same for Anthony. Therefore, the extant records we have from Anthony probably reflect some pruning that might otherwise be even more vivid and reflective of a contemplative desire and delight in enjoyment of God.[61]

Less than a year later Anthony recorded this event:

> [Feb 13, 1751]: Last Monday, Feb. 11, at night, my soul was led to contemplate the being and perfections of the blessed God. Here I stood and gazed, until all my soul was fixed with unutterable attention. O, how did the glory of this divine, infinite, self-existing, self-sufficient Being, raise my contemplation, and draw out the strength of my soul, with vigor and ardor, to dive as far, and take in as much as a finite mortal being could contain! O, how glorious, how infinitely glorious, did the exalted, immense, immortal incomprehensible

---

[59]Susanna Anthony, *The Life and Character of Miss Susanna Anthony*, ed. Samuel Hopkins, 2nd ed. (Worcester, MA, 1810), 91 (emphasis original).

[60]Brekus, *Sarah Osborn's World*, 112.

[61]Isaac Watts felt a similar need to caution readers about Elizabeth Singer Rowe's erotic "language of rapture addressed to the Deity" when he edited her *Devout Exercises of the Heart* following her death in 1737. Belden C. Lane, *Ravished by Beauty: The Surprising Legacy of Reformed Spirituality* (New York: Oxford University Press, 2011), 122.

Deity then appear, to my enlarged, adoring soul! And while I gazed, my soul was filled with in expressible astonishment at the many and great affronts and indignities I had offered to this divine, infinite Majesty. . . . Verily my soul is here lost in wonder. O infinite goodness and love! This is dignity, even contemplation and enjoyment of thyself, that the most daring sons of men would never have dared to ask, had not thou, thou only, who was able and willing, thus dignified our nature.[62]

Significantly Anthony employed the word *gaze* twice to describe her focused attention on the all-glorious and all-powerful God. This meditation deepened her contemplation and filled her with as much delight as a human finite soul could taste and see of the divine goodness. The effect was that her adoring soul swelled more fully. It is critical to recognize that as Anthony perceived more clearly the perfection of God that she was overcome with the sinful rebellion of her own heart. However, instead of being turned to dust she was lost in the wonder and enjoyment of God. When she spoke of gazing on God's glory, she declared that it drew out all of her strength. This language has often been used in the history of Christian spirituality to speak of being ravished by God.

Additionally, throughout Hopkins's *Life and Character*, readers see frequent references to descriptive expressions of transport, ravishment, intense desire to love and know God more fully, and thoughts of sweetness and being swallowed up in God. This is identical to the love language of the Song of Songs that was used by medieval writers such as Bernard of Clairvaux (1090–1153). Similar expressions are also evident in the exchange of letters between Anthony and Sarah Osborn.[63] Since one of the sharp criticisms that many raise against contemplation is that it isolates a person from the world, it is significant that Anthony, who never married, engaged in a ministry of caring for the poor and sick through her ministry of letter writing.

Sarah Jones. This passionate usage of the bridal language of the Song of Songs was not exclusive to New England Congregational members. One finds an equally vibrant personal piety among the Wesleyans. One example is Sarah Jones (1753–1794), who spent her entire life in southern Virginia.

---

[62] Anthony, *Life and Character*, 92-93.
[63] *Familiar Letters, Written By Mrs. Sarah Osborn, and Miss Susanna Anthony* (Newport, RI, 1907). These letters cover the period from 1740 to 1779.

She has attracted the attention of various scholars of early American and Methodist history[64] and was renowned for her strongly ascetical and intense ecstatic spiritual experiences. Jones was one of the "Mothers of Israel," validating her importance to early Methodism. This position of leadership referred to Deborah the Old Testament judge. Clearly the life and ministry of Deborah did not reflect the typical expectation of a submissive woman who avoided the roles normally expected of men during the eighteenth century.[65] While there is no record of women licensed by the Methodists in the American colonies, Jones did preach on occasions and essentially fulfilled the duties of a preacher except for administering the sacraments.[66] In addition to her active correspondence with a wide variety of members of the early Methodist movement including Francis Asbury, she composed numerous poems and hymns.

In a letter to her pastor and spiritual mentor, Rev. Jeremiah Minter, she wrote:

> Wednesday morning the 28th [1790] I arose with some deep exercise not without some temptation, which drove me to close work; yet cheerful to those around me. I don't know how it may be with you; but with me, when the blaze of ecstasy slacks in my soul, there stands the Devil with ten thousand darts—but he gets nothing by it. I flew to God and his word, and got a search, and found the serpent's haunt, twisted him out, and he flew like lightning from me, and I was caught up into the third Heaven, and was rapt in such flames of dying love, I can by no means express it. This was while in my room at work, Mr. Jones [her husband] and family by. Such seas of bursting glory rolling from Heaven, I screamed out—weakness overpowered my limbs—my dear companion smiled in pleasing wonder, and joy and pleasure filled my room. I grasped happiness; and gazed in admiration; and swam in the full rivers that issued from the throne of God. I strained up the steep of Excellent, and sunk in the flames of love divine. My brother; Austin reckons up 288 opinions among the Philosophers about happiness, but they all would come short, yea very short of telling what I this

---

[64]See, e.g., the indexes in Lester Ruth, *Early Methodist Life and Spirituality: A Reader* (Nashville: Kingswood, 2005); Cynthia Lynn Lyerly, *Methodism and the Southern Mind, 1770–1810* (New York: Oxford University Press); James D. Bratt, ed., *By the Vision of Another World: Worship in American History* (Grand Rapids: Eerdmans, 2012); and Rhonda D. Hartweg, "All in Raptures: The Spirituality of Sarah Anderson Jones," *Methodist History* 45, no. 3 (2007): 166-79.

[65]Lyerly, *Methodism and the Southern Mind*, 96.

[66]Ibid., 110, 111; cf. Hartweg, "All in Raptures," 172.

moment enjoy. My soul trembles as the needle beneath the loadstone. O, what is it? What is it, I say? It is joy, and gladness. What joy? Spiritual joy, a sweet delightful passion, arising from Heaven, to fence me in against troubles.[67]

This moving passage from Jones's letter is a detailed repudiation of the critics of evangelical contemplation. Her deep desire was for closer communion with God. Jones confessed the spiritual truth that many have testified to over the centuries of the church, the closer one grows toward God the more the devil tempts and seeks to create doubt and confusion in the believer's life. It is noteworthy that Jones turned to God's Word for her defense and protection. Like Paul she struggled to find words to communicate the depth of her experience of God in the third heaven (2 Cor 12:2). The entire focus was directed to the delight and enjoyment of God and not herself. Twice she mentioned "the flames of dying love" and "flames of love divine." This illustrates Richard Foster's observation that "the two most common words to describe the contemplative way of life are fire and love."[68] While both Edwards and Anthony made frequent usage of the bridal love language of the Song of Songs, they did not include the imagery of flames or fire. This is not to say it is absent in their writings, for Edwards declared his love for Jesus Christ resembled "a due fervor, ardency and sweet flames of love,"[69] but it does occupy a more prominent place in the writings of Sarah Jones.

Rhonda Hartweg helpfully summarizes Jones's exuberance and the fervent pitch of her piety in articulating that she was "in the throws of ecstasy, her emotions run rampant and her pen can hardly keep pace with her passionate discourse of love. . . . [Her] spiritual journey led her to places of rapture where she most nearly escaped the confines of her earthly existence. At times, it seems as if her physical body was all that kept her tethered to the earth."[70] Lester Ruth reminds readers that Sarah Jones was not unique

---

[67]Sarah Jones, *Devout Letters: or, Letters Spiritual and Friendly*, ed. Jeremiah Minter (Alexandria: Samuel Snowden, 1804), 9-10.

[68]Foster, *Streams of Living Water*, 49 (emphasis original).

[69]Jonathan Edwards, *Works of Jonathan Edwards Online*, vol. 13, *The "Miscellanies": Entry Nos. a-z, aa-zz, 1-500*, ed. Thomas A. Schafer (New Haven, CT: Yale University Press, 1994), 165. In his *Religious Affections*, Edwards also spoke of the "flame of fire" and "pure heavenly flame of fire." Jonathan Edwards [1754], *Works of Jonathan Edwards Online*, vol. 2, *Religious Affections*, ed. John E. Smith (New Haven, CT: Yale University Press, 1959), 114, 130.

[70]Hartweg, "All in Raptures," 169. Some of Jones's hymns also reflect this same sense of ecstatic rapture. See Ruth, *Early Methodist Life and Spirituality*, 172-73.

among early Methodist leaders and that she should be seen "as a more intense form of something inherent in Methodist piety."[71] Therefore, Jones provides a paradigmatic icon into which we can explore the nature and dynamics of early evangelical spirituality.

In another letter, composed on November 18, 1790, to her cousin the Rev. William Spencer, Jones wrote:

> Brother, I want more than a little religion, I sicken for enlargement, and want my desires and soul in every faculty extended, that I may drink seas, and rivers and running streams, of Jesus' dying love, and what I cannot drink, I want to swim in continually: my Jesus is no broken cistern, but he is a well of life without bottom. Boundless, matchless, adorable Jesus! Sometimes I feel like my breath would cease in his embraces. And such floods of dying love dashing through my whole frame, I cry, stay me with flagons, comfort me with apples, send them from the Tree of Life, for I am sick of love. . . .
>
> Now I return to close these lines. I am now sitting about half a mile from my dwelling, in the silent wood, near two hours in solemn engagement with the tremendous Jehovah, with my Bible open in sight of those eyes that run to and fro like flames of fire. . . . Could you see the lid of my heart; could you have seen me these two hours past with my face bathed in brine, my Bible lifted towards God . . . I believe, because I have tasted his love. I know he is here, even in my heart. I do not attempt just now, to write you how great my exercise at this moment is, as it must be long, but you may guess that Gideon's God is with me. I want to be holier, I want to be humbler, I want to live in God's will.[72]

The intensity of her unfathomable desires can only be satisfied in Jesus, "the well of life" that has no boundaries and can ever enlarge to meet the longings of the believer's heart. Again, the erotic language of the Song of Songs is present as well as the centrality of Scripture as Jones has her Bible open on her lap, poring over God's message to her. Jones also spoke of her exercise or spiritual disciplines. Her rigorous spiritual life was characterized by an ascetical intensity reminiscent of the early desert Christians of the fifth century. She would often fast and eliminate sleep to cultivate her spiritual practices.[73] While this might seem excessive in our overly consumption-oriented Western society, this was far more the norm, as Ruth reminds us,

---

[71]Ruth, *Early Methodist Life and Spirituality*, 37.
[72]Jones, *Devout Letters*, 61-62.
[73]Ruth, *Early Methodist Life and Spirituality*, 12-13.

of the early evangelicals. Additionally, it relates to the charge of "enthusiasm" that was frequently used as a denigration of the affective expressions of piety and strong dependence on the Holy Spirit. Many of the early American evangelical preachers and lay leaders were accused of this. But it must be realized that this receptivity to the affective was not at the cost of biblical knowledge. One of John Wesley's biographers neatly captures this in his book title *Reasonable Enthusiast*.[74]

Francis Asbury. Unlike Sarah Jones, who spent her entire life in one small region of Virginia, Francis Asbury (1745–1816), our second Methodist, is better known as one of John Wesley's primary evangelists in America. Asbury was born and raised in England and arrived in the colonies in 1771 and spent the rest of his life conducting an itinerant ministry that closely followed the pattern of John Wesley. Thomas Coke ordained Asbury as the second American Methodist bishop in the colonies. Like Susanna Anthony, Asbury lived a celibate life to devote himself more fully to the cause of Christ. Similar to Sarah Jones, Asbury cultivated great spiritual discipline and was often frustrated by the laxity that he discovered in many of the colonial religious societies. This coupled with his strong emphasis on preaching about sanctification and holiness guided his ministry. John Wigger, Asbury's most recent biographer, summarizes the intensity of his spiritual practices: He would typically rise at four in the morning for an hour of prayer, and he spent much of his day on horseback as he traveled the various routes to preach and call people to faith in Jesus. He would frequently use this time for reading various works of theology encouraged by John Wesley. It is estimated that he preached over ten thousand sermons during his forty-five years of ministry in America. Similar to Sarah Jones, he formed an austere lifestyle in both his diet, the intensity in which he pushed himself, and even requiring a simplicity of saddles and riding gear, using only the most inexpensive horses.[75]

Because of the hectic nature of Asbury's ministry, he did not write any major treatises, but we do have his journal and letters. And unlike a single

---

[74]Henry D. Rack, *Reasonable Enthusiast: John Wesley and the Rise of Methodism*, 3rd ed. (Peterborough, UK: Epworth, 2002). This term also appears in a recent study of contemplation within evangelicalism in another southern microcosm. See Samuel C. Smith, *A Cautious Enthusiasm: Mystical Piety and Evangelicalism in Colonial South Carolina* (Columbia: University of South Carolina Press, 2013).

[75]John Wigger, *American Saint: Francis Asbury and the Methodists* (New York: Oxford University Press, 2009), 3.

journal entry of Susanna Anthony and Sarah Jones that could cover five or more pages, Asbury's time restrictions produced many brief and uneven passages. The other disappointing feature of Asbury's writings is that they are more likely to address the effects of his preaching and travels and the conditions of weather than provide an illuminating glimpse into his soul. Nonetheless there are numerous succinct descriptions of his practice of and sensitivity to contemplation. What is also instructive is that Asbury's language was unique when compared with the previous three authors. That does not in any way diminish the intensity of his experience, but he often employs vocabulary that is less specific and not as exuberant.

Clearly the desires of Asbury's heart were for a deep and abiding sense of God's presence. On one occasion he wrote, "Monday 22. I found Christ in me the hope of glory: but felt a pleasing, painful sensation of spiritual hunger and thirst for more of God. On Tuesday I rode to Burlington, and on the way my soul was filled with holy peace, and employed in heavenly contemplations."[76] There is an urgency that one notices in reading Asbury's journal; he longed for heaven and the fullness of life in Christ and cried out, "When shall my soul be adorned as a bride for her bridegroom?"[77] Asbury enlarged on that hunger for God elsewhere when he borrowed language from the Song of Songs and confessed, "Wednesday 20. My soul was refreshed with the love of God. How do I long for a mind thoroughly refined, filled with perfect purity, and constantly devoted to God! The prospect and hope of this frequently transports my soul—Lord hasten the blessed period! Let all my soul be swallowed up in love!"[78] This passage also reflects perfectionism, John Wesley's teaching on perfect love. The term *transport* can often be used for the more ambiguous word *ravishment* that in a positive sense speaks of being drawn out to God by the tender power of God's love. The culmination of this intense longing sometimes ushered Asbury into God's presence that produced joyful communion:

> Lord's day, 30. I kept close house till evening. And O! what happiness did my soul enjoy with God! So open and delightful was the intercourse between God

[76]Francis Asbury, *An Extract from the Journal*, August 7, 1771, to December 29, 1778, vol. 1 (Philadelphia: Joseph Crukshank, 1792), 211.
[77]Ibid.,165.
[78]Ibid., 98.

and my soul, that it gave me grief if any person came into my room, to disturb my sweet communion with the blessed Father and the Son. When my work is done, may I enter into that fullness of joy which shall never be interrupted, in the blissful realms above![79]

Because he had tasted the enjoyment of God, Asbury looked ahead to a time in heaven when there would be no longer interruptions to being in God's presence. But for now he continued his peripatetic pace of itinerate preaching. He employed a range of adjectives to describe his communion with God. On this occasion he spoke of "sweet communion," which is his most common term.[80] He also employed the modifiers of "deeper" or "delightful" or "close" communion with God.[81] Additionally, being in God's presence can replicate David's experience: "you will fill me with joy in your presence" (Ps 16:11). Elsewhere Asbury proclaimed that he desires "nothing but to enjoy more of God."[82]

In one of the most captivating entries in Asbury's journal he again spoke of his deep longing for God:

Monday 30. . . . My soul is in constant search after more of God, and sweetly sinks deeper and deeper into the abyss of his fullness. I am much employed in the spirit and duty of prayer; but earnestly desire to be more so. My desire is, that prayer should mix with every thought, with every wish, with every word, and with every action; that all might ascend as a holy, acceptable sacrifice to God.[83]

Here Asbury sounds more like Johannes Tauler (ca. 1300–1361), who was read by some eighteenth-century evangelicals, or another medieval mystic in speaking of God as the ever-expanding abyss. In yet another entry his language is similar in voicing his desire to be in the "boundless ocean of [God's] love."[84] Regardless of how much he had already tasted of God, Asbury is desirous of more. More fully, he longed for an integration of all his life that resembled David's prayer,

---

[79]Ibid., 153.

[80]Ibid., 153, 224, 238, 240, 315.

[81]Ibid., 299, 210; and Francis Asbury, *An Extract from the Journal*, January 1, 1779, to September 3, 1780 (Philadelphia: Ezekiel Cooper, 1802), 20.

[82]Asbury, *Journal* (1792), 234, cf. 153, 224; and Asbury, *Journal* (1802), 12.

[83]Asbury, *Journal* (1792), 347.

[84]Ibid., 346.

give me an undivided heart,
>   that I may fear your name.
>
> I will praise you, LORD my God, with all my heart. (Ps 86:11-12)

Asbury also parallels the Ignatian principle of contemplation in action when he confesses, "I long to be made perfect in love, to have all my heart wrapped up in Christ Jesus, to have my conservation in heaven; and to be completely prepared for every duty."[85] That truly is the balance that Christians have sought over the centuries, to enjoy God fully and love our neighbor faithfully.

CONCLUSION

This chapter has demonstrated that contemplation, the vibrant enjoyment of God, was common among eighteenth-century American evangelicals. Regardless of gender, both men and women, regardless of theological tradition, both Calvinist and Arminian, all reveal deep appreciation for contemplation. Each person recognized the centrality of Jesus Christ as their Savior and Lord and the central role Scripture plays in the Christian life. None of them sought to achieve these deep spiritual experiences by their own efforts apart from God's enabling grace. Further, if questioned about being contemplatives, they would have most likely confessed that they were simply Christians whose deepest desire was to love Christ and grow in intimacy with God. The resulting enjoyment and sweetness of being near to God was simply the gift of the desires of their heart. For them their identity as evangelical Christians was refreshed by contemplation rather than contemplative Christians who were inspired by evangelicalism. In other words, contemplation was a modifier to their core evangelical convictions.[86] These four early evangelicals strongly authenticated Bruce Demarest's conclusion: "Living contemplatively is not a luxury. It is the habit of living in the presence of God, and it provides the solid foundation for the whole of the Christian life and service."[87]

---

[85]Ibid., 340.

[86]Brian K. Rice, "Contemplation and the Holy Scriptures," *Evangelicals on the Ignatian Way* (blog), March 21, 2011, http://lci.typepad.com/evangelicalsignatianway/2011/03/contemplation -and-the-holy-scriptures.html.

[87]Bruce Demarest, *Satisfy Your Soul: Restoring the Heart of Christian Spirituality* (Colorado Springs, CO: NavPress, 1999), 158.

CHRISTIAN CONTEMPLATION AND THE CROSS

The Pathway to Life

DIANE CHANDLER

INTRODUCTION

During a trip to a country in Asia, our church's medical outreach team visited the country's largest Buddhist monastery and temple in the capital city. We desired to understand the Buddhist worldview of the nation's majority in order to pray for them and to reach them with the truth of the gospel. Over two hundred Buddhist monks resided at the monastery, also housing the largest indoor Buddhist statue in the world, within the adjoining Gandan temple. The several-stories-high gold-plated statue was surrounded by hundreds of smaller statues, each representing a different Buddhist deity. While outside the temple, scores of people spun prayer wheels, each seeking to please a deity that they could neither touch, see, nor know. The monks inside were either deep in meditation or were chanting in order to further their pathway to nirvana, hoping for a complete state of liberation.

Like the apostle Paul, who felt distressed after seeing how Athens was replete with idols (Acts 17:16-23), I too felt grieved, as well-meaning people were seeking what they could neither know nor comprehend. Although engaged in a contemplative state, they were unable to achieve the ultimate peace and salvation for their souls that they desired. Contemplation has been a practice of different religions and worldviews for centuries. The search, however, is misguided, if this pathway disregards the living and true God, whose Son Jesus Christ offered himself on a cross to redeem humankind to the Father. It is through the cross that God in Christ offers the free gift to those who receive him. This union between God and humankind is only possible through the crucified Christ, who, through the cross, made a way for humankind to be restored to relationship with the Father. The triune God is worthy of our focus, our worship, our entire being—and our contemplation.

This chapter covers three primary, yet interwoven, sections in order to ascertain the tremendous purpose and opportunity followers of Christ have to experience union with the living God who causes followers to live and move and have their being (Acts 17:28). The first section describes the significance of Christian contemplation by addressing what contemplation is and why it is a necessary Christian practice that needs to be retrieved today. This section also highlights how thoughtful Christian seekers and writers have experienced union with God, from which we can glean in our own contemporary era.

The second section addresses the significance of the cross, the very foundation of the Christian faith. As the emblem of Christianity, the cross can so easily be relegated to steeple tops and Good Friday sermons, with scant reflections at other times of the year as to its centrality to the Christian faith. Christ crucified establishes our faith in lived experience, as we recognize that without the cross there is no life. All facets of the Christian life—the past, the present, and the future—all revolve around the cross.

The third section conjoins the first two sections by demonstrating how contemplation, specifically of the cross, has been a formidable Christian practice over the centuries. Contemplation of the cross brings all facets of the Christian life together, making the cross the central raison d'être of our identity, our practices, our fellowship, our suffering, our hope, and our contemplation.

In this chapter, I hope to encourage retrieval of the lost art of Christian contemplation into contemporary praxis in a way that brings us to the cross and causes us to pray and live victoriously in light of it—not as some symbol devoid of power, as I witnessed in the Asian Gandan temple, but rather as one that fosters union with the living and true God of love and hope. The significance of contemplation clearly evidences through historical overview.

THE SIGNIFICANCE OF CONTEMPLATION:
HISTORICAL OVERVIEW

I begin by first addressing what Christian contemplation is and then by providing an overview as to those who have engaged in this practice through the centuries. Generally speaking, contemplation has been a practice of transcendence in order to know and love God in spiritual union.[1] Union with God leading to inner transformation into Christlikeness frames the core of Christian contemplation. The word *contemplation* derives from the Latin word *contemplatio*, meaning to look at, observe, or to gaze attentively. The word originally meant to mark out a place for observation.[2] Regarding Christian contemplation, the word connotes making God the place of genuine observation by being spiritually attached (Jn 15:1-8). David conveyed this idea of observation when he expressed his heart's desire of gazing on the beauty of the Lord and of seeking him in his temple (Ps 27:4).

Having written extensively about such experiences throughout church history, Bernard McGinn refers to contemplative practices as mystical experiences, which include "preparation for the consciousness of and the effect of what the mystics themselves have described as a direct and transformative presence of God."[3] In other words, the goal of contemplation is for the human spirit, mind, will, and emotions to be unencumbered in order to commune with God, as God eagerly waits to be beholden. God knows us (Ps 139:1; Jer 1:5), and our lives are to be hidden in Christ (Col 3:3).

Contemplation began with the ancients and continues to today, with the practice developing over time. McGinn, whose multivolume series titled *The Presence of God: A History of Western Christian Mysticism*, maintains that this practice developed in three major stages: (1) the monastic period, encompassing the early fathers and the Middle Ages, (2) the new mysticism period between the twelfth to the seventeenth century, and (3) then the crisis of mysticism period from the mid-seventeenth century to

---

[1] John Peter Kenney, *Contemplation and Classical Christianity: A Study in Augustine* (Oxford: Oxford University Press, 2013), 3.
[2] The Latin word *contemplatio* derives from the verb *contemplari*, which historically referred to marking out the space for the augurs to read the auguries.
[3] Bernard McGinn, ed., *The Essential Writings of Christian Mysticism* (New York: Modern Library, 2006), xiv.

the twentieth century.[4] Regardless of era, however, contemplative practice acknowledges that a spiritual reality exists beyond physicality in pursuit of union with God. McGinn prefers the word *presence* over *union*, as the former connotes a relationship with God that is more supple in accounting for "the variety of ways that mystics have expressed how God comes to transform their minds and lives."[5]

Many Christian figures engaged in contemplation, yet one person or approach neither fully explores the breadth of contemplative practices nor the circumstances that prompt the desire for deeper union with God. A sampling of twelve authors, representing McGinn's identified three church eras, are briefly described below. They include (1) the monastic/Middle Age period—Gregory of Nyssa, Augustine, and Anselm of Canterbury; (2) the new mysticism period—Francis of Assisi, Thomas Aquinas, the anonymous author of the *Cloud of Unknowing*, Thomas à Kempis, Teresa of Ávila, and John of the Cross; and (3) the crisis of mysticism period—Dietrich Bonhoeffer.

In the monastic period, Gregory of Nyssa (335–394) viewed contemplation as three movements in the soul's approach to God, comparing these movements to three Wisdom books: Proverbs is likened to purification, a stage of infancy; Ecclesiastes is related to illumination, or the youth stage; and the Song of Songs as maturity beyond contemplation to union through love.[6] Gregory also likened contemplation to the soul's entrée into light, cloud, and darkness, drawn from Moses' seeing God in the light (burning bush), then the cloud (at Mt. Sinai), followed by "thick darkness where God was" (Ex 20:21). To Gregory, this divine darkness connoted the incomprehensibility of God. Utilizing the simile of a mirror, Gregory asserted that the soul first can become increasingly like God through purification in virtue. Virtue alone, however, does not lead to union; rather union occurs when,

---

[4]Ibid. For an expansive history of the practice of contemplation, or what Bernard McGinn broadly calls mysticism, see his five-volume series titled *The Presence of God: A History of Western Christian Mysticism: The Foundations of Mysticism: Origins to the Fifth Century*, vol. 1 (New York: Crossroad, 1991); *The Growth of Mysticism: Gregory the Great Through the Twelfth Century*, vol. 2 (New York: Crossroad, 1996); *The Flowering of Mysticism: Men and Women in the New Mysticism, 1200–1350*, vol. 3 (New York: Crossroad, 1998); *The Harvest of Mysticism in Medieval Germany*, vol. 4 (New York: Crossroad, 2005); and *The Varieties of Vernacular Mysticism, 1350–1550*, vol. 5 (New York: Crossroad, 2012).

[5]McGinn, *Essential Writings*, xv.

[6]Andrew Louth, *The Origins of Christian Mystical Tradition from Plato to Denys*, 2nd ed. (Oxford: Oxford University Press, 2007), 79-80.

through the cloud and the darkness, the soul feels the presence of God through God's Word.[7] For Gregory, this union of love is "beyond the senses and beyond the intellect," as the soul "penetrates more deeply into the knowledge and presence of God."[8]

Church father Augustine (354–430) experienced contemplative practices after being primed through exposure to pagan Platonic practices of transcendence that introduced him to a noncorporeal sense of the ethereal world and to human wisdom. These pagan practices could not, however, fulfill the deepest longings of his heart, which Augustine recounted in *Confessions*.[9] As he described, "We must fly to our beloved homeland. There the Father is, and there is everything."[10] Augustine highlighted three dimensions of life: the contemplative, the active, and the mixed, which presupposes balance: "As to these three modes of life . . . he [the believer] may choose any of them without detriment to his eternal interests. . . . No man has a right to lead such a life of contemplation as to forget in his own ease the service due to his neighbor; nor has any man a right to be so immersed in the active life as to neglect the contemplation of God."[11] Augustine proposed a unity between loving God and loving others without conflating the contemplative and active, so well-illustrated in his sermon highlighting the differing dispositions of Mary and Martha.[12] Clearly, Augustine operated out of a hierarchical relationship where contemplation superseded the active but did not deny its importance, with love being the unifier.[13]

Pertaining to the second period of the new mysticism, Anselm of Canterbury (1033–1109) viewed contemplation as the means to know God, in a way similar to Augustine's espousal of the same before him. In chapter one of *Proslogium*, titled "The Mind Aroused to Contemplate God," Anselm highlighted the role of the mind in contemplation: "It [the mind] casts aside cares, and excludes all thoughts, save that of God, that it may seek Him. . . .

[7]Gregory of Nyssa, *Commentary on the Song of Songs* 11.1001 B-C.

[8]Louth, *Origins*, 93-94.

[9]Augustine, *Confessions* 7.10.16; 7.17.23.

[10]Augustine, *The City of God*, trans. Marcus Dods (New York: Modern Library, 1950), 9.17.

[11]Augustine, *City of God* 19.19.

[12]Augustine, *Sermons 91A-150*, trans. Edmund Hill, The Works of St. Augustine: A New Translation for the 21st Century III/4 (New York: New City Press, 1992), 104.4, p. 83.

[13]Charlotte Radler, "*Actio et Contemplatio*/Action and Contemplation," in *The Cambridge Companion to Christian Mysticism*, ed. Amy Hollywood and Patricia Z. Beckman (Cambridge: Cambridge University Press, 2012), 213.

Man was created to see God."[14] Yet Anselm acknowledged, "Man cannot seek God, unless God himself teaches him; nor find him, unless he reveals himself."[15] For Anselm, contemplation of the living God involved a mind that was free and accessible to God.

For Francis of Assisi (1181/1182–1226), contemplation of God incorporated an appreciation of nature and the natural world, which inspired awe and wonder of Creator God.[16] However, contemplation was not to stop there. Francis saw contemplation as integral to being transformed into Christlikeness, as noted by Bonaventure (1221–1274), who viewed Francis as a model contemplative when commenting: "In all the virtues he imitated it as perfectly as he could, and at last, completing and perfecting [himself] in Jesus through the impression of the sacred stigmata, he was totally transformed into him."[17]

Moving to Thomas Aquinas (1225–1274), contemplation was linked to "the vision of God's essence in heaven,"[18] as union considers "the simple consideration of the truth" involving natural and supernatural means.[19] For Thomas, encountering divine love became the essence of contemplation, "because a person delights in gaining what is loved, the contemplative life finds its goal in the delight that is in the faculty of desire, on the basis of this delight love is also part of the intention."[20]

In the mid to late fourteenth century, the anonymous English author of the *Cloud of Unknowing* served as a guide for contemplative prayer and exhorted readers to surrender themselves into a state of unknowing in order to behold God. The author took a very practical approach to contemplation, explaining the cloud of unknowing is above, which is between the individual and God, whereas the cloud of forgetting is below and is between oneself

---

[14]Anselm of Canterbury, *Proslogium*, trans. S. N. Deane, in *St. Anselm's Basic Writings: Proslogium, Monologium, Gaunilo's in Behalf of the Fool, Cur Deus Homo*, 2nd ed. (Peru, IL: Open Court, 1998), 49.

[15]Ibid.

[16]St. Francis of Assisi, "The Canticle of Brother Sun," in *Francis and Clare: The Complete Works*, trans. Regis J. Armstrong and Ignatius C. Brady, Classics of Western Spirituality (Mahwah, NJ: Paulist Press, 1982), 37-39.

[17]McGinn, *Flowering of Mysticism*, 120.

[18]McGinn, *Harvest of Mysticism in Medieval Germany*, 32.

[19]Thomas Aquinas, *Summa theologiae*, vol. 46, *Action and Contemplation*, trans. Jordan Aumann (Chicago: Blackfriars, 1966), 25 (see IIa-IIae, q. 180, a. 4, ad 2).

[20]Thomas Aquinas, *Summa theologiae*, IIa-IIae, q. 180, a. 1c.

and all other creatures. Moving more deeply into the cloud, the contemplative finds that love guides with the result of "self-forgetting,"[21] whereby the true self finds completeness in Christ. Like other classic contemplatives, the author invites the reader to focus on one single word, which served as a defense when confronted with interruption or conflict. The author suggested using a one-syllable word, like *God* or *love*, as the locus of contemplation.[22]

The *Cloud*'s author identifies four phases of growth, namely, the Common, the Special, the Singular, and the Perfect, calling the reader to the interior life, motivated by love's longing for God in a posture of humility. Throughout the brief seventy-five chapters, the repeated theme is divine love: "Though this loving desire is certainly God's gift, it is up to you to nurture it. . . . And all he asks of you is that you fix your love on him. . . . Close the doors and windows of your spirit against the onslaught of pests and foes and prayerfully seek his strength."[23] The seeker is cautioned that a feeling of nothingness and darkness will come, as a cloud of unknowing, but this darkness is precisely where one's spirit finds God. The author warns that those called to contemplation will not always feel "the stirring of love continually and permanently,"[24] but can be assured that the contemplative life "will continue without end into eternity."[25] Thus contemplation must supersede the active life.

Thomas à Kempis (1380–1471), whose book *Imitation of Christ* has become an enduring classic, exhorted his readers to love solitude and silence. Thomas wrote quite practically, "Seek a proper time for yourself and think often upon the blessings of God."[26] Further, Thomas instructed, "He, therefore, who seeks to reach that which is hidden and spiritual must with Jesus slip away from the crowd."[27] For Thomas, the godly path of imitating Christ predicated on union with him in the secret place, which he refers to as friendship. He continued, "It is a great art to know how to live with Jesus,

---

[21]William Johnston, ed., *The Cloud of Unknowing and The Book of Privy Counseling* (Garden City, NY: Image, 1973), 172.

[22]Ibid., 56.

[23]Ibid., 47.

[24]Ibid., 145.

[25]Ibid., 58.

[26]Thomas à Kempis, *The Imitation of Christ*, trans. E. M. Blaiklock (Nashville: Thomas Nelson, 1981), 46 (1.20.1).

[27]Ibid., 47 (1.20.3).

and great wisdom to know how to hold him."[28] Holding Jesus is not passive but rather augments friendship with God.

During the time of the Reformation, Teresa of Ávila (1515–1582) described the spiritual life as an interior castle, made up of seven dwelling places.[29] For Teresa, greater union with God meant proceeding from the outer dwelling places to the interior castle, the dwelling place of God. Whereas the first three dwellings are achieved through personal initiative, the remaining four are only accessible to those who come through the prayer of the Quiet. In the fifth mansion, Teresa describes intimate union with Christ as a spiritual betrothal, applying the metaphor of a silkworm where "the soul begins to live and nourishes itself on this food, and on good meditations, until it is full grown."[30] Contemplation provides the path to mansion seven, where Jesus becomes the center of the soul through spiritual marriage.

A contemporary of Teresa, John of the Cross (1542–1591), emphasized the soul's emptying and purification through contemplation that leads to union with Christ. Similar to most mystical writers, John viewed meditation as the preliminary step to contemplation, particularly when the soul became dissatisfied. Through detachment of worldly things and experiencing the "dark night of the soul," the soul moves from purification to illumination, followed by union with God. John viewed contemplation as "that love [a]s the soul's inclination, strength, and power in making its way to God, for love unites it with God. The more degrees of love it has, the more deeply it enters into God and centers itself in God."[31] Thus for John, contemplation "is nothing else than a secret and peaceful and loving inflow of God, which, if not hampered, fires the soul in the spirit of love, as is brought out in the following verse: Fired with love's urgent longings."[32]

Others throughout Christian history, too numerous to mention, serve as guides in the practice of Christian contemplation. Contemporary authors

---

[28]Ibid., 74 (2.8.3).

[29]Because of unfortunate space limitations, other female figures not mentioned here but of equal importance include Catherine of Siena, Clare of Assisi, and Saint Thérèse of Lisieux.

[30]St. Teresa of Ávila, *The Interior Castle*, trans. and ed. E. Allison Peers (Mineola, NY: Dover, 2007), Mansion 5, chap. 2.

[31]John of the Cross, "The Living Flame of Love," in *John of the Cross: Selected Writings*, ed. Kieran Kavanaugh, Classics of Western Spirituality (Mahwah, NJ: Paulist Press, 1987), 298.

[32]John of the Cross, *The Dark Night of the Soul*, in Kavanaugh, *John of the Cross: Selected Writings*, 186 (1.10.6).

reveal how contemplative practices lead to life transformation. One such example is Dietrich Bonhoeffer (1906–1945), though hardly considered a mystic. Yet Bonhoeffer's commitment to the Word of God and to meditation is noteworthy.[33] Although Bonhoeffer mentioned two types of meditation—one on Scripture and the other he called free meditation, he clearly favored meditation on Scripture, for which he taught his seminarians at Finken-walde, Germany. He offered simple reasons for his practice: because he was a Christian, a preacher of the Word, and in need of the discipline of prayer.[34] For him, meditation was "a source of peace, of patience, and of joy; it is like a magnet that draws together all the forces of our life that make for order; it is like deep water that reflects the clouds and the sun on its clear surface."[35]

Contemplation is a spiritual practice worth retrieving, especially as it relates to the reality of the cross and Christ crucified—the very core of the Christian faith—which constitutes the next section.

THE CROSS AS THE FOUNDATION FOR CONTEMPLATION

As demonstrated above, the practice of contemplation is evident throughout church history. More specifically, contemplation of the cross strikes a fa-miliar chord throughout many authors' praxis and writings. Before ad-dressing contemplation of the cross, which is addressed in the third section of this chapter, this second section provides an interlude by laying a foun-dation regarding the centrality of the cross, so emblematic of the crucified Christ in the Christian faith. Without understanding the centrality of the cross, contemplation loses its significance.

The centrality of the cross within New Testament writings, along with Old Testament writings, point to the crucified Christ. The Old Testament pointed to the cross yet to come, whereas the New Testament proclaimed the cross, with the Redeemer having come. Whereas Psalm 22:14-15 narrates the agony that Christ would suffer ("I am poured out like water, / and all my bones are out of joint; / my heart is like wax; / it is melted within my breast; / my mouth

---

[33] Although meditation is often associated with lectio divina rather than contemplation, it is worth highlighting Bonhoeffer's practice, which kept him in vibrant union with Christ.

[34] Dietrich Bonhoeffer, *Meditating on the Word*, ed. and trans. David McI. Gracie, 2nd ed. (Cambridge, MA: Cowley, 1986), 22-23.

[35] Ibid., 43.

is dried up like a potsherd, / and my tongue sticks to my jaws; / you lay me in the dust of death"), Isaiah 53:5 explains why ("But he was wounded for our transgressions; / he was crushed for our iniquities; / upon him was the chastisement that brought us peace, / and with his wounds we are healed"). Jürgen Moltmann said it well: "Christian faith stands and falls with the knowledge of the crucified Christ, that is, with the knowledge of God in the crucified Christ, or, to use Luther's even bolder phrase, with the knowledge of the 'crucified God.'"[36]

In the Gospels, Jesus reminds his followers that whoever refuses to take up the cross and follow him is not only unworthy of him but cannot be his disciple (Mt 10:38-29; Lk 14:27). The Synoptic Gospel accounts each include the pathway of the cross that Jesus declared prior to his death, announcing that his followers must take up his cross, deny themselves, and follow him (Mt 16:24; Mk 8:34; Lk 9:23). The cross became the doorway for following Christ, as it were, because all facets of the Christian life point to it and derive from it.

Few contemporary theologians frame the centrality of the cross in Christianity more strongly than John Stott.[37] Noting the cross as the primary Christian emblem, Stott observes with irony "the horror with which crucifixion was regarded in the ancient world,"[38] which explained in part why Paul's message of the cross was considered foolishness to unbelievers, as the cross was considered culturally shame-filled. To Jews, crucifixion connoted a curse (Deut 21:23). Notwithstanding that the cross was an offense to those who are perishing (1 Cor 1:18), Jesus chose this symbol prior to his crucifixion to vividly illustrate his mission to redeem humankind (Mt 16:24; Mk 8:34; Lk 9:23; 14:27). As black theologian James Cone notes, the cross, as symbol, "inverts the world's value system with the news that hope comes by way of defeat, that suffering and death do not have the last word."[39] Stott highlights the centrality of the cross when quoting P. T. Forsyth: "You do not understand Christ till you understand the cross."[40]

---

[36]Jürgen Moltmann, *The Crucified God: The Cross of Christ as the Foundation and Criticism of Christian Theology*, trans. R. A. Wilson and John Bowden (New York: SCM Press; Harper & Row, 1974), 65.

[37]John R. W. Stott, *The Cross of Christ* (Downers Grove, IL: InterVarsity Press, 1986), 18-46.

[38]Ibid., 23.

[39]James H. Cone, *The Cross and the Lynching Tree* (Maryknoll, NY: Orbis, 2011), 2.

[40]Stott, *Cross of Christ*, 43.

After Christ's death, the apostles, most notably Paul, emphasized the cross, the paradox of human evil superseded by divine purpose. Paul declared that while we were still enemies of God, Christ's death reconciled us to the Father through the cross in order to give us all things (Rom 5:10; 8:32). To the Corinthians, Paul proclaimed the gospel "not with eloquent wisdom, so that the cross of Christ might not be emptied of its power" but as God's power (1 Cor 1:17-18). Paul's superlative goal was "to know nothing among you except Jesus Christ and him crucified" (1 Cor 2:2). Furthermore, Paul boasted in nothing else save the cross of the Lord, believing that he had been crucified to the world and the world to him (Gal 6:14). As Pauline scholar Michael Gorman notes, "Paul came to believe that the crucified Jesus was not only the revelation of true divinity but also the paradigm of true humanity."[41]

The significance of the cross for contemplation relates to the past and present, which frames our outlook for the future. Regarding the past, contemplation of the cross soberly calls us to reflect back regarding the great cost of self-giving love that paid for humanity's salvation and redemption. As Miroslav Volf contends, the cross reflects the ultimate self-giving of Christ personally and the triune God corporately.[42] As a result of this restored relationship through reconciliation of sin based on Christ's sacrifice, eternal life is promised (Eph 2:16; Col 1:20). Contemplation of this reality is cause for joy, regardless of present circumstances. As a result of the cross, Christ ascended into heaven, thus making way for the Holy Spirit to become the divine presence in believers' lives. Contemplation of the cross indirectly leads to appreciation of the Holy Spirit's indwelling, the conduit for union with Christ.

As for the present, contemplation of the cross reminds us that through Christ we become his disciples through the Holy Spirit's empowerment. Discipleship involves denial of self, taking up one's cross, and following Christ (see Mk 8:34), which includes sharing in his sufferings. Dietrich Bonhoeffer observed, "Suffering and rejection sum up the whole cross of Jesus."[43] As disciples, we contemplate the cross and the path that Jesus

---

[41]Michael J. Gorman, *Cruciformity: Paul's Narrative Spirituality of the Cross* (Grand Rapids: Eerdmans, 2001), 19.

[42]Miroslav Volf, *Exclusion and Embrace: A Theological Exploration of Identity, Otherness, and Reconciliation* (Nashville: Abingdon, 1996), 25.

[43]Dietrich Bonhoeffer, *The Cost of Discipleship*, trans. R. H. Fuller (New York: Macmillan, 1937), 96.

walked, as we too are called to die to self so that we can live for Christ, even through pain and suffering. As such, contemplation of Christ's suffering provides a bridge to our own sufferings (see Phil 2:8-9). As Bonhoeffer elaborated, there is no need to look for a cross or to run after suffering.[44] One's cross begins with dying to self and "meets us at the beginning of our communion with Christ."[45]

Bonhoeffer noted that part of this communion involves forgiveness, a form of suffering in itself: "Forgiveness is the Christlike suffering which it is the Christian's duty to bear."[46] Volf concurs, observing, "The passion of Christ is the agony of a tortured soul and wrecked body offered as a prayer for the forgiveness of torturers."[47] Thus Volf identifies forgiveness as a form of suffering, stating: "When I forgive I have not only suffered a violation but also suppressed the rightful claims of strict restitutive justice."[48]

Contemplation of the cross also fosters an appreciation and expectation for healing, which occurs in the present but will be ultimately fulfilled in the kingdom to come. Through Christ's wounds we are healed (Is 53:5)—both in this life and the life to come. Christ not only paid the price so that we can be healed of sin's dire penalty but also so that spiritual, emotional, mental, and physical infirmities can be healed.[49]

Furthermore, contemplation of the cross gives added significance to the sacraments of baptism and the Eucharist. In baptism, we are buried with Christ in his death so that new life can emerge.[50] Through participation in the Eucharist, we reflect on Christ's death on the cross, remembering that his body was broken and his blood was shed on our behalf.[51] The Eucharist also proclaims the Lord's death until he comes (1 Cor 11:23-26). Through the Lord's Supper, communion with Christ and fellowship in the body of Christ are intended to strengthen *koinōnia*, or genuine community, thus fostering

---

[44]Ibid., 98.

[45]Ibid., 99.

[46]Ibid., 100.

[47]Volf, *Exclusion and Embrace*, 125.

[48]Ibid.

[49]In Jesus' earthly ministry, many were healed of sickness and disease and delivered from demons: the leper in Galilee (Mt 8:1-4), the paralytic at Capernaum (Mk 2:3-12), the demoniac in the Gerasenes (Lk 8:26-39), Jairus's daughter (Mt 9:18-26), the deaf (Mk 7:31-35), and the blind (Mt 20:29-34).

[50]See Laird, *Into the Silent Land*, 12-13.

[51]Ibid., 14-15.

unity, while also looking forward to the ultimate union with Christ when we are united with him in eternity (Rev 19:3-6). Contemplating the cross within the context of the Eucharist reinforces that "union with Christ apart from the community is impossible."[52]

When realizing all of the ways that God through the cross anchors our lives and practices (i.e., redemption, reconciliation, forgiveness, fellowship of Christ's sufferings, the sending of the Holy Spirit, anticipation of healing, the sacraments of baptism, and the Eucharist resulting in *koinōnia*), contemplation of the cross ultimately points to the future, which produces joy, when considering our destiny with Christ in eternity. It was for the joy that was set before Christ that he "endured the cross, despising its shame, and is seated at the right hand of the throne of God" (Heb 12:2). Joy buoyed by divine hope and love outpoured are outcomes of contemplation of the cross.

CONTEMPLATION OF THE CROSS: A RICH HERITAGE

This third and final section provides noteworthy examples of those whose lives were deeply influenced through contemplation, specifically of the cross and Christ's passion. By being spurred on to contemplate the robust realities of the cross that touch on every area of life, we reestablish the central reality of the Christian life: Christ's inexpressible sacrifice that leads to life. The lives of those who contribute to the rich heritage regarding contemplation of the cross are briefly described below and include Ignatius of Antioch, Justin Martyr, Tertullian, Bernard of Clairvaux, Bonaventure, Julian of Norwich, Thomas à Kempis, Catherine of Genoa, Desiderius Erasmus, and Ignatius of Loyola. These exemplars, who have paved the way for rich fellowship with the crucified Lord, beckon us to follow in their footsteps.[53]

Beginning with the first two centuries, martyred bishop Ignatius of Antioch (d. 117) lived a life of contemplation of the cross, so much so that he

---

[52]Michael J. Gorman, *Becoming the Gospel: Paul, Participation, and Mission* (Grand Rapids: Eerdmans, 2015), 30.

[53]For further resources, see Robin M. Jensen, *The Cross: History, Art, and Controversy* (Cambridge, MA: Harvard University Press, 2017), esp. chaps. 7 and 8; along with the trilogy by Richard Viladesau, *The Beauty of the Cross: The Passion of Christ in Theology and the Arts from the Catacombs to the Eve of the Renaissance* (Oxford: Oxford University Press, 2006); *The Triumph of the Cross: The Passion of Christ in Theology and the Arts from the Renaissance to the Counter-Reformation* (Oxford: Oxford University Press, 2008); *The Pathos of the Cross: The Passion of Christ in Theology and the Arts; The Baroque Era* (Oxford: Oxford University Press, 2014).

identified with the crucified Christ as an essential mark of discipleship, which led him down his own Calvary road. Ignatius took up his own cross in death in order to "imitate the Passion of my God."[54]

Christian apologist Justin Martyr (100–165) saw the cross in all aspects of everyday life through the visual demonstrations that he beheld.[55] When viewing the human face and the placement of the eyes, he saw the cross. When he saw cross-shaped tools, he was led to contemplate the cross. And when considering how a vessel crosses the sea, he again contemplated the cross. Justin Martyr evidenced the cross everywhere, causing him to reflect regularly on Christ's passion and sacrifice.[56]

North African lawyer and theologian Tertullian (155–240) wrote about the crucified God, as he confirmed the reality of Christ's sufferings (*Deus crucifixus*) and underscored the assurance of salvation: "The powers of the Spirit of God proved Him to be God, His sufferings attested the flesh of man."[57]

Moving to the twelfth century, Bernard of Clairvaux (1090–1153), whose work influenced Martin Luther's own perspectives of the cross a few centuries later, emphasized humility, so emblematic of the cross. According to Bernard, humility is completely personified in the crucified Christ, a constant source of contemplation.[58] Bernard's identification with the sufferings of Christ caused him to ask: "What can be so effective a cure for the wound of conscience and so purifying to keenness of mind as steady meditation on the wounds of Christ?"[59] Like the spirituality of so many in the Middle Ages, contemplation of the cross was central to Bernard's spirituality.[60]

---

[54]Ignatius, "Letters of Ignatius: Romans," in *Early Christian Fathers*, ed. Cyril Richardson (New York: Macmillan, 1979), 105.

[55]Justin Martyr, *First Apology* 1.5, "Symbols of the Cross."

[56]See Stott, *Cross of Christ*, 45.

[57]Tertullian, *On the Flesh of Christ* 5 (in *Ante-Nicene Fathers*, ed. Alexander Roberts and James Donaldson (repr., Peabody, MA: Hendrickson, 1994), 525, www.ccel.org/ccel/schaff/anf03 .v.vii.v.html.

[58]Bernard of Clairvaux, Sermon 42; *Bernard of Clairvaux: On the Song of Songs*, trans. K. Walsh, Cistercian Studies 7 (Kalamazoo, MI: Cistercian Publications, 1976), 216.

[59]Bernard of Clairvaux, *Sermon 62* 4.7; *Bernard of Clairvaux: Selected Works*, trans. G. R. Evans (Mahwah, NJ: Paulist Press, 1987), 250-51. Also see Graham Tomlin, *The Power of the Cross: Theology and the Death of Christ in Paul, Luther, and Pascal* (Carlisle, UK: Paternoster, 1999), 130-33.

[60]John R. Tyson, introduction to *Invitation to Christian Spirituality: An Ecumenical Anthology*, ed. John R. Tyson (New York: Oxford University Press, 1999), 25.

Franciscan theologian Bonaventure (1221–1274) was deeply influenced by his contemplation of the cross, as evidenced in his writings. In *Meditations*, Bonaventure focused heavily on Christ's passion. Bernard McGinn notes that in Bonaventure's book the nativity takes up eight chapters, whereas the passion takes up thirteen chapters.[61]

Particularly poignant, Julian of Norwich (1342–1461), who while dying in the streets of the English city of Norwich, received sixteen visions, or showings, of the crucified Christ over two days. She recovered and wrote these visions down into twenty-five chapters. Later after receiving further revelation, Julian expanded the text with renewed reflections to create a longer book version, titled *A Revelation of Love*, comprising eighty-six chapters.[62] Julian desired above all else that she see with her own eyes "our Lord's Passion which He suffered for me, so that I might have suffered with Him as others did who loved Him. . . . My intention was, because of that revelation, to have had truer recollection of Christ's passion."[63] Through these showings of Christ's passion, Julian received a profound sense of God's love, without beginning or end, which brought about redemption, while having "space and time to contemplate it."[64] Julian's autobiographical writings and reflections appealed to a broad spectrum of believers, both lay and religious.

As mentioned earlier, in the late medieval era, Thomas à Kempis (1380–1471) wrote of the cross in his enduring classic, *The Imitation of Christ*, a compendium of writings in four books, instructing readers to contemplate Christ and his passion. Thomas would also affirm, "Look, it all consists in the cross, and it all lies in dying; and there is no other way to life and true peace within, save the way of the holy cross."[65]

Italian mystic Catherine of Genoa (1447–1510), who suffered depression and loneliness resulting from an unhappy marriage, encountered God's transforming love. The realization of her own sinfulness highlighted all the more Christ's passion on her behalf. One commentator noted that in her bedroom hung a picture of Christ being taken down from the cross. When

---

[61]McGinn, *Flowering of Mysticism*, 120.
[62]McGinn, *Varieties of Vernacular Mysticism*, 425.
[63]Julian of Norwich, "The First Vision," in *Julian of Norwich: Showings*, trans. James Walsh, SJ (New York: Paulist Press, 1978), 125-26.
[64]Ibid.
[65]Thomas à Kempis, *Imitation of Christ*, 82 (2.12.3).

she entered the room and gazed on the picture, she simultaneously experienced both profound grief and love, considering the extreme suffering that God had endured because of divine love.[66] For Catherine, contemplation of the cross was a daily occurrence.

Dutch priest and theologian Desiderius Erasmus (1466–1536) wrote about contemplation of the cross as being the remedy for temptation. Erasmus believed that the cross was "the refuge for those who toil, and the weapon for those in the fray," adding that for successful contemplation of the cross "you must have a plan of action, realizing that you are fighting a life-and-death battle . . . so that when the time comes for you to make use of your plan, you will know exactly what to do."[67] Mentioning various temptations such as envy, gluttony, lust, and avarice, Erasmus maintained, "There is no temptation or vice for which Christ did not furnish a remedy on the Cross."[68]

Founder of the Society of Jesus (Jesuits), Ignatius of Loyola (1491–1556) became a religious leader following military service, debilitating wounding, and eventual conversion. Cloistered in a cave and encouraged by the example of Francis of Assisi, Ignatius prayed for long periods of time, where it is believed that he wrote the *Spiritual Exercises*. Ignatius maintained that conformity to Christ involved prayerful contemplation of the life, death, and resurrection of Christ. Specifically, week three of the *Spiritual Exercises* focuses on contemplation of Christ's passion.[69] Each day of the week offers a different contemplation, accompanied by prayer, in following the journey of Christ from Bethany to Jerusalem for the Last Supper, from the Last Supper to the garden through to the crucifixion, and then finishing with contemplating the passion as a whole.

All of these historical figures were challenged into a deeper union with God in Christ through contemplation of Christ's sacrificial love as evidenced on the cross. This reality drove them into deeper communion with God through prayer. Thus the cross became the place where encounter with God's presence led to deeper gratitude resulting in inner transformation.

---

[66]Paul Gavin, trans., *The Life and Sayings of Catherine of Genoa* (Staten Island, NY: Alba House, 1964), 22-23.

[67]Desiderius Erasmus, "The Handbook of the Militant Christian" (Seventeenth Rule), in *The Essential Erasmus*, trans. John P. Dolan (New York: New American Library, 1983), 80-81.

[68]Ibid., 81.

[69]St. Ignatius of Loyola, *The Spiritual Exercises of Saint Ignatius of Loyola*, trans. Anthony Motolla (New York: Image, 1964), 91-95.

CONCLUSION

In this chapter I have tied together three interwoven sections. Beginning first with the significance of Christian contemplation within historical tradition, the second section focused on the biblical and theological significance of the cross as faith's cornerstone. The third section described exemplars who incorporated contemplation of the cross into their life rhythms. Finding our own personal rhythms to commune with God as contemporary Christians involves overcoming constant competitors—busy schedules, competing priorities, and multiple distractions, including some good things like social media and entertainment.

Overcoming competitors, however, is only one aspect in spending time in contemplation with God. In other words, spending time with God involves more than simply finding quiet in the midst of noise and chaos. Rather, being in God's presence necessitates a deep and abiding value that acknowledges one's vital need for God and one's poverty without this intimate and divine longing and beholding. Establishing a value for communion with God and contemplation and overcoming competitors for one's time and attention both must work together in tandem.

Contemporary author Ruth Haley Barton offers hope to all who struggle with seeking the necessary silence and solitude for communing with God, or what others call the "practice of stillness" and "the art of letting go."[70] Acknowledging that we are starved for intimacy, rest, and quiet, Barton reflects: "I needed to let the twin engines of desperation and desire lift me out of the stuck places into the realm where the spiritual life happens at God's initiative rather than the pushing and forcing that often characterizes my effort."[71] Entering the presence of God in silence and solitude is a first step in offering God our undivided attention so that we not only "experience God as our ultimate reality"[72] but also enter into contemplative prayer to the Father through Christ and by the Spirit. Contemplative prayer, then, is a focus on God in adoration.

So practically speaking, how can we nurture this rest in God, without which our lives become dry, distant, and often desperate? I would like to

---

[70]Martin Laird, *Into the Silent Land: A Guide to the Christian Practice of Contemplation* (New York: Oxford University Press, 2006), 5.

[71]Ruth Haley Barton, *Invitation to Solitude and Silence: Experiencing God's Transforming Presence* (Downers Grove, IL: InterVarsity Press, 2004), 32.

[72]Ibid., 34-35.

propose some practical steps that we can take to open space for God and with God in contemplation.

First, we need to establish a core value that prioritizes spending time with God. Internal and external expectations for personal performance assertively challenge this priority. Hence, we need to resist our tendency toward performance orientation and "hurry sickness," a term referring to the chronic condition of our age that is in constant pursuit of accomplishing more. In other words, we need to practice slowing down.[73] A personal situation brought this home to me several years ago. I had planned to plant flowers in my garden early one Saturday morning. However, many interruptions caused the planting to move to the evening hour prior to sunset—not the best time for gardening! As I furiously planted and watered the dozen red geranium plants in the front yard after the street lights had come on, I heard my elderly neighbor call to me as he was walking by, "Slow down and pace yourself!" Knowing that I would not have any time to plant the flowers the next day because of church responsibilities nor that upcoming week, I had to acknowledge the wisdom of his admonition amid my own scheduling quandary and bout with hurry sickness. I did need to slow down and make space for planting when I was less rushed. But I jammed the planting into my schedule anyway. The same is true with our time with God. We need to slow down in order to allow the Holy Spirit to plant God's Word in our hearts and to hear God's words minister to our souls. This slowing down is essential for contemplation.

Second, we need to plan our schedules in a way that prioritizes time alone with God. Just as my misplaced schedule contributed to my frenzy in planting flowers, so our misplaced schedules contribute to shallow and truncated time with God. I find that early in the morning is my best time for reading Scripture and in engaging in worship, which leads to contemplation and contemplative prayer. If time allows, morning walks in a selected spot also contribute to a sense of solitude and communion with God. Establishing rhythms of solitude and rest in God helps to overcome speed addiction. For example, although Jesus was on a divine timetable, he never hurried, nor do we read in the Gospels that he ever ran.[74] Not only do we need daily rhythms, we also need

---

[73]See John Ortberg, *The Life You've Always Wanted: Spiritual Disciplines for Ordinary People* (Grand Rapids: Zondervan, 1997), chap. 5.

[74]See Alan Fadling, *An Unhurried Life: Following Jesus' Rhythms of Work and Rest* (Downers Grove, IL: InterVarsity Press, 2013).

weekly rhythms. Observing a Sabbath where we cease from work for one day a week is vital for a life of ongoing renewal and contemplation. Engaging in Sabbath might include detaching from social media in order to focus on the Lord in contemplation.

Third, we need periodic and extended time alone with God in retreat. We retreat in God in order to reengage with others. My most memorable times with the Lord have been during times where I can legitimately detach from various responsibilities in order to spend time with God in extended solitude and contemplation. Having a place to go to such as a retreat center, or another place other than one's home, is the ideal arrangement. For some, spending time outdoors camping or taking a cabin in the woods might provide the same resulting respite.

In summary, establishing a value for contemplation, planning our schedules for daily and weekly time with God, and also factoring in periodic times of retreat provide practical steps for opening up time with God in contemplation. Specifically, contemplation of the cross contributes to deepening compassion for Christ and others, so that we might become more like him in all facets of life. Unlike the Buddhist monks praying to an unknown God, described at the beginning of this chapter, we know that the true and living God is always close, beckoning us to behold his Son, whose cruciform example offers eternal love and hope. Contemplation of the cross is indeed the pathway to life.

PART 2

CONSTRUCTIVE PROPOSALS

BIBLICAL SPIRITUALITY AND CONTEMPLATIVE SPIRITUALITY

STEVEN L. PORTER

Keep yourselves in the love of God.

JUDE 21

INTRODUCTION

My goal in this chapter is not to offer direct biblical support for contemplative prayer or spirituality. Rather, my intent is to motivate a biblical spirituality—that is, a biblical theology of life in the Spirit—that grounds a contemplative dimension of the Christian life.[1]

While putting forward direct biblical support for contemplation is certainly feasible, we would have to first arrive at a definition of contemplation and then hunt for the required biblical backing. The problem with this methodology is that we might then be primed to perceive biblical evidence for our predetermined understanding of contemplation where it is not fully present. This is sometimes referred to as *eisegesis*: reading into (*eis-*) the biblical text a meaning that is not properly derived out of the text itself (*exegesis*).[2]

---

[1] I am using the term *biblical spirituality* synonymously with a *biblical theology of life in the Spirit*. By both phrases I mean the attempt to identify a unified biblical teaching across, in this case, the canonical New Testament on the theme of life in the Spirit. For a discussion of the nature of biblical theology, see Craig G. Bartholomew, "Biblical Theology," in *Dictionary for Theological Interpretation of the Bible*, ed. Kevin J. Vanhoozer (Grand Rapids: Baker Academic, 2005), 84-90. For a treatment of biblical spirituality, see Frances M. Young, *Brokenness and Blessing: Towards a Biblical Spirituality* (Grand Rapids: Baker Academic, 2007).

[2] For more on *exegesis*, *eisegesis*, and hermeneutics more generally, see Grant Osborne, *The Hermeneutical Spiral: A Comprehensive Introduction to Biblical Interpretation* (Downers Grove, IL: InterVarsity Press, 1991), 41.

This potential problem can be at least partly avoided by developing a thoroughly biblical spirituality first and then examining what aspects of contemplative spirituality fit within that biblical portrait. Of course, the potential bias of this route is that we might develop our "biblical" spirituality proleptically, in anticipation of the defense of our preferred understanding of contemplation. *Surprise, surprise,* my reader thinks, *a chapter on contemplative spirituality that ends up developing a biblical spirituality that undergirds contemplation.*

My hypothetical reader is right. The potential for bias exists with either methodology. And yet, there is a methodological integrity to beginning with a robust biblical spirituality in that such a route provides a better chance of yielding a biblically chastened understanding of contemplation. Indeed, the biblical spirituality developed here will, at best, ground a contemplative dimension to the Christian life. This conclusion falls short of viewing the Christian life as entirely or even largely contemplative in nature. It also falls short of grounding particular forms of contemplative prayer. In fact, the biblical spirituality presented here will be in the position to critique and constrain at least some aspects of what might be included in contemplative spirituality or contemplative prayer.

PRELIMINARY POINTS

Before turning to the development of this biblical spirituality, a few preliminary points are in order. First, and thankfully, a biblical spirituality can attempt to be thoroughly biblical without being comprehensive in scope. That is to say, the thoroughly biblical spirituality developed here will fail to be a comprehensive biblical theology of life in the Spirit. The best that can be done in the space available is to develop a few relevant New Testament principles on the sanctifying work of the Holy Spirit and explore the degree to which these principles ground a contemplative dimension of the Christian life.[3]

A second preliminary point is that to call something a biblical spirituality does not entail that all other views of Christian spirituality that depart to one degree or another from what is presented here are therefore unbiblical. Biblical theology is a contentious field in that biblical exegetes and biblical

---

[3]For a more comprehensive biblical theology of life in the Spirit, see Robert L. Saucy, *Minding the Heart: The Way of Spiritual Transformation* (Grand Rapids: Kregel, 2013).

theologians contend for particular ways of interpreting, organizing, and applying what Scripture has to say about the topic in question. I am endeavoring to develop an understanding of Christian spirituality that looks to the Bible as its primary source of evidence. It is thoroughly biblical in that sense. But as is the case in biblical interpretation, and theological work more generally, there are others who will disagree with the interpretative moves and applications made in this chapter, and for them a different view will lay better claim to the moniker *biblical spirituality*. This is simply how theological progress is made: we articulate and defend as best we can a particular interpretation or theological judgment and others are invited to provide reasoned agreement and/or disagreement.

Third, a biblical theology of Christian spirituality is by design a limited and narrow methodological approach to the doctrine of sanctification. Systematic theology, for instance, while necessarily tethered to the deliverances of biblical exegesis, meaningfully includes other legitimate theological sources in its construction of doctrine. For instance, we might think of systematic theology as synthesizing historical theology, philosophical theology, spiritual theology, biblical theology, as well as extrabiblical sources of knowledge (e.g., the sciences). But that grand and important task is not before us here. Rather, I seek to do some of the biblical-exegetical work that is foundational to the higher-order work of systematics.[4]

Last, it bears mentioning that biblical spirituality refers to a view of new covenant life in the Spirit that is grounded in the teaching of the Bible and not necessarily a spirituality that centers on engagement with the Bible. The role of the Bible in the Christian life is one of the many issues that a comprehensive biblical theology of life in the Spirit will address.[5] Indeed, one

---

[4]This is not to say, however, that biblical theology is done in a historical, philosophical, or experiential vacuum. One's presuppositions and preunderstandings are involved in biblical hermeneutics, and yet there remains a way for the biblical theologian to allow the biblical text to be the primary focus and epistemic priority. See Osborne, *Hermeneutical Spiral*, 263-84. For more on an integrative theological methodology, see Steven L. Porter, "Wesleyan Theological Method as a Theory of Integration," *Journal of Psychology and Theology* 32, no. 3 (2004): 190-99; and Porter, "Theology as Queen and Psychology as Handmaid: The Authority of Theology in Integrative Endeavors," *Journal of Psychology and Christianity* 29, no. 1 (2010): 3-14.

[5]See, for instance, M. Robert Mulholland Jr., *Shaped by the Word: The Power of Scripture in Spiritual Formation* (Nashville: Upper Room, 1985); and John Jefferson Davis, *Meditation and Communion with God: Contemplating Scripture in an Age of Distraction* (Downers Grove, IL: IVP Academic, 2012).

seminal issue of Christian spirituality is the degree to which the propositional truths of the Bible are the focus of life in the Spirit and the degree to which the Godhead itself—Father, Son, and Holy Spirit—is the central focus. It is precisely to this and related issues that I turn in proposing four foundational principles of biblical spirituality.

FOUR FOUNDATIONAL PRINCIPLES OF BIBLICAL SPIRITUALITY

Principle 1: The gracious availability of the agapeic reality of God. An essential principle of any biblical spirituality has to be the gracious availability of the agapeic reality of God. That Father, Son, and Spirit have unilaterally breached the deadly resistance of human sinners with unlimited and never-ending, perfect love (divine agape) is no mere propositional truism or Christian nicety. Instead, this claim refers to the realistic and, therefore, revolutionary availability of the triune God to the psychological structures of the embodied human personality as persons develop individual lives and communities increasingly conducive to receiving such divine agape. As John Baillie states:

> What is directly revealed to us . . . is not truths or doctrines about God but God himself. Our doctrines about God are always secondary to our direct finding of God in the realities of our experience, and are never wholly adequate to that finding or wholly exhaustive of its meaning. God does not [just] communicate with us: He does something far better—He communes with us. Not the communication of propositions but the communion of spirits is the last word about divine revelation.[6]

Reflecting on Baillie's statement, Paul Moser writes, "Such communion . . . would be agent-to-agent (person-to-person), and not just agent-to-proposition. It would involve the direct acquaintance of one personal agent with another, even if human beliefs accompany the acquaintance."[7] While it is important and essential that the unmerited, agapeic reality of God be conceptualized in true biblical-theological propositions, it is a mistake to think Christians merely have access to those propositions when, in fact, Christians have direct acquaintance with the one to whom those propositions refer.[8] In other

---

[6] As quoted in Paul K. Moser, "Agapeic Theism: Personifying Evidence and Moral Struggle," *European Journal for Philosophy of Religion* 2 (2010): 4.

[7] Ibid., 4.

[8] For a further discussion of knowledge by acquaintance in reference to God, see Brandon Rickabaugh, "Eternal Life as Knowledge of God: An Epistemology of Knowledge by

words, we love the Lord our God with all our heart, mind, soul, and strength; we do not love the statement that "the Lord our God exists" with all our heart, mind, soul, and strength.

Paul poignantly makes this point, writing, "and hope does not put us to shame, because God's love [*agapē*] has been poured into our hearts through the Holy Spirit who has been given to us" (Rom 5:5). This pouring out of God's agape by the Spirit draws attention to the substantial and ongoing reality of God's loving, influential contact with the motivational center of human personality (i.e., the heart).[9] Noting the perfect verb tense of "has been poured into" (*ekkechytai*), which indicates an ongoing result of a completed action, John Stott writes, "the initial outpouring remains a permanent flood."[10] This flood of divine love does not refer to the propositional truth that God loves us, or the historical demonstration of God's love on the cross, or God's love at an abstract, heavenly distance, but rather, the psychologically tangible love of God that has objectively flooded the core of human personality via the person of the Spirit.[11]

Similarly, Paul writes to the Galatians that because Christians are the adopted sons and daughters of God, "God has sent the Spirit of his Son into our hearts, crying, 'Abba, Father!'" (Gal 4:6). Here again we see a pneumatological realism, a nonpropositional acquaintance, or what John Jefferson Davis has called an "inaugurated ontology."[12] Through placing our confidence in Christ's person and work and receiving the abiding presence of his life-infusing Spirit as adopted children of God, direct access to Abba, Father has commenced. Of course, while this direct access to God awaits full realization in the new heavens and new earth (Rev 21:3; cf. 1 Jn 3:2), even now "the love of Christ controls us" and in him human persons are a "new creation" (2 Cor 5:14, 17). The human heart is revitalized and reborn through real, influential, reconciled contact with the

---

Acquaintance and Spiritual Formation," *Journal of Spiritual Formation and Soul Care* 6, no. 2 (2013): 204-28.

[9]For a masterful discussion of the heart in biblical anthropology and sanctification, see Saucy, *Minding the Heart*.

[10]John R. W. Stott, *The Message of Romans* (Downers Grove, IL: InterVarsity Press, 1994), 142.

[11]See Douglas Moo, *The Epistle to the Romans*, New International Commentary on the New Testament (Grand Rapids: Eerdmans, 1996), 304-5.

[12]For Davis, an inaugurated eschatology brings with it an inaugurated ontology: "a comprehensive new paradigm of reality." Davis, *Meditation and Communion with God*, 66.

being of God in Christ by the Spirit with whom the believer is to "keep in step" (Gal 5:25).[13]

Another key text for the availability of the agapeic reality of God is John 14:16-23. Here Jesus is explaining to his disciples that, while he will no longer be physically present with them (Jn 14:18-19), he will not abandon/orphan them but will manifest/reveal/disclose/show (*emphanisō*) himself to them (Jn 14:21). The other Judas insightfully asks how this manifestation or showing will be apparent only to the disciples and "not to the world" (Jn 14:22). Jesus carefully responds, "If anyone loves me, he will keep my word, and my Father will love him, *and we will come to him and make our home with him*" (Jn 14:23).[14] Similar to Paul, Jesus teaches that the immaterial reality of him and his Father will come through love to a receptive human by means of the Holy Spirit (see Jn 14:16-17, 25-26).

Reflecting on Jesus' teaching in this passage, D. A. Carson writes, "This must not be construed as merely creedal position. The Spirit is to be experienced; otherwise the promise . . . of relief from the sense of abandonment is empty."[15] Carson goes on to quote Rudolf Schnackenburg approvingly: "In the twentieth century . . . consciousness of the presence of the Spirit has to be [*sic*] a very great extent disappeared, even in the believing community. It is possible to say that the only person who will understand words about the Spirit is the one who has already experienced the presence of the Spirit."[16] J. I. Packer agrees. In discussing the various aspects of the ministry of the Spirit, Packer writes:

> When, however, experiential aspects of life in the Spirit come up for treatment (as distinct from convictional, volitional, and disciplinary aspects) . . . Evangelicals for the most part seem to be at a loss. In this terrain of direct

---

[13]Moyer Hubbard argues that Paul's new-creation motif indicates a Spirit-wrought anthropological change with ongoing relational implications. See Moyer V. Hubbard, *New Creation in Paul's Letters and Thought* (Cambridge: Cambridge University Press, 2002), 233-41.

[14]While Jesus is most likely referring to his postresurrection appearances in Jn 14:19-20, it seems clear in his response to Judas's question that he primarily has in mind the abiding ministry of his Spirit. For this view, see Rodney A. Whitacre, *John*, IVP New Testament Commentary (Downers Grove, IL: InterVarsity Press), 361-62; George R. Beasley-Murray, *John*, Word Biblical Commentary, 2nd ed. (Nashville: Thomas Nelson, 1999), 258-59; and D. A. Carson, *The Gospel According to John*, Pillar New Testament Commentary (Grand Rapids: Eerdmans, 1991), 501-4.

[15]Ibid., 500.

[16]As quoted in Carson, *John*, 500-501.

perceptions of God—perceptions of his greatness and goodness, his eternity and infinity, his truth, his love, and his glory, all as related to Christ and through Christ to us—understanding was once much richer than is commonly found today. This is a place where we have some relearning to do.[17]

Perhaps part of the relearning Packer references stems from an evangelical tendency to reduce "experiential aspects of life in the Spirit" to mere cognitive and behavioral relations with God. But the availability of the triune God to the human person is not exhausted by belief in certain propositions about God and/or actions in keeping with his commands. The scribes and Pharisees cognitively knew the Scriptures, but they did not come to Jesus to whom those Scriptures pointed (Jn 9:39-40). And while they looked behaviorally clean on the outside of their "cups," they did not allow Jesus to clean their insides (Mt 23:25-26). Indeed, Jesus testifies, "On that day many will say to me, 'Lord, Lord, did we not . . . do many mighty works in your name?'" and he declares in response, "I never knew you . . . you workers of lawlessness" (Mt 7:22-23). It appears that correct theological language ("Lord, Lord") and impressive religious behavior ("mighty works in your name") in actual fact amount to a violation of the law of God when one is not personally known by Jesus. While accurate theology and obedience are important facets of life with God, there is a robust relational knowing at the core of the divine-human relationship in Christ Jesus.

An important biblical emphasis here is that God's real presence to humans is a communicative, meaningful presence. Just as the incarnate Jesus came with physical presence and the expression of meaning, the Spirit remains with spiritual presence and meaning. God's presence and meaning in the new covenant is often understood biblically in the language of Spirit and word. The indwelling Spirit cries out, "Abba! Father!" (Gal 4:6) and "bears witness with our spirit that we are children of God" (Rom 8:16).[18] Or, as Jesus says to his disciples, "I still have many things to say to you, but you cannot bear them now. When the Spirit of truth comes . . . he will take what

---

[17]J. I. Packer, *Keep in Step with the Spirit: Finding Fullness in Our Walk with God* (Grand Rapids: Baker, 2005), 62.

[18]In reference to Rom 8:16, the editors of the NET Bible state, "The objective data, as helpful as they are, cannot by themselves provide assurance of salvation; the believer also needs (and receives) an existential, ongoing encounter with God's Spirit in order to gain that familial comfort" (NET Bible, Rom 8:16, n. 21, https://net.bible.org/#!bible/Romans+8).

is mine and declare it to you" (Jn 16:12-13, 15).[19] As the mediating presence of God, the Spirit cries out, testifies, and declares true words to the human heart/spirit. Indeed, the word of God is the "sword of the Spirit" (Eph 6:17). But the word or truth (Jn 17:17) that the Spirit powerfully declares should not be immediately understood as the Bible itself. God's self-communication of who he is and what he intends his children to understand precedes and gave rise to the inspiration of the Bible, and so God as person remains full of meaning in and with his written word. The word or meaning of God himself is "living and active" (Heb 4:12; cf. Heb 1:3; 1 Pet 1:23) and by his Spirit that life-giving reality extends to the written words of Scripture. There is, as John Calvin puts it, an "indissoluble union" of God's person and the written word.[20] This is to say that the Bible is not a closed system, but rather an open system that remains connected to God and thereby provides a channel of communion with God. Robert L. Saucy helpfully summarizes:

> Thus we are not simply reading the words of God in the Scriptures. We are encountering and incorporating the living Word himself. The Scriptures give us life and healing because they give us Christ, the living personal Word of God, and all that he is for us. Both Scripture and Christ are living and active. . . . By continually consuming the Word we are nourishing ourselves through communion with Christ. We taste the goodness of the Lord himself (1 Pet 2:2).[21]

So, the first point of our biblical spirituality pertains to the gracious, un-merited availability of the agapeic reality of God to those clothed in Christ Jesus. God's love is a real personal presence and communicative meaning to which the Christian is acquainted however much or in whatever ways he or she is consciously aware of it.[22] "In this is love," John has it, "not that we have loved God but that he loved us." (1 Jn 4:10). Notice that the primacy of love

---

[19]Carson emphasizes that this passage is *primarily* directed to the apostles and only *derivatively* to the Spirit's work in later, nonapostolic believers. In light of other treatments of the Spirit's ongoing ministry (e.g., Rom 8:16; Gal 4:6) and the broader context of Jn 14–17, it seems right to see the declaratory ministry of the Spirit as having a primary inspirational/revelatory role when it comes to the apostles and a derivative illuminating role when it comes to the later, nonapostolic believers. See Carson, *John*, 541-42.

[20]John Calvin, *Institutes of the Christian Religion* 1.9.1.

[21]Saucy, *Minding the Heart*, 138. See also, Robert L. Saucy, *Scripture: Its Power, Authority, and Relevance* (Nashville: Thomas Nelson, 2001), 240-42.

[22]The Spirit is crying out "*Abba*, Father" even if we have never consciously discerned that testimony. Davis writes, "Like a sleeping infant in her mother's arms, we can be receiving love even

is "not that we have loved God," rather "that he loved us."[23] And yet, in the Christian life it can be tempting for us to move too quickly and linger too long on our attempts to love God rather than remaining "rooted and grounded" in God's permanent agape for us (Eph 3:17) and seeing our love for him (and others) emerge from his "first love" (1 Jn 4:19; cf. Gal 4:9; 1 Cor 8:3).

Principle 2: The agapeic reality of God is inherently transformational. This leads me to lay emphasis on a second foundational principle of biblical spirituality, which is the biblical notion that God's Spirit and word—his real presence and meaning—are inherently transformational of human moral experience. The transformational or sanctifying dynamics of the Spirit and word tend to be passed over quickly or left in the realm of mystery. While there are no doubt various ways that God's presence and meaning affect the human psyche, some of which are indeed mysterious, there are clear indications in Scripture that God's relational presence is itself inherently transformational in a manner that befits interpersonal relationships.[24] Saucy writes, "The power of God's Word to transform lives rests in the truth that it is more than theological doctrines and instructions for life. It is not teaching and learning like that of the philosophies in the Greek academies. It is the powerful voice of the risen Lord—the truth in Person—communicating himself to us today."[25]

But how does the "powerful voice of the risen Lord" transform us? Consider the psalmist's bald claim that "in your presence there is fullness of joy" (Ps 16:11). Or, as Jesus teaches his disciples, "Abide in me, and I in you. . . . My words abide in you. . . . Abide in my love. . . . These things I have spoken to you, that my joy may be in you, and that your joy may be full" (Jn 15:4, 7, 9, 11). Notice that the fullness of joy is not the result of Jesus merely telling the disciples these truths about their mutual indwelling in him, but the

---

when we are not consciously aware of the presence of the one who loves" (Davis, *Meditation and Communion with God*, 68-69).

[23]For a discussion of this passage in relation to contemplation, see Hans Urs von Balthasar, *Explorations in Theology*, vol. 3, *Creator Spirit*, trans. Brian McNeil, CRV (San Francisco: Ignatius, 1967), 173.

[24]For a discussion of an interpersonal model of the Spirit's sanctifying work, see William P. Alston, "The Indwelling of the Spirit," in *Divine Nature and Human Language*, ed. William P. Alston (Ithaca, NY: Cornell University Press, 1988), 121-50.

[25]Saucy, *Minding the Heart*, 138.

fullness of joy is found in the mutual indwelling—the union and communion with Christ—to which Jesus refers.[26] That is, it is abiding in Jesus (Jn 15:4), his word (Jn 15:7), and in his love (Jn 15:9) that his joy is in his disciples and their joy is made full.[27] In reference to this passage, Carson writes, "What is presupposed is that human joy in a fallen world will at best be ephemeral, shallow, incomplete, until human existence is overtaken by an experience of the love of God in Christ Jesus, the love for which we were created, a mutual love that issues in obedience without reserve."[28]

Of course, that God's loving presence brings fullness of joy should not be surprising to us. It is a common human experience to have one's emotions and attitudes take a positive turn when in the presence of a person or persons who know and love them deeply. Indeed, the human psyche has to resist in some way the other's loving attention in order to avoid the positive emotional result that would otherwise follow. While there can be various psychological blockages to the normal result of experiencing relational love (e.g., depression), the general human tendency to feel increasing joy in the presence of another's loving attention remains. If imperfect human relationships tend to do that, it is an easy extrapolation to imagine the psychological effects of the perfect, unlimited agape of our heavenly Father. Of course, divine love too can be resisted, but ideally joy would be one of the natural byproducts of even a small degree of receptivity to divine love.[29]

While the psychological benefits of receiving God's presence and meaning are more than the emergence of joy, it is striking to consider how many other virtues more or less automatically follow from an attitudinal state of joy. Perhaps thinking of joy as a pervasive sense of overall and ultimate well-being will help us consider the various attitudes and ways of being that would be largely eradicated in one's character should joy

---

[26]See W. L. Kynes, "Abiding," in *Dictionary of Jesus and the Gospels*, ed. Joel B. Green, Scot McKnight, and I. Howard Marshall (Downers Grove, IL: InterVarsity Press, 1992), 2-3.

[27]Gerald McDermott presents Jonathan Edwards's view that it is saints' participation in the coinherence of the divine persons that brings godly affections, including joy. See McDermott, "Jonathan Edwards on the Affections and the Spirit," in *The Spirit, the Affections, and the Christian Tradition*, ed. Dale M. Coulter and Amos Yong (Notre Dame, IN: University of Notre Dame Press, 2016), 280.

[28]Carson, *John*, 521.

[29]The psychologist David G. Benner offers a nice treatment of the transformational dynamics of love in his *Surrender to Love: Discovering the Heart of Christian Spirituality* (Downers Grove, IL: InterVarsity Books, 2003), 71-88.

become a more and more dominant attitude.[30] For instance, it is difficult to imagine intentionally cutting someone off on the freeway or yelling at your children if you are experiencing anything approximating fullness of joy. For that matter, most of what starts arguments (snide remarks, harsh tones, passive comments, and the like) would be stopped dead in its tracks by joy.[31]

As another example of the inherently transformational nature of God's presence and meaning, we can look at the connection 1 John places on how the human reception of God's love brings about the human disposition to love others. John believes God's love to be so formational of the human disposition to love that he claims, "If we love one another, God abides in us and his love is perfected in us" (1 Jn 4:12). In other words, the believer's love for another is evidence that God's abiding love is being perfected in that believer.[32] John makes the same point again a few lines later: "So we have come to know and to believe the love that God has for us. God is love, and whoever abides in love abides in God, and God abides in him. By this is love perfected with us" (1 Jn 4:16-17). It is important to see here that the "By this" [en toutō] is best understood as referring back to the believer abiding in God and God abiding in them, and so it is due to the believer's remaining (rooted and grounded) in the relational reality of God's love that the disposition to love others is perfected.[33]

Perhaps seeing that peace also (and inversely related to peace, the diminishment of anxiety) is a psychological benefit of living life more and more

---

[30]Dallas Willard writes, "Joy is natural in the presence of such [God's] love. Joy is a pervasive sense—not just a thought—of well-being: of overall and ultimate well-being. Its primary feeling component is delight in an encompassing good well-secured." Dallas Willard, *Renovation of the Heart: Putting on the Character of Christ* (Colorado Springs, CO: NavPress, 2002), 132-33.

[31]This is not Stoicism. The Stoic is unperturbed by misfortunes because of the perspective they have taken on those misfortunes. The Christian is unperturbed because they abide in and with a loving and caring friend. The first route is fundamentally cognitive, while the second is essentially relational. On this point, see Willard, *Renovation of the Heart*, 131-33.

[32]God's love for us is not conditional on our love for another. Rather, the construction allows that our love for others is dependent on God's love for us. This is put more clearly in 1 Jn 4:16-17. See Colin G. Kruse, *The Letters of John*, Pillar New Testament Commentary (Grand Rapids: Eerdmans, 2000), 161-62.

[33]I. Howard Marshall argues that this reading is more natural. See Marshall, *The Epistles of John*, New International Commentary on the New Testament (Grand Rapids: Eerdmans, 1978), 194-95. See also the extensive discussion in n. 42 of 1 Jn 4:17 in the NET Bible, https://net.bible .org/#!bible/1+John+4:17.

with God will firm up the notion that relational connectedness to the agapeic reality of God is inherently transformational.

First, there is Jesus' teaching in Matthew 6:25-34 that his followers need not be anxious about the basic necessities of life (food, clothing, water) because, as Jesus teaches there, the Father values his children (Mt 6:26), he competently cares for those he values (Mt 6:28-30), and he knows what his children need (Mt 6:32). It is in seeking first the kingdom reality of being valued, cared for, and known by God the Father that debilitating anxiety is eliminated. There is, quite literally, nothing to worry about if we are primarily oriented to the relational reality of the loving rule and reign of God (i.e., the kingdom and righteousness of God). In treating this passage, Charles Talbert writes, "This text, then, is designed to serve as a catalyst for the formation of the character of disciples in the direction of trust in God's providential goodness by enabling them to see a different kind of world, one in which creatures live out of their trust in divine providence and are free of debilitating anxiety."[34] And if the follower of Jesus is not worrying about food, clothing, and water because of a singular reliance on the Father's competent care, then there is a good chance they won't be worried about anything higher up on their hierarchy of needs. While the lack of undue anxiety is not quite the same as the positive experience of peace, the gradual diminishment of anxiety found in orienting oneself to the kingdom of God is certainly an essential ingredient in coming to peace (see Jn 14:27).

When it comes to peace itself, Paul instructs the Colossians to "let the peace of Christ rule in your hearts, to which indeed you were called in one body" (Col 3:15; cf. Phil 4:7). Notice here that it is the peace of Christ; that is, it is either the peace that Christ himself had or the peace that comes from being united to Christ.[35] Either way, such peace is not produced independently of Christ but as a result of allowing Christ's peace to rule their hearts. As Paul puts it elsewhere, "to set the mind on the Spirit is life and peace" (Rom 8:6). Or, as Isaiah has it,

---

[34]Charles H. Talbert, *Reading the Sermon on the Mount: Character Formation and Ethical Decision Making in Matthew 5–7* (Grand Rapids: Baker Academic, 2004), 129-30.

[35]F. F. Bruce notes that Deissmann refers to this phrase as the "mystical genitive": "the peace which is yours in union with Christ." See F. F. Bruce, *The Epistle to the Colossians, to Philemon, and to the Ephesians*, New International Commentary on the New Testament (Grand Rapids: Eerdmans, 1984), 157n142.

> You keep him in perfect peace
> whose mind is stayed on you,
> because he trusts in you. (Is 26:3)

While peace in the context of Colossians 3 has to do with harmony with other believers, there should be no doubt that outward peaceful relations is made possible by an inner peaceful repose. Indeed, biblical peace is "that sense that everything is right."[36] Stanley E. Porter writes, "In Greek thought 'peace' is a relational word which speaks of a state of objective well-being, leading to harmonious relations between people or nations."[37] We let our "objective well-being" in Christ rule in our hearts, which leads to peace with those around us.

Now, if love, joy, and peace, which are the initial fruit of walking with the Spirit (Gal 5:22), are beginning to dominate one's affective experience of the world, it seems quite easy to see how the remaining fruit would naturally emerge. A permanent flood of divine love leading to a disposition to love others combined with a pervasive sense and objective state of ultimate well-being provides a firm moral basis and motivational structure for patience, kindness, goodness, faithfulness, gentleness, and self-control. To put it another way, it is very difficult to imagine a human mind pervaded by love, joy, and peace that regularly produces actions and words that are impatient, cruel, evil, disloyal, harsh, and out of control. Those vices just wouldn't stand a chance in such a human moral psychology.[38] Such a view of biblical spirituality brings us to our third fundamental principle.

Principle 3: Persons-in-Christ can avail themselves of the agapeic reality of God to greater and lesser degrees. While God's real, agapeic presence is available to persons-in-Christ and is in and of itself transformational of the human personality, a third foundational principle of biblical spirituality is that persons-in-Christ can avail themselves of the gracious availability of God's presence and meaning to greater and lesser degrees. This is to say, God's fully available presence and meaning can be resisted and received by persons to greater and lesser degrees. This is why the "permanent flood" of

---

[36]Saucy, *Minding the Heart*, 26.

[37]Stanely E. Porter, "Peace, Reconciliation," in *Dictionary of Paul and His Letters*, ed. Gerald F. Hawthorne, Ralph P. Martin, and Daniel G. Reid (Downers Grove, IL: InterVarsity Press, 1993), 696.

[38]For a brief discussion of the connection between the Spirit, transformed affections, and virtue formation in Jonathan Edwards's theology, see McDermott, "Jonathan Edwards," 279-92.

divine agape does not bring about entire sanctification immediately. As Scripture notes in various places, persons-in-Christ can "quench the Spirit" (1 Thess 5:19), "grieve the Holy Spirit" (Eph 4:30; cf. Is 63:10), or be filled with other things in place of the fullness of the Spirit (e.g., Eph 5:18).[39] Moreover, Paul speaks of "divided" and "undivided devotion to the Lord" (1 Cor 7:34-35), and Jude encourages his congregations to "keep yourselves in the love of God" (Jude 21), which entails that there are degrees in which a person can remain apart from the love of God.

Another clear, biblical indication that there are greater and lesser degrees of receptivity to divine agape is found in Paul's prayer that the saints in Ephesus, having been "rooted and grounded in love, may have strength to comprehend with all the saints what is the breadth and length and height and depth, and to know the love of Christ that surpasses knowledge, that you may be filled with all the fullness [plērōma] of God" (Eph 3:16-18). Paul's prayer makes it clear that even though the Ephesians are already rooted and grounded in agape, there nevertheless remain multiple dimensions (breadth, length, height, depth) to Christ's love that quite literally surpass the knowledge they already have. It is not that they are epistemologically un-aware that they are loved by Christ. Rather, it is that there is a greater degree of Christ's love than what they currently comprehend or are acquainted with. Paul's prayer is that the Ephesians would more completely comprehend (to take into one's self or appropriate) a greater degree of the richness of Christ's love so that they would be "filled with all the fullness of God" (Eph 3:18).[40]

The language of resistance, receptivity, filling, and being full can be mis-takenly pictured as interaction with some kind of divine juice that is either consumed or avoided. This is to depersonalize God and thereby turn spiritu-ality into an impersonal affair. Rather, as we have seen, Father, Son, and Spirit are interpersonally and therefore influentially available to persons-in-Christ, and yet the formational influence of another person is capable of being dampened, avoided, neglected, and defused or, alternatively, received,

---

[39]In his *Filled with the Spirit*, John R. Levison writes, "While the holy spirit, therefore, can be re-ceived by and fill believers, it can also be the object of resistance. . . . The gospel of Luke, Acts, Ephesians, and Hebrews together indicate that followers of Jesus also have the potential to op-pose the spirit—to blaspheme, to lie to it, to grieve it, and to outrage it." See John R. Levison, *Filled with the Spirit* (Grand Rapids: Eerdmans, 2009), 231.

[40]It is important to note here that in Jesus "the fullness [plērōma] of God was pleased to dwell" (Col 1:19; cf. Col 2:9).

welcomed, focused on, and fully embraced. To see that the filling of the Spirit is an interpersonal, relational process rather than an impersonal, materialistic process makes the dynamics of spiritual growth somewhat analogous to the dynamics of human, interpersonal relationships.[41]

Paul's ethical use of "flesh" (*sarx*) can provide further insight into the dynamics of relational resistance and receptivity to the Spirit's transformational work.[42] For instance, consider 1 Corinthians 3:1-5:

> But I, brothers, could not address you as spiritual people, but as people of the flesh, as infants in Christ. I fed you with milk, not solid food, for you were not ready for it ["not yet able to receive it," NASB]. And even now you are not yet ready, for you are still of the flesh. For while there is jealousy and strife among you, are you not of the flesh and behaving only in a human way ["walking like mere men," NASB]? For when one says, "I follow Paul," and another, "I follow Apollos," are you not being merely human?

Here Paul utilizes the metaphor of an infant's digestive system to illustrate the impact of the flesh on spiritual maturity (cf. Heb 5:11-15). The idea is that just as an infant is "not yet able to receive" solid nourishment and must sustain growth on milk, so too the Corinthian Christian who is "still of the flesh" is not yet able to receive the solid nourishment by the Spirit (e.g., words "taught by the Spirit," 1 Cor 2:13) and must sustain their growth on a kind of nourishment only fit for spiritual infancy.[43]

The problem with this picture is that the Corinthian Christians need to move beyond their infancy in Christ and yet the only way to mature is to be able to receive more fully the presence and meaning of the Spirit. What Paul makes clear is that flesh stands in the way of the Corinthians' reception of this deeper nourishment. Flesh, in this context, amounts to the attempt to live life in a "merely human" manner apart from God's resources (1 Cor 3:3). The concrete example to which Paul points is the Corinthian's attempt to find value/meaning/significance through comparing themselves to one another based on whom they follow (Paul, Apollos, Cephas, Christ,

---

[41]See H. H. Farmer, "Experience of God as Personal," *Religion in Life* 2 (1933): 234-46.

[42]The following four paragraphs borrow substantially from my "The Gradual Nature of Sanctification: *Sarx* as Habituated, Relational Resistance to the Spirit," *Themelios* 39, no. 3 (2014): 470-83.

[43]As Morna Hooker puts it, the Corinthians don't grow as "the result of their own inability to digest what he is offering them." Quoted in Gordon Fee, *The First Epistle to the Corinthians*, New International Commentary on the New Testament (Grand Rapids: Eerdmans, 1987), 126.

1 Cor 1:11-12). Paul's diagnosis of the Corinthians' problem is that they were trusting/resting on the "wisdom of men" instead of trusting/resting in the "power of God" (1 Cor 2:5). While there is nothing intrinsically wrong with looking to the wisdom of human persons, the problem was that the Corinthians were doing so as a replacement for trust in God's power. Notice here that it is an idolatrous, relational resistance to the Spirit that leads to the lack of receptivity to the Spirit's transforming presence and meaning.

Additionally, as Paul makes clear in Galatians, the human person does contain a mix of desires, some of which—the desires of the flesh—are opposed to the desires of the Spirit "to keep you from doing the things you want to do" (Gal 5:17). Paul clearly identifies one set of desires as the "desires of the Spirit" (Gal 5:17). So the Spirit desires to empower the Christian for fruitful living, and yet these desires of the Spirit are in contrast to the desires of the flesh, which are in opposition to the Spirit, seeking to find life apart from him.[44] Since the Christian can still attempt to live a fleshly existence in autonomy (see Gal 3:3; 5:16), trusting in his or her own resources (i.e., gratifying the desires of the flesh), it is fair to say that the indwelling Spirit's desires are in opposition to human fleshly desires to live in autonomy from the Spirit. Hence, the conflict for the Galatian Christians is not a conflict of their desires to sin as opposed to their desires not to sin. Rather, it is a relational conflict between trusting in the desires of the Spirit by walking in the Spirit or trusting in one's fleshly desires to find life apart from the Spirit. In this vein, Robert Jewett defines *sarx* in Galatians 5 as "Paul's term for everything aside from God in which one places his final trust."[45] Or, as Oliver O'Donovan puts it, "Whether it appears as law or as license, the ultimate fact about life according to the flesh is that it is a refusal of life in the Spirit."[46] So we see here that *sarx*—or the desires of the flesh—amount to a relational resistance to the Spirit.[47]

---

[44]Frederick W. Danker, Walter Bauer, William F. Arndt, and F. Wilbur Gingrich, *Greek-English Lexicon of the New Testament and Other Early Christian Literature*, 3rd ed. (Chicago: University of Chicago Press, 2000), 372, notes that *epithymei kata tinos* means "rise up in protest" or "desire against."

[45]Robert Jewett, *Paul's Anthropological Terms: A Study of Their Use in Conflict Settings* (Leiden: Brill, 1971), 103.

[46]Oliver O'Donovan, *Resurrection and Moral Order: An Outline for Evangelical Ethics*, 2nd ed. (Grand Rapids: Eerdmans, 1994), 13.

[47]See Ronald Y. K. Fung, *The Epistle to the Galatians*, New International Commentary on the New Testament, 2nd ed. (Grand Rapids: Eerdmans, 1988), 252.

Principle 4: Persons-in-Christ can make efforts to increase their receptivity to the agapeic reality of God. Paul's exhortation for the Galatians to "keep in step with the Spirit" (Gal 5:25) implies that despite the flesh's lingering resistance to God, Christians have been given some measure of responsibility to turn toward the Spirit, embodying in that turn greater receptivity to the desires of the Spirit. It is not just that Christians can be receptive to God to greater and lesser degrees; it is that their choices have something to do with increasing or decreasing their level of receptivity. This brings us to our fourth and final principle of biblical spirituality, namely, that persons-in-Christ can make embodied efforts to increase their receptivity to the agapeic presence and meaning of God. These embodied efforts involve sense-perceptible practices (i.e., spiritual disciplines) that are meant to direct the human mind/person to the immaterial, non-sense-perceptible reality of God's presence and meaning. While a full biblical theology of Christian spiritual practice is not possible here, I will examine two important passages.[48]

First, not only did Jesus himself engage in various embodied practices of dependence on his Father (e.g., his forty-day fast), his early teaching in Matthew 6:1-18 stresses three practices that, when approached correctly, increase one's receptivity to God. As Jesus puts it in Matthew 6, "when you give to the needy" (Mt 6:2), "when you pray" (Mt 6:5), "and when you fast" (Mt 6:16), "you must not be like the hypocrites" (Mt 6:5; cf. Mt 6:2, 16). Rather, Jesus' followers are to give, pray, and fast "in secret" and "your Father who sees in secret will reward you" (Mt 6:4, 6, 18).[49] It is important to note several points here.

First, while there is no suggestion that these three practices exhaust a full-orbed spiritual existence in Christ, Jesus does assume that his followers are engaging in at least these three practices. "Thus, when you give," "when you pray," "when you fast" (Mt 6:2, 5, 16) implies the expectation that these

---

[48]For a more complete treatment of Christian spiritual practice, see Dallas Willard, *The Spirit of the Disciplines: Understanding How God Changes Lives* (San Francisco: HarperSanFrancisco, 1988).

[49]Craig Keener argues that Matthew intends that these practices apply to his own mid-first-century audience in addition to Jesus' initial, contemporary context. There is no reason to think that these practices wouldn't also apply to followers of Jesus today. See Craig A. Keener, *The Gospel of Matthew: A Socio-rhetorical Commentary* (Grand Rapids: Eerdmans, 2009), 206, 536-37.

activities will occur.[50] While these three practices were indeed common in first-century Judaism as well as in the history of Israel, Jesus reauthorizes their legitimacy among his kingdom followers.[51] Moreover, we see these practices in the early church (e.g., Acts 2:42, 45-46; 13:3; cf. Phil 4:9). The phrase "Pray then like this" (Mt 6:9) is even more forceful and, of course, the Lord's Prayer has been treated as an essential form of prayer throughout the church's history. So while Jesus' main teaching here would apply to other practices as well, it does seem right to hold these three practices in particular as fundamental for followers of Jesus.

Second, Jesus not only highlights these three practices but, much more to the point of the passage, teaches that it is essential to practice them in a particular way of which there is a negative requirement (a way not to engage them) and a positive requirement (a way to engage them). Negatively, Jesus' followers are to resist the prevailing motivation for these practices within their immediate context, which was to do these things to be "seen by others" (Mt 6:2, 6, 16). The reason to resist engaging in that way is that such an approach has extremely limited results. The hypocrites who practiced in that way "have their reward" (Mt 6:2, 5, 16) and, more significantly, have "no reward from your Father who is in heaven" (Mt 6:1).

What does have a significant benefit in Jesus' inaugurated kingdom is to positively engage these practices in secret so as to strip oneself of the possibility of seeking the approval of others and to thereby cast one's self entirely onto the care of the Father, who is the only one who "sees in secret" (Mt 6:6). Jesus is not teaching that God will be impressed with the secretive performance of these practices, but rather that once a person refrains from doing these things to impress others, the only other motivation to do them is with a deep sense of one's utter reliance on the Father. Why else would one engage in such activities—indeed, from a mere human perspective these practices are counterproductive—unless one is thereby exercising their trust in God's reign? Giving of one's own resources to those in need, praying that God's will be done over one's own, and foregoing one's daily nourishment embodies a deep dependence and trust in God's goodness and love. For instance, Craig

---

[50]Ibid., 209.

[51]For some discussion of these practices in ancient Israel, see Michael J. Wilkins, *Matthew*, NIV Application Commentary (Grand Rapids: Zondervan, 2004), 271-82.

Keener observes, "One should pray not because one thinks that one's prayer or formulas earn God's favor, but as an expression of trust in a Father who already knows one's need and merely waits for his children to express their dependence on him (6:8, 32)."[52] These practices done in the way Jesus teaches are bodily ways of exercising one's inner disposition to seek first the reign of God that can then become habituated over time.[53] Moreover, what becomes habituated is not merely fasting, prayer, and almsgiving but an overall way of life of wholehearted trust in the inexhaustible resources of God's kingdom goodness.

A second significant passage for examining Scripture's teaching regarding embodied practices of receptivity to God is Colossians 3:1-4. On the basis of the Colossian Christians' having been raised to new spiritual life with Christ, Paul exhorts them to "seek the things that are above, where Christ is, seated at the right hand of God. Set your minds on things that are above, not on things that are on earth" (Col 3:1-2). It is important to step back and ponder what exactly Paul was enjoining in his exhortation to "seek" and to "set your minds" on "things that are above." First, what are these "things"? F. F. Bruce writes that the Colossians "must therefore pursue those things which belong to the heavenly realm where [Christ] reigns; their mind, their attitude, their ambition, their whole outlook must be characterized by their living bond with the ascended Christ."[54] As Bruce implies, the only object Paul mentions that is located above is the risen, ascended, and exalted Christ, who is envisioned in a position of rest (seated) and authority (at the right hand) with the Father (cf. Rom 8:34; Eph 1:20).[55] The Colossians having "received Christ Jesus the Lord" are to "walk in him" (Col 2:6), setting

---

[52]Keener, *Matthew*, 213. Regarding fasting, Keener writes, "In biblical and Jewish tradition, fasting was a time of drawing close to God by demonstrating one's commitment to him . . . such fasting is not asceticism for asceticism's sake" (227).

[53]Jesus' particular examples of secretive giving, praying, and fasting (e.g., not letting one hand know what the other is doing or going into a closet) are best taken hyperbolically and not literally. For instance, most of Jesus' private prayers took place outside (e.g., Mt 14:23) and not in a closet. Indeed, to the degree that Jesus' teaching about secretive prayer is to be understood as private prayer, there is in his teaching an implicit commendation of the practice of solitude. See Keener, *Matthew*, 211.

[54]Bruce, *Colossians*, 131.

[55]Craig Keener writes, "For Colossians, the heavenly focus must be on Christ alone. . . . The only content of these heavenly matters specified is the exalted Christ." See Craig A. Keener, "Heavenly Mindedness and Earthly Good: Contemplating Matters Above in Colossians 3.1-2," *Journal of Greco-Roman Christianity and Judaism* 6 (2009): 181, 183.

their minds—orienting the entirety of their beings—on the living Christ, who is "the image of the invisible God, the firstborn of all creation. . . . Before all things, and in him all things hold together" (Col 1:15, 17; cf. Mark 8:33). Having one's focus on the Lord of all enthroned above would dramatically alter one's perspective on everything else. Indeed, it appears that it is in setting one's mind on Christ that the enablement arises to "Put to death therefore what is earthly in you" (Col 3:5) and "put on . . . compassionate hearts, kindness, humility, meekness, and patience" (Col 3:12).[56] As the well-known hymn has it,

> Turn your eyes upon Jesus,
> look full in his wonderful face,
> and the things on earth will grow strangely dim,
> in the light of his glory and grace.

But what activities are involved in setting one's mind on Christ and the "above" where he reigns? Of course, Paul and the Colossians understood this to be figurative language and did not think of Christ literally enthroned at the Father's right hand.[57] Indeed, because Christ "has been elevated to the position of highest sovereignty over the universe, he pervades the universe with his presence."[58] Still, the mere decision to have the thought that one's Lord pervades the universe and is sovereign over it is itself an embodied practice. That is to say, one cannot think about Jesus in that way without intending to do so, which would involve, first of all, deciding not to dwell on whatever else might be on or before one's mind. For the Colossians that choice would include not focusing on the "elementary principles of the world" (Col 2:8 NASB), whereas for us it might involve turning off the daily news. Whatever the thoughts and images away from which one needs to shift attention, Paul enjoins the Colossians to intentionally bring Christ before their minds choosing to see him in a position of relaxed authority over everything, including whatever else might be vying for their attention. Those things—"earthly things"—would be put in their place, such that sexual immorality, evil desires, and wanting whatever one wants when one wants

---

[56] For a helpful discussion of Paul's connection between focusing on Christ and the moral sections of Col 3, see ibid., 184-88.
[57] See Bruce, *Colossians*, 133.
[58] Ibid.

it (i.e., covetousness) would be able to be put to death (Col 3:5). And so, to set one's mind on Christ involves an intentional thought, imagination, and meditation on the truth that in Christ "are hidden all the treasures of wisdom and knowledge" (Col 2:3) and that he "is the head of all rule and authority" (Col 2:10). Such an intentional focus might turn us to confess the ways in which we trust in our own or others' control instead of placing ourselves under Christ's all-knowing authority. This confession might then lead to prayer about our deep need for Christ's rule and reign in our lives. The injunction, then, to seek the things that are above can be understood as a multifaceted practice that would involve, among other things, intentional thought, imagination, meditation, confession, and prayer.[59] This is to "present [our] bodies as a living sacrifice" (Rom 12:1; cf. Rom 6:13-19).

As was the case in Matthew 6, each of the practices involved in setting one's mind on Christ is done in and with the body as a way of posturing oneself in receptivity to the agapeic reality of God. In some bodily manner, the follower of Jesus steps out on her desire to direct herself more fully to God in trust and love. Her embodiment of that intention (e.g., in prayer, fasting, or setting her mind on Christ) expresses her desire for deeper dependence on the presence and meaning of God, which, as was noted earlier, has the inherent potential to transform her moral experience (e.g., bring about love, joy, and peace).[60] As Paul says, "What you have learned and received and heard and seen in me—*practice these things*, and the God of peace will be with you" (Phil 4:9, emphasis added). Human reliance on the God of peace is appropriated through spiritual practices. And it is precisely here that language of contemplation can be helpful.

BIBLICAL SPIRITUALITY AND A CONTEMPLATIVE DIMENSION TO THE CHRISTIAN LIFE

The four principles of biblical spirituality developed above generate the following picture of the Christian life: (1) there is for persons-in-Christ the

---

[59]Keener writes, "In the context, then, Colossians speaks of no abstract contemplation detached from present earthly existence. Rather, the focus on heaven is a focus on Christ, not only as he is enthroned above, but as that reality of his lordship impinges on the living of daily life" (Keener, "Heavenly Mindedness," 185).

[60]Dallas Willard provides a trenchant analysis of the role of the body in spiritual disciplines in *Spirit of the Disciplines*, 30-32, 75-94. See also, James K. A. Smith, *Imagining the Kingdom: How Worship Works* (Grand Rapids: Baker Academic, 2013).

gracious, unmerited availability of the agapeic reality of God's presence and meaning; (2) ongoing receptivity to God's presence and meaning is inherently transformational of human moral experience; (3) there exist degrees of habituated receptivity as well as resistance to God's presence and meaning; and (4) persons-in-Christ can make choices to intentionally engage in embodied practices of increased receptivity. These practices— such as prayer, giving, fasting, meditation on Scripture—all involve embodied, physical, sense-perceptible means of grace that have as their intended goal relational communion with the immaterial God of grace.[61] Paul exhorts the Philippians to practice what they had learned, received, heard, and seen in him not as ends in themselves or as meritorious deeds, but as conduits of receptivity to being with the "God of peace," who was already available to them in Christ by the Spirit (Phil 4:9).

For instance, when we pray on our knees with head bowed or with palms opened upward (sense-perceptible, embodied postures of surrender) speaking the words "Our Father . . . thy kingdom come, thy will be done" (sense-perceptible, embodied indications of dependence), we engage in this practice as a means of directing our attention to and receiving from a non-sense-perceptible, gracious divine reality—namely, God in Christ by the Spirit. Our spiritual practices are not ends in themselves, but means to the end of God himself. These practices make God present to us, for in Christ by the Spirit he is already fully available. Rather, spiritual practices avail us of God's ongoing, gracious availability. Until the dwelling place of God is among us (Rev 21:3) and we see "face to face" (1 Cor 13:12), we engage in various practices to set our minds on Christ.

But most of us need assistance to look beyond and through our embodied, sense-perceptible activities to an immaterial, non-sense-perceptible person whose agape-love is graciously available to us. It is here that the language of contemplation can aid us. At least in modern parts of the world, non-sense-perceptible, immaterial objects and persons are not typically thought of, let alone believed in.[62] Thus the modernized world increasingly lacks a

---

[61]For more on means of grace and their role in sanctification, see my "Why Should We Read Spiritual Classics?," in *Reading the Christian Spiritual Classics: A Guide for Evangelicals*, ed. Jamin Goggin and Kyle Strobel (Downers Grove, IL: IVP Academic, 2013), 15-30.

[62]See Louis Dupré, *Religion and the Rise of Modern Culture* (Notre Dame, IN: University of Notre Dame Press, 2008), 14.

conceptual framework, terminology, and imagination to conceptualize human experience of an invisible, immaterial world.

Perhaps turning to a bit of the history surrounding the language of contemplation can help at this point. For Plato and other ancient Hellenists, contemplation (or *theōria*) was understood as a kind of mental insight or intuitive understanding of incorporeal, non-sense-perceptible realities and was, therefore, distinct from sense perception of corporeal realities. Jacob Sherman writes, "For Plato, *theoria* denoted an exalted species of vision, both a vision of and a communion with (*koinōnia*) the Forms that lie within and, at the same time, beyond the mutability of the material world. . . . One sees the Forms, or even the Good that lies beyond both being and the Forms, only by integrally participating in the reality of that which one beholds."[63] While on Plato's view the forms were impersonal and material reality was disparaged, the language of contemplation nonetheless sheds light on an approach to human experience that sees through material things to transcendent, immaterial objects.

While biblical spirituality understands ultimate reality as personal and does not disparage God's creation of matter, there remains a crucially important contemplative dimension to life in the Spirit. The follower of Jesus is meant to engage sense-perceptible, physical, and embodied practices as the means of directing attention to and communing with God. Speaking of his invisible, immaterial Father, Jesus said to the Jewish leaders, "His voice you have never heard, his form you have never seen, and you do not have his word abiding in you, for you do not believe the one whom he has sent. You search the Scriptures because you think that in them you have eternal life; and it is they that bear witness about me, yet you refuse to come to me that you may have life" (Jn 5:37-40). The Jewish leaders were looking at the sense-perceptible Word of God written (the Scriptures) and the sense-perceptible living Word of God incarnate (Jesus), but they failed to see that these Scriptures pointed to Jesus as the Messiah and that Messiah-Jesus pointed to the Father. Both the sense-perceptible written Word and incarnate Word were divinely given means of directing humanity's attention to God the Father and making communion with him possible (Jn 1:18).

---

[63]Jacob Holsinger Sherman, *Partakers of the Divine: Contemplation and the Practice of Philosophy* (Minneapolis: Fortress, 2014), 8.

It is such an understanding of the Christian life that led early Christians to critically integrate the Hellenistic language of contemplation. Sherman writes:

> Early Christians, however, following Philo, adopted the term *theoria* but applied it to the God who called all of creation both to be and to be in relation to Godself. For early Christian contemplative writers such as Origen and Gregory of Nyssa, contemplation became not simply the beholding of immutables but, rather, a supremely personal *theoria theou*; a loving vision of the God who created all things and who became incarnate out of love for a wayward creation.[64]

"Contemplation," Sherman concludes for the Christian, "thus becomes not an exercise in abstraction but a practice of personal communion."[65] In treating Augustine's understanding of contemplation, A. N. Williams argues that on Augustine's epistemology,

> to know God certainly entails mastery of information, but it also entails personal contact. Knowledge of God is personal knowledge in the fullest sense, in that it encompasses both knowledge-about and acquaintance-with. . . . The rubric under which Augustine above all understands the mind's transformative engagement with God is contemplation. . . . Such a view is neither original or unique to Augustine. On the contrary, the centrality of contemplation is evident in both Eastern and Western theologians from the earliest Fathers to the Middle Ages. It is modern theology that has lost the concept of contemplation, and with it the sense that the knowledge of God differs radically from knowledge of a subject or discipline.[66]

And yet, while biblical spirituality grounds this sort of contemplative dimension to the Christian life, there is nothing in the biblical view presented here that leads to all that might be included in this or that understanding of contemplative spirituality or contemplative prayer. For

---

[64]Ibid., 19.

[65]Ibid., 18.

[66]A. N. Williams, "Contemplation: Knowledge of God in Augustine's *De Trinitate*," in *Knowing the Triune God: The Work of the Spirit in the Practices of the Church*, ed. James J. Buckley and David S. Yeago (Grand Rapids: Eerdmans, 2001), 130, 137, 145. John Peter Kenney also argues that Augustine developed a distinctly Christian understanding of contemplation. See John Peter Kenney, *Contemplation and Classical Christianity: A Study in Augustine* (Oxford: Oxford University Press, 2013). See also Bernard McGinn, *The Presence of God: A History of Western Christian Mysticism*, vol. 1, *The Foundations of Mysticism: Origins to the Fifth Century* (New York: Crossroad, 1994), 23-61.

instance, the degree to which or the ways in which a person can be consciously aware of God's personal presence are not decided by the four principles developed here.[67] Neither is the question of whether contemplation is infused or acquired, whether there are particular prayer practices that lead one into contemplation, or whether there are stages of contemplative prayer.[68]

In fact, contemplative prayer, depending on how it is understood, could easily be too narrow of a framework for robust biblical prayer. For example, the third foundational principle of biblical spirituality discussed above— that there exists ongoing human resistance to receiving God's gracious presence—suggests that biblical prayer will always involve a wrestling with God. Alternatively, the conceptual framework of contemplative prayer might suggest that the ultimate goal of prayer is some sort of pure attending to God. But such a pure communion (or union) seems out of step with the desires of the flesh being opposed to the desires of the Spirit. Even Jesus' experience in Gethsemane demonstrates that struggle to surrender— agony in prayer—is a normal part of earthly communion with God. "Father, if you are willing, remove this cup from me. Nevertheless, not my will, but yours, be done. . . . And being in agony he prayed more earnestly" (Lk 22:42, 44). This is what Moser refers to as agonic and kenotic prayer: "agonic, because Jesus struggles against his initial preference and submission to God's will; and kenotic, because Jesus empties, or denies, his initial preference in order to obey God's call to self-giving obedience for the sake of others (cf. 2 Corinthians 8:9)."[69] In this and other ways, the biblical spirituality presented here presents a challenge to ways of understanding contemplative prayer that fail to integrate agonic and kenotic dimensions to prayer.

---

[67]It is important to remember that the conscious awareness of God and the experiential influence of God do not amount to the same thing. Just as I can be experientially influenced by my wife's love for me even though I am not consciously thinking about or occurrently aware of my wife's love, so too I can be experientially influenced by God's love for me even though I am not consciously thinking about or occurrently aware of God's love. For instance, the Spirit is crying "*Abba*, Father" and no doubt that is having its experiential effect even though I am not consciously thinking about or occurrently aware of the Spirit's cry (i.e., I have never *heard* it).

[68]For what has become a classic discussion of these and other questions regarding contemplation, see Reginald Garrigou-Lagrange, *Christian Perfection and Contemplation* (St. Louis: Herder, 1937).

[69]See Moser, "Agapeic Theism," 9.

CONCLUSION

The conclusion, then, of this chapter is a rather modest one when it comes to contemplation. The conclusion is that biblical spirituality grounds a contemplative dimension to life in the Spirit. But how far and in what directions that contemplative dimension can be expanded remains largely unaddressed.

It might be thought that this conclusion is so modest that, in the end, no biblical case has been made for contemplative spirituality and contemplative prayer. The biblical case presented here does not lead to the conclusion that we need language of contemplation in our understanding and practice of Christian spirituality. Just as a mother can lovingly gaze at her child without language of motherly affection, so too a disciple of Jesus can set their mind on Christ at the right hand of the Father without language of contemplation. For that matter, Christians could successfully abide in Christ and love God without language of "abiding in the vine" or "loving the Lord your God with all your heart, mind, soul, and strength." Though, of course, if too much of this language is missing from our understanding of life in the Spirit, we would be in danger of losing essential, biblical concepts. Language helps us hone in on a way of conceptualizing and thereby engaging life in the Spirit, and it is quite clear in Scripture that there are better and worse ways of conceptualizing and thereby engaging life in the Spirit (e.g., Gal 3:1).

Furthermore, while Jesus, Paul, and the other New Testament writers did not utilize language of contemplation (*theōria*), they did make use of nearby concepts, such as "having the eyes of your heart enlightened" (Eph 1:18), "to know the love of Christ that surpasses knowledge" (Eph 3:19), "Seek the things that are above, where Christ is" (Col 3:1), "though you have not seen [Christ], you love him" (1 Pet 1:8), and so on.[70] They also certainly thought of the presence of the Lord as an experiential reality. Paul lifts the lid on his own experience at one point, telling Timothy, "At my first defense no one came to stand by me, but all deserted me. . . . But the Lord stood by me and strengthened me" (2 Tim 4:16-17). It appears Paul had a keen awareness of the experiential and transformational reality of the risen and present Jesus.

---

[70]The word *theōria* only occurs once in the New Testament, in Lk 23:48. Cognates of *theōreō* occur often, but all of these uses describe vision in the ordinary sense.

So, while we do not need language of contemplation per se, we do need a biblical-theological framework and related terminology that makes it clear that we are dealing with the real presence of God in Christ by his Spirit. Otherwise our views of sanctification and spiritual practice will grind toward being largely understood in cognitive, behavioral, and/or emotional categories.[71] In the end, we will end up with some sort of lifeless, deistic spirituality that substitutes beliefs, behaviors, or felt experience for God himself. Indeed, in our materialistic, empirically minded, sensate setting, it seems fair to think that many Western Christians have lost the ability to imagine, let alone meaningfully interact with, invisible, immaterial, non-sense-perceptible reality.

In his biblical theology of God's presence, J. Ryan Lister writes, "Talk of God's presence is part of the white noise of evangelicalism, a catchphrase that means as little to the one saying it as it does to the one hearing it."[72] Or, as Packer put it, "When it comes to experiential dimensions of life in the Spirit . . . we have some relearning to do."[73] To understand this point—that we have some relearning to do—should be enough to motivate us to carefully consider a long tradition of philosophical and explicitly Christian reflection on what it would involve for the human mind to be in meaningful contact with an immaterial person. Unless one goes in for deism, to serve a risen and living Savior who non-sense-perceptibly stands beside us demands that we carefully consider the real availability of him and his Father's agapeic reality and the ways that we might through the Spirit avail ourselves more fully of that reality.

---

[71]It bears noting that the contemplative dimension of the Christian life blocks seeing relationship with God as primarily driven by felt, emotional experience. Relational awareness of another is certainly emotionally laden, but there are ways to be aware of others that are not primarily about the emotional impact. Indeed, a focus on emotions is a focus on how the other makes me feel and not on the other person himself or herself. For instance, I may feel comforted or joy, but it is awareness of the other's faithful presence that causes that effect. Contemplation is the focus on the other, not on the emotional impact of the other.

[72]J. Ryan Lister, *The Presence of God: Its Place in the Storyline of Scripture and the Story of Our Lives* (Wheaton, IL: Crossway, 2015), 21.

[73]Packer, *Keep in Step with the Spirit*, 62.

CONTEMPLATION BY SON AND SPIRIT

Reforming the Ascent of the Soul to God

KYLE C. STROBEL

INTRODUCTION

The way Jonathan Edwards set up the notion of contemplation focuses not on the question, should we engage in contemplation? but rather, what are we contemplating? For Edwards, to be human entails that we are captivated by whatever our hearts find beautiful.[1] Our hearts are often captivated by lesser beauties, things that were meant to point beyond themselves to God's beauty. We become enamored of things that were supposed to point us to God, and we accept their secondary beauty instead of what is more glorious. We spend a lot of time contemplating the latest sporting events, movies (and their stars), and, maybe more than anything else, the objects of our romantic affections. We are not short on contemplation as a culture, but what is absent is the contemplation of God.

The goal of this essay is to provide a distinctively theological approach to the question of both contemplation as such and prayer more broadly.[2] But the main goal concerns the former. The category of contemplation, historically, has concerned Christian knowledge of God. Augustine has

---

[1]For more on Edwards's view of contemplation, see Kyle Strobel, *Formed for the Glory of God: Learning from the Spiritual Practices of Jonathan Edwards* (Downers Grove, IL: IVP Academic, 2013); and Strobel, introduction to *Jonathan Edwards: Selected Writings*, ed. Kenneth P. Minkema, Adriaan C. Neele, and Kyle C. Strobel, Classics of Western Spirituality (Mahwah, NJ: Paulist Press, 2018).

[2]Several friends provided critical feedback as I developed this from the original article, and particular thanks should go out to Matthew Levering, Jamin Goggin, and Ty Kieser.

this inclination, as put helpfully by A. N. Williams, "For Augustine . . . contemplation does not signify an advanced form of prayer. What it does designate is a form of knowledge of God."[3] Before turning to the notion of contemplative prayer, if we are to accept such a notion, we have to first address contemplation as such. Building on Edwards's insights, that contemplation is at the heart of what it means to be human, we need to distinguish between natural contemplation and supernatural contemplation. It is helpful to start, in one sense, with natural contemplation, in that we come to understand, in generic terms, what the word *contemplation* means. But this approach is limited, and if we rest here too long our understanding of contemplating God will be stifled. In contrast, while we can affirm that natural contemplation provides an initial (albeit limited) description, when we turn to contemplation of God there is a necessary reforming of contemplation we need to attend to.[4] All natural contemplation points beyond itself to this more perfect calling—humankind's created purpose to glorify God.

In focusing on the contemplation of God as the orienting feature of all contemplation, we must push beyond natural notions to God's self-giving and the overall telos of his creatures. In this sense, contemplation is the precursor to the beatific vision, which entails becoming like him "because we shall see him as he is" (1 Jn 3:2).[5] Contemplation, therefore, is partaking

---

[3]A. N. Williams, "Contemplation," in *Knowing the Triune God: The Work of the Spirit in the Practices of the Church*, ed. James J. Buckley and David S. Yeago (Grand Rapids: Eerdmans, 2001), 137. "It is the rubric of contemplation that allows us to understand that theological speech in this life is inexorably bonded to the vision of God in the next. Theology understood as contemplation is therefore the consummate discipline, the discipline shaped by paradise because it belongs most essentially to paradise." Ibid., 146.

[4]My friend Matthew Levering provided helpful pushback to my initial article on this point specifically. He was worried (correctly) that I ignored natural contemplation entirely. At the end of the day he may not be entirely satisfied with where I've landed on the issue, but his thoughts have been incredibly helpful to me as I reconsidered my original position. See my article, "'In Your Light They Shall See Light': A Theological Prolegomena for Contemplation," *Journal of Spiritual Formation and Soul Care* 7, no. 1 (2014): 85-106.

[5]This notion has deep roots in the tradition. "The happy congruence of subject-matter and methodology is particularly true of the Fathers' doctrine of contemplation, from Origen to Evagrius, Macarius, and Augustine, and down to Gregory the Great and Maximus the Confessor, all of whom teach an inward and upward ascent that reaches the point where the eternal light transfigures the still veiled earthly forms of salvation. Contemplation here is the flashing anticipation of eschatological illumination, the presaging vision of transparent glory in the form of the Servant." Hans Urs von Balthasar, *The Glory of the Lord: A Theological Aesthetics*, vol. 1, *Seeing the Form*, trans. Erasmo Leiva-Merikakis (New York: Crossroad, 1982), 39.

in the access we are given to the Father in Christ by the Spirit (Eph 2:18-19). Contemplation is an act of faith by which we attend deeply to the divine revelation given in Christ by the Spirit. As such, contemplation is grounded on an act of love in God. Love "alone restores knowledge," John Webster declared, and the mode by which Christians receive that love is through the knowledge received in contemplation.[6] Therefore, contemplation of God has certain key characteristics that will be developed below: First, contemplation is both receptive and responsive to divine revelation, and is not primarily a generative act. In other words, we do not create or achieve contemplation, but instead contemplation is a "receptive act," as it is a human response to divine revelation.[7] Second, contemplation of God is personal-relational, and is therefore not solely an act of the intellect, but is an affective act; or, better, contemplation is an act of the whole person before the face of God. Third, because of this, contemplation is governed by God's revelation, and as such entails a kind of reciprocal relation between God's self-giving and the ascent of the mind (or, better, heart) to God.[8] God's self-giving is known in Son and Spirit, and a proper reception of Son and Spirit entails a contemplative act. (This is, for instance, what Edwards's notion of religious affections was articulating.)

---

[6]John Webster, *God Without Measure: Working Papers in Christian Theology*, vol. 1, *God and the Works of God* (London: T&T Clark, 2015), 84.

[7]Or, in the words of von Balthasar, "Genuine Christian contemplation is derived wholly from the biblical hearing of the word of God." Hans Urs von Balthasar, *Explorations in Theology*, vol. 3, *Creator Spirit*, trans. Brian McNeil, CRV (San Francisco: Ignatius, 1993), 181n1.

[8]This notion of a reciprocal relation has deep roots in the spiritual tradition. Bonaventure, for instance, in his *Itinerarium Mentis in Deum* states, "When in faith the soul believes in Christ as in the uncreated Word, who is the Word and splendor of the Father, it recovers its spiritual sense of hearing and of sight; its hearing so that it might receive the words of Christ, and its sight that it might consider the splendors of that light. . . . With its spiritual senses restored, the soul now sees, hears, smells, tastes, and embraces its beloved." Furthermore, "When these things have been accomplished, and our spirit has been brought into conformity with the heavenly Jerusalem, it is ordered hierarchically so that it can ascend upward. For no one enters into that city unless that city has first descended into the person's heart by means of grace." Bonaventure, *Itinerarium Mentis in Deum*, in *Works of St. Bonaventure*, ed. Philotheus Boehner, OFM, and Zachary Hayes, OFM (St. Bonaventure, NY: Franciscan Institute, 2002), 2:99, 101. For Bonaventure, the soul is brought into conformity with the heavenly realm, because the soul must become ordered by this descent for the purpose of ascent. We are using very different theological machinery to make the same point. The believer's soul is ordered by the love of God received in the descent of Christ and the Spirit, and as such, the believer is prepared to ascend to the Father, in the Son, by the Spirit. This formulation refocuses the notion of ascent around a relational union and communion with the Son by the Spirit such that the believer has access to the Father from within Christ's own Sonship.

To advance theological prolegomena for contemplation, therefore, we first turn to the possibility and ground of contemplation.[9] While natural contemplation can serve as a given—we all know what it means to set our hearts on the object of our desire—it is far from clear how we contemplate God himself. It is not intuitively obvious how one might contemplate God and if it is even truly possible. The possibility and ground of contemplation provides the foundation for our second focus, the contemplation of God discovered in God's revelation, which leads us to a relational understanding of the contemplative act. Christian contemplation can never simply be attending to an object; it is contemplating the God who has revealed himself in Christ Jesus. This then sets up the conclusion, where I will attend to how this may help us consider the question of contemplative forms of prayer.

THE POSSIBILITY OF CONTEMPLATION

The possibility of contemplation begins with the assumption that humankind cannot generate knowledge of God, as if knowing God were some a priori construal of deity.[10] Grounding contemplation theologically entails the recognition that contemplation is not simply a technique or practice, as if we could skillfully ascend to God through reason alone. A Christian account of contemplation must be formed by the self-revelation of God and the shape of redemption. To help give structure to our theological prolegomena for contemplation, therefore, I begin by outlining how contemplation is possible, and only then turn to provide an account of what grounds the Christian's contemplation of God. Both the possibility and ground will be ordered by, and receive their contours from, the economic movement of God to reveal himself in Son and Spirit.

Contemplation is made possible in the economic movement of Son and Spirit to unite humanity to the life of God, first in the incarnation and then individually through union and communion with the Son in the Spirit. As Paul says in Ephesians 2:18, "For through him [Jesus] we . . . have access in one Spirit to the Father." This self-giving of God provides access to the Father through the Son by the Spirit, establishing the contours for both salvation

---

[9]I set up the material this way after attending to the helpful development of Hans Urs von Balthasar in his book *Prayer*, trans. Graham Harrison (San Francisco: Ignatius, 1955).

[10]Or, in other words, contemplation is not simply *about* God qua deity, but is knowledge of him as Father, Son, and Holy Spirit from within the Son by the Holy Spirit.

and contemplation. Furthermore, contemplation is grounded by God's own contemplative life, and within that life, God's contemplation of us within the Son. The first movement of God's economic existence to unite humanity to the life of God creates the possibility for contemplation.[11] The second movement, God's contemplation of his people in his Son, grounds contemplation in a twofold manner. First, humanity does not stand before God unannounced. Those who set their minds on things above, as Paul commands in Colossians 3, are the elect; they are those who are known in Christ. This fact establishes the second, namely, that contemplation of God is only understood eschatologically—from the consummation of all things. In other words, the beatific vision serves to ground contemplation proleptically. Faith will dissolve into sight in glory, and therefore, the sight of glory orients faith now (1 Cor 13:12).

Addressing the possibility of contemplation requires deliberate attention to particular aspects of Christ's role as mediator.[12] In Jesus Christ we are confronted with Immanuel—God with us. Christ ushers into human history the personal presence of God in a way unknown prior. The presence of God in Jesus creates a new reality not complete until the consummation of all things. Christ's presence points forward to the future work of God, but it does so through the abundance of types in the Old Testament. More specifically, the types of God's presence, such as the temple broadly and the holy of holies more narrowly, lay the groundwork for Christ's coming. Christ's presence within the created order undermines the relevance of the temple because the new temple has arrived.[13]

---

[11] I follow Hans Urs von Balthasar here who states, "This is exactly where Christ, with his twofold motion—to the Father and from the Father—can help to make contemplative prayer possible." Balthasar, *Prayer*, 53-54. Balthasar makes his point in reference to contemplative prayer, but it is fitting for contemplation as such as well.

[12] Notice Augustine's focus in this regard, as told by Andrew Louth: "Only through the Incarnation of the Word is the possibility of union with God opened to us. This is very important, for here Augustine cuts himself off completely from his neo-Platonist background. It is important to notice, too, that his doctrine of the Mediator is integral to his understanding of man's response to God. What God requires of man, we have seen, is continence, single-minded devotion to Himself, purity of heart. But without God's condescension to us in the Incarnation to respond to, we will either—in Augustine's view—be provoked to despair by our awareness of sin, or seek to ascend to God under the inspiration of pride." Andrew Louth, *The Origins of the Christian Mystical Tradition: From Plato to Denys*, 2nd ed. (Oxford: Oxford University Press, 2007), 140.

[13] The temple serves as the context to understand contemplation, and the idea of contemplation is really just a conceptual gloss on Psalm 27:4: "One thing have I asked of the LORD, / that will I seek after: / that I may dwell in the house of the LORD / all the days of my life, / to gaze upon

The temple, as the sign of God's presence, is the greatest antitype of Immanuel; it was the mode of God's presence that pointed ahead to God's fullness descending. Jesus' entrance into Jerusalem, therefore, signs the temple's death warrant; the new and better temple had arrived, so the old one was superfluous. Importantly, the concept of the temple is not eradicated by Jesus, since the physical temple was only meant to be a shadow of heavenly realities (Heb 8:5). These heavenly realities remain (Heb 8:1-2), so that in Christ's ascension to the Father he ascends to his right hand as our faithful high priest (Heb 2:17). It is within the context of Jesus' role as high priest that the writer to the Hebrews states, "Let us then with confidence draw near to the throne of grace, that we may receive mercy and find grace to help in time of need" (Heb 4:16). Because of this reality, "We have this as a sure and steadfast anchor of the soul, a hope that enters into the inner place behind the curtain, where Jesus has gone as a forerunner on our behalf" (Heb 6:19-20). Jesus, as the true high priest, is the "better hope . . . through which we draw near to God" (Heb 7:19), and "he is able to save to the uttermost those who draw near to God through him, since he always lives to make intercession for them" (Heb 7:25).

The Son's role as high priest is particularly important for the Son's leading believers before the Father, but it must not serve as the foundational image. Jesus' identity as high priest is one of his offices in relation to humanity, and it is grounded on his primary and eternal identity as the Son of the Father. This identity, grounding his entire mission in redemption history, unveils the deeper truth lurking in the gospel. The Sonship that is Jesus' by nature can become ours by grace. To put that another way, Jesus breaks open the Sonship of the Son—his Sonship—to us, so that the Father's love for the Son is given over to us (Jn 17:26).[14] In Galatians 4:4-7 Paul argues,

> When the fullness of time had come, God sent forth his Son, born of woman, born under the law, to redeem those who were under the law, so that we might receive adoption as sons. And because you are sons, God has sent the Spirit

---

the beauty of the LORD / and to inquire in his temple." This never ceases to be the formal reality of contemplation, but "temple" is now understood as Christ. Even the word *contemplation*, claims Andrew Louth, originally meant something like "what goes on in a temple." See Andrew Louth, "Theology, Contemplation and the University," *Studies in Christian Ethics* 17 (2004): 73.

[14]Note that the failure to live by the grace of God in virtue is equated with being excluded from the *life* of God (Eph 4:17).

of his Son into our hearts, crying "Abba! Father!" So you are no longer a slave, but a son, and if a son, then an heir through God.

God sends forth his Son because adoption is the governing issue of soteriology. This adoption as sons and daughters of God is received in the Son and accomplished by the uniting presence of the Holy Spirit. In other words, it is in Christ's Sonship that believers come to stand before the Father as sons and daughters. Christians come to participate in the Sonship of Christ and are therefore able to proclaim with Christ, "Abba! Father!" Therefore, in this grace of God we begin to pray, not our prayer, but Jesus' prayer before the Father. Jesus is the one who prays "Abba! Father!" but that prayer is now ours as we partake of his life by the Spirit. It is within this new reality, the reality of adoption in Christ's own Sonship, that contemplation is made possible.

Against the backdrop of Christ's work to lead us before the Father, it is important to read Colossians 3:1-3: "If then you have been raised with Christ, seek the things that are above, where Christ is, seated at the right hand of God. Set your minds on things that are above, not on things that are on earth. For you have died, and your life is hidden with Christ in God."[15] This passage follows Paul's admonition against a worldly spirituality, one with a misguided asceticism, and one that ultimately fails to hold fast to the head—namely, Christ. It is here that we can begin to see the contours of a distinctively Christian account of contemplation; we find that we are called to set our minds on things above, but only because Christ is there, and we are in Christ. We can approach the throne of grace with confidence because we are ushered before that throne of grace within the very person of Christ. Following the Reformed notion of ascent, we ascend to the Father within the person of the Son through communion with him.[16] Contemplation is made possible, therefore, because we are united to the Son and because that Son

---

[15]In a real sense, in contemplation one comes to find oneself. This discovery of self is not an inner gazing, but is the fruit of setting one's mind on God and realizing that "your life is hidden with Christ in God" (Col 3:3). Who you are is alien to yourself. It is in this vein that Balthasar will state, "Simon the fisherman could have explored every region of his ego prior to his encounter with Christ, but he would not have found 'Peter' there; for the present, the 'form' summed up in the name 'Peter,' the particular mission reserved for him alone, is hidden in the mystery of Christ's soul." Balthasar, *Prayer*, 60.

[16]Julie Canlis helpfully narrates the Reformed impulse in her work on ascent and ascension in Calvin when she writes, "Ascent is into *sonship*, but never as *the Son*." She clarifies this notion by claiming, "The mystical ascent is this deeper and deeper burrowing into Christ (always pneumatologically conceived), not our effort to do so. His ascent is our path and goal. His

leads us before the Father.[17] Putting this in terms of prayer, we pray to the Father, in the Son, and by the Holy Spirit, because the form of our prayer follows the contours of God's self-giving. The form by which God has revealed and given himself to us in Jesus Christ and his Spirit provides the contours of contemplation.[18]

THE GROUND OF CONTEMPLATION:
THE ASCENSION OF CHRIST

Contemplation is made possible through the sending of the Son and Spirit to provide access to the Father, but to ground contemplation, to articulate its theological structure, we must address the present activity of the Son and Spirit in us and through us before the Father. There is a twofold orientation to the christologically conditioned notion of contemplation we are describing: First, humanity does not come before God unannounced, but as those who are known—contemplated—in Christ. Second, contemplation is understood eschatologically; the dark sight of faith is the reality of all knowledge of God prior to the consummation of all things. These two points serve to organize the material in this section. What unites these two points is the present ministry of Christ. We are known in Christ, and Christ himself leads us before the Father. This leading of Christ is done, second, with an eye toward eternity when we shall see "face to face,"[19] when Christ will

---

narrative has become our own." Julie Canlis, *Calvin's Ladder: A Spiritual Theology of Ascent and Ascension* (Grand Rapids: Eerdmans, 2010) 237-38, 51.

[17]"The goal of the Trinity's work in history, then, is to draw us into contemplative friendship with the Trinity. This contemplative friendship, Augustine is clear, cannot fully be enjoyed prior to the vision of God, eternal life. Yet in faith the firstfruits have arrived. In this state of imperfect contemplation, Christians 'ought to think about the Lord our God always, and can never think about him as he deserves; . . . at all times we should be praising him and blessing him, and yet no words of ours are capable of expressing him.'" Matthew Levering, "Friendship and Trinitarian Theology: Response to Karen Kilby," *International Journal of Systematic Theology* 9, no. 1 (2007): 49.

[18]"Christian prayer can attain to God only along the path that God himself has trod; otherwise it stumbles out of the world and into the void, falling prey to the temptation of taking this void to be God or of taking God to be nothingness itself." Hans Urs von Balthasar, *The Threefold Garland: The World's Salvation in Mary's Prayer*, trans. Erasmo Leiva-Merikakis (San Francisco: Ignatius, 1978), 19.

[19]If we were to push beyond the ground and possibility of contemplation, we could ask the deeper question concerning the *object* of contemplation. Jesus claims that "whoever has seen me has seen the Father" (Jn 14:9); therefore we could push the question forward and ponder whether this is circumstantial in the scheme of redemptive history (in the age of faith), which will therefore dissolve into a sight of the Father and the Son in the Spirit.

consummate his work of redemption. Taking these in turn, we see that Jesus has already drawn near to the Father in our stead, and Jesus already draws near to the Father in prayer for us.[20]

In Christ: Contemplation conditioned by election. Christ, our great high priest, stands in the "presence of God on our behalf" (Heb 9:24). This is not simply the work of the Son in the economy, but is the Spirit's work as well. As Paul notes in Romans 8: "Likewise the Spirit helps us in our weakness. For we do not know what to pray for as we ought, but the Spirit himself intercedes for us with groanings too deep for words. And he who searches hearts knows what is the mind of the Spirit, because the Spirit intercedes for the saints according to the will of God" (Rom 8:26-27). Just as we boldly approach the throne of grace in confidence, not in ourselves but in Christ, so too we boldly approach God as one who has already been approached by God. We enter into prayer through Christ, by his indwelling Spirit, so that we can set our minds on things above, where Christ is, and where we are in Christ.

At the heart of contemplation we find not our action but God's, which breaks open its possibility. He is the Alpha and Omega in the affairs of this reality. The possibility of contemplation, as outlined above, is created by God's movement to us and for us in Son and Spirit, and by tracing this movement further we can see the structure of contemplation in the prayer life of the Son and Spirit for us, in us, and through us. Contemplation is established on the fact that our God is the God who abides in us (1 Jn 4:15), and that God's act of abiding grounds our abiding in Christ (Jn 15:4). Even as Christ is "able to save to the uttermost those who draw near to God through him," we come before him as those known deeply by the Father because Christ "always lives to make intercession for them" (Heb 7:25). In the affairs of redemption, in their entirety, we proclaim, All is from you,

---

Or, on the other hand, we could follow the likes of John Owen and argue that the sight of the Son is the only true sight available for creatures—even glorified creatures. See my chapter "Jonathan Edwards's Reformed Doctrine of the Beatific Vision," in *Jonathan Edwards and Scotland*, ed. Ken Minkema, Adriaan Neale, and Kelly van Andel (Edinburgh: Dunedin Academic Press, 2011), 171-88; and my article "A Spiritual Sight of Love: Constructing a Doctrine of the Beatific Vision," Union, www.uniontheology.org/resources/bible/biblical -theology/a-spiritual-sight-of-love-constructing-a-doctrine-of-the-beatific-vision.

[20]In Augustine's words, "As it is, our faith has now in some sense followed him in whom we have believed to where he has ascended." Augustine, *The Trinity*, Works of St. Augustine: A New Translation for the 21st Century I/5 (New York: New City Press, 1991), 4.4.24., p. 170.

through you and to you, to you be glory forever and ever (see Rom 11:36). The freedom of the Christian rests in this reality: all is from God, through him and to him, and Christ is our intercessor, mediator, and substitute. We can approach the throne of grace boldly because we do not ride the wave of our own ability or value, but, in Balthasar's words, we "find ourselves afloat like a ship above the immense depths of an entirely different element,"[21] which is nothing less than the unfathomable love of the Father in the Son and the Spirit. Within God's praying, we are not simply received as valid observers of the divine life but are, in the words of Peter, "partakers of the divine nature" (2 Pet 1:4). These unfathomable depths are grounded not only in God's action for us but also in the eternal decree—before time we were known and received—elected, in him (Eph 1:4-6). Within the fullness of God's gazing on us, his contemplation of us in Christ—grounded eternally and known already in Christ—we are received ("your life is hidden with Christ in God," Col 3:3).[22] Furthermore, Balthasar claims, "In the Son, the Father contemplates us from before all time, and is well pleased. It is in the Son that the Father can predestine and choose us to be his children, fellow children with the one, eternal Child, who, from the beginning of the world, intervenes as sponsor for his alienated creatures."[23]

Therefore, the ultimate grounding of contemplation is being contemplated in Christ, being seen and known in the love of the Father on the Son (Jn 17:26). Christ revealed himself as the one who was fully known, and yet also the one who had seen the Father, an act we are repeatedly told is impossible, lest one die (see Judg 13:22; Jn 1:18; 6:46). Christ is the one who has seen the Father, and in him we see through the mirror dimly, anticipating when we will know God as we have been known by him (1 Cor 13:12). Jesus' relation with the Father is broken open for us such that we share the knowledge he sanctified for humanity in his own life. The beatific vision,

---

[21]Balthasar, *Prayer*, 44.

[22]Balthasar notes, "God's gaze is not passive (otherwise it would not be a *divine* gaze); he does not merely 'read off' or ascertain: his gaze is creative, generative, originative, by his utterly free decree." Ibid., 40. Balthasar continues, "The creature comes into being out of the bottomless freedom of God; this coming-to-be began with God's loving gaze, in which he chose the creature before all eternity. This election is made known to us in time through our calling and justification, and is perfected in that utterly sovereign act of judgment in which God finally takes the creature out of time and sets him in His eternity to 'glorify' him." Ibid., 42.

[23]Balthasar, *Prayer*, 51.

known in Christ, is the fulfilment of our dim knowledge by faith, whereas contemplation is proleptically oriented by this perfect vision. As a vision in Christ, it is located within a filial vision of Father on the Son, and therefore the Father's love of the Son is the context of our seeing God as Father in our gazing on Christ ("Whoever has seen me has seen the Father," Jn 14:9). We come to share in Christ's sight of the Father, as we come to partake internally in Christ's receiving the Father's gaze ("This is my beloved Son, with whom I am well pleased," Mt 3:17). This is a personal-relational knowing that entails knowing as one is known, such that the sight of God is both penetrating and revealing; it is the sight as one undone by the Word that leaves one "naked and exposed" before God (Heb 4:13) while simultaneously upholding the person in the love and knowledge of God. It is an anticipation of the beatific vision where love is known in full.

In Christ: Contemplation conditioned by eschatology. In Christ we are known, and in Christ we come to know—this is the christological medium of contemplation. The reality of being in Christ serves to delineate both the possibility and the ground for contemplation, a contemplation available because Christ took on our human nature and is now our high priest. The believer has been given this access point to contemplation in the Son, but it is more than a mere entrance: the Son is the path of knowing itself. He is the light of God; or, as put by the psalmist, "in your light do we see light" (Ps 36:9).[24] The light of God's economic existence is the medium that illumines the knowledge of God (or, with Paul, "that the God of our Lord Jesus Christ, the Father of glory, may give you the Spirit of wisdom and of revelation in the knowledge of him, having the eyes of your hearts enlightened" Eph 1:17-18). In Christ we have been called "out of darkness into his marvelous light" (1 Pet 2:9), and as is promised in the new Jerusalem, the glory of God will be the light that illumines reality for the Christian—a light known in the darkness of faith here, but that will illumine all in the presence of God in eternity. It is this light that we see dawning in our own era of redemption history, a light that is dim but still functions to order society around the Lamb, the light of the world.

---

[24]The immediate context of this section of Ps 36 focuses on God's abundance, delight, and overflow of his life. In fact, a mixed metaphor is used: "For with you is the fountain of life; / in your light do we see light." Both light and water (fountain) entail the image of overflow and abundance. This overflow is the economic movement of Son and Spirit to bring God's very life to his people.

It is within the illuminating presence of the Spirit that we come to see Christ. Understanding contemplation within this context helps to focus our attention on the nature of contemplation as knowing and being known. Contemplation anticipates the face-to-face knowing of eternity; this is its goal. Face-to-face knowledge denotes both proximity as well as intimate knowledge within a specifically relational register. Knowledge of God is partaking in God's self-knowledge; it is coming to know within the Sonship of the Son, and is therefore coming to know as a child. This reality pushes all knowledge of God into a specific mold that is relational, Christocentric, and eschatologically oriented. In other words, we are those who live in anticipation of the face-to-face sight of eternity; here, our sight is through the dark mirror of faith, but it always longs for what will come. "No man shall ever behold the glory of Christ by sight hereafter," John Owen asserts, "who doth not in some measure behold it by faith here in this world."[25] In the consummation of all things, God's people will, in some sense, see him, but whatever that sight entails in eternity, in our stage of redemption history this reality is a sense of the heart that captivates the "eyes of the heart." This is a sight by faith, and is therefore only visual in a spiritual sense. In eternity we will be like him, because we will see him as he is (1 Jn 3:2), yet even now, "we all, with unveiled face, beholding the glory of the Lord, are being transformed into the same image from one degree of glory to another" (2 Cor 3:18), and "God, who said, 'Let light shine out of darkness,' has shone in our hearts to give the light of the knowledge of the glory of God in the face of Jesus Christ" (2 Cor 4:6). God's people see God in Christ by the Spirit in the dim sight of faith, and this sight is transformative but incomplete. In eternity, this darkness will fade away.

The grounding of contemplation: A summary. By way of summary, contemplation has always been understood as a kind of seeing God. In Christ, prior to his return, this seeing is by faith. This sight by faith is contemplation— it is more than simply knowledge about God, but is knowledge in a particular

---

[25]John Owen, *Meditations and Discourses on the Glory of Christ in his Person, Office, and Grace: with The Differences Between Faith and Sight; Applied Unto the Use of Them that Believe*, in *The Works of John Owen*, ed. W. Gould (London: Johnstone and Hunter, 1850–1855), 1:288. Owen states, "There are, therefore, two ways or degrees of beholding the glory of Christ, which are constantly distinguished in the Scripture. The one is by *faith*, in this world—which is 'the evidence of things not seen'; the other is by *sight*, or immediate vision in eternity, 2 Cor. V. 7, 'We walk by faith, and not by sight.'" Ibid., 288.

relational register—it is beholding the glory of the Lord. This sight is made possible by the movement of the Son and Spirit to draw creatures into the life of the Son by the Spirit so that they have access to the Father. The structure of this vision is the continuing activity of Son and Spirit for, with, and through a person as they set their minds on things above. This development of contemplation has a twofold orientation: First, contemplation is grounded in God's contemplation of his people in Christ, which is itself grounded in the fact that the Son who took on human nature is the One who has seen the Father (Jn 6:46). It is in him that we are received and in him that we come to stand before the Father. By taking on human nature, the Son has become the mediator of all knowledge of God in his person. The Son is the pilgrim, the child and the person of faith, and it is in union with the Son that we can know God as our Father. Second, contemplation is oriented by the beatific reality of glory, where we will see God face to face, a notion that denotes both proximity and relationality. All knowledge of God is colored by Christ's work and the eschatological reality of our existence. Therefore, it is within this matrix that we have to understand contemplation.

My account, as offered here, has yet to really speak to the act of contemplation, focusing more on its possibility and its grounding. Articulating the act of contemplation is necessary for a full-fledged account of contemplation and/or contemplative prayer (which is beyond the scope of this chapter). But it must be emphasized that contemplation entails a subjective and experiential reality that is founded on the objective reality as described here. This means that contemplation has internal within it an existential and affective movement of the heart as it is an ascent of love within the person of the Son, by the Spirit, to the Father, as it is a receptive act of receiving the love poured into one's heart by the Spirit (Rom 5:5), upholding them in this ascent. In the Son and by the Spirit believers are sanctified for the presence of God and ushered into that presence through the Son and Spirit's continued ministry, and this ascent to God is in communion with God in the person of the Son by the Spirit. This is an ascent of relational knowing within the love of God, such that God's love awakens the desire for its completion.

Therefore, here and now, the act of contemplation will open the believer's heart, in the midst of its brokenness and sin, to the reality of God and the indwelling corruption still at work. John notes the necessity of assuring one's heart before God when our "heart condemns us," because "God is greater than our heart, and he knows everything" (1 Jn 3:20). The assurance the heart needs in God's presence is an assurance that the ground of our contemplation and presence is not our own ability, value, or virtue, but is Christ's. When our heart condemns us, the movement of the heart should be a wholesale abandonment of ourselves in the hands of the Father, trusting that it is only there where we are truly secure. This is why it is imperative to recall that the current of contemplation follows the contours of love, where we come to know and trust in the love of God only truly in our brokenness, anxiety, and fear. The beginning of wisdom is the fear of the Lord, we are told, but we trust that it is not the end; it is only as we come to experientially know the love of God that our fears are cast away (Prov 9:10; 1 Jn 4:18).

In our contemplation we come to know ourselves, our true selves, before the face of God. In the words of John Calvin, "It is certain that a man never achieves a clear knowledge of himself unless he has first looked upon God's face, and then descends from contemplating him to scrutinize himself."[26] But it is in this movement from God to ourselves that the Christian must come to recognize their life hidden with Christ in God. The movement of the heart always leads back to God in love, in whom we know life as we discover ourselves upheld by the love of another. This is the love received and known in Christ Jesus, made available by the Spirit, which we receive as we come in faith. The act of contemplation by faith is the experimental reception and trust of this truth, being open to how much of our hearts still want to discover life, not in God, but in oneself. Contemplation by faith, therefore, is the act of resting in God's loving presence in Jesus, holding open the truth of oneself to God and trusting that "there is therefore now no condemnation for those who are in Christ Jesus" (Rom 8:1).

In light of this, let me draw these various threads together. I argued that the possibility of contemplation is established through the economic movement of God to draw his people into his own life. This movement breaks open the Father-Son relationship so that Christ's own Sonship is made available to fallen humanity. We do not approach the Father in

---

[26]John Calvin, *Institutes of the Christian Religion*, ed. John T. McNeill, trans. Ford Lewis Battles, Library of Christian Classics (Philadelphia: Westminster, 1960), 1.1.2.

isolation, but within the intercession of both Son and Spirit. This will prove to be true for contemplation as well. As we are indwelt by the Spirit and united to the life of the Son—the seeing One—we come to see within his life and come to know ourselves as those seen by God in him.[27] Our relationship to the Father is paved by God's unrelenting love, known in Christ through the Spirit's light of love. Likewise, all knowledge of God is pushed into this mold. Our knowing by faith is knowing in the Son's own knowledge. Our pilgrim knowledge is given this specific christological orientation and is formed by its teleology, that one day we too shall see. This, I suggest, provides the ground and possibility of contemplation, and as such, offers specific direction for addressing at least one form of prayer.

CONCLUSION: CONTEMPLATIVE PRAYER?

To conclude, let me point ahead in several ways I believe this account of contemplation might help form at least one kind of prayer along a specific trajectory. Christian theologies of prayer should not be governed by notions of mental health, conscious states, or the quest for transcendence, but should be ordered by the God who has given himself to his people in Jesus Christ. By focusing on God's self-revelation in Christ by the Spirit, and by orienting contemplation by faith with an eye to the beatific vision, we are given a specific context in which to talk about prayer as such and, in particular, inquire into the possibility of an evangelical form of silent or wordless prayer (that, for the sake of common usage, can be called *contemplative prayer*).[28] In brief, the goal of this conclusion is simply to utilize my foregoing development to suggest an account of contemplative prayer from within the movement of God's self-giving that would count as a distinctively evangelical

---

[27]Christ is the one who has seen the Father (Jn 6:46), and in him we too see clearly. But once again, this seeing is not abstracted from redemption, such that we view an object as if we could be detached from it. Rather, seeing God is seeing the Father, *our* Father, and therefore seeing as his children. This seeing is seeing *in* the Son and therefore in his Sonship. Note Edwards's focus on the beatific vision in glory, "The saints shall enjoy God as partaking with Christ of his enjoyment of God, for they are united to him and are glorified and made happy in the enjoyment of God as his members. . . . They being in Christ shall partake of the love of God the Father to Christ, and as the son knows the Father so they shall partake with him in his sight of God, as being as it were parts of him as he is in the bosom of the Father." Jonathan Edwards Center archive, Unpublished Sermon, Rom. 2:10, #373 [L. 44v.].

[28]It is unclear in my mind if the language of contemplative prayer is helpful, but I'll use it here simply because it has become a widely accepted term.

kind of contemplative prayer. While this is not the only way to construe contemplative prayer, even of a supposedly evangelical variety, the contours outlined above help to focus our attention on a specific way we can do so. Here, contemplative prayer is not an attempt to circumnavigate God's self-revelation, nor is it an attempt to achieve a transcendent state or union with Being (or any other such notion). Contemplation is the experiential corollary, on my model, to faith. Contemplation entails grasping onto Christ, who has gone beyond the veil, and who serves as our anchor of the soul in the presence of God (Heb 6:19). Contemplative prayer, then, is simply putting our faith in this reality. It is coming before God as the one who truly does trust that on the cross, "It is finished" (Jn 19:30), and casting one's soul on his promise.

What makes this contemplative, therefore, rather than another sort of prayer, is that it is a mode of prayer whose goal is to rest entirely on the work of Christ and the Spirit. In this sense, silent or wordless prayer is resting on the intercession of Son and Spirit, trusting that their words are enough for you. Furthermore, silence in prayer is repentant, as we come to recognize that our words are often selfish attempts to manipulate God rather than submit to him. The reality of one's heart in contemplative prayer, positively or negatively, provides opportunities to hand oneself over to God in full. This kind of prayer is utter submission—it is a giving-over of oneself to God—such that everything in one's heart is fodder for self-giving. Anything that the heart provides in this silence, whether thought, image, or experience, can be handed over to God as something he has atoned for, such that the whole of the person rests in the objective work of Christ. This is the wordless posture of heart that seeks to embody Psalm 121:

> I *lift up my eyes* to the hills.
> From where does my help come?
> My help comes from the LORD,
> who made heaven and earth. (Ps 121:1-2)

This prayer is a lifting of the eyes of the heart to God, trusting that it is in him alone that help truly comes. Put in another way, this is the prayerful equivalent to our "upward call of God in Christ Jesus" (Phil 3:14). Our upward call is the call to ascend in the person of the Son to the Father, because the Father himself loves us (Jn 16:27). Because this upward call is in Christ Jesus, we lift our eyes because the help that comes from the hills is the love of God known in Christ Jesus and offered in abundance in the Spirit.

It is from within this love that we can understand a distinctively evangelical form of contemplative prayer. The love of God that surpasses knowledge (Eph 3:19) is precisely the love of God that calls us into silence and trust. In this sense, contemplative prayer is a silent trust of God with a fourfold orientation:[29] First, contemplative prayer leads in silence as it stands before the God of wonder and rests in his gracious abundance. This silence is not a rejection of words, but is the childlike trust of faith. In silence, one is choosing not to trust in their own words, but in the intercessory prayers of the Son and the Spirit, who pray for all believers (Rom 8:26-27; Heb 7:26). In silence the believer comes to see how much their heart longs to atone for its own sins, to hide from God, and to use faithfulness as a way to keep God at arm's length. In silence the believer is awoken to their heart's continued sinfulness and depravity in the same moment that it is receiving and abiding in the love of the Son. In contemplation the believer is simultaneously left "naked and exposed" before God (Heb 4:12-13) and clothed with his robes of righteousness and received in the love of the Father on his Son (Jn 17:26).

Second, the person practicing contemplative prayer recognizes that they stand before the judge, and therefore their heart breaks open in fear, anxiety, guilt, and shame, and even, perhaps, anger and sadness at the thought of one such as them before a God such as this. This is the space where humility is forged. But it is also the place where Christ is grasped all the more, remembering that we do not ascend the throne of God climbing our own virtues, but through the righteousness of Christ alone. This is why the imperative to "draw near" is connected to Christ's priestly work on our behalf (Heb 7:11-25). In drawing near to God within the person of the Son, one comes to know that they are only ever upheld as they are held by the Son before the Father.

---

[29]I am utilizing Bernard's four kinds of contemplation here to articulate four features of contemplative prayer. The four are (1) to wonder at majesty; (2) look on the judgments of God; (3) remember kindness; and (4) rest wholly in the expectation of what is promised. See Bernard of Clairvaux, *On Consideration*, in *Bernard of Clairvaux: Selected Works*, Classics of Western Spirituality, trans. G. R. Evans (New York: Paulist Press, 1987), 171-72.

Third, the contemplative attends to the gracious goodness and mercy of God, not only for one's justification, but even for their sanctification (1 Cor 1:30). God is our all in all, and as such, he is the abundant goodness we seek. In so doing, the contemplative offers themselves in this prayer, holding their heart open to God and trusting that he will uphold them in his love. Contemplation by faith, in this sense, is setting our mind on the unseen, and not on the seen (2 Cor 4:18), so that our hearts can be calibrated to the goodness, truth, and beauty of God himself. It is not only in our objective knowing but in the existential recalibration of one's soul in gazing on the beauty of the Lord, that one comes to see Christianly in this age of faith.

Last, the one praying contemplatively sets their hearts on the promises embraced in Christ, trusting that whatever is true of our circumstances now, they are not to be compared with the abundant glory to be known then. This prayer "forgets what is past, rests wholly in the expectation of what is promised (Phil 3:13), which nourishes patience and nerves the arm of perseverance, for what is promised is eternal," Bernard of Clairvaux declares. He continues with the admonition, "He must still be sought who has not yet been found (Mt 7:7) fully, but he is perhaps sought more worthily and found more easily by prayer than discussion."[30] The texture of this silence, therefore, takes on the reality of one's heart before God in lament, struggle, praise, or even the simple longing for God's will to be done on earth as it is in heaven. This prayer is the wordless longing of hope before every tear is wiped away, and as such, it is the natural movement of the human heart being formed by faith, hope, and love.

A distinctively evangelical form of contemplative prayer rests fully on the work of Christ in his justification of the unrighteous and continues to rest fully on him as one's sanctification (1 Cor 1:30). Far from a spiritually elitist vocation, contemplative prayer is a prayer of utter abandon and trust of the God who saves. Contemplative prayer, therefore, is never to be the only prayer of God's people, but it is a mode of Christian praying. In this prayer Christians lay themselves at the foot of the cross and reach out for their Lord to carry them when they cannot carry themselves. The wordlessness of this prayer is not, in one sense, wordless, because it entails the heart taking the posture of "Amen" to the intercession of Son and Spirit, as the Son holds

---

[30]Bernard of Clairvaux, *On Consideration*, 172.

the believer before God as their great high priest and as the Spirit cries out with groanings too deep for words.[31] In faith, the person praying contemplatively is seeking "the things that are above, where Christ is, seated at the right hand of God" (Col 3:1). In Christ, this person discovers that they are already "hidden with Christ in God" (Col 3:3) and, as such, can rest fully in his love.

---

[31]Jonathan Edwards's wife, Sarah, and one of his main archetypes for true Christian spirituality, once wrote, "The sweet language of my soul continually was, 'Amen, Lord Jesus! Amen, Lord Jesus!'" This is at the heart, I think, of the evangelical nature of contemplative prayer. *Works of Jonathan Edwards Online*, vol. 41, *Family Writings and Related Documents*, accessed February 17, 2017, http://edwards.yale.edu/archive?path=aHR0cDovL2Vkd2FyZHMueWFsZS5lZHUvY2dp LWJpbi9uZXdwaGlsby9nZXRvYmplY3QucGw/Yy4zzOToyLndqZW8=.

GOSPEL-CENTERED CONTEMPLATION?

A Proposal

RYAN A. BRANDT

A MODERATE PERUSAL OF EVANGELICAL LITERATURE reveals a lack of understanding and appreciation of contemplation. We incessantly speak about theology but seldom discuss its relevance in the contemplative or prayerful life. A. W. Tozer once quipped of this problem: "Once [Christians] have found God, they no longer need to seek Him."[1] Perhaps we could state his point more expressly: once Christians have understood God, they no longer need to experience him. Of course, few evangelicals would confess this, but the intellectualist way some do theology leads to the problem at hand.

This chapter intends to be a theological apologetic for contemplation, defending and advancing a gospel-centered[2] understanding of contemplation for the purposes of Christian theology and life. The thesis is that contemplation is entailed by theological constructs within Christianity. This chapter will make five interrelated arguments, each one focusing on specific theological categories wherein contemplation is shown to be inseparable from Christianity and its gospel: Contemplation is (1) grounded in the Trinity, (2) entailed by the concept of union with Christ, (3) expressed through the believer's experience of love in Christ, (4) reflected in a transformational reading of Scripture, and (5) highlighted as a foretaste of the beatific vision.

---

[1] A. W. Tozer, *The Pursuit of God* (Las Vegas: Martino, 2009), 16-17.
[2] In other words, while there are other conceptions of contemplation, this chapter seeks to defend a particularly Christian variety of contemplation that is founded on and focused on themes of the Christian gospel.

Before continuing with the argument, I will briefly define what I mean by contemplation, since there are many varieties of the word and concept. As I define it, echoing Thomas Aquinas and John Webster, contemplation is captivated attention to the triune God.[3] It consists of a gospel-centered gazing and enjoying God, and it culminates in personal transformation, experience of love, and spiritual rest and peace in communion with Christ.

CONTEMPLATION IS GROUNDED IN THE TRIUNE NATURE OF GOD

The first argument for contemplation is that the triune God is its ontological basis. God is the perfect gazer of himself, and his gazing becomes the foundation of our gazing.[4] The triune God is perfect, which means, as Gregory of Nyssa notes, that he is the standard of all things good and "he admits diminution in nothing."[5] While God's perfection is evident in each iota of his nature and activity, this chapter will limit its discussion to God's perfect relationship (Trinity) and glory (beauty) for the purposes of understanding the basis of contemplation.

First, the triune God is the standard of relationship. In his earthly ministry, Jesus Christ attests to his intimate relationship with his Father: "All

---

[3]This definition refers specifically to Christian contemplation. Contemplation consists of "the simple act of gazing on the truth" (Thomas Aquinas, *Summa theologiae*, trans. Laurence Shapcote, OP, ed. John Mortensen and Enrique Alarcón [Lander, WY: The Aquinas Institute, 2012], IIa-IIae, q. 180, a. 3, ad 1). Or John Webster: "Contemplation is rapt attention to God the cause of all things rather than to the things of which he is the cause" (John Webster, "What Makes Theology Theological?," *Journal of Analytic Theology* 3 [May 2015]: 24).

[4]Like all theological propositions, God's gaze here must be understood in an analogical sense. When we describe the human gaze, we typically denote a visual sense. However, God does not visualize or see as we see. When we speak of God's gaze, consequently, we refer to at least two aspects of God's gaze in himself: it is (1) intellectual, that is, God knowing himself, and (2) experiential, God loving himself. This definition would find favor with Aquinas, who suggests that the contemplative life is intellectual and emotive, though he does seat the final blessedness primarily in the intellect (Thomas Aquinas, *Summa theologiae*, IIa-IIae, q. 180, a. 1 and 7; cf. Ia-IIae, q. 3, a. 4), and also Jonathan Edwards, who often suggests that God's existence, understanding, and love (and thus happiness/delight) are each reciprocally related (Jonathan Edwards, *Discourse on the Trinity*, in *The Works of Jonathan Edwards*, vol. 21, *Writings on the Trinity, Grace, and Faith*, ed. Sang Hyun Lee [New Haven, CT: Yale University Press, 2003], 113, 143).

[5]Gregory of Nyssa, *On the Holy Spirit: Against the Followers of Macedonius*, in *The Nicene and Post-Nicene Fathers*, ed. Philip Schaff, Series 2 (repr., Peabody, MA: Hendrickson, 2004), 5:318. Beforehand, he clarifies, God "exhibits perfection in every line in which the good can be found. If it fails and comes short of perfection in any single point," it cannot "be or be called Deity at all" (ibid., 316).

things have been handed over to me by my Father, and no one knows the Son except the Father, and no one knows the Father except the Son and anyone to whom the Son chooses to reveal him" (Mt 11:27). The relationship within the Godhead is, at the very least, characterized by an intimate, extensive knowledge. It is likewise characterized in terms of a family metaphor, since, as Paul elaborates, we become in Christ "citizens with the saints and members of the household of God" (Eph 2:19).[6] The triune God is perfect relationship, and through Christ we are brought into this perfect family relationship.

God is also the standard of beauty. As he is intimate relationship, so also he is glorious sublimity, the most beautiful thing on which to gaze. The Gospel of John often affirms this idea. For example, Jesus speaks about his glory that he wants to share with believers: "Father, I desire that they also . . . may be with me where I am, to see my glory that you have given me" (Jn 17:24). Paul affirms this kind of reasoning, as recorded in his wonderful exclamation of the "depth of the riches and wisdom and knowledge of God" (Rom 11:33). Indeed, various biblical authors often associate God—or godly things—with beauty (Ps 50:2; Is 60:9; Ezek 28:12; 31:8, 9). For it is God who has "made everything beautiful in its time," as the author of Ecclesiastes writes (Eccl 3:11). God is the most beautiful existence, and nothing that exists or could ever exist even approaches his beauty.

To draw these discussions together, God is perfect relationship; he is also perfect beauty. Therefore, as God is perfect relationship and beauty, so also he is the perfect gazer, knower, and enjoyer of himself. The Trinity thus implicates contemplation within the three persons. Jonathan Edwards cryptically explains, the Son's beholding is his existing.[7] For the triune God to exist is to gaze on himself, and vice versa. The triune God is thus necessarily defined as the contemplator par excellence. He is the supreme beauty, and thus he gazes on himself first and

---

[6]We also overhear this idea in a conversation between the Son and the Father in Jn 14–17: Jesus explains, "Those who love me will keep my word, and my Father will love them, and we will come to them and make our home with them" (Jn 14:23). For indeed, he, the Father, and the Spirit are one (Jn 17:21-23).

[7]The Son "beholds himself in himself," so that the Son's gazing is "nothing else but his existing." Furthermore, "The idea's beholding is the idea's existing" (Edwards, *Discourse on the Trinity*, 143).

foremost. As he gazes on himself, he grounds our ectypal gazing of God in Christ.[8]

This initial argument, consequently, sets contemplation on its ontological foundation, rather than speculating its pragmatic fruits—a common but understandable mistake in the history of the church. God gazes and enjoys himself fully. Therefore, when we speak of contemplation, we refer not to a work done by us, first and foremost; rather, we speak of God's eternal act within himself: his perfect reciprocal gaze.

CONTEMPLATION IS ENTAILED BY UNION WITH CHRIST

Second, contemplation follows from the reality of union with Christ. Namely, we contemplate for the very reason that we are in union and communion with Christ.

Union with Christ is a polyvalent metaphor, one that can be applied to numerous discussions in theology, especially those concerning the atonement, salvation, and ethics.[9] Union with Christ typically summarizes the person's identity upon repentance and faith. The union itself does not implicate a Neoplatonic, mystical absorption of the self into the divine, though it does inspire a sense of mystery and awe. While in Adam previously, believers are now in Christ and are given his identity and all his benefits implied therein.

Substantiating the argument of this chapter, contemplation exists for believers because God indwells them in Christ: Just as Jesus Christ claims that he is "in my Father," so also believers are in him and him in them (Jn 14:20; cf. 1 Jn 2:5-6; 4:15). Indeed, people previously in Adam, upon faith and repentance, transfer their allegiance to Christ, the head; accordingly, they are

---

[8]The Trinity, in Lewis Ayres's apt words, "is drawn from Scripture through the Spirit's work as an initial glimpse of that which will be our sight in eternity" (Lewis Ayres, "As We are One: Thinking into the Mystery," in *Advancing Trinitarian Theology: Explorations in Constructive Dogmatics*, ed. Oliver Crisp and Fred Sanders [Grand Rapids: Zondervan, 2014], 109).

[9]For example, especially in Reformed theology, union with Christ is understood to be the undergirding or overarching metaphor of salvation, namely, salvation as election, calling, regeneration, conversion, justification, sanctification, and glorification. Calvin makes this clear (John Calvin, *Institutes of the Christian Religion*, ed. John T. McNeill, trans. Ford Lewis Battles, Library of Christian Classics [Philadelphia: Westminster, 1960], 3.1.1-4; 3.2.24). For a contrasting view, which understands union with Christ as experiential, and thus one step in the *ordo salutis*, see Bruce Demarest, *The Cross and Salvation: The Doctrine of Salvation*, Foundations of Evangelical Theology (Wheaton, IL: Crossway, 1997), 326-29.

united to Christ.[10] Contemplation is that spiritual discipline whereby they, sons and daughters, gaze and enjoy God, the source of their salvation. It involves communion with Christ and a deepening knowledge of God, which is epitomized by theological reasoning ending in meditation. More profoundly, it involves a deep-seated appreciation of the vast mysterious depths of God that knowledge cannot possibly attain, and for which we simply gaze and enjoy, resting in his ineffable love. As Aquinas notes, "The contemplative life . . . pertains to the intellect" but also "terminates in delight."[11] It is by the means of contemplation that we experience the psalmist's earnest desire:

> One thing have I asked of the LORD . . .
> that I may dwell in the house of the LORD
>   all the days of my life,
> to gaze upon the beauty of the LORD,
>   and to inquire in his temple. (Ps 27:4)

Contemplation thus establishes the notable difference between knowing God propositionally and knowing him by acquaintance. Contemplators have experienced God's beauty, transcendence, and love. They long evermore to experience God (in Christ through the Spirit) through rest and enjoyment. Indeed, when we contemplate God, we sense the grace of the one who joins us to God.

This kind of argument should sit well with the evangelical tradition. Union with Christ is part and parcel with communion; communion implies a real, substantial connection with the triune God in Christ. This connection, I would argue, is illustrated by contemplation: gazing and enjoying God in love. It is central to the Trinity (as I previously explained) and also union and communion with Christ.

---

[10]Calvin expressively writes, "First, we must understand that as long as Christ remains outside of us, and we are separated from him, all that he has suffered and done for the salvation of the human race remains useless and of no value for us. Therefore, to share with us what he has received from the Father, he had to become ours and to dwell within us. For this reason, he is called 'our Head,' and 'the first-born among many brethren.' We also, in turn, are said to be 'engrafted into him,' and to 'put on Christ.' For, as I have said, all that he possesses is nothing to us until we grow into one body with him" (Calvin, *Institutes* 3.1.1, p. 537). Indeed, salvation is accomplished in the life, death, and resurrection of Jesus himself (Gal 2:20; Eph 3:17; Col 2:6-7), and sinners are saved as they are joined to Christ by the Spirit through faith.

[11]Thomas Aquinas, *Summa Theologiae* IIa-IIae, q. 180, a. 1, co.

CONTEMPLATION IS AN EXPRESSION OF LOVE IN CHRIST

Third, part and parcel with the former discussion, contemplation involves the experience of love in Christ. Love here refers to the gracious bond of the triune God. As God loves, we experience this love through the restful gaze of contemplation as we are united with Christ. Along these lines, the following section shall articulate the reality of contemplation by appealing to limits of human understanding and the telos of love. The basic assertion is that contemplation is an instrument in achieving personal-acquaintance knowledge.

The human experience of the divine, while often concurrent with understanding, also transcends understanding; it is suprareasonable but not infrareasonable. This idea parallels David's experience throughout the Psalms: God's thoughts are vast (Ps 139:17) and his greatness and understanding are unsearchable (Ps 145:3; Is 40:28). As he reflects on the surpassing wisdom of God, David also admits that God's knowledge is ultimately too wonderful for him (Ps 139:6). God alternatively dwells in "thick darkness" (1 Kings 8:12) and "unapproachable light" (1 Tim 6:16). He is ultimately a breadth, length, height, and depth "that surpasses knowledge" (Eph 3:18-19). As Paul concludes elsewhere, "O the depth of the riches and wisdom and knowledge of God! How unsearchable are his judgments and how inscrutable his ways!" (Rom 11:33). Explaining the biblical data, the great Cappadocian father Basil suggests that the triune God is ultimately "unapproachable in thought."[12] Herman Bavinck similarly explains, "God infinitely surpasses our understanding, imagination, and language."[13] While God can be understood through his revelation, his essence is beyond our capacity to reason (though not against it).

This discussion should not imply that contemplation is emptying the mind before God or that God contradicts our knowledge; rather, contemplation involves the recognition that our relationship with God cannot be reduced to propositional knowledge or understanding but often exceeds them. Contemplation thus accounts for the fact that the human experience,

---

[12]Basil the Great, *On the Spirit*, in Schaff, *Nicene and Post-Nicene Fathers*, 22.53 (8:34). For a good contemporary resource, which makes a historical and theological case for the incomprehensibility of God, see Steven D. Boyer and Christopher A. Hall, *The Mystery of God: Theology for Knowing the Unknowable* (Grand Rapids: Baker Academic, 2012).

[13]Herman Bavinck, *Reformed Dogmatics*, vol. 2, *God and Creation*, ed. John Bolt, trans. John Vriend (Grand Rapids: Baker Academic, 2004), 40-41, cf. 29.

including love, sometimes transcends the cognitive capacities. As we reach the limits of understanding, we journey in personal trust and love—both of which are at the basis of the practice of contemplation.

Job experienced this kind of moment. He faced a kind of suffering that made no sense to him—or to us, for that matter. His friends—Eliphaz, Bildad, and Zophar—thought that Job's suffering was understandable, explaining to Job their reasoning. They each thought they understood the mind of the Lord in particular situations. In the end,

> the LORD answered Job out of the whirlwind and said:
> "Who is this that darkens counsel by words without knowledge?"
> (Job 38:1-2)

As the story of Job illustrates, some things are beyond our intellectual comprehension; they are "things too wonderful for me, which I did not know" (Job 42:3).

At this juncture, it may also be helpful to distinguish propositional knowledge from knowledge by acquaintance.[14] Job's friends thought that they could reason out God propositionally to make sense out of the horror of Job's suffering; while they were reasoning, however, they lacked fuller understanding and personal acquaintance with God as the loving, holy, and sovereign Lord. In fact, as the story of Job displays, there is not a theological answer to our suffering beyond seeking and knowing God in a personal way. Sometimes life—even God—does not seem sensible to our mental faculties. Herein lies the significance of contemplation. It journeys beyond our understanding, beyond the darkness from a lack of disclosure, and enters into the presence of God, humbly, beggingly, and resting in his love. It does not contradict propositional knowledge, but it does move beyond it, humbly seeking understanding and acquaintance with God himself.

---

[14]Using the distinctions of epistemology, there are at least three types of knowledge: (1) propositional knowledge, which includes the knowledge of facts; (2) skill knowledge, which refers to knowledge of how to do something; and (3) knowledge by acquaintance, which is a direct knowledge of a person. Brandon L. Rickabaugh summarizes several characteristics of knowledge by acquaintance. His conclusion is helpful: "Knowledge by acquaintance is the type of knowledge we have of other persons and of our self along with other kinds of objects. It is direct knowledge, not dependent on language or concepts, which is gained through encounter and often interaction with reality and does not require certainty" (Brandon L. Rickabaugh, "Eternal Life as Knowledge of God: An Epistemology of Knowledge by Acquaintance and Spiritual Formation," *Journal of Spiritual Formation and Soul Care* 6, no. 2 [2013]: 215, cf. 208-15).

In other words, we have a deeper knowledge of God when we recognize that our capacities cannot fully know him. Gregory of Nyssa made this keen observation: as people know God more, they eventually enter the "dark cloud of unknowing" where, in the face of little understanding, they are forced to hold firm to faith and love.[15] Sometimes it is only in darkness that people can see God. Andrew Louth summarizes Gregory: "As the soul responds to God's love, as it comes closer to the unknowable God, it enters into deeper and deeper darkness, and knows Him in a way that surpasses [mere propositional] knowledge."[16] That is, people have knowledge by acquaintance of God through personal trust and love. "This direct acquaintance with the love of God," Brandon Rickabaugh elaborates, "provides a non-propositional cognitive foundation for knowledge of God, of his activity, and of his reality."[17] While people may not have the words to express their experience of God, they have an awareness of his personal presence. Moreover, as people turn to God, they recognize that God's nature and ways surpass their capacities to understand fully, which then encourages them to trust and love God for who he is—even when who he is is beyond their capacities.

The former discussion finds particular clarity in Paul's claim that love is the ultimate goal for the Christian as well as the cosmos. It recognizes that, as Paul claims, while "love never ends . . . as for knowledge, it will pass away" (1 Cor 13:8). Paul here contrasts the present way of knowing with the future (eschatological) way of knowing. The present way of knowing—that is, the spiritual gift of knowledge—is inferior in virtue of the noetic effects of sin, but in the end, we will know God face-to-face; namely, we will know him directly.[18] Paul's basic point is that, unlike the spiritual gifts, love

---

[15]Gregory of Nyssa, *Commentary on the Canticle* 888C-893C, quoted in Gregory of Nyssa, *From Glory to Glory: Texts from Gregory of Nyssa's Mystical Writings*, trans. and ed. Herbert Musurillo (repr., Crestwood, NY: St. Vladimir's Seminary Press, 2014), 201-2.

[16]Andrew Louth, *The Origins of the Christian Mystical Tradition: From Plato to Denys*, 2nd ed. (Oxford: Oxford University Press, 2007), 79, see also 92-93. It is important to note here that Gregory is suggesting that the soul's ascent to God only happens in and through the triune God (see Gregory of Nyssa, *Commentary on the Canticle* 1000C-1004C, quoted in Gregory of Nyssa, *From Glory to Glory*, 246-50).

[17]Rickabaugh, "Eternal Life as Knowledge of God," 220; cf. Paul K. Moser, *The Evidence for God: Religious Knowledge Reexamined* (New York: Cambridge University Press, 2010), 136.

[18]See Gordon D. Fee, *The First Epistle to the Corinthians*, New International Commentary on the New Testament (Grand Rapids: Eerdmans, 1987), 648-49. As he rightly notes, "What is not quite

never ends: it characterizes both the present and future ages.[19] As Anthony Thiselton boldly asserts, "The sermons of prophets and the 'knowledge' of theologians are rendered redundant, while the character and fruit of love does not fall apart."[20] Paul also highlights a difference between present knowledge and eschatological knowledge. Now we know "in part," now we speak/reason "like a child," "now we see in a mirror dimly"; but then we "gave up childish ways," then we see "face to face," then we will "know fully, even as I have been fully known" (1 Cor 13:8-12). While our present knowledge (propositional and acquaintance) is true, it is partial nonetheless: God has not fully revealed himself, and we are not fully acquainted with him, that is, until we undergo a different mode of existence in our glorified bodily state. Our full and direct ("face to face") knowledge—"even as I have been fully known"—comes at the final revealing in the beatific vision (to be discussed later).

Contemplation, in this sense, is practicing for the end: envisioning it, savoring it, and acknowledging that our present knowledge cannot always grasp what the end will be. Consequently, contemplation is a means of producing proper knowledge (by acquaintance) of God. It strives to experience God in a way that theology can fail to describe, and it allows us to "taste and see that the LORD is good" (Ps 34:8). I fear that if we reduce theology to propositional knowledge, if contemplation ends without being acquainted with God's presence, then we may quickly become like Job's friends, assuming and acting like we have the answers, when in fact the answer is "I don't understand," and the theological response is mourning and lament.

CONTEMPLATION REFLECTS THE TRANSFORMATIONAL READING OF THE SCRIPTURES

As I previously discussed, Christians are united with Christ and thus contemplate the one to whom they are bonded, an act that ends with the experience of trust and love. Contemplation also blends into discussions of

---

clear is the exact nuance of the final clause that expresses the nature of that final knowing, 'even as I am fully known'" (ibid.).

[19]Paul spends "the entire chapter expounding the eschatological permanence of love alone" (Anthony C. Thiselton, *The First Epistle to the Corinthians*, New International Greek Testament Commentary [Grand Rapids: Eerdmans, 2000], 1071).

[20]Ibid., 1061.

properly reading Scripture for personal transformation; namely, contemplation explains how Christians read Scripture in light of its God-given basis and formational end. In the following section I will argue that contemplation, as epitomized in the ancient method of lectio divina,[21] best fulfills the transformational, prayer-filled focus of Scripture.

An ancient method of reading Scripture, the lectio divina (divine reading) involves a synthesis of knowing Scripture and a personal desire for God. It often consists of four interrelated and overlapping phases:[22] read, meditate, pray, and contemplate.[23] The first phase includes a prepared stillness wherein readers ask for the Spirit to come alongside them as the plain meaning of the passage is thoughtfully and accurately read. The second phase involves, after several readings, a deep and multiperspectival reflection of the text that points the readers to the gospel in Christ. In this phase, readers personally understand the passage well enough to apply it to themselves, and they allow the text to reprove or console as necessary. The third phase speaks (or prays) out loud the meditation to God. In particular, the readers request God to allow the truth to change them inwardly and guide them as they live out the meaning of the passage. The fourth stage

---

[21] An excellent place to start to understand the lectio is *The Rule of St. Benedict: In Latin and English with Notes*, ed. Timothy Fry (Collegeville, MN: Liturgical Press, 1981), 249-52. See also Jean Leclercq, *The Love of Learning and the Desire for God: A Study of Monastic Culture*, trans. Catharine Misrahi (New York: Fordham University Press, 1982), 15-22; D. Rees, *Consider Your Call* (London: SPCK, 1978), 261-73; and D. Gorce, *La Lectio Divina* (Paris: Picard, 1925). More recent discussions can be found in Michael Casey, *Sacred Reading: The Ancient Art of Lectio Divina* (Liguori, MO: Liguori, 1995); Tim Gray, *Praying Scripture for a Change: An Introduction to the Lectio Divina* (West Chester, PA: Ascension, 2009); James C. Wilhoit and Evan B. Howard, *Discovering Lectio Divina: Bringing Scripture into Ordinary Life* (Downers Grove, IL: InterVarsity Press, 2012); and Enzo Bianchi, *Lectio Divina: From God's Word to Our Lives* (Brewster, MA: Paraclete, 2015), esp. 95-107.

[22] In other words, the reader should not think of the lectio as a progression whereby the person moves out of one phase and into another. Rather, these phases ought to be seen as formally distinct but overlapping in their content, expression, and goal. For example, when the person contemplates (fourth phase), the person does not disengage the mind from meditation, but rather the person, in the presence of the Almighty, recognizes that God is ultimately beyond knowledge and understanding and enjoys the vision of God.

[23] In Latin: *lectio, meditatio, oratio,* and *contemplatio*. I am following the influential fourfold description of Guigo II (the Carthusian) of the late twelfth century (see Guigo II, *The Ladder of Monks and Twelve Meditations by Guigo II*, trans. Edmund Collegde and James Walsh [repr., Kalamazoo, MI: Cistercian, 1979]). Of course, different traditions have added/subtracted phases. For a full discussion, see Henri de Lubac, *Medieval Exegesis: The Four Senses of Scripture*, trans. Mark Sebanc and E. M. Macierowski (Grand Rapids: Eerdmans, 1998–2009). A contemporary example is Tim Gray, who helpfully adds a final phase called *operatio*, which refers to the person's practical resolution as a result of the *lectio* (Gray, *Praying Scripture for a Change*, 109-20).

involves the personal recognition that, through the Spirit's groanings, the meditation is no longer a monologue; rather, the readers through faith experience the love of God in communion with Christ. This fourth phase captures the total experience and appreciation of the person bonded to Christ as they see and savor the Lord.

The lectio may be compared to the process of eating food or conversing with a person. In the first example, one takes a bite, chews, savors, and then digests and absorbs the food. In a similar manner, the contemplator bites Scripture (reads), chews it (meditates), savors (prays), and finally absorbs it (contemplates). In the second example, the lectio is similar to conversing with a person. Enzo Bianchi explains it well: when we speak with another person, "we make an exodus from ourselves, die to our own narcissism, listen to the other person, look closely at her face for a glimpse into her soul, who she is deep down. We come to know the other person when we respect how he is different and other, and when we can accept who we are in relation to him."[24]

While God is not a peer equal to us, the analogy suffices to show that the proper reading of Scripture is not a studious monologue but rather an entrance into a dialogue, that is, an I-Thou experience of personal acquaintance.

In order to express the intent and practice of the lectio divina for the purposes of gospel-centered transformation, a concise example of a lectio reading should suffice: "Jesus said to them, 'I am the bread of life; whoever comes to me shall not hunger, and whoever believes in me shall never thirst'" (Jn 6:35). The lectio reader begins by asking descriptive questions similar to any modern analytical reading (e.g., what Jesus meant by "bread," how his audience would interpret this kind of statement, the literary context of John's organization, authorial intention). Then, after reading the passage aloud in context several times, the person ruminates (lit., masticates) or meditates on the passage, perceiving connections between Jesus' words here and Israel's wilderness wanderings, for example. Using words from the passage as a sort of concordance hook for the rest of Scripture, the person would continue to pray the Scripture for their own self and the world. In other words, the reader would not so much intellectually dissect the meaning of "bread of life" but rather seek to ingest, chew, and digest Jesus Christ as

---

[24]Bianchi, *Lectio Divina*, 98.

the bread. At this point, the lectio reader ventures beyond the plain sense of the analytical reading and journeys toward personal, devotional readings. They want to know Scripture, certainly; but they want this knowledge to intersect and change their hearts. Indeed, they do not only desire to read the text but to allow the text to read them. They want to understand Scripture, not so much as a text to be studied, but as the living Word with Christ as the center. In other words, the lectio reader suggests that the point of reading Scripture is not merely hearing, knowing, and recalling; rather, it is the gazing and treasuring of Jesus himself. A lectio reading is fulfilled when, like Mary, people have "treasured up all these things, pondering them" in their hearts (Lk 2:19).[25]

In the end, through the lectio divina, contemplation seeks out personal transformation. It concedes that there is more going on in scriptural reading and prayer than the knowing process; rather, reading and prayer are part of a direct I-Thou encounter. Contemplators want to know God in a personal way, recognizing that they only truly know God when they are morally responsive to his will. Contemplation thus affirms Paul K. Moser's epistemological point that the kind of knowledge that God ultimately values is "volitionally transformative," seeking the "change of human will."[26] People change as the Spirit meets them in their (lectio) reading of Scripture. As they are bonded to Christ, so they wish to act like him. It is no surprise that monks always sounded out the words while reading, weighing all words to release their full flavor of the divine reading (hence the term from Benedict and others, "divine readings").[27]

---

[25]Summarizing the basic difference between this monastic method and scholastic theology (more akin to analytic methods), Jean Leclercq notes, "Rather than speculative insights [in scholastic theology], it gives them a certain appreciation, of savoring and clinging to the truth and, what is everything, the love of God" (Leclercq, *Love of Learning*, 4, cf. 72-73). Benedict, for example, wanted his monks to experience the gospel in their "divine reading"; the best way to do so, he believed, was by reading Scripture as speaking (not only to the ancient context but also) to them (see *Rule of St. Benedict*, chap. 48). As Leclercq avers again, "Theology, spirituality, cultural history: these three realities were not separated in the real life of the monks, and they can never be dissociated" (Leclercq, *Love of Learning*, 6, cf. 28-34).

[26]Paul K. Moser, *The Elusive God: Reorienting Religious Epistemology* (Cambridge: Cambridge University Press, 2008), 90. He explains elsewhere that faith is "the affirmative response to God of yielding oneself to (participating in) God's experienced moral character and will. Clearly, such faith is no merely intellectual response of assent to a proposition" (Paul K. Moser, "Gethsemane Epistemology: Volitional and Evidential," *Philosophia Christi* 14, no. 2 [2012]: 268).

[27]Leclercq, *Love of Learning*, 15, cf. 16-22. Indeed, Benedict assumed that the personal practice of the *lectio* would disturb the resting monks (*Rule of St. Benedict*, 249-52).

Without the lectio divina, without contemplation, readers easily may fail to read Scripture in light of its intent and goal: the personal and reflective knowledge of Jesus Christ as their Lord. Without the lectio, or at least the contemplative and transformational aspects of it, one simply reads to understand the meaning of Scripture and not necessarily its direct intent for the person. Reading Scripture is—and ought to be—inescapably bound with both knowledge and transformation. Contemplation is the capstone of this holistic experience.

CONTEMPLATION IS A TRANSFORMATIONAL FORETASTE OF THE BEATIFIC VISION

Fifth, contemplation is a transformational foretaste of the beatific vision. Contemplative practices thus serve the Christian, united to Christ, in preparation for the beatific vision. Christians are made sons and daughters of God so that they might gaze and enjoy God dimly now but in perfection later.

What are the characteristics of the beatific vision? The beatific vision is the final vision of God upon death when Christians enjoy "the direct vision of the Godhead" as they see his "divine majesty face to face."[28] The vision is typified by the infamous request of Moses for God to "show me your glory" (Ex 33:18) and fulfilled in the final revelation, that is, of course, only ectypally. While we cannot speak in detail about the characteristics of the future beatific state, Charles Hodge explains eight elements that can be known, the first of which deserves our attention: "That this incomprehensible blessedness of heaven shall arise from the vision of God. This vision is beatific. It beatifies. It transforms the soul into the divine image; transfusing into it the divine life, so that it is filled with the fullness of God."[29] Notably, this beatifying element—along with several other elements of the consummation, according to Hodge—also occurs during this lifetime. Christians gaze God in the present. They see him, know him, and thus are beatified, that is, made more in the image of Christ.

---

[28]Calvin, *Institutes* 2.14.3. The vision includes the moment when we, "partakers of heavenly glory," as Calvin writes, "shall see God as he is" (ibid.). A biblical example is seen in Stephen. Luke describes the moment just before he is stoned: "Filled with the Holy Spirit, he gazed into heaven and saw the glory of God and Jesus standing at the right hand of God. 'Look,' he said, 'I see the heavens opened and the Son of Man standing at the right hand of God!'" (Acts 7:55-56).

[29]Charles Hodge, *Systematic Theology* (repr., Peabody, MA: Hendrickson, 2003), 3:860-61.

This gaze and transformation occurs through the new covenant and ends in the eschatological vision. Regarding the new covenant, Paul explains, "And we all, with unveiled face, beholding the glory of the Lord, are being transformed into the same image from one degree of glory to another. For this comes from the Lord who is Spirit" (2 Cor 3:18). We behold God, experiencing a direct knowledge of acquaintance in an I-Thou encounter. In other words, we experience who God is, who we are, and are thereby transformed. John reflects this idea eschatologically as he explains the benefits of being children of God: "when [God] appears, we shall be like him, because we shall see him as he is" (1 Jn 3:2). Like a mirror reflects its object, Christians will reflect the likeness of Christ; as sons and daughters of God, they will reflect their Father.[30]

Peter further elaborates the final experience of transformation into the image of God. One day, as Peter reflects, you "may escape from the corruption that is in the world because of lust, and may become participants of the divine nature" (2 Pet 1:4 NRSV).[31] While this does not mean that Christians will be consubstantial with the Godhead, they will, through communion with Christ, be "granted all things that pertain to life and godliness" through the Godhead (2 Pet 1:3-4). Christians thereby partake in the divine nature (not *ousia*) as they are granted divine characteristics or qualities such as immortality, holiness, and love.[32] Bluntly stated, God's things become our things.[33] As Calvin further highlights, Christians are "participants not only

---

[30]Therefore, "the privileges which we now enjoy in a partial manner will then be ours fully and completely" (I. Howard Marshall, *The Epistles of John*, New International Commentary on the New Testament [Grand Rapids: Eerdmans, 1978], 172).

[31]The idea within this phrase ("become partakers of the divine nature") is well attested in both the Greek (Plato, Epictetus, etc.) and Jewish literature (Philo and Josephus) (see Peter H. Davids, *The Letters of 2 Peter and Jude*, Pillar New Testament Commentary [Grand Rapids: Eerdmans, 2006], 172-74; Gene L. Green, *Jude and 2 Peter*, Baker Exegetical Commentary on the New Testament [Grand Rapids: Baker Academic, 2008], 186).

[32]Participating in the "divine nature" refers not to participating in God's essence but rather to his qualities or virtues (Green, *Jude and 2 Peter*, 186-87; Thomas R. Schreiner, *1, 2 Peter, Jude*, New American Commentary [Nashville: B&H, 2003], 294). Additionally, given that Peter contrasts "partakers of the divine nature" with "the corruption that is in the world because of sinful desire" (2 Pet 1:4), it is likely that Peter has in mind both restoration from decay and corruption in general (i.e., immortality) and the moral transformation of the individual in particular (holiness and love), though the latter is more chiefly his concern in context (Green, *Jude and 2 Peter*, 186-87; cf. Davids, *The Letters of 2 Peter and Jude*, 173-75).

[33]As Michael W. Austin highlights, "We *participate* in God's knowledge, virtue, and love; we do not *become* God's knowledge, virtue, and love" (Michael W. Austin, "The Doctrine of *Theosis*: A

in all his benefits but also in himself" through union with Christ.[34] Therefore, the beatific vision is in fact "the end of the gospel" as it renders "us eventually conformable to God, and, if we may so speak, to deify us."[35] The Spirit bonds, transforms, and beautifies us in Christ, giving us God's communicable virtues. According to Peter, the beatific vision transforms the person into the renewed image of God.

In one sense, then, the beatific vision is the final revelation that contemplation seeks: "to gaze upon the beauty of the LORD" (Ps 27:4). It is the ultimate I-Thou encounter as it transforms us according to beauty itself. Gregory of Nyssa poetically articulates that we will "discover that which alone is worthy of our desire," and thus "become beautiful because" we are "near to Beauty."[36] In another sense, contemplation—as I have developed it in this chapter thus far—seeks this relationship now. Contemplators rest in the reality that they are presently united with Christ and have communion with the triune God; thus they recognize that they are also partaking in a mysterious fellowship, gazing God as God first gazes them, and thus being transformed into him. The triune economy is not just something external to Christians; rather, as they gaze Christ's beauty through the Spirit, they are brought into God's inner contemplation so that they are beautified (that is, sanctified) as well. As Augustine asserts, our nature is completed in the knowledge of God: "This contemplation is promised us as the end of all activities and the eternal perfection of all joys."[37] Contemplation is thus a central practice for the Christian because, through it, the Christian enjoys God and is transformed in anticipation of the final vision.

Contemplation is simultaneously the acknowledgment that, at the end of the day—after hard work thinking and studying—our knowledge is limited, our thinking imperfect, and our analogies falter. "For now we see in a mirror

---

Transformation Union with Christ," *Journal of Spiritual Formation and Soul Care* 8, no. 2 [2015]: 181).

[34]Calvin, *Institutes* 3.2.24.

[35]John Calvin, *Commentaries on the Catholic Epistles*, trans. and ed. John Owen (repr., Grand Rapids: Baker, 2009), 371. For an excellent discussion of Calvin's understanding of the ascent of Christ (and likewise our ascent in him), see Julie Canlis, *Calvin's Ladder: A Spiritual Theology of Ascent and Ascension* (Grand Rapids: Eerdmans, 2010).

[36]Gregory of Nyssa, *On Virginity* 46.364A-369B, quoted in Gregory of Nyssa, *From Glory to Glory*, 109, cf. 110-11.

[37]Augustine, *The Trinity*, trans. Edmund Hill, ed. John E. Rotelle, 2nd ed. (Hyde Park, NY: New City Press, 2015), 1.3.17: 83.

dimly, but then face to face. Now I know in part; then I shall know fully, even as I have been known" (1 Cor 13:12). Contemplation recognizes that, while the gift of knowledge is helpful now, while the work of theologians matters in the present, and while knowledge can bring us to some recognition of the truth, it is not the telos. Karl Barth wonderfully summarizes, "Because the sun rises all lights are extinguished."[38] One day we will participate and enjoy the love and gaze of God directly.

Bonaventure summarizes the beatific vision, undergirding the present preparation and anticipation of this vision. His words reflect well its connection to contemplation and so offer a fine conclusion:

> I pray, O God, that I may know you and love you, so that I may rejoice in you. . . . Let your [knowledge and] love grow in me here, and there be made complete, so that here my joy may be great with expectancy, and there be complete in reality. . . . Until then, let my mind meditate on it, let my tongue speak it, let my heart love it, let my mouth express it. Let my soul hunger for it; let my flesh thirst for it; my whole being desire it, until I enter into the joy of my Lord, who is God three and one, blessed forever! Amen.[39]

CONCLUSION

Contemplation is captivated attention to the triune God. It consists of a gospel-centered gazing and enjoying God, and it culminates in transformation, the experience of love, and spiritual rest and in communion with Christ. In this chapter I have made a case for gospel-centered contemplation. I have suggested that contemplation is normative to Christianity by appealing to various theological ideas wherein contemplation is necessary, or at least insightful.

The chapter moved from discussing the ontological substructures of contemplation (the Trinity and union with Christ), to the experience of the person in Christ (the failure of mere propositional knowledge, the telos of love), and finally culminated with a discussion of the transformation that necessarily happens through contemplation in Christ (the lectio divina and beatific vision).

---

[38]Karl Barth, *The Resurrection of the Dead* (London: Hodder & Revell, 1933), 86.
[39]Bonaventure, *Breviloquium*, in *Works of St. Bonaventure*, trans. and ed. Dominic V. Monti (Saint Bonaventure, NY: Franciscan Institute Publications, 2005), 9:300-301.

I will close by noting six areas of significance for Christians today.

First, because contemplation is grounded in the triune God and only expressed through union with Christ, it is integral to theology, prayer, and the experience of the gospel itself. Basil the Great thus suggests that failing to contemplate leads to a lackluster spiritual life. He writes, "The carnal man, who has never trained his mind to contemplation, but rather keeps it buried deep in lust of the flesh, as in mud, is powerless to look up to the spiritual light of the truth."[40] Contemplation keeps our eyes on things above, that is, on matters of the gospel.

Second, contemplation is a means by which we experience the peace of justification. The restful process allows room for the Spirit to calm minds and provide peace. As Paul reminds us, "to set the mind on the Spirit is life and peace" (Rom 8:6; cf. Rom 8:9-11). John Owen expresses the value of the contemplative mindset well: "The Holy Spirit enables Christians to sit in dungeons, rejoice in flames and glory in troubles. If he brings to mind the promises of Christ for our comfort, neither Satan nor man, neither sin nor the world, nor even death itself shall take away our comfort. Saints who have communion with the Holy Spirit know this only too well."[41]

Third, contemplation is the healthy admission that we are not God and cannot know what he knows. It is a personal response to the overwhelming awesomeness of God. Theology is not merely writing words on a page. The two-dimensional God we describe, even while "accurately" depicting the God of Scripture, falls exceedingly short of the living, infinite God. Theology is not about increasing our stock of true propositions but rather gaining knowledge of God by being acquainted with him and transformed unto him.

Fourth, and closely related, as contemplation is part of the sanctifying process on the part of the believer, so it leads to an increased personal knowledge of God. Intellect is not enough. Paul Moser rightly cautions, "We would come to know God's reality more profoundly as God increasingly becomes our God, the Lord of our lives, rather than just an object of our contemplation or speculation."[42] A (transformational) contemplation is,

---

[40]Basil the Great, *On the Spirit* 22.53.

[41]John Owen, *Communion with God*, ed. R. J. K. Law (Edinburgh: Banner of Truth Trust, 1991), 178-79.

[42]Moser, *Elusive God*, 122.

among other things, the medicine that overcomes puffed-up theological minds and prideful hearts. It reminds us that intellectual disputation cannot stand without personal reformation. Therefore, our theologies ought to be framed in light of the end, in light of the center and the source, the triune God, who calls us back to him through the gospel.

Fifth, contemplation empowers us to read Scripture as a book written for us, as the lectio so wonderfully demonstrates. Let Scripture change your heart and not only nourish your mind.

Sixth, contemplation provides the restful, quiet space necessary for discerning spiritual need and growth. As Blaise Pascal infamously quipped, "I have often said that the sole cause of man's unhappiness is that he does not know how to stay quietly in his room."[43] Contemplation often consists in a passivity before God, a mere listening. In so doing, contemplation enables people to experience themselves and God. It naturally leads to the recognition that they are finite, and God transcends their propositional thoughts and prayers. Contemplation thus requires the presence of humility in the face of the mystery of an Almighty God. The Psalms reflect much silence. The chapter closes with one example, Psalm 131:1-2, which is also a superb exemplar of the contemplative mindset.

> O LORD, my heart is not lifted up,
>   my eyes are not raised too high;
> I do not occupy myself with things
>   too great and too marvelous for me.
> But I have calmed and quieted my soul,
>   like a weaned child with its mother;
>   like a weaned child is my soul within me.

[43]Blaise Pascal, *Pensées*, trans. A. J. Krailsheimer (New York: Penguin, 1995), 136, 37.

THE BEATIFIC VISION

Contemplating Christ as the Future Present

HANS BOERSMA

SEEING GOD IN CHRIST (1):
CONTEMPLATION IN THE GOSPEL OF JOHN

When in social gatherings people ask me what I am working on and I answer, "The beatific vision," this regularly earns me a puzzled look: It turns out that the beatific vision is a topic Christians do not commonly discuss, and many are entirely unfamiliar with it. As a result, I have learned to give a somewhat longer response to the question: I now say that I'm studying what it means to see God in the hereafter, in the eschaton. Whatever the reasons for the lack of familiarity with the topic of the beatific vision, it poses a serious problem, considering the Bible and the broad tradition of the church understand the beatific vision as the final purpose or aim of human existence. We have every reason, therefore, to reflect on the topic of seeing God. Such reflection is important especially because the beatific vision in the eschaton is intimately connected to our contemplation of God today. The main point of this chapter is that the vision of God begins to take initial shape already in our contemplative practices today. Learning about the beatific vision, therefore, teaches us also about our everyday spirituality that anticipates this vision. And, conversely, the more we learn what it means to contemplate God in Christ, the better prepared we are for the eschatological vision of God.

One of the most well-known biblical passages that speaks of the vision of God (*visio Dei*) occurs in Jesus' farewell discourse to his disciples (Jn 13–17). As he encourages them by explaining that he is leaving them so as to prepare a place for them ("In my Father's house are many rooms," Jn 14:2), Thomas and Philip engage Jesus in discussion. Thomas expresses his incomprehension: He doesn't know where Jesus is going, let alone how to get there. In response, Jesus points to himself: "I am the way, and the truth, and the life. No one comes to the Father except through me" (Jn 14:6). In some sense, it would seem from this that the Father is the destination, while Jesus is the means through which one arrives at it. But Jesus then adds a comment that complicates this understanding. He points to the eternal mystery of the Father-Son relationship: "If you had known me, you would have known my Father also. From now on you do know him and have seen him" (Jn 14:7).[1] Jesus indicates, therefore, that when we look at him, we already see the Father as well. At least for those who look with eyes of faith, there is no distance separating the Father from the Son.

This gift of spiritual sight seems to be in short supply with Philip. He presses the point: "Lord, show us the Father, and it is enough for us" (14:8). Philip, like many others in John's Gospel, displays culpable ignorance: Jesus has just indicated that by knowing and seeing him, we also know the Father; yet Philip is still asking to see the Father. As Philip makes this request of Jesus, the answer is (quite literally) staring him in the face: When we contemplate Jesus, we contemplate the Father. Since the Father and the Son are one (see Jn 10:30; 12:45; 13:20), it makes no sense to look for the Father behind Jesus. Though it is true that Jesus is the means to the Father, it would be erroneous to suggest that another divine person is hiding behind Jesus. To explain this to Philip, therefore, Jesus makes the matter as plain as possible: "Have I been with you so long, and you still do not know me, Philip? Whoever has seen me has seen the Father. How can you say, 'Show us the Father'? Do you not believe that I am in the Father and the Father is in me?" (Jn 14:9-10). According to Jesus' dialogue with Thomas and Philip, then, Jesus is the way to the Father, and the reason is

---

[1]Biblical scholars commonly suggest that this passage primarily refers to the Son's mission and only in a secondary sense speaks of the ontological unity between Father and Son (e.g., Raymond E. Brown, *The Gospel according to John XIII–XXI*, Anchor Bible 29A [Garden City, NY: Doubleday, 1970], 632; Andreas J. Köstenberger, *John*, Baker Exegetical Commentary on the New Testament [Grand Rapids: Baker Academic, 2004], 431). I agree with this assessment, distinctly keeping in mind, however, that from the economy we know of the inner trinitarian life. We need not downplay the latter in favor of the former. In and through God's self-revelation in Christ, we come to know God as he truly is.

that Father and Son are one. Seeing the Son necessarily entails seeing the Father.

One of the key lessons to draw from this dialogue is that contemplation of God is centered on the incarnate Christ. It is by seeing Christ in the flesh and by recognizing in him, through eyes of faith, the eternal I Am that we gain life (or happiness, beatitude). We may put it even stronger: Seeing Christ with eyes of faith not only leads to beatitude, it is beatitude. In Christ, end and means converge. When we see Christ, we see God. It is with good reason that many in the tradition have taken a Christ-centered approach to the vision of God. The basis for this lies in Jesus' allusions to the doctrines of the Trinity and the incarnation. His remark to Thomas, "I Am the way, and the truth, and the life" (Jn 14:6)—the sixth of seven "I am" sayings in this Gospel—is a claim of identity with the Father. When Jesus states that he is the I Am (*egō eimi*), he identifies with the I Am who revealed himself to Moses at the burning bush with the name, "I AM WHO I AM" (Ex 3:14).

Thus, when the prologue to John's Gospel identifies Jesus as the "true light" (Jn 1:9), the Evangelist is suggesting nothing less than that in Jesus the glory of God's own presence has come to dwell with his people.[2] Much like God used to come down in the theophany of fire within the pillar of cloud in the tabernacle and in the temple (Ex 33:9; 40:34-35; 1 Kings 8:10-11), so he has now come down in Christ in human flesh and blood: "And the Word became flesh and dwelt [or tabernacled—*eskēnōsen*] among us, and we have seen his glory, glory as of the only Son from the Father, full of grace and truth" (Jn 1:14). The vision that renders us truly happy (the Latin *beatus* meaning "happy")—or, as John's Gospel would put it, the vision that genuinely gives life (Jn 1:4; 8:12)—is the vision of Jesus Christ as the eternal Son of God who has taken on flesh and blood (Jn 3:16; 6:50-54). Vision of God is always vision in and through the human Jesus who is identified as the Son of God, in and through whom alone we come to know the Father. The future beatific vision is, therefore, not a stage beyond the vision of Christ (though we will see God in Christ much more clearly in the beatific vision than ever before). Rather, we see God himself (and as such we could even say that we see the divine essence) when we indwell the incarnate tabernacle of God through

---

[2]Cf. Jesus' comment in Jn 8:12: "I am the light of the world. Whoever follows me will not walk in darkness, but will have the light of life."

union and communion with Jesus. Sacrament and reality coincide in him. The divine essence does not lie behind or beyond Christ; rather, those who have eyes of faith can see the very character or being of God in the unity of the person of Christ.

Jesus' conversation with Thomas and Philip in the Gospel of John is key to understanding the beatific vision, even though the passage does not mention the eschatological vision of God directly. Biblical passages that explicitly address the topic are obviously central (and there are quite a few of them), but we need to incorporate these into a broader theology of seeing God (and of contemplation of God), which we draw from the Scriptures as a whole. Since Jesus is the true and ultimate revelation of God (Heb 1:2), Jesus manifests him in a way unmatched by any previous manifestations and unsurpassed by any future revelation: Jesus is the true and ultimate sacramental theophany of God, made present in and through the hypostatic union of the divine and human natures in the Son of God. We know about the beatific vision by turning with eyes of faith to the Christ whom we behold in the gospel and in the sacrament.[3]

Thus, though an eschatological barrier prevents us from obtaining direct access to the beatific vision, we do have recourse to reliable insight into what this beatific vision entails: God's self-manifestation in Christ does not mislead; when in faith we look to him, we come face to face with God himself. Whenever we look to God through faith in Christ, we engage in contemplation of him. As such, contemplation is not in the first place a kind of ecstasy (though I don't mean to exclude such experiences); nor is it something reserved for elite Christians. Rather, it is an activity in which many of us engage without recognizing it as such: Whenever we take time to reflect on who Christ is and what he has done for us, we contemplate also the Father. When we do this we share, therefore (albeit provisionally), in

---

[3]Herbert McCabe comments: "The story of Jesus is nothing other than the triune life of God projected onto our history, or enacted sacramentally in our history, so that it becomes story." (Herbert McCabe, "The Involvement of God," in *God Matters* [London: Continuum, 1987], 39-51, at 48). McCabe goes on to write, "Watching, so to say, the story of Jesus, we are watching the processions of the Trinity. . . . They are not just reflection but sacrament—they contain the reality they signify. The mission of Jesus is *nothing other* than the eternal generation of the Son" (ibid. 48-49 [emphasis original]). I am indebted to Fr. John Behr for this reference. For Jesus as the "primordial sacrament" (*oersacrament*), see Edward Schillebeeckx, *Christ the Sacrament of the Encounter with God* (Lanham, MD: Sheed & Ward, 1963).

the eschatological vision of the Father himself. The reason is simply that Christ makes the future present.

SEEING GOD IN CHRIST (2):
BEATIFIC VISION IN THE NEW TESTAMENT

My suggestion that we approach the doctrine of the beatific vision christologically has implications for the way we read the many biblical passages that directly refer to the beatific vision. Without dealing exhaustively with the biblical witness, it may nonetheless be helpful to discuss some of the key verses. In his sixth Beatitude, Jesus comments, "Blessed are the pure in heart, for they shall see God" (Mt 5:8). Jonathan Edwards, in a 1730 sermon on this verse, makes clear that just as God once spoke on Mount Sinai to Israel, so he speaks here on a mountain to his disciples—though God reveals himself here in the incarnate Christ much more clearly and perfectly than he once did on Mount Sinai.[4] In Christ, God is present once again, only this time in a much more glorious manner. This means, for Edwards, that the vision of God is not just mentioned in the Beatitudes but actually takes place on this momentous occasion. The disciples see God in Christ; they see him in a way that used to be foreclosed to the ancient people of Israel—for only in Christ does God assume human flesh.

On my understanding, therefore, it seems to me that the Beatitudes (and in particular the one that holds out the vision of God to the pure in heart) have Jesus himself as their focus. Jesus does not position himself as a third party between God (the promised object) and his audience (who are told to be pure in heart); Jesus is not an outsider imposing on others an extraneous condition (purity of heart) for seeing God. Rather, in his Beatitude on the *visio Dei*, Jesus puts himself forward as the subject of both the first and the second part of his saying. In terms of the first part, it seems obvious that Jesus is the very definition of what it means to be "pure in heart." We obtain purity only by participating in his purity. We participate in the life of God—in his purity—only inasmuch as we are united to Christ. The second part of Jesus' saying makes clear that this purity of heart enables us to discern who

---

[4]Jonathan Edwards, "The Pure in Heart Blessed," in *Works of Jonathan Edwards*, vol. 17, *Sermons and Discourses, 1730–1733*, ed. Mark Valeri (New Haven, CT: Yale University Press, 1999), 59. See edwards.yale.edu.

God is in Jesus. If Jesus is the true revelation of God, then in him we see the character or being of God. Jesus' words, then, hold out to the disciples the way to greater intimacy with himself. Both parts of this Beatitude dispel any notion of Jesus standing aloof from or in-between the two parties (God and humanity) that he reconciles. It is in the hypostatic union of the Son of God that we come to know ourselves as well as God. Jesus does not simply pronounce this Beatitude; he is himself its subject. He is both the one in whom we are blessed ("blessed are the pure in heart") and the contents of the promise ("they shall see God"). Again, therefore, in Jesus means and end converge: Since the three persons of the Trinity are not three individuals, but are one in substance, there is no vision of the Father outside of Jesus Christ.

The apostle Paul, in his encomium on love (1 Cor 13:1-13), holds out the promise of face-to-face vision of God, saying that "now we see in a mirror dimly, but then face to face" (1 Cor 13:12). He explains that in this beatific vision, partial (*ek merous*) knowledge (1 Cor 13:9) will give way to full knowledge (*epignōsomai*), corresponding to God's full knowledge of us (*epegnōsthēn*) (1 Cor 13:12).[5] Thus, both in terms of sight and in terms of knowledge, the eschaton marks a transition to a much more glorious future. The Puritan theologian John Owen expounds on this transition in his post-humously published *Meditations and Discourses on the Glory of Christ* (1684). As long as we see Christ's glory merely by faith, explains Owen, we have a view that is "obscure, dark, inevident, reflexive"[6] and thus unsteady and uneven.[7] By contrast, our vision of the glory of Christ in heaven will be "immediate, direct, intuitive," and therefore "steady, even, and constant."[8] Owen then goes on to say:

> Christ himself, in his own person with all his glory, shall be continually with us, before us, proposed unto us. We shall no longer have an *Image*, a

---

[5]Though Paul contrasts knowing in part with knowing fully (*epignōsomai*), we should not give too much weight to the use of *epi* in the verb. Rudolf Bultmann comments that "ἐπιγινώσκειν [*epiginōskein*] is often used instead of γινώσκειν [*ginōskein*] with no difference in meaning" ("γινώσκω," in *Theological Dictionary of the New Testament*, ed. Gerhard Kittel, trans. Geoffrey W. Bromiley [Grand Rapids: Eerdmans, 1964], 1:703) and that "even in 1 C. 13:12 the alternation is purely rhetorical" (ibid., 704).

[6]John Owen, *Meditations and discourses on the glory of Christ, in his person, office, and grace with the differences between faith and sight: applied unto the use of them that believe* (London, 1684; Wing O769), 174.

[7]Ibid., 178.

[8]Ibid., 179 (emphasis omitted).

Representation of him, such as is the delineation of his Glory in the Gospel. We *shall see him*, saith the Apostle, *face to face*; 1 Cor. 13. 12. which he opposeth unto our seeing him *darkly as in a glass*, which is the utmost that faith can attain to.[9]

Owen does not explain here the reason for his christological reading of the passage. Presumably, what drives it is his conviction that God reveals himself fully in Christ and that we can be "fully known" only when God accepts us in him. Christ, according to Owen, will forever be the means of communication between God and his saints. Owen's theological disposition seems to me exactly right: The virtue of love that abides (1 Cor 13:13) is the saints' eternal participation in the love that defines God in Christ, that is to say, the character or the essence of God. To know God in Christ—whether on earth today or in heaven in the hereafter—is to know (something of) the character or essence of God. There simply is no other vision of God.

Just as 1 Corinthians 13:12 contrasts today's partial (*ek merous*) knowledge with the full knowledge (*epignōsomai*) of the hereafter, so John's first epistle too emphasizes the ineffable character of the future face-to-face vision: "Beloved, we are God's children now, and what we will be has not yet appeared; but we know that when he appears we shall be like him, because we shall see him as he is [*kathōs estin*]" (1 Jn 3:2). The meaning of this saying is not immediately transparent. What does it mean to "see him as he is"? Who is "him"? Is it the Father or is it the Son?[10] And what does "as he is" entail? The exegetical questions are numerous and complex. One thing is undisputed, however: the eschatological vision will far surpass anything we may experience by way of contemplation today.

Those who think it is the Father whom we will see "as he is" (*kathōs estin*) often conclude that in the eschaton (and, therefore, not today) we will see

---

[9]Ibid.

[10]Simon Francis Gaine argues that John has the Father in mind, since (1) John has just mentioned our adoption as "God's children" in the same verse; and (2) John also seemed to have the Father in mind as the one who "appears" in 1 Jn 2:28 and the one of whom we are born in 1 Jn 2:29 (since elsewhere in the letter John makes clear that we are born of *God*, 1 Jn 3:9; 4:7; 5:1). Simon Francis Gaine, *Did the Saviour See the Father? Christ, Salvation and the Vision of God* (London: T&T Clark, 2015), 26-29. Others, however, argue that John has the Son in mind: In 1 Jn 3:5, 8, John says of the Son that he "appeared," and so it may seem more likely that the Son is also the subject of "he appears" in 1 Jn 2:28 and in 1 Jn 3:2. Rudolf Bultmann, *The Johannine Epistles: A Commentary on the Johannine Epistles*, trans. R. Philip O'Hara, Lane C. McGaughy, and Robert W. Funk, Hermeneia (Philadelphia: Fortress, 1973), 48.

the divine essence itself. This is Thomas Aquinas's argument. After stating that face-to-face vision (1 Cor 13:12) implies seeing God's essence, the thirteenth-century Dominican adds: "Further, it is written (1 Jo. iii. 2): *When He shall appear we shall be like to Him, because we shall see Him as He is.* Therefore we shall see Him in His essence."[11] Now, Thomas is appropriately cautious in how he affirms this vision of the divine essence. In an important sense, he acknowledges that this vision of God's essence does not mean that we will comprehend God.[12] This built-in reservation, meant to safeguard God's transcendence or otherness vis-à-vis the creature, seems to me important: Regardless of what it means that we will see God "as he is," it cannot mean that the Creator-creature distinction will disappear.

This does raise the question of what we mean by seeing the divine essence. Eastern and Protestant theologians often—though the latter by no means universally—avoid saying that the beatific vision involves seeing God's essence. The underlying reason is the same in both traditions. Notwithstanding Saint Thomas's claim to the contrary, there is a lingering concern among Orthodox and Protestants that the prospect of an eschatological vision of God *per essentiam* entails a denial of divine transcendence. It is a concern we should not dismiss lightly. Thomas Aquinas speaks a great deal about seeing the divine essence, but to my knowledge he does not speak of the beatific vision as a vision of Christ. This cannot but lead to the question of whether Aquinas thought that the final object of our vision is something that lies beyond Christ, namely, the very essence of God.

The questions that we face here are difficult. The seventh-century theologian Saint Maximus the Confessor, in response to questions from the Libyan monk Thalassius points out that our understanding of these matters

---

[11]Thomas Aquinas, *Summa theologica* (*ST*), trans. Fathers of the English Dominican Province, 5 vols. (1948, repr.; Notre Dame, IN: Christian Classics, 1981), suppl. q. 92, a. 1 (emphasis original); cf. *ST* I, q. 12, a. 1.

[12]*ST* I-II, q. 4, a. 3. Thomas explains here that our eschatological comprehension of God is not the kind in which God (the comprehended) is included in us (the comprehensors). Instead, comprehension here means "holding something already present and possessed: thus one who runs after another is said to comprehend him when he lays hold on him." In *ST* I, q. 12, a. 1 Thomas briefly comments that God is "not comprehended." And in *ST* I, q. 12, a. 7, he explains that no created intellect can know God infinitely, so God cannot be comprehended in the sense that he would be included within a finite being. Saint Thomas does claim, however, that in some sense it is possible to comprehend God, "for he who attains [*attingit*] to anyone is said to comprehend him when he attains to him" (*ST* I, q. 12, a. 7). Thomas means to convey that in some way we can reach or attain the essence of God without grasping or including it within our finite being.

is limited. He discusses the question of how to hold together the ignorance that John appears to confess ("Beloved, we are God's children now, and what we will be has not yet appeared," 1 Jn 3:2) with Paul's claim to knowledge ("For the Spirit searches everything, even the depths of God," 1 Cor 2:10).[13] Maximus suggests that though the two verses both speak of the eschatological future, each deals with a different aspect of it. We already know the divine aim, or *skopos*—we know that we will be deified—but we do not yet know precisely what this will entail; we do not know how exactly we will be deified. As Norman Russell puts it, according to Maximus "the reality of the form of future goods has not yet been revealed. For the present we walk with faith."[14] The question of how we will be deified or how we will see God is one that reason cannot adequately or fully address.[15]

Especially in the light of Maximus's word of caution, it seems to me that St. Thomas gives an unduly speculative answer to the question of how the *visio Dei* is possible.[16] He would not have faced this question in the same way had he not separated the light of faith (which allows for indirect vision today) and the light of glory (which enables us to see the essence of God directly in the hereafter). If we truly see the character or *ousia* of God in Christ, then it is the same God in Christ who has been seen in a variety of ways in history and whom in the hereafter we will see in glory. God does not reveal a different part or aspect of himself at different points of salvation history, so that at death the one aspect that remains veiled would be the

---

[13]Maximus the Confessor, *Ad Thalassium*, no. 9. See Norman Russell, *The Doctrine of Deification in the Greek Patristic Tradition* (Oxford: Oxford University Press, 2006), 284-85.

[14]Russell, *Doctrine of Deification*, 285.

[15]Maximus distinguishes between essence and energies, arguing that though human beings can participate in the divine energies of God, they will never see his essence. Gregory Palamas codified this distinction in the fourteenth century. See John Meyendorff, *A Study of Gregory Palmas* (Crestwood, NY: St. Vladimir's Seminary Press, 1998), 202-27. If the essence-energy distinction is meant as a real, rather than just a nominal distinction, it may be difficult to retain the simplicity of God—and it is unlikely that Palamas had in mind nothing more than a nominal distinction. It seems to me that we alleviate the Palamite concern about seeing the essence of God by recourse to Christology: All vision of God (and of his essence) has always been and always will be only a partial and theophanic vision of God's being in Christ.

[16]Thomas suggests that the light of glory (*lumen gloriae*) will serve as a created gift elevating the natural intellect so that it can see the divine essence (*ST* 1, q. 12, a. 2). But this raises the question of how a created light can have a deifying effect. Aquinas's defense that God gives the created light of glory this deifying power seems to me inadequate: Only God's own power suffices to enable us to see him. For a similar critique, see Nicholas J. Healy, *The Eschatology of Hans Urs von Balthasar: Being as Communion* (Oxford: Oxford University Press, 2005), 172. See further Michael M. Waddell, "Aquinas on the Light of Glory," *Tópicos* 40 (2011): 105-32.

vision of the divine essence. Rather, throughout history God has trained his people to see him by means of self-revelation. It is just that we can see his character much more clearly in the incarnate Christ than in any manifestation of God prior to this. But at all times—even in the eschaton—this self-manifestation (or disclosure of the divine essence) is a manifestation of God in Christ.

The Puritan theologian Thomas Watson, while affirming that 1 John 3:2 depicts the sight of God as transforming in character, remains cautious in how he expresses this. Commenting in his 1660 treatise on the Beatitudes that the saints "shall have some rayes and beams of Gods glory shining in them,"[17] Watson then makes the following comparisons:

> As a man that rowles himself in the Snow, is of a Snow-like whiteness; as the Crystal by having the Sun shine on it, sparkles and looks like the Sun; so the Saints by beholding the brightness of Gods glory, shall have a tincture of that glory upon them; not that they shall partake of Gods very essence; for as the iron in the fire becomes fire, yet remains iron still; so the Saints by beholding the lustre of Gods Majesty shall be glorious creatures, but yet creatures still.[18]

Watson's language is fascinating. He claims that the saints will have a "tincture" of God's own glory. And though he doesn't explicitly use the language of deification, by saying that "the iron in the fire becomes fire," the unspoken inference is that those who participate in God become divine. At the same time, in order to safeguard the Creator-creature distinction, Watson then explains that we will not partake of the divine essence itself. As I have already made clear, I am not convinced that we need to avoid the language of seeing the divine essence: There is every reason to say that, inasmuch as God's theophanic appearances in the Old Testament Scriptures were sacramental appearances of God in Christ, God revealed himself from the beginning the way he really is. Still, Watson's underlying concern is salubrious: As human beings we will never usurp the place of the transcendent God. His love in Christ is infinite; our capacity properly to apprehend it always finite.

It is hardly coincidental that the Puritans, including Watson—and, in the eighteenth century, also Jonathan Edwards—often connected the beatific

---

[17]Thomas Watson, *The beatitudes: or A discourse upon part of Christs famous Sermon on the Mount* . . . (London, 1660; Wing [2nd ed.]: W1107), 261.
[18]Ibid., 261-62.

vision with seeing Christ in the hereafter. It is in and by seeing Christ that we also see God himself. Through union with the humanity of Christ we will not just see his divinity, but inevitably we will see (in a spiritual sense) each of the divine persons, since they are one God. Edwards puts this beautifully: "The spouse of Christ, by virtue of her espousals to that only begotten son of God, is as it were, a partaker of his filial relation to God, and becomes the 'King's daughter' (Ps. 45:13), and so partakes with her divine husband in his enjoyment of his Father and her Father, his God and her God."[19] Even in the eschaton, it is through union with Christ in his human nature that we attain to the eternal Word of God and so to union with the triune God.

If the argument thus far holds—namely, that we have to construct the doctrine of the beatific vision as a vision of Christ—then this means that whenever and wherever we see Christ on earth, we anticipate the beatific vision. This is the case most clearly in the incarnation—hence Jesus' comment to Philip, "Whoever has seen me has seen the Father" (Jn 14:9). By contemplating Christ we also contemplate the Father. We simply cannot separate seeing Christ during his sojourn on earth from seeing the Father in the eschaton. When by faith we are united to Christ, we already participate, in a proleptic way—sacramentally—in the beatific vision. Indeed, whenever and wherever we see truth, goodness, and beauty, it is as though the eschaton comes cascading into our lives and we receive a glimpse of God's beauty in Christ. While the eschatological face-to-face vision is the reality (*res*) of our deifying union with God in Christ, rays from the light of God's presence already shine into our lives today. In these rays, God himself—none other than he—appears to us; these rays are theophanies (divine appearances), sacraments (*sacramenta*), which render the future present to us.[20]

---

[19]Jonathan Edwards, "True Saints, When Absent from the Body, Are Present with the Lord," *Works of Jonathan Edwards*, vol. 25, *Sermons and Discourses, 1743–1758*, ed. Wilson H. Kimnach (New Haven, CT: Yale University Press, 2006), 234. Kyle C. Strobel helpfully comments: "Our call is not simply to gaze on the beauty of Christ, to see Christ as beautiful, but to be caught up into this beauty itself—that our whole being would consent to his, and that we would partake in his filial relationship with the Father." Kyle Strobel, "Theology in the Gaze of the Father: Retrieving Jonathan Edwards's Trinitarian Aesthetics," in *Advancing Trinitarian Theology: Explorations in Constructive Dogmatics*, ed. Oliver D. Crisp and Fred Sanders (Grand Rapids: Zondervan, 2014), 147-70, at 160-61.

[20]Cf. John Panteleimon Manoussakis's comment that "a *pre*-eschatological vision of God is precisely made possible only retrospectively by eschaton itself—that is by the kingdom—which is to come and yet always coming, flowing, as it were, into history." John Panteleimon Manoussakis,

VISION AS PEDAGOGY:
CONTEMPLATION IN IRENAEUS OF LYONS

The second-century theologian Irenaeus of Lyons (ca. 130–202) was keenly aware that the eschatological vision of God in Christ is already given to us in the revelatory anticipations (or sacraments) that precede it. The bishop of Lyons repudiated the Gnostic and Marcionite devaluation of both the created order and the Old Testament narratives of ancient Israel. Through his Logos, God reveals himself in both, Irenaeus maintained, so that in some fashion one can contemplate God in both. Saint Irenaeus had a high view of the materiality of the created order.[21] He purposely used earthy vocabulary such as *plasma, plasmatio, caro, artifex Verbum, plasmare,* and *fabricare* to speak of the origin of creation.[22] Irenaeus regarded the Redeemer and the Creator as one and the same God—seeing as the "one God . . . by the Word and Wisdom created and arranged all things"[23]—so that the vision of God at the end of time meant for him the completion of a manifestation of God that began with creation itself.

Irenaeus articulated this conviction in his famous words: "For the glory of God is a living man; and the life of man consists in beholding God. For if the manifestation [*ostensio*] of God which is made by means of the creation, affords life to all living in the earth, much more does that revelation [*manifestatio*] of the Father which comes through the Word, give life to those who see God [*qui vident Deum*]."[24] For Irenaeus, we first see God in creation, and so the process leading to the beatific vision begins with his self-manifestation in creation. The created order, we could say, functions for Irenaeus as a theophany that makes God present in some way, so that to see

---

"Theophany and Indication: Reconciling Augustinian and Palamite Aesthetics," *Modern Theology* 26 (2010): 76-89, at 86.

[21]This stands in contrast to the Gnostics, for whom material substance originated in "ignorance and grief, and fear and bewilderment." *Irenaeus against Heresies* (hereafter *haer.*), in *The Apostolic Fathers with Justin Martyr and Irenaeus,* ed. Alexander Roberts, James Donaldson, and A. Cleveland Coxe, *Ante-Nicene Fathers* (Buffalo, NY: Christian Literature Company, 1885), 1.2.3 [1:318].

[22]J. T. Nielsen, *Adam and Christ in the Theology of Irenaeus of Lyons: An Examination of the Function of the Adam-Christ Typology in the Adversus Haereses of Irenaeus, Against the Background of the Gnosticism of His Time* (Assen, Netherlands: Van Gorcum, 1968), 16-17. See also John Behr, *Asceticism and Anthropology in Irenaeus and Clement* (Oxford: Oxford University Press, 2000), 38.

[23]*haer.* 4.20.4: 488.

[24]*haer.* 4.20.7: 490.

him there—and to treat creation accordingly—is to engage in contemplation of God.[25]

In book four of *Against Heresies*, the bishop outlines the pedagogical process through which God slowly but surely apprentices his human creatures so as to enable them to see him. The entire salvation history is a narrative in which God takes his children by the hand and with pedagogic skill leads them to maturity so that in the end they will be able to sustain the sight of God in his kingdom.[26] This divine pedagogical approach moves through three successive stages, according to Irenaeus. With prophetic vision the prophets saw beforehand, through the Spirit, God's coming in the flesh, when he would be seen, not according to his greatness and glory but "in regard to His love, and kindness, and as to His infinite power."[27] Next, in adoptive vision God manifests himself to us today through his Son. Finally, paternal vision is the ultimate vision of the Father, a vision of such brilliance that it will render human beings incorruptible in the eschaton. Irenaeus summarizes this gradual increase in vision by commenting:

> For as those who see the light are within the light, and partake of its brilliancy [*claritatem*]; even so, those who see God are in God, and receive of His splendor [*claritatem*]. But (His) splendour [*claritas*] vivifies them; those, therefore, who see God, do receive life. And for this reason, He, (although) beyond comprehension [*incomprehensibilis*], and boundless and invisible, rendered Himself visible, and comprehensible [*comprehensibilem*], and within the capacity of those who believe, that He might vivify those who receive and behold Him through faith.[28]

---

[25]Eastern theology often speaks in this connection of "noetic contemplation" (*theōria physikē*). See Bruce V. Folz, *The Noetics of Nature: Environmental Philosophy and the Holy Beauty of the Visible* (New York: Fordham University Press, 2014).

[26]Irenaeus argues that God could have created Adam and Eve perfect from the beginning but did not do so because they were mere infants. Even when in Christ God recapitulated all things, he did not come in his glory, but instead merely "as we were capable of beholding Him. He might easily have come to us in His immortal glory, but in that case we could never have endured the greatness of the glory" (*haer.* 4.38.1: 521). Cf. *haer.* 3.22.4: 455; Irenaeus, *Proof of the Apostolic Preaching*, trans. Joseph P. Smith, Ancient Christian Writers 16 (New York: Paulist Press, 1952), 14:56.

[27]*haer.* 4.20.5: 489. Statements such as this led to the Eastern distinction between the essence and energies of God. We should keep in mind, however, that Irenaeus does not use this technical language, and we should probably read no more into it than an acknowledgment that we cannot grasp or comprehend the entirety of God's infinite life.

[28]*haer.* 4.20.5: 489; parentheses original.

Salvation history, for Irenaeus, is a process of increasing perception of the light of God's brilliance (*claritas*), which gives one a share in this light and so in the divine life.[29]

The three stages are not separate, as if the saints see a different object at each stage. Rather, according to Irenaeus, at each stage they see the same God—though both ontologically and epistemologically, the stages differ from each other in important ways, especially since only in Christ does God take on human flesh.[30] Vladimir Lossky comments that each stage "is virtually contained in the other," so that the prophetic "vision of 'the likenesses of the splendour of the Father' already contains the premises for the perfect vision which will be realized later."[31] Put differently, for Irenaeus, although the prophets did not yet see the actual face of God, the final telos was in a mysterious sense present from the beginning of God's self-manifestation. Irenaeus's understanding of the beatific vision was sacramental inasmuch as he believed that the eschatological reality was in some way already present in both of the stages leading up to it.[32]

Irenaeus's understanding of salvation history, therefore, is not simply one that progresses chronologically from creation, via the fall, to redemption and consummation. Rather, the bishop understood this history as the progressive revelation of the Christ, who in an incipient, inchoate manner was always already present.[33] Speaking of the relationship between the (Old

---

[29] Cf. Mary Ann Donovan, "Alive to the Glory of God: A Key Insight in St. Irenaeus," *Theological Studies* 49 (1988): 283-97, at 288-89.

[30] Although Irenaeus depicts the Logos as already present in Old Testament theophanic appearances and visions (*haer.* 4.20.11: 491-92), he regarded the Old Testament theophanies and prophetic visions as nonbodily manifestations of the Logos and as such inferior to God's physical self-manifestation in the incarnation. Jackson Jay Lashier, "The Trinitarian Theology of Irenaeus of Lyons" (PhD diss., Marquette University, 2011), 144-50.

[31] Vladimir Lossky, *The Vision of God*, trans. Asheleigh Moorhouse, 2nd ed., Library of Orthodox Theology 2 (Leighton Buzzard, UK: Faith Press, 1973), 34. Irenaeus takes the expression "similitudes of the splendour of the Lord" from Ezek 1:28 (2:1) (*haer.* 4.20.11: 491). Ezekiel actually speaks of "the appearance of the likeness of the glory of the LORD" (see *haer.* 4.20.10). For Irenaeus, the genitival construct indicates distance: The prophets did not see the Father himself; he remained invisible.

[32] Irenaeus makes this particularly clear when he comments: "In this manner, therefore, did they also see the Son of God as a man conversant with men, while they prophesied what was to happen, saying that He who was not come as yet *was present*; proclaiming also the impassible as subject to suffering, and declaring that He who was then in heaven *had descended* into the dust of death" (*haer.* 4.20.8: 490 [emphasis added]).

[33] Cf. John Behr's word of caution regarding the term *salvation history*: "'Salvation history' certainly unfolds in scripture as a narrative, as we read from the opening verses of Genesis onwards, but

Testament) Scriptures and the gospel, John Behr comments on their relationship as follows:

> Irenaeus does not understand this in terms of a history recorded in the "Old Testament" continuing on to a new phase in the "New Testament," as two bodies of literature between which, if we so wish, we might be able to discern correspondences, or "types," and continuities. There is, rather, a strict identity between the Scriptures and the Gospel, both speaking of the "once for all" work of God in Christ: at length and diachronically, on the one hand, through various figures in the Scriptures; in brief, on the other hand, recapitulated together, synchronically, in the Gospel, drawing from the Scriptures.[34]

The strict identity of which Behr speaks indicates that Christ was not just foreshadowed, but was actually already present within the Scriptures themselves. The difference between the various stages of God's pedagogy is the increasing clarity with which he reveals himself. Like a good teacher, God constantly adjusts himself to his students' capacity.

THREE THEOPHANIES: MOSES' CONTEMPLATION OF GOD

It is not only the overall history of salvation that is akin to a pedagogical program leading toward the *visio Dei*. When we isolate a narrow slice of this history, namely, the book of Exodus, we see that here too God makes himself increasingly visible and more intimately present, both to Moses individually and among the people of Israel corporately. Although we could turn to a variety of biblical passages, the exodus narrative is particularly instructive, since it forms the backdrop to the Pauline promise that in the hereafter we will see God face-to-face (1 Cor 13:12).[35] Perhaps, therefore, we need to turn to the book of Exodus in order to see how it anticipates (and sacramentally instantiates) the face-to-face vision of God in the eschaton. The narrative makes clear that from the beginning God has been unveiling himself to his people, so that the beatific vision lies anchored sacramentally within the

---

reading this narrative as 'salvation history' is nonetheless a statement of how these scriptures appear retrospectively in the light of Christ" (*The Mystery of Christ: Life in Death* [Crestwood, NY: St. Vladimir's Seminary Press, 2006], 88).

[34]John Behr, *Irenaeus of Lyons* (Oxford: Oxford University Press, 2013), 139 (emphasis added).

[35]The theology of God's progressive self-manifestation through theophanies begins in the book of Genesis. For reasons of economy I will restrict myself to some highlights from the book of Exodus.

very early stages of salvation history. From the beginning, the Son of God was the treasure hidden in the field (see Mt 13:44) and could be discerned by those who had eyes to see.[36]

So, how does the book of Exodus concretely depict God as the divine tutor, leading his people to the beatific vision in glory? Moses first encounters God in the burning bush (Ex 3:1-6). It is the "angel of the LORD" who "appeared" (*yērāʾ*) to Moses (Ex 3:2)—though God himself calls to him from the bush (Ex 3:4). Moses, awed by the appearance of the God of his fathers, "hid his face [*pānāyw*], for he was afraid to look [*mēhabbîṭ*] at God" (Ex 3:6). God's appearance in created form—as the angel of the Lord in a burning bush—comes in the context of God's redemptive love for his people: The narrative is bracketed by expressions of God hearing, seeing, remembering, and knowing (Ex 2:24-25; 3:7), indicating his attentive care for his oppressed people. The theophanic experience opens up a call narrative, in which God enlists Moses to become their leader.

Once Moses has led the Israelites out of Egypt and they have arrived at Mount Sinai, God appears to him a second time. He instructs Moses to consecrate the people and to have them wash their clothes, since he will come down upon the mountain "in the sight of [*lə ʿênê*; literally, "before the eyes of"] all the people" (Ex 19:11). To be sure, they have already experienced God's presence throughout their journey: He has traveled with them continuously in a pillar of cloud and of fire (Ex 13:21-22).[37] But the requirement of purification intimates that he is about to manifest himself in a more direct fashion. Still, even this time, the divine self-revelation is veiled and takes the form of "thunders and lightnings and a thick cloud on the mountain and a very loud trumpet blast" (Ex 19:16), with the mountain being "wrapped in smoke because the LORD had descended on it in fire" (Ex 19:18). The Lord warns Moses that the people will perish if they "break through to the LORD to look [*lirʾōt*]" (Ex 19:21). After giving Israel the Book of the Covenant (Ex 20:1–23:33), God then invites Moses, Aaron, Nadab, and Abihu, as well

---

[36]For Irenaeus's use of Mt 13:44 in support of his sacramental reading of the Scriptures, see *haer.* 4.26.1: 496. Cf. Hans Boersma, *Scripture as Real Presence: Sacramental Exegesis in the Early Church* (Grand Rapids: Baker Academic, 2017), 16-17.

[37]Carl Friedrich Keil and Franz Delitzsch comment that "we have to imagine the cloud as the covering of the fire, so that by day it appeared as a dark cloud in contrast with the light of the sun, but by night as a fiery splendour." Carl Friedrich Keil and Franz Delitzsch, *Commentary on the Old Testament* (Peabody, MA: Hendrickson, 1996), 1:346.

as seventy of the elders to "come up to the LORD" to "worship from afar" (Ex 24:1). Once they have gone up, these leaders experience an encounter with God that is much more intimate than what the rest of the people have witnessed: "They saw [*wayyir'û*] the God of Israel. There was under his feet as it were a pavement of sapphire stone, like the very heaven for clearness. And he did not lay his hand on the chief men of the people of Israel; they beheld [*wayyeḥezû*] God, and ate and drank" (Ex 24:10-11). The text mentions emphatically that despite their vision of God, the leaders of the people do not perish. Instead, they celebrate a meal of fellowship in God's presence.[38] When Moses and Joshua proceed even higher up the mountain, on the seventh day Moses approaches the cloud and actually enters it (Ex 24:18). His second encounter with God thus concludes with Moses entering the very place of God's presence. The absence of a description this time around surely is an indication of the ineffably glorious character of the experience.

God then makes preparations for a more permanent presence among his traveling people. He gives detailed instructions for the building of a tabernacle (Ex 25-31), and the book concludes with a description of its actual construction (Ex 35-40). In between these two sections, we find the narrative of the golden calf, followed by the account of Moses' third vision of God and of his plea for God to accompany his people on their journey. God initially shows himself reluctant to do so after the golden calf incident, indicating he will send an angel before them instead (Ex 33:2). This attitude toward the people contrasts sharply with God's stance vis-à-vis Moses. Moses speaks with the Lord in the tent of meeting, with the pillar of cloud standing at the entrance (Ex 33:9). The intimacy of the encounter is thus far unparalleled: "Thus the LORD used to speak to Moses face to face [*pānîm 'el- pānîm*], as a man speaks to his friend" (Ex 33:11). In what follows, God does end up promising that his face (*pānay*) will accompany the Israelites, after all (Ex 33:14).

Moses, however, continues to worry whether or not God will actually be true to this promise, and he exclaims, "Please show me your glory [*kəbōdekā*]" (Ex 33:18). The Lord's response makes clear that there are limits to one's ability—even that of Moses—to endure the light of God's face:

---

[38]The meal is commonly interpreted as a covenant meal. For an alternative view, based on historical-critical considerations, see E. W. Nicholson, "The Interpretation of Exodus xxiv 9-11," *Vetus Testamentum* 24 (1974): 77-97.

"I will make all my goodness pass before you and will proclaim before you my name 'The LORD.' And I will be gracious to whom I will be gracious, and will show mercy on whom I will show mercy. But," he said, "you cannot see my face [pānay], for man shall not see me and live." And the LORD said, "Behold, there is a place by me where you shall stand on the rock, and while my glory [kəbōdî] passes by I will put you in a cleft of the rock, and I will cover you with my hand until I have passed by. Then I will take away my hand, and you shall see my back ['ăḥōrāy], but my face [pānay] shall not be seen." (Ex 33:19-23)

God reveals his gracious character but stipulates that despite this unveiling of his name (and so of his identity), he will in some sense remain veiled: Moses can only see God's back.[39]

Many theologians have mulled over this passage, since God's refusal to show Moses his face (Ex 33:20, 23) seems directly to contradict the earlier statement that Moses had already seen God face-to-face (33:11). An Irenaean lens may help us make sense of this puzzle. That is to say, it seems to me that God is educating Moses, revealing himself with increasing clarity.[40] The Lord first appears to Moses in a burning bush (Ex 3:1-6). Next, he shows himself to Moses on Mount Sinai, initially in the company of the other leaders and subsequently by himself within the cloud (Ex 24:9-18). Finally, God speaks to Moses face to face in the tent of meeting, and Moses is allowed to see God pass by, as Moses watches within a cleft of the rock (Ex 33:7-23). Within this progression of increasingly direct and intimate contact, God's word of caution that "man shall not see me and live" (Ex 33:20) serves as an indication that God's face-to-face encounter with Moses as his friend has not erased the Creator-creature distinction. In some ways, God remains veiled, even in this remarkably personal and intimate encounter. Moses' sight of the merciful character of God (Ex 33:19; 34:6-7)

---

[39]Cf. Walter Brueggemann's comment: "The culmination of this chapter is a vision of God (vv. 22-23). It is, however, a vision that embodies exactly the tension and juxtaposition we have seen all through the chapter. Moses does get to see God—but not God's face. Moses' 'seeing' is honored—but not fully. Moses anticipates Paul: 'For now we see in a mirror, dimly, but then we will see face to face' (1 Cor 13:12 NRSV)." Walter Brueggemann, "The Book of Exodus: Introduction, Commentary, and Reflections," in The New Interpreter's Bible, ed. Leander E. Keck (Nashville: Abingdon, 1994), 1:942-43.

[40]John Calvin has a similar understanding of a face-to-face vision of God that develops throughout salvation history in line with a divinely accommodated pedagogy. See Arnold Huijgen, Divine Accommodation in Calvin's Theology: Analysis and Assessment, Reformed Historical Theology 16 (Göttingen: Vandenhoeck & Ruprecht, 2011), 217-19.

does not mean that he now comprehends God. In its very nature, God's mercy is infinite and cannot be exhausted by human sight.

This inexhaustibility of God's being is precisely what Gregory of Nyssa had in mind in his reflections on Moses' ascent up the mountain: "He [i.e., Moses] shone with glory. And although lifted up through such lofty experiences, he is still unsatisfied in his desire for more. He still thirsts for that with which he constantly filled himself to capacity, and he asks to attain as if he had never partaken, beseeching God to appear to him, not according to his capacity to partake, but according to God's true being [*hos ekeinos esti*]."[41] Gregory rightly postulates that regardless of the intimacy of our vision of God, we will never capture or comprehend the infinity of his being. Even in the eschaton, God continues infinitely to transcend us. Our progression into the life of God will continue forever—a teaching to which Jean Daniélou referred as *epektasis*, an eternal stretching forth into the life of God.[42] Contemplation of God progresses without end, even in the eschatological reality of the beatific vision itself.

CONCLUSION

Contemplation is a practice we learn by recognizing the presence of God in theophanies—manifestations of God. From the moment of creation God's ultimate aim and purpose for human beings is that they may see him. Irenaeus's celebrated saying that "the glory of God is a living man; and the life of man consists in beholding God" captures the key insight that the purpose of humanity is always to see God.[43] The biblical narrative, therefore, shows us that God gives ever-greater opportunity for contemplating him, so that we may get a foretaste of the beatific vision through these early sacramental anticipations of it. The created order itself, as Irenaeus recognized, is such a theophanic anticipation. And the Old Testament presents us with numerous narratives of God making himself present to his people by way of theophanies. A christological understanding of divine revelation implies that we should recognize Christ's presence already in the creation and in these Old

---

[41]Gregory of Nyssa, *The Life of Moses*, trans. and ed. Abraham J. Malherbe and Everett Ferguson (New York: Paulist Press, 1978), 2.230.1-6: 114.

[42]Jean Daniélou, *Platonisme et théologie mystique: Doctrine spirituelle de Saint Grégoire de Nysse*, rev. ed., Théologie 2 (Paris: Aubier, 1944), 291-307.

[43]*haer.* 4.20.4: 488.

Testament theophanies. Christian contemplation, therefore, is not something outlandishly esoteric or strange. It is, first and foremost, recognizing Christ as the real presence of creation and of Old Testament theophanies. Every adumbration of the Christ event is a kind of sacrament, which makes the reality of Christ present to those who have eyes to see. Christian contemplation, therefore, is a sacramental way of seeing: It means we approach creation and the Scriptures as filled with the presence of Christ.

The contemplation that I have just mentioned is in some ways rather ordinary: It involves simple acceptance in faith that what we see in the natural world and in the Scriptures is not something purely natural but is stamped with the presence of Christ. Still, degrees of contemplation vary. The Christian tradition contains multiple accounts of saints who hoped to ascend into the presence of God so as to contemplate him more intimately and to see him more immediately. This seems to me a quite legitimate desire, which is rooted in the biblical understanding of the beatific vision. Moses himself had three theophanic appearances and in each one progressively contemplated God more intimately and directly. Even though Moses already had a face-to-face vision of God (Ex 33:11), he still longed to see God's face more clearly (Ex 33:18). What is more, John's Gospel makes unambiguously clear that there is no more brilliant theophany than the incarnation of the Word in Jesus Christ. When we contemplate him in faith, we see the Father (Jn 14:7, 9). When we turn to Christ, therefore, this transforms us far beyond anything that even Moses experienced: we change "from one degree of glory to another" (*apo doxēs eis doxan*, 2 Cor 3:18). And even this contemplation is merely preliminary to a vision that will be "face to face" (1 Cor 13:12) in a way that Moses' vision cannot possibly have been "face to face" (Ex 33:11). The expression "face to face," therefore, is one that allows for degrees: God's face in Christ is an inexhaustible source of life. So as to enter more deeply into this boundless life of God, Christians deliberately take time to reflect on who God is for them in Christ—how the future is present in Christ. After all, it is such contemplation that enables them to see the face of God more clearly.

I suspect we sometimes think of contemplation as something strange and out of bounds for ordinary Christians. I have tried to make clear that this is not so. To be sure, contemplation does sometimes lead to remarkable spiritual experiences. But it is the presence of Christ, not the experience, that is central. Although Moses reaches astounding heights of contemplation, none of the narratives describe him as interested in an experience as such. Moses is consistently concerned for his people, as he wants the face of God to journey along with them ("Is it not in your going with us, so that we are distinct, I and your people, from every other people on the face of the earth?," Ex 33:16). Perhaps the most startling aspect of the book of Exodus is its ending. Once more it describes the presence of God, this time after the construction of the tabernacle is finished. At that point the glory of the Lord fills the tabernacle (Ex 40:34), and God continues to travel with his people through his presence in the tabernacle: "The cloud of the LORD was on the tabernacle by day, and fire was in it by night, in the sight of [lə 'ênê; literally, "before the eyes of"] all the house of Israel throughout all their journeys" (Ex 40:38). The book of Exodus does not conclude with one of the theophanies of Moses; it ends with God's presence among his people, reminding us that contemplation is by no means an isolated activity. The beatific vision is the result of God's indwelling of his people. As such, we never have to fear that it is out of bounds for ordinary Christians. When Christ is made present to us, both in Word and in sacrament, we experience the future present—the theophanic brilliance of the glory of God—a genuine anticipation of the beatific vision itself.

CONTEMPLATIVE AND CENTERING PRAYER

JAMES WILHOIT

TO FAITHFULLY ATTEND TO THE QUESTIONS concerning contemplation broadly, and contemplative prayer more specifically, one should read generously and seek out the best examples to engage. This essay is an attempt to do just that. Focusing our attention on centering prayer is an opportunity to put before us one of the most well-developed techniques of prayer in modern Roman Catholic spirituality.[1] It is only after we faithfully attend to this method and its theological underpinnings, and generously listen to its guidance, that we can assess its usefulness and appropriateness for evangelical

---

[1]Centering prayer is a unique instantiation of contemplative prayer designed to be very accessible for those new to contemplative practices. This prayer method has received a wide following in the United States and around the world. The organization Fr. Thomas founded to support and disseminate this practice, Contemplative Outreach, has about 160 chapters in the United States and twenty other countries and offers programs and resources on contemplative spirituality to many people of all Christian traditions and supports centering prayer groups throughout the world (Susan Komis of Contemplative Outreach, interview by author and email correspondence, May 24, 2016). Centering prayer has gained some national prominence, having been reported on in major newspapers and periodicals like the *New York Times* and *Newsweek*, and its effectiveness in shaping brain structure has been the subject of recent empirical research. Jerry Adler et al., "In Search of the Spiritual," *Newsweek*, August 29 2005; Rich Barlow, "Some Drawn to 'Centering' Prayer," *Boston Globe*, September 21 2002, 1; Peter Steinfels, "Ideas and Trends: Trying to Reconcile the Ways of the Vatican and the East," *New York Times*, January 7 1990, 1; Daniel Goleman, "A Slow, Methodical Calming of the Mind," *New York Times*, March 21, 1993. See also: Michael Spezio, "Mindfulness in the Brain: A Study of Contemplative Practice in Relation to Neural Networks of Social Judgment and Meta-awareness" (paper presented as part of the USC Templeton Lecture Series, October 25, 2006); Andrew B. Newberg and Mark Robert Waldman, *How God Changes Your Brain: Breakthrough Findings from a Leading Neuroscientist* (New York: Ballantine, 2009), 48-49; and for comprehensive review of the pertinent literature see Kirk A. Bingaman, "The Art of Contemplative and Mindfulness Practice: Incorporating the Findings of Neuroscience into Pastoral Care and Counseling," *Pastoral Psychology* 60, no. 3 (2011): 477-89.

spirituality. This essay will conclude with some reflections on evangelical criticisms and my own suggestions for how to receive this practice of contemplative prayer.

THE METHOD OF CENTERING PRAYER

Centering prayer is intended to be an individual prayer practice that is best learned in a group setting and maintained through periodic retreats, where it is intensely practiced. While centering prayer is rightly classified as a contemplative practice, Thomas Keating has tended to portray it as preparation for contemplative prayer. This preparation comes through facilitating "the development of contemplative prayer by preparing our faculties to cooperate with this gift."[2] The emphasis is that this prayer provides a method to respond to God's initiative, in giving one the gift of infused contemplation. Centering prayer is intended to provide a context and perspective for one's prayer practice, not to become one's primary form of prayer.

The method of centering prayer is very straightforward. In terms of technique, the pray-er is asked to sit in silence for an established period of time (twenty minutes is suggested) with the intention of being present before God. The emphasis on the intentionality to be present is a distinctive feature of Keating's counsel. His careful and well-articulated balancing of what might be termed infused contemplation, coupled with an emphasis on our personal responsibility in participating in an intentional openness to God, are distinctive of Keating's position. Often meditative and contemplative prayer becomes very technical, skill-oriented, and portrayed as an achievement of disciplined concentration. Centering prayer is not an achievement, but making and keeping an appointment with God. At the beginning of the time of prayer, you simply declare to God your desire to sit in his loving presence, and during your practice you seek to honor this intention.

Because the practice of intentional and focused silence is a learned discipline, there is significant teaching devoted to cultivating this practice in Keating's writings and Contemplative Outreach's retreats. There is an assumption that lectio divina is the entryway into centering prayer. Keating writes,

---

[2]Thomas Keating, *The Method of Centering Prayer* (Butler, NJ: Contemplative Outreach, 2006), n.p.

"Centering prayer is a method designed to deepen the relationship with Christ begun in *lectio divina*."[3] The person with a well-developed practice of lectio divina has learned some measure of stillness, an appreciation for contemplative prayer, and a stance of quietly receiving from God. The commitment of the originators to lectio divina as preparation for centering prayer is often ignored when this method is presented on retreats or to youth groups.

The method employed by centering prayer has two dimensions. The first dimension is one's intention. Many forms of contemplative prayer place great emphasis on attention, but for Keating the emphasis is on intention, that is, our desire to be with God. In contrast, a popular book on meditation by an American Buddhist indicates that "meditation takes gumption,"[4] and the concentration needed for it is "developed by force, by sheer unremitting willpower."[5] Keating does not discount the effort involved in prayer, but he portrays centering prayer as a way of grace in which we "cooperate with the gift" of God's presence.[6] Our intention can be represented as hands open to receive. The second dimension is a strategy for respecting one's intention by remaining mentally engaged with the prayer practice. In large measure this dimension consists of strategies for dealing with distracting or wandering thoughts.

Keating provides four guidelines to help us consent to God's presence and remain with this engagement. The first is "choose a sacred word as the symbol of your intention to consent to God's presence and action within."[7] The prayer is to ask in prayer for a word from the Holy Spirit that will uniquely help him or her to focus in prayer. Keating advises one not to change this word during a prayer session but does not indicate that one must keep this word for the indefinite future. It is also important to note that this word is not a classic mantra. The word is not viewed as powerful in and of itself, but merely serves as a shorthand for one's consent. Instead of declaring, "I intend to place myself in the loving presence of God with open hands of receptivity," one merely repeats the prayer word as a summary of this intention.

---

[3]Thomas Keating, *Foundations for Centering Prayer and the Christian Contemplative Life: Open Mind, Open Heart, Invitation to Love, the Mystery Of Christ* (New York: Continuum, 2002), 118.
[4]Henepola Gunaratana, *Mindfulness in Plain English* (Boston: Wisdom Publications, 2002), 7.
[5]Ibid., 149.
[6]Thomas Keating, *Foundations*, 118.
[7]Thomas Keating, *Method*, n.p.

The second guideline is "sitting comfortably and with eyes closed, settle briefly and silently introduce the sacred word as the symbol of your consent to God's presence and action within."[8] There are just a few passing references to how to sit for prayer. He emphasizes the need to find a posture that embodies respect and receptivity. In centering prayer there is a sensitivity to embodied spirituality, but there is not the precise attention to posture and sitting that one finds in some approaches to meditation. The second step points to the essence of this prayer form, self-surrender.[9] This prayer word is to be used gently to recall one's intention and not as a club to beat away distractions or drown out mental noise. Keating asks the pray-er to "introduce the sacred word . . . as gently as laying a feather on a piece of absorbent cotton."[10] In his writings he demurs from calling the sacred word a mantra and uses the practice of the sacred word to highlight what he perceives as differences between centering prayer and Eastern forms of prayer.

> This brings me to the chief difference between centering prayer, Vipassana, and Hindu mantric practice. Centering prayer comes out of the Christian contemplative heritage, inspired in the first instance by the Desert Mothers and Fathers and the Hesychastic tradition of the Eastern Orthodox Church, both of which cultivate interior silence and purity of heart. In the methods of meditation in the Eastern religions, the emphasis is on concentration for the sake of developing clarity of mind. . . . Centering Prayer is a passage from concentrative practices to alert receptivity through consenting to God's presence and action within us. . . . This is attentiveness not of the mind but of the heart. Its source is pure faith in God's presence leading to surrender to the interior action of the Holy Spirit in the here and now.[11]

While words and images are not used in his prayer form, a distinct feature is that you are communicating with a divine person whom you have come to understand through your engagement with the church and its teachings, and through reading and meditating on Scripture. He repeatedly reminds his readers that "Centering Prayer does not 'empty the mind,'" it provides a way

---

[8]Ibid.

[9]Cynthia Bourgeault, "Centering Prayer as Radical Consent," *Sewanee Theological Review* 40, no. 1 (1996): 52. See also Cynthia Bourgeault, *Centering Prayer and Inner Awakening* (Lanham, MD: Cowley, 2004) for an extended discussion of Keating's emphasis on intention.

[10]Keating, *Method*, n.p.

[11]*The Thomas Keating Reader* (Brooklyn: Lantern Books, Kindle Edition, 2012), 84-85.

of engaging the God who loves us more than we imagine and whose fellowship and affirmation we do desperately need.[12]

His third guideline asks one, "When you become aware of thoughts, return ever-so-gently to the sacred word."[13] This advice shows his Benedictine commitment to John Cassian and his concern about thoughts.[14] His choice of the term *thought* is carefully chosen, and he elects to avoid terms like *distractions*. Keating does not advocate an "emptying of the mind," but does favor a prayer posture similar to what is often described as "no-thought." Consequently, he does not encourage the use of mental images in centering prayer. The swirls of thoughts are not defeated by a direct frontal attack, but are allowed with the confidence that God, in his grace, will deal with them: "As soon as a thought emerges, one returns 'ever-so-gently' to the sacred word. The gentleness is important here. One invites God to do the work. Grace moves one away from each and every distraction toward the silent presence of God within. The pray-er's role is to intend to return to God's presence through the use of the sacred word."[15] Unlike some forms of meditation, centering prayer does not seek to suppress thoughts or "empty the mind," but exercises a "willingness to let go of thoughts as they arrive and return to the sacred word as a symbol of one's consent to rest in God."[16]

Fourth, one is to conclude the prayer by remaining "in silence with eyes closed for a couple of minutes."[17] It is suggested that this gentle ending be accompanied by a prayer such as the Lord's Prayer and a statement of gratitude to God.

THEOLOGICAL FOUNDATIONS

Keating's writings are marked by a gentle certainty and clarity. He is content to posit his position, explain it, and suggest applications, but he seldom argues for or defends his position. He locates his work as standing squarely in the Christian contemplative tradition and credits *The Cloud of Unknowing*

---

[12]Ibid., 35.

[13]Ibid.

[14]For a clear practical introduction to Cassian and his emphasis on thoughts, see Mary Margaret Funk, *Thoughts Matter: The Practice of the Spiritual Life* (New York: Continuum, 1998).

[15]Thomas Ward, "Centering Prayer: An Overview," *Sewanee Theological Review* 40, no. 1 (1996): 24.

[16]Bourgeault, *Radical Consent*, 48.

[17]Keating, *Method*, n.p.

with suggesting this prayer practice: "It is an attempt to present the teaching of earlier times (e.g., *The Cloud of Unknowing*) in an updated form."[18] He sees his project as making accessible the riches of the contemplative tradition: "It is a way of bringing procedures to be found in the contemplative teachings of the spiritual masters of the Christian tradition out of the dusty pages of the past into the broad daylight of the present."[19]

The present indwelling of Christ in each believer is his theological touchstone. In what is essentially the official tract for centering prayer, written by Keating and widely distributed by Contemplative Outreach, he provides the following one-paragraph statement of "Theological Backgrounds":

> The source of centering prayer, as in all methods leading to Contemplative Prayer, is the indwelling Trinity: Father, Son, and Holy Spirit. The focus of centering prayer is the deepening of our relationship with the living Christ. It tends to build communities of faith and bond the members together in mutual friendship and love.[20]

The "indwelling Trinity" and "relationship with the living Christ" are constructs that appear throughout his writings. While quite orthodox in his official writings, his statements on the indwelling of Christ belie a universalism more evident in his lectures. He is willing to push the envelope with his language of indwelling: "The risen Jesus is among us as the glorified Christ. Christ lives in each one of us as the Enlightened One, present everywhere and at all times."[21] The language he employs to describe this indwelling is more evocative than precise, and he seems bent on portraying this principle as utterly attractive. The primacy of this construct can be seen in a statement like the following: "The fundamental principle of the spiritual journey is the Divine Indwelling." Despite its stated importance he does not nuance or develop this perspective.[22] His concern is to suggest ways for Christians to live and pray in light of this reality.

The main practice of the spiritual life, then, is to "be in" and participate in the indwelling Trinity through Christ. For Keating, origins of centering

---

[18]Ibid., 118.
[19]Keating, *Foundations*, 31–32.
[20]Keating, *Method*, n.p.
[21]Keating, *Foundations*, 117.
[22]Thomas Keating, *Fruits and Gifts of the Spirit* (New York: Lantern, 2007), 3.

prayer are trinitarian; this union is not a direct communion of the soul with God, for this intimacy is always through Christ.[23] The language of intimacy in current spirituality often evokes an image of interpersonal warmth, support, care, and romance. For Keating, the intimacy emphasizes transparency, vulnerability, receiving care, and participation. There is the "embrace element" in his intimacy, but he places more emphasis on a therapeutic intimacy. He writes, "As we sit in centering prayer, we identify with Christ on the cross and are healed of our emotional wounds."[24] Keating sees that centering prayer allows us to experience the reality that "perfect love casts out fear" (1 Jn 4:18 NRSV) and that our vulnerability, fostered by this unconditional love, allows "the fullness of grace to flow through us" healing "these wounds."[25]

In contemplative prayer the Spirit places us in a position where we are at rest and disinclined to fight. By his secret anointings the Spirit heals the wounds of our fragile human nature at a level beyond our psychological perception, just as a person who is anesthetized has no idea of how the operation is going until after it is over.[26]

The solitude offered by centering prayer becomes a place of transformation. While it is a retreat from the world, it is not an escape. It is a time to do serious business with God. Keating's understanding echoes that of Henri Nouwen: "Solitude is the furnace of transformation."[27] His language is never as raw as that of Thomas Merton, who describes meditation as being "brought naked and defenseless into the center of that dread where we stand alone before God in our nothingness."[28]

CENTERING PRAYER AS A WAY OF PROMOTING MINDFULNESS

An outcome of centering prayer that does not receive significant attention in Keating's writings is its enhancement of the life skill of mindfulness. Mindfulness is a broad term used in everyday language when we urge

---

[23]Gustave Reininger, "Centering Prayer and the Christian Contemplative Tradition," *Sewanee Theological Review* 40, no. 1 (1996): 34.

[24]Thomas Keating, "The Theological Foundations of Contemplative Outreach: A Commentary by Thomas Keating," *Contemplative Outreach News* 15 (Spring/Summer 2001): 2.

[25]Keating, *Foundations*, 84.

[26]Ibid, 42.

[27]Henri Nouwen, *The Prayer of the Heart* (New York: Ballantine, 2003), 15.

[28]Thomas Merton, *Contemplative Prayer* (New York: Herder & Herder, 1969), 85.

someone to "be mindful of what you say"—meaning essentially, be careful—or the declaration of Psalm 8:

> What is mankind that you are mindful of them,
>> human beings that you care for them? (Ps 8:4 NIV)

Here *mindful* seems to mean essentially to "lovingly pay attention to," as it does in Mary's Magnificat when she confesses

> for he has been mindful
>> of the humble state of his servant. (Lk 1:48 NIV)

You may hear of a friend who is suffering with chronic pain and has found relief through learning mindfulness meditation. It is this last use, what might be called clinical mindfulness, that is most relevant to this discussion. It is a cultivated way of being present to ourselves, others, God, and the world around us. It includes the practice of focusing our attention and awareness on the present moment with an appreciative curiosity.

A large and growing body of research provides evidence that mindfulness changes both subjective and physiological states. Those who engage in mindfulness practices find feelings of anxiety and depression lessened, they experience greater self-compassion, they are less reactive, and they experience deeper satisfaction in their relationships. Not only does a sense of well-being improve, but overall health improves. Mindfulness is associated with a stronger immune system, decreased blood pressure, and better sleep patterns, and facilitates changes in brain activity, enabling a more calm and focused state of attention.[29]

Mindfulness is perhaps most easily defined by its opposite, mindlessness, which is the tendency to run on autopilot, to be so preoccupied as to miss the interpersonal cues around one, to fail to savor the delights of life. So mindfulness is simply "knowing what we are doing while we are doing it."[30] The ability to be present is a basic move in the spiritual life; without it, one is not able to deeply attend to the text of Scripture or be present in prayer and worship.

---

[29]The following source provides a clear overview of the positive therapeutic benefits by one of the early advocates of mindfulness meditation as a clinical practice. Jon Kabat-Zinn, *Full Catastrophe Living: Using the Wisdom of Your Body and Mind to Face Stress, Pain, and Illness*, 2nd ed. (New York: Bantam, 2013), 242-68.

[30]Nathaniel Branden, *The Art of Living Consciously: The Power of Awareness to Transform Everyday Life* (New York: Simon and Schuster, 1997), 66.

By the 1970s mindfulness had made its way into the literature of psychology and personal growth texts in the United States. Certainly, multiple factors contributed to the growing interest in this construct; however, two persons served as remarkably effective proponents of it. The first is Thích Nhất Hạnh, a Vietnamese Buddhist who gained notoriety through his compassionate and creative outreach to the victims of the violence in his country and who held brief but high-profile teaching positions in the United States that brought mindfulness to the attention of Westerners.[31] The medical researcher Jon Kabat-Zinn began to use mindfulness in medical treatment in the 1970s and went on to empirically demonstrate the efficacy of mindfulness in treating a variety of diseases. His method of Mindfulness-Based Stress Reduction (MBSR) has been widely adopted around the world and has given rise to therapies such as Mindfulness-Based Cognitive Therapy (MBCT).[32]

The initial successes in medicine and psychiatry caught the attention of researchers in related areas, and by the 1990s mindfulness research was being conducted in education, psychology, management, and related fields. In the emerging field of positive psychology, mindfulness is seen as robust contributor to human flourishing.[33]

Christians have a rich tradition of interest in mindfulness, although this term has not been favored. The simple call of Peter to "pay attention" (2 Pet 1:19 NIV) to the Scriptures or Paul's call to "set your minds on things above, not on earthly things" (Col 3:2 NIV), which is echoed in Philippians 4:8, "if anything is excellent or praiseworthy—think about such things" (NIV). Through the pages of the Bible, there is an emphasis on the self-regulation of attention—the importance of directing our attention ("I made a covenant with my eyes / not to look lustfully," Job 31:1 NIV; "I will not set before my eyes / anything that is worthless," Ps 101:3). This paying attention and directing our attention requires training but is necessary to be fully present to and open before God and the Scriptures. As Dallas Willard

---

[31] Thích Nhất Hạnh, Mobi Ho, and Dinh Mai Vo, *The Miracle of Mindfulness: An Introduction to the Practice of Meditation* (Boston: Beacon, 1987).

[32] Jon Kabat-Zinn, *Full Catastrophe Living: Using the Wisdom of Your Body and Mind to Face Stress, Pain, and Illness* (New York: Bantam, 1990).

[33] Peter Malinowski, "Flourishing Through Meditation and Mindfulness," in *The Oxford Handbook of Happiness*, ed. Susan A. David, Ilona Boniwell, and Amanda Conley Ayers (Oxford: Oxford University Press, 2013), 384-96.

quipped, "God does not ordinarily compete for our attention."[34] The construct of mindfulness is discussed by many early Christian writers, most notably Evagrius and Cassian, with their emphasis on attentiveness to our thinking.[35]

While *mindful* is used a few times in English translation of the Bible (ten times in the KJV), the term could easily be substituted with a synonym like *attentive*. The construct of mindfulness is not to be uncovered through a simple word search. Some Orthodox writers cite *nēphō*, "well-balanced, self-controlled" ("But the end of all things is at hand: be ye therefore sober, and watch unto prayer," 1 Pet 4:7 KJV) as an equivalent term for *mindfulness*.[36] In the *Philokalia*, *nepsis* has an emphasis on guarding the perimeter of one's mind more than cultivated quality of thought. *Nepsis* is not so much a stand-in for *mindfulness* as it is a watchfulness of thought that would cultivate a certain quality of mindfulness. It must be noted that the desert tradition, seen in Evagrius and Cassian, does not esteem the modern clinical mindfulness that is content-neutral, but wants to develop a heart that will "fix your thoughts on Jesus, whom we acknowledge as our apostle and high priest" (Heb 3:1 NIV).

Certainly a number of biblical passages call for care in one's thought life in a way that goes beyond the content of one's thoughts. For example, the quality of one's heart is to be safeguarded above all things (Prov 4:23). This is done in part through the eyes and ears, which are its gates, and in some way shape it (Prov 2:2; 4:21-23). The quiet and humble faith of the childlike in Psalm 131 pictures something akin to mindfulness. Certainly, Jesus' concern about the futility of worry in the Sermon on the Mount is also another related attribute of mindfulness. Paul, in Philippians 4:4-10, describes the content or object of one's thinking as well as a humble and nonstriving quality that should mark it.

---

[34]Dallas Willard, *The Great Omission: Reclaiming Jesus's Essential Teachings on Discipleship* (San Francisco: HarperOne, 2006), 36.

[35]An excellent discussion of thoughts in these two ancient authors can be found in Dennis L. Okholm, *Dangerous Passions, Deadly Sins: Learning from the Psychology of Ancient Monks* (Grand Rapids: Brazos, 2014); and Diogenes Allen, *Spiritual Theology: The Theology of Yesterday for Spiritual Help Today* (Cambridge, MA: Cowley, 1997).

[36]Frederick W. Danker, Walter Bauer, William F. Arndt, and F. Wilbur Gingrich, *Greek-English Lexicon of the New Testament and Other Early Christian Literature*, 3rd ed. (Chicago: University of Chicago Press, 2000), s.v. "νήφω." Accessed via Accordance.

The construct of mindfulness per se is not central in Keating's teachings, although he advocates centering prayer as a way of growing into a state of equanimity where one is less captivated by the opinions of others and more able to hear from God. Several researchers have examined centering prayer to see if it produces measurable changes in brain functioning. The number of studies is small, but they do show that like its more clinical counterpart, mindfulness meditation, centering prayer does produce lasting neurological changes associated with lowered reactivity and greater serenity.[37] In a review article that examined the potential positive benefits of centering prayer, Bingaman concluded, "Repeating a 'spiritually powerful phrase' in the context of centering prayer has the capacity to resculpt the brain over time, until as contemplative practitioners would say, we feel it taking up residence in our heart."[38]

THE UNIQUENESS OF CENTERING PRAYER

Writers on centering prayer tend to want to have it two ways when they appeal to history. On the one hand, they portray centering prayer as part of the long tradition of Christian contemplative prayer, and on the other hand, they promote centering prayer is a new and distinct method. For this discussion I will grant both claims and am most interested in what might be unique about it, especially in terms of other contemporary approaches to Christian contemplative prayer. I see four unique emphases of centering prayer:

> Centering prayer places a unique emphasis on intentionality rather than on willpower.
> Centering prayer asks that one not only pray but also locate one's prayer in a contemplative construal of the world.

---

[37]Andrew B. Newberg and Mark Robert Waldman, *How God Changes Your Brain: Breakthrough Findings from a Leading Neuroscientist* (New York: Ballantine, 2009), 48-49; Joshua J. Knabb, "Centering Prayer as an Alternative to Mindfulness-Based Cognitive Therapy for Depression Relapse Prevention," *Journal Of Religion And Health* 51, no. 3 (2012): 908-24; Jane K. Ferguson, Eleanor W. Willemsen, and MayLynn V. Castañeto, "Centering Prayer as a Healing Response to Everyday Stress: A Psychological and Spiritual Process," *Pastoral Psychology* 59, no. 3 (2010): 305-29; Kirk A. Bingaman, "The Promise of Neuroplasticity for Pastoral Care and Counseling," *Pastoral Psychology* 62, no. 5 (2013): 549-60.

[38]Kirk A. Bingaman, "The Art of Contemplative and Mindfulness Practice: Incorporating the Findings of Neuroscience into Pastoral Care and Counseling," *Pastoral Psychology* 60, no. 3 (2011): 477-89.

Centering prayer as a movement has developed a clear and concrete method of prayer and a widespread and effective network of training. Centering prayer promotes mindfulness in the sense of being more present to what is going on and less reactive and judgmental.

Emphasis on intentionality. Keating makes it clear that the practice of centering prayer is enhanced by careful attention to practices like seated pose, posture, breathing, and attention to the space in which you pray. However, he places his primary focus on having a proper intention as you go to prayer. Many forms of meditation and quiet prayer place a great emphasis on cultivating your attention. One can find instruction in attention-oriented meditation books on how to sit motionless for multiple hours.

Cynthia Bourgeault writes, "Centering Prayer works with an entirely different property—not attention, but intention."[39] During centering prayer the pray-er is invited to repeat a sacred word, but this is not to become the focus of one's thoughts; it is intended to be a "reminder of one's intent for the duration of the prayer period to relinquish attachment to one's surface flow of thoughts and associations, and to rest in God's presence."[40] The contrast with methods that focus on attention can be seen in a story Keating has told. At a centering prayer training, a nun approached him to confess that her session had been an utter failure. "In twenty minutes," she says, "I must have had twenty thousand thoughts." Keating replies, "How wonderful! Twenty thousand opportunities to return to God."[41] Keating seeks to carefully articulate a middle path between a laissez-faire "just show up" and a willful concentration. He emphasizes that one often begins with an emphasis on concentration, but "Centering Prayer is a passage from concentrative practices to alert receptivity through consenting to God's presence and action within us, which places the emphasis on purity of intention."[42]

Keating's emphasis on intentionality is a remarkable gift. A perusal of the current literature on forms of meditation and contemplative prayer, unless informed by centering prayer, shows that by and large meditation is

---

[39]Bourgeault, *Radical Consent*, 48.
[40]Ibid.
[41]Ibid.
[42]*Keating Reader*, 84-85.

portrayed as a human achievement obtained through increasing one's powers of focus and concentration. Keating's emphasis on intention allows for a gracious tenor to pervade this prayer practice. It is not a practice of human achievement, but one of intentionality, receptivity, and openness to God's grace.

Centering prayer as a construal of the world. Keating sees centering prayer as more than a technique. A robust practice of centering prayer includes the cultivation of a particular way of viewing the world. Keating writes, "God's presence is available at every moment, but we have a giant obstacle in ourselves—our world view. It needs to be exchanged for the mind of Christ, for His world view."[43] This new perspective is understood to be both an outlook we cultivate and a perspective we receive as a gift through the practice of centering prayer, "with the world view that Christ shares with you in deep silence. His view of things becomes more important to you, than your own. Then he asks you to live that new life in the circumstances of everyday."[44] The importance of cultivating and receiving this new worldview can be seen in the amount of space Keating devotes to putting off the false self and its self-protective strategies and consciously practicing love. He says that this includes not acting out of anger and living in the reality of God's presence. The vast majority of Keating's books focus not on the techniques of centering prayer, but on a construal of the world that is compatible with contemplative prayer.

Method and training. One story of how centering prayer developed has Keating tasking his monks with finding a clear, simple, and historically Christian method for introducing the practice of contemplative prayer. After various attempts, Fr. William Menniger proposed a method he attributed to the popular medieval prayer book *The Cloud of Unknowing*. Originally the prayer was called the "Cloud Prayer." This prayer was introduced to retreatants to St Joseph's Abbey, and Keating constantly worked on ways of presenting it with clarity and focusing on its essentials. Through his retreats, writings, conferences, and leadership, an effective network of supporters of centering prayer has developed around the world.

---

[43]Thomas Keating, *Open Mind, Open Heart: The Contemplative Dimension of the Gospel* (New York: Continuum, 1994), 45.
[44]Ibid., 120.

Centering prayer promotes mindfulness in the sense of being more present to what is going on and less reactive and judgmental. Clinical mindfulness is understood as a way of cultivating a third-person perspective toward one's thoughts, noticing and observing what one is thinking instead of being overly identified with them, and to help one become less reactive. In the late 1970s medical researcher Jon Kabat-Zinn began to study the use of mindfulness in helping patients cope with chronic pain. He has demonstrated its efficacy in treating a variety of conditions. His method of Mindfulness-Based Stress Reduction (MBSR) has been widely adopted around the world and has given rise to therapies such as Mindfulness-Based Cognitive Therapy (MBCT). The initial successes in medicine and psychiatry caught the attention of researchers in related areas, and by the 1990s mindfulness research was being conducted in education, psychology, management, and related fields. One of the most common methods for promoting mindfulness is through what is known as sitting meditation.[45] A limited number of studies have shown that the practice of centering prayer seems to be as effective as sitting meditation in promoting mindfulness and its clinical benefits.[46]

CENTERING PRAYER AS A POSSIBLE EVANGELICAL PRACTICE

Centering prayer has enjoyed remarkable widespread support in its forty-year existence, but it is not without its critics. The criticisms are wide-ranging. Some writers focus on concerns about the theological proclivities of the founders of the movement (Keating, Pendleton, and Menniger), but the most strident critiques locate centering prayer in what they see as a broad and pernicious movement of theological compromise in which orthodox Christianity is being supplanted by New Age mysticism. Centering prayer is also caught in the net of evangelical critiques that object to patterns of devotion that are not explicitly taught in Scripture. They assert that

---

[45]While there are significant differences between the God-oriented present moment awareness supported by centering prayer and the mindfulness state engendered by mindfulness meditation, there is evidence to suggest that contemplative practices like centering prayer have salutatory benefits similar to those of mindfulness meditation. See, Fernando Garzon, "Christian Devotional Meditation for Anxiety," in *Evidence-Based Practices for Christian Counseling and Psychotherapy*, ed. Everett Worthington, Eric Johnson, Joshua Hook, and Jamie Aten (Downers Grove, IL: IVP Academic, 2013), 59-78.

[46]See the sources listed in note 1 of this chapter.

Scripture is the sole authority and source of guidance concerning practices of faith and devotion. A wise and moderate advocate of this position wrote to me about centering prayer: "I would think that the question of the sufficiency of Scripture 'for life and godliness' must be addressed. In my view, one would be hard-pressed to find centering prayer taught or modeled in Scripture as a method of prayer." To this author, centering prayer is ruled out as an evangelical practice because it is not explicitly practiced in Scripture. Our confession of Scripture as our ultimate authority certainly does not entail that it is the sole authority or source of knowledge on Christian spirituality. To the extent that Christian spirituality is the study of the lived reality of persons, why should we exclude insights from the study of spiritual practices and at the same time allow the introduction of empirical findings in the area of medicine or psychology? More sympathetic critiques tend to focus on concerns about the centering prayer movement and some of its emphases, especially its explicit foundational document, the Neoplatonic *Cloud of Unknowing*.[47] Others raise concerns about the widespread use of centering prayer in some programs because they contend that contemplative prayer is something that one grows into and should not be presented as an attractive introduction to the life of prayer.

While these critiques raise a variety of concerns about centering prayer, I do not believe they disqualify centering prayer from being an appropriate evangelical practice. However, I am cautious about introducing centering prayer into evangelical churches and ministries. I must underscore that I see the practice and underlying theology of centering prayer as bound together. It seems naive to speak of centering prayer as a theologically neutral method, a mere spiritual technique. While the broad theological assumptions of centering prayer may be compatible with evangelical theology, they are not deeply evangelical in terms of emphasis. For those interested in introducing this practice to an evangelical context, I offer the following suggestions:

---

[47]Three thoughtful and thoroughgoing critiques of centering prayer can be found in the following books by evangelical authors. These authors appear to base their critiques on centering prayer as presented in well-respected secondary sources rather than on Keating and Pennington texts. Donald G. Bloesch, *The Struggle of Prayer* (Colorado Springs, CO: Helmers & Howard, 1988); John Jefferson Davis, *Meditation and Communion: Contemplating Scripture in an Age of Distraction* (Downers Grove, IL: IVP Academic, 2012); Timothy Keller, *Prayer: Experiencing Awe and Intimacy with God* (New York: Dutton, 2014).

1. Centering prayer should be presented as a complete package. Keating understands centering prayer as a practice grounded in a contemplative view of the world, and he suggests that the practice of lectio divina could serve as an appropriate introduction and context for centering prayer. His writings have something like a ratio of about five parts foundations (theology/psychology) to one part method. The contemplative context is necessary for the practice to be done with a grace-oriented stance.

2. Centering prayer needs to be grounded in the gospel. Keating grounds the Christian's assurance of God's love in creation and baptism. As evangelicals, we must ground our sense of intimacy with God in our union with Christ made available in our regeneration. In my perusal of several evangelical adaptations of centering prayer, I did not find a clear grounding for our courage to enter God's presence in the cross. Also, an evangelical will want to see that the tendency in centering prayer to privilege God's immanence is balanced by an appropriate emphasis on divine transcendence.

3. Centering prayer should be seen as an advanced form of prayer. I think evangelicals, with our radical democratic impulse, recoil at the idea of levels of prayer, but we need to respect the wisdom of the church that contemplative forms of prayer grow out of a well-developed practice of vocal prayer.

4. Centering prayer must be shown to be missional. In Keating's writings one cannot escape the call to use this prayer practice as a way of becoming a new person more deeply committed to loving others. However, it can be taught in a very narcissistic way with the aim of promoting personal peace and self-satisfaction. This distorts Keating's sense that the times of prayer are often terribly disquieting, as we come to see and experience our sins in new ways, and that it continually calls us away from our false self with its myriad of self-protective strategies. He says that centering prayer is "preparation for action."[48]

5. One will need a discerning stance toward Keating's vast corpus of writing. An internet search for the term "centering prayer" turns up a

---

[48]Keating, *Foundations*, 58.

very wide continuum of practices, from the solidly Christian to the vaguely spiritual and non-Christian in orientation. The etiology of this lack of precision is difficult to determine, but Keating has not always been as theologically judicious in his freewheeling talks, which are now widely distributed in video form, as he generally has been in print. He does have a universalistic tendency and makes pantheistic-like statement such as, "The silence opens us to the Other who is in our midst and who wills that all be one."[49] And, "Once we understand that the Gospel is addressed to a presence within us that already exists, listening to the Word of God becomes a process of gradual enlightenment."[50] Like many spiritual writers before him, he offers a well-developed practice that is grounded in historic Christian practices and was initially grounded in a solid biblical and theological framework, but as his interests have broadened, he has explored related issues seemingly without the same theological commitments in place.

Keating has certainly succeeded in his quest to make the riches of the contemplative tradition available to a wider audience. He has also accomplished his apologetic aim of showing young people that Christianity offers a rich contemplative tradition. He has shown the power of a clear technique, coupled with compelling foundational teaching, to provide a lifelong method of prayer. I think Keating's most enduring legacy will be his emphasis on intention. In the past fifty years many writers have sought spiritual guidance on contemplation from Eastern religions, which place a great deal of emphasis on attention and concentration in prayer. In his quiet way Keating has challenged this orientation by his gracious words: "Centering prayer is not so much an exercise of attention as intention . . . you intend to go to your inmost being, where . . . God dwells. You are opening to Him by pure faith."[51] His writings show contemplative prayer not as an achievement of human will, but the gracious gift of the God who loves his children and longs to embrace and heal them.

---

[49]Thomas Keating, *The Divine Indwelling: Centering Prayer and Its Development* (New York: Lantern, Kindle Edition), Location 265.
[50]Ibid., Locations 78-79.
[51]Keating, *Foundations*, 36.

CONTEMPLATIVE PRAYER IN THE EVANGELICAL AND PENTECOSTAL TRADITIONS

A Comparative Study

SIMON CHAN

INTRODUCTION

Any attempt to compare evangelical and Pentecostal responses to contemplative prayer faces two difficulties. First, how do we compare two traditions that share many common beliefs, tendencies, and impulses? Both traditions are evangelical in that they place special emphases on the gospel, conversion, and personal relationship with Jesus. Would this vast overlap not make a comparison suspect? Second, within each tradition, there is a broad spectrum of views regarding contemplation. There are conservative evangelicals and Pentecostals who reject contemplation as too Catholic. Any comparison between them would be irrelevant. But there are "open" evangelicals and Pentecostals who share similar reasons for and attitudes toward contemplation. Any comparison between them would be redundant. Despite these difficulties, I will argue in this essay that there are significant differences in their respective spiritualities to form a legitimate basis for comparison. Evangelical spirituality is shaped by certain theological tendencies that make it more difficult, though not impossible, for the cultivation of contemplative prayer, whereas Pentecostal spirituality contains beliefs and impulses that make it more conducive to the development of contemplation. The value of a comparative study is that it not only leads to a more nuanced appreciation of their different contributions to Christian spirituality, but also shows the different ways in which contemplative prayer is assimilated into the two traditions.

UNDERSTANDING CONTEMPLATION

We need to make two preliminary observations about the nature of contemplation in order to set the context of our task at hand. First, contemplation as a distinct spiritual practice is generally recognized to be part of an older, nonevangelical mystical tradition. Over time, the Catholic tradition has also developed a mystical theology. In the teaching of Teresa of Ávila, for example, contemplation forms part of a continuum with ascetical or active prayer. According to Teresa, ascetical prayers, including vocal prayers, petitions, and meditation, are a more basic form of prayer, which should lead one to deeper levels of contemplation.[1] The move from meditation to contemplation, that is, from active to passive prayer, is part of the life of growth in prayer, or growth in relationship with God marked by increasing knowledge of and intimacy with him. People who meditate deeply on the Word may find themselves ineluctably drawn into contemplation. The growth process may be compared to growth in interpersonal relationship at the human level: the deeper the relationship, the lesser the need for words. Casual acquaintances have more need for words to understand each other; intimate lovers, who over time have developed a shared world of thought and experiences, need fewer words or no words at all to communicate: The twinkle in the eye, the raising of an eyebrow, that peculiar snort or smile— each gesture sends a clear, unmistakable message known only to themselves. Healthy spiritual growth should lead one naturally from vocal prayer and meditation to contemplative silence. To stop short of contemplative prayer is to short-circuit the growth process. In short, contemplative prayer is an intrinsic part of the growth process. For the devout soul, it is not even a question of choice. It should come as effortlessly as a child sucking its mother's breast. Teresa of Ávila uses this analogy to describe the "prayer of quiet" which, in her schema, is the beginning of contemplation.[2]

---

[1] In *The Interior Castle* Teresa distinguishes between an active or ascetical phase of "meditations and petitions," which brings "consolations" (4.1.4) and a passive phase, which she terms "the prayer of quiet," which brings "spiritual delight" (4.2.2). See *The Collected Works of St. Teresa of Ávila*, vol. 2, trans. Kieran Kavanaugh and Otilio Rodriguez (Washington, DC: ICS, 1980).

[2] Teresa of Ávila, *The Way of Perfection*, in Kavanaugh and Rodriguez, *Collected Works*, 31.9.

Second, there is a need to distinguish between a phenomenological and a theological definition of contemplation. Phenomenologically, Christian contemplation shares certain common features with those found in other philosophical and religious traditions. But from their similarity Christians draw very different conclusions. Some conservative Christians would, on that account, reject contemplation as a non-Christian practice (as noted in Schwanda's critique of some evangelicals). Others at the opposite end of the theological spectrum would proceed to validate any kind of contemplative tradition as equally valid ways to union with God. While there are phenomenological similarities, what is more important are theological discontinuities. As Kyle Strobel notes in his essay, it makes a real difference whether our contemplative practice is derived from a "generic account of contemplation" or is "formed by God's life and revelation."[3] The significance of the distinction between the phenomenological and theological is aptly captured in C. S. Lewis's illustration of mystical experience. All mystical experiences are like the experiences of sailing: They all feel the same, but they tell us nothing about the ship's final destination.

> All who leave the land and put to sea will "find the same things"—the land sinking below the horizon, the gulls dropping behind, the salty breeze. Tourists, merchants, sailors, pirates, missionaries—it's all one. But this identical experience vouches for nothing about the utility or unlawfulness or final event of their voyages—
>
> *It may be that the gulfs will wash them down,*
> *It may be they will touch the Happy Isles.*[4]

Making the distinction between the phenomenology and the theology of contemplation is not only helpful in clarifying some thorny issues among evangelicals, it is also particularly appropriate to the task at hand: If theology does make a difference, are there theological nuances that may explain the different responses to contemplation by evangelicals and Pentecostals as evangelicals and Pentecostals? I think there are.

---

[3]Kyle Strobel, "In Your Light They Shall See Light: A Theological Prolegomena for Contemplation," *Journal of Spiritual Formation and Soul Care* 7 no. 1 (2014): 105. See also Kyle Strobel's chapter in this volume.
[4]C. S. Lewis, *Letters to Malcolm: Chiefly on Prayer* (Glasgow: Fount, 1978), 67.

THE NATURE OF EVANGELICAL SPIRITUALITY

The evangelical attitude toward contemplation cannot be properly understood without first considering the nature of evangelical spirituality. Evan Howard's succinct description of evangelical spirituality will serve as our point of entry.[5] The first characteristic of evangelical spirituality is its protest against Catholicism. According to Howard, evangelicalism made a decisive break "with the scholasticism of Catholic theology, the hierarchy of Catholic ecclesiology, the mechanics of late medieval spirituality, and the basic structure of late medieval Catholic ascetic and mystical consciousness."[6] Its reaction against Catholic "mystical consciousness" would make it difficult to appreciate contemplation since in the Catholic scheme contemplation is part of mystical prayer. To reject its "mystical consciousness" is ipso facto to reject contemplative prayer.

Another characteristic is activism. Evangelical spirituality is marked more by doing than resting. It creates a certain temper that goes against the grain of contemplative prayer, which is, as will be seen shortly, a kind of resting. Evangelicals are not comfortable with a spirituality that stresses passivity. Although a quietistic stream seen in Keswick spirituality flourished for a time, it did not gain wide acceptance across the broad spectrum of evangelicalism and was treated in some evangelical circles with suspicion.[7] Today, the Keswick Convention has lost much of its appeal. The reason could only be guessed at, but one possible explanation is that evangelicalism, until recently, had not developed a coherent spiritual theology capable of integrating these seemingly opposing streams. Its activism tends to preclude spiritual passivity. In Catholic spiritual theology, growth in the Christian life could be explicated in

---

[5]Evan Howard, "Evangelical Spirituality," in *Four Views of Christian Spirituality*, ed. Bruce Demarest (Grand Rapids: Zondervan, 2012). Howard's understanding appears apropos to the evangelicalism from the mid-nineteenth century—the kind that is also characteristic of much of modern evangelicalism. If the revival movements of the mid-eighteenth century are included, the nature of evangelical spirituality would have to be qualified somewhat differently. E.g. the Wesleyan revival had a strongly eucharistic dimension, which was not apparent in the Wesleyan-Holiness movement of the mid-nineteenth century. See Geoffrey Wainwright's introduction to John and Charles Wesley, *Hymns on the Lord's Supper*, facsimile reprint (Madison, NJ: The Charles Wesley Society, 1995), v-xiv. On the Wesleys' eucharistic spirituality, see Lorna Khoo, *Wesleyan Eucharistic Spirituality: Its Nature, Sources, and Future* (Adelaide, Australia: ATF Press, 2005).

[6]Howard, "Evangelical Spirituality," 162.

[7]See ibid., 181.

terms of progressing from an active phase to a more passive phase. One starts with vocal prayer and other mediating ascetical practices before entering into the "prayer of quiet" and "infused" contemplation.[8] Without the foundation in active prayer, one is in danger of falling into the heresy of quietism.[9]

Another mark of evangelical spirituality is the primacy of the word: "Bible study is *the* discipline of evangelical Protestantism."[10] The problem of evangelical spirituality is not that it is word-centered, but that it tends to be exclusively so. Further, the word is reduced to the verbal-rational at the expense of the nonverbal and nonrational. Spiritually, it creates a certain mindset that is not conducive to contemplation. For instance, evangelicals, following the magisterial Reformers, profess Word and sacrament as constitutive of the church, but in practice most evangelical churches observe the sacrament of Holy Communion less frequently than they would preaching. Preaching takes center stage while the sacrament is sidelined. Thus their spirituality is not as decisively shaped by the sacrament as it is by preaching. This has consequences on the choice of spiritual disciplines. They are more comfortable with spiritual practices involving the use of the intellect rather than the imagination. Discursive meditation is preferred over imaginative meditation of the Ignatian type. Most evangelicals would not proceed further into passive forms of prayer where one loses intellectual control. Generally, any nonrational approach to spirituality is viewed with suspicion. Most hold to a memorialist view of the Lord's Supper or Holy Communion for precisely this reason.[11] A memorialist view comports better with its rational approach to the Christian life. It's easier to explain that Communion provides visible, object lessons on the gospel—there is nothing mystical about it—than that communicants mysteriously receive the body of Christ. Many would readily go along with Calvin that the Lord's Supper is "visible word,"[12] but not many would go along with his idea that at the Lord's Supper "Christ's

---

[8]See note 1 above.

[9]See *The New Dictionary of Catholic Spirituality*, ed. Michael Downey (Collegeville, MN: Liturgical Press, 1993), s.v. "Quietism."

[10]Howard, "Evangelical Spirituality," 181 (emphasis original).

[11]Even the term *Eucharist* is shunned by many evangelicals because of its association with Catholicism.

[12]See John Calvin, *Institutes of the Christian Religion* 4.14.3.

flesh, separated from us by such great distance, penetrates to us, so that it becomes our food" by "the secret power of the Holy Spirit."[13]

Yet another feature of evangelicalism is its free church ecclesiology or parachurch mentality, arising as an alternative to and a protest against clericalism. The church is understood in functional rather than ontological terms. Church is only a better way of organizing Christians for the cultivation of their personal spiritual lives and for mission. The Christian life is defined largely in terms of the individual's personal relationship with God (with some help from the church). It is not intrinsically linked to the church and its sacraments and thus is free from clerical control. The strength of evangelical spirituality is that it gives to each individual a sense of personal responsibility. It encourages each person to have a personal and warm relationship with the person of Jesus Christ. But there are serious weaknesses. Its failure to see the church as an ontological reality that exists both in and through time means that the larger Christian tradition plays only a minimal role in the cultivation of spirituality.[14] Take, for example, the use of the creed. Evangelicals may accept the contents of the Nicene Creed,[15] but they rarely, if at all, recite it. This omission is quite revealing of the evangelical mindset and spirituality. To recite the creed is to engage in a speech-act that affirms ecclesial identity and historic continuity with the ancient church—much in the same way as singing the national anthem is a way of affirming a people's national identity. To recite the creed is to say that the church that formulated this creed in this particular form is the church to which I belong, not just the church from which I can draw lessons for my own faith and practice. Evangelicals tend to see the church merely as "my tutor" but not as "our Mother." Freedom from Mother Church gives evangelicals the freedom to pick and choose her teachings and doctrines. It allows them to turn their "protest" against the church and her sacraments into a settled conviction. All these characteristics of evangelical spirituality create a mindset that makes it difficult for evangelicals to embrace contemplative prayer.

But evangelical spirituality is not necessarily governed by these tendencies. The fact that an increasing number of modern evangelicals are

---

[13]Calvin, *Institutes* 4.17.10.

[14]As Orthodox Bradley Nassif points out in his "Response to Evan Howard," in Demarest, *Four Views on Christian Spirituality*, 187-88.

[15]Howard, "Evangelical Spirituality," 163.

becoming receptive to older spiritual traditions since the 1970s[16] suggests that perhaps these evangelical tendencies can be (and should be) modulated. Why must evangelical spirituality be so exclusively word-centered to the extent that the sacrament, especially the Lord's Supper, plays no significant role in forming its spirituality despite the fact that, by definition, evangelicals would agree with the magisterial Reformers that the church is constituted by Word and sacrament? If evangelicals take their own understanding of the church seriously—if indeed the Christian life is shaped by Word and sacrament—should they not be more open to imaginative meditation and contemplation rather than confine themselves to discursive meditation? And if the sacraments are more than a memorial (nonmemorialist views were in fact predominant among the magisterial Reformers) and more than visible word (*verbum visibile*), should not evangelicals be more open to encountering God as mystery, which in turn should open the way into contemplative prayer?

THE NATURE OF PENTECOSTAL SPIRITUALITY

Pentecostal spirituality is notoriously difficult to define. There are seemingly contradictory impulses. On the one hand, it manifests a tendency toward enthusiasm, such as the emphasis on direct, divine intervention in miracles and supernatural healings; the Holy Spirit as the agent who communicates directly to the human spirit; the human agent being "moved by the Spirit" to give a "prophetic word" to the church; and so on. On the other hand, it displays a strong sacramental tendency: prayer for divine healing is often accompanied by the use of anointing oil, the anointed cloth or "blessed water."[17] Space does not permit us to examine the possibility of integrating these two tendencies.[18] For our present purpose I will look at the sacramental dimension of Pentecostalism, which has an important bearing on contemplative prayer.

---

[16]See my article "New Directions in Evangelical Spirituality," *Journal of Spiritual Formation and Soul Care* 2, no. 2 (2009): 219-37. Cf. Howard, "Evangelical Spirituality," 186.

[17]The use of "blessed water" and various ritual actions is more prominent among the African Independent Churches. See J. Ade Aina, "The Church's Healing Ministry," in *A Reader in African Christian Theology*, ed. John Parratt (London: SPCK, 1987), 104-8; Allan Anderson, *Zion and Pentecost: The Spirituality and Experience of Pentecostal and Zionist/Apostolic Churches in South Africa* (Pretoria: University of South Africa Press, 2000); Anderson, "African Initiated Churches of the Spirit and Pneumatology," *Word and World* 23, no. 2 (2003): 178-86.

[18]The issue is addressed in my book *Pentecostal Ecclesiology: An Essay on the Development of Doctrine* (Blandford Forum, UK: Deo, 2011), 91-125.

Pentecostal attitude toward sacraments. The Pentecostal understanding of sacraments opens a fruitful avenue for exploring its difference with evangelicalism with regard to contemplation. In contrast to the generally non-sacramental evangelical understanding, Pentecostals are generally more sacramental in both theory and practice. As Daniel Tomberlin, a Church of God pastor notes, "Early Pentecostals intuitively knew that there is a 'real presence' in the celebration of the sacraments. . . . In the early published writings of the Church of God, the Lord's Supper was known as 'the Sacrament.'"[19] The early Pentecostals might not have a well-developed sacramental theology, but a number of things they did shows that Holy Communion occupied a place of special significance in their worship. Jonathan Black, a researcher from a classical Pentecostal denomination, the Apostolic Church of the United Kingdom, gives an interesting account of the way the early Apostolics worshiped. The high point of their worship was the Communion, which itself could last for more than forty minutes. Unlike the modern "contemporary worship," there was less music and singing. Worship was about being in God's presence at the Lord's Table "as if the people had already entered into heaven."[20] They composed hymns for Communion and even compiled a hymnal for the occasion titled *Hymns at the Holy Table*.[21] The belief that Communion holds special significance can also be seen in an early Assemblies of God teacher who describes the Lord's Supper as a "healing ordinance," that is, a means by which divine healing takes place.[22] Besides the Lord's Supper, other sacramentals were observed, such as the widespread use of the anointed cloth and anointing oil for healing.[23] Unlike evangelicals, who only began to make use of

---

[19]Daniel Tomberlin, *Pentecostal Sacraments: Encountering God at the Altar* (Cleveland, TN: Center for Pentecostal Leadership and Care, 2010), 76-77.

[20]Jonathan Black, "A Foretaste of Heaven: Early Pentecostal Thoughts on Worship," Apostolic Theology (blog), June 2015, http://apostolic-theology.blogspot.com/2015/06/a-foretaste-of-heaven -early-pentecostal.html. Note its similarity with the Orthodox understanding of worship. Apostolic sacramentality is well documented in Black's recent work, *Apostolic Theology: A Trinitarian Evangelical Pentecostal Introduction to Christian Doctrine* (Luton, UK: Apostolic Church, 2016), 557-623.

[21]Ian Macpherson, ed., *Hymns at the Holy Table* (London: Evangel Press, 1974).

[22]P. C. Nelson, *Bible Doctrines* (Springfield, MO: Gospel Publishing House, 1948), 73. The book is an exposition of the Assemblies of God's sixteen "Tenets of Faith" and was used in Assemblies of God Bible institutes and colleges worldwide.

[23]Daniel Tomberlin, *Pentecostal Sacraments: Encountering God at the Altar* (Cleveland, TN: Center for Pentecostal Leadership and Care, 2010); Kimberly Alexander, *Pentecostal Healing: Models in*

nonevangelical spiritual practices in recent times, there are strong evidences of a pervasive sacramentology in early Pentecostal history. The sacraments, however, were neglected as Western Pentecostals realigned themselves with evangelicals[24] and then rediscovered in the late twentieth century.[25] Quite clearly, Pentecostals were more sacramental in practice and temperament than evangelicals.[26]

This difference has an important bearing on their respective practices of contemplation. This is because sacrament and contemplation sustain an intimate relationship to one another. To affirm the sacramentality of created things is another way of saying that ordinary things can be a vehicle of spiritual reality: the finite can contain the infinite. Underlying this sacramental outlook is the mystery of the incarnation. The Word became flesh— and we beheld the glory of God in the humanity of Jesus (Jn 1:14). Jesus in all his earthly actions was fulfilling God's redemptive plan for the world through which his glory is revealed. Jesus in his humanity is the "primordial sacrament" of God;[27] that is to say, the incarnate Christ is the basis of all other sacraments but most supremely the Eucharist, the "sacrament of sacraments."[28] To participate in the sacrament, then, is to be open to an encounter with the mystery of the person of Jesus. In this respect, contemplation shares the same logic as sacrament. To encounter Christ in the Eucharist is at once to be drawn into contemplation. In his homily on the Feast of Corpus Christi in 2012, Benedict XVI explains the interconnectedness

---

Theology and Practice, JPT Supplements (Blandford Forum, UK: Deo, 2006); R. Marie Griffith "Material Devotion—Pentecostal Prayer Cloths," The Material History of American Religion Project, accessed February 1, 2011, www.materialreligion.org/journal/handkerchief.html.

[24]For example, William W. Menzies and Stanley M. Horton, *Bible Doctrines: A Pentecostal Perspective* (Springfield, MO: GPH, 1993). The work is an update of Nelson's *Bible Doctrines* and could be regarded as representing the official Assemblies of God position. On the Lord's Supper it takes a clearly antisacramental view (111). As noted above, Nelson understands the Lord's Supper as "a healing ordinance," but the phrase no longer appears in Menzies and Horton.

[25]See my "The Use of Prosper's Rule in the Development of Pentecostal Ecclesiology," *International Journal for The Study of the Christian Church* 11, no. 4 (2011): 305-17.

[26]The Pentecostal sacramental instinct refuses to go away, but it surfaces in highly questionable forms among the New Apostolic Reformation charismatics. The recent craze of grave-sucking or grave-soaking is a case in point. It is believed that by lying on or having physical contact with the tomb of well-known Pentecostal preachers one could imbibe their "anointing" to continue their miraculous ministry. It looks like a crude parody of Catholic devotion to saints and religious relics.

[27]Edward Schillebeeckx, *Christ the Sacrament of Encounter with God* (London: Sheed & Ward, 1963), 16.

[28]*Catechism of the Catholic Church* (Mahwah, NJ: Paulist Press, 1994), no. 1330.

between celebration and adoration of the Eucharist, and how the Eucharist and contemplation are complementary.

> To be all together in prolonged silence before the Lord present in his Sacrament, is one of the most genuine experiences of our being Church, which is accompanied in a complementary way with the celebration of the Eucharist, listening to the Word of God, singing, approaching together the table of the Bread of life. Communion and contemplation cannot be separated, they go together. To really communicate with another person I must know him, I must be able to be in silence close to him, to hear him and to look at him with love. True love and true friendship always live of[f] the reciprocity of looks, of intense, eloquent silences full of respect and veneration, so that the encounter is lived profoundly, in a personal not a superficial way.[29]

If Christ is sacramentally and mysteriously present in the eucharistic celebration (leaving aside the question of how he is present), it would be but natural and proper to adore him in and through the eucharistic celebration. And in adoring him one is awed and drawn into the "eloquent silences full of respect and veneration"—in short, into contemplative prayer.[30] Such contemplative prayer will not arise, however, if one is occupied with merely drawing out spiritual lessons through discursive meditation.[31]

The distinguishing mark of Pentecostal spirituality. If there is in fact a profound connection between sacrament and contemplation, and if Pentecostals are instinctively sacramental, it follows that contemplative prayer should also be an intrinsic part of Pentecostal spirituality in a way that it is not of evangelical spirituality. I will argue that this is in fact the case. The key to understanding Pentecostal spirituality is to be found in the quintessentially Pentecostal teaching on the baptism in the Spirit and its initial evidence of glossolalia. It is the one thing that distinguishes Pentecostals from evangelicals, making it the Pentecostals' main identity marker.

---

[29]"Pope's Corpus Christi Homily," *Zenit*, June 7, 2012, http://zenit.org/articles/pope-s-corpus -christi-homily/.

[30]One can begin at least to understand, if not appreciate, the Catholic practice of the adoration of the host.

[31]This is not to deny the value of this type of sacramental meditation, which was widely recommended by seventeenth-century Puritan devotional writers such as Lewis Bayly (1575–1631), *The Practice of Piety* (1611); Arthur Hildersham (1563–1632), *The Doctrine of Communicating Worthily in the Lord's Supper* (8th ed., 1633); and Henry Tozer (1563–1632), *Directions for a Godly Life* (10th ed., 1688).

Whether glossolalia should be understood as the initial evidence of Spirit-baptism is debated among modern Pentecostal scholars.[32] As I have explained elsewhere, the initial-evidence doctrine may not be the best way to explain the link between glossolalia and Spirit-baptism, but there is no question that among early Pentecostals glossolalia regularly accompanied their experience of Spirit-baptism and continued to be a regular feature in their devotional life.[33] Without taking account of this consistent correlation in Pentecostal experience, it would be difficult to explain why most classical Pentecostal denominations have an initial evidence doctrine in their statements of faith.[34] The Pentecostal doctrine of Spirit-baptism faithfully reflects the *sensus fidelium* of the early Pentecostals.[35] This is abundantly evident in early Pentecostal literature: "In about an hour and a half, a young man was converted, sanctified, and baptized with the Holy Ghost, and spoke with tongues"[36]—observations and testimonies like this occurred with consistent frequency in the Azusa Street Revival.

Two points need to be made about these testimonies. First, they tend to conform to the Pentecostal community's expectation, that is, the Pentecostal *ordo salutis*: salvation by the blood of Christ, followed by sanctification, and baptism in the Spirit accompanied by tongues. Theologically, this is the Wesleyan-Holiness Pentecostal's understanding of the threefold works of grace.[37] Telling their stories according to this theological framework is their way of validating their experience as Pentecostals. Second, and more importantly, the language used to describe their experience before and after

---

[32]See Gary B. McGee, ed., *Initial Evidence: Historical and Biblical Perspectives on the Pentecostal Doctrine of Spirit Baptism* (Peabody, MA: Hendrickson, 1991).

[33]Simon Chan, "The Language Game of Glossolalia, or Making Sense of the Initial Evidence," *Pentecostalism in Context: Essays in Honor of William W. Menzies*, ed. Wonsuk Ma and Robert P. Menzies (Sheffield: Sheffield Academic Press, 1997), 80-95.

[34]The Pentecostal/Charismatic Churches of North America, an association of thirty-five large Pentecostal denominations, affirms initial evidence as part of its statement of faith. "Statement of Faith," Pentecostal/Charismatic Churches of North America, accessed March 13, 2016, www .pccna.org/about_statement.aspx.

[35]In Catholic teaching the *sensus fidelium* plays a more critical role in the development of doctrine compared to Protestantism. See *Lumen Gentium*, Dogmatic Constitution on the Church, November 21, 1964, §12.

[36]Eddie Hyatt, ed., *Fire on the Earth: Eyewitnesses Report from the Azusa Street Revival* (Lake Mary, FL: Creation House, 2006), 16.

[37]Hyatt, *Fire on the Earth*, 12, 154, 156, etc. (emphasis added).

Spirit-baptism resembles the language of the contemplatives.[38] In preparation for the coming of the Spirit, one is to "let all go and just yield to Him."[39] This is clearly a carryover of the Keswick tradition. But when the Spirit came, they use such expressions as "though never unconscious, I was quite oblivious to those around, just worshipping"; "I am launched out into the fathomless ocean of God's love, joy and peace"; "unspeakable joy that flooded my soul when I, in simple faith, let my whole heart go"; "Jesus himself and the Holy Spirit entering in like a flood. . . . He [the Spirit] so melted me that I allowed Him to come in. I took Him in all His fullness"; "I feel that I want to be like the bed of a river, perfectly still, but wide enough to admit a flood."[40] If we compare the effects of the Pentecostal experience of Spirit-baptism with the effects of the "prayer of quiet" in Teresa of Ávila, the linguistic similarities are quite unmistakable:

> He [God] produces this delight with the greatest peace and quiet and sweetness in the very interior part of ourselves. I don't know from where or how, nor is that happiness and delight experienced, as are earthly consolations, in the heart. I mean there is no similarity at the beginning, for afterward the delight fills everything; this water overflows through all the dwelling places and faculties until reaching the body. That is why I said that it begins in God and ends in ourselves. For, certainly, as anyone who may have experienced it will see, the whole exterior man enjoys this spiritual delight and sweetness.[41]

But judging from their background and education, these early Pentecostals were probably not even aware of the fact that their experience of Spirit-baptism was phenomenologically quite indistinguishable from that of medieval mystics. If they had known, they would have been quite appalled. Certainly they were not seeking to frame their testimonies to conform to Catholic mysticism. A plausible explanation is that Spirit-baptism bears deep spiritual affinity to contemplative prayer. The tongues-speakers were closer to the mystics than they realized. Yet despite the similarities, the

---

[38]The functional similarities between glossolalia and certain contemplative elements found in other Christian traditions have long been acknowledged. See Richard A. Baer Jr., "Quaker Silence, Catholic Liturgy, and Pentecostal Glossolalia—Some Functional Similarities," in *Perspectives on the New Pentecostalism*, ed. Russell P. Spittler (Grand Rapids: Baker, 1976), 151-64.
[39]Hyatt, *Fire on the Earth*, 150.
[40]Ibid., 147-150 et passim.
[41]Teresa of Ávila, *Interior Castle* 4.2.4.

Pentecostals were reluctant to unequivocally identify the other manifesta-tions such as unspeakable joy as the baptism in the Spirit. Why was glos-solalia singled out as the initial evidence?

The contemplative tradition may provide an answer. Teresa distinguishes between "consolations," which come from ascetical prayers ("through our own efforts"),[42] and "spiritual delight," which comes from the prayer of quiet.[43] Teresa further observes that consolations may be accompanied by deep emotions such as joy and tears, "tightening in the chest and even ex-ternal bodily movements that they cannot restrain."[44] But these emotions and involuntary physical manifestations may well be just natural phe-nomena, like the joy that spontaneously wells up when "someone suddenly inherits a great fortune" or the natural tears that come with sadness. This is because the consolations of ascetical prayer "have their beginning in our own nature and end in God,"[45] whereas the "spiritual delight" that comes with the prayer of quiet "begins in God and ends in ourselves";[46] that is to say, "spiritual delight" is a gift ("infused") and not dependent on our action. Early Pentecostals, too, experienced many other emotions and physical manifestations associated with the presence of the Spirit, but they did not regard them as the most distinctive sign of baptism in the Spirit. Whatever theological rationales modern Pentecostals offer for their doctrine of initial evidence,[47] one thing is indisputable: Glossolalia is a form of nondiscursive, passive prayer, arising from one's yielding fully to the Spirit. This is clearly evidenced by the way many traditional Pentecostals seek to distinguish baptism in the Spirit from the Spirit's work in salvation. "We receive, as it

---

[42]Teresa of Ávila, *Interior Castle* 4.2.3.

[43]See note 1 above.

[44]Teresa of Ávila, *Interior Castle* 4.2.1.

[45]Teresa of Ávila, *Interior Castle* 4.1.4.

[46]Teresa of Ávila, *Interior Castle* 4.2.4. It should be noted that for Teresa the prayer of quiet is only the beginning of contemplation or the transition from ascetical prayer to infused contemplation. It occurs at the fourth "Mansion" or "Dwelling Place." There are still three more to go.

[47]Classical Pentecostals offer different arguments for the initial evidence doctrine. William G. Mac-Donald suggests that since the tongue is the most unruly member of the body (see Jas 3:1-8), glossolalia signals the complete yielding the whole person to the Spirit. William G. MacDonald, "Biblical Glossolalia: Thesis 6," *Enrichment Journal*, accessed July 27, 2018, http://enrichment journal.ag.org/200501/200501_Glossolalia_6.cfm. Roger Stronstad, understanding Luke's theology of the Spirit as essentially charismatic, sees tongues as "the appropriate physical symbol" of the disciples' vocation to witness to the gospel throughout the world. Roger Stronstad, "They Spoke with Tongues and Prophesied," *Enrichment Journal*, accessed March 24, 2016, http://enrichment journal.ag.org/200501/200501_081_tongues.cfm.

were, a drink of the Holy Spirit when we are saved, but when we are baptized in the Spirit, it is as if that initial drink becomes an ocean that completely surrounds us."[48] Here is another:

> The Holy Spirit is living within every child of God (1 Corinthians 3:16); however, the Spirit does not maintain continual and complete control of every one of God's children. If we are saved, we have the Spirit (Romans 8:9). If we are filled, the Spirit has us. At salvation, the Holy Spirit comes in to abide (Jn 14:16). At the filling, the Holy Spirit takes over to preside.[49]

In singling out glossolalia, were the early Pentecostals in their inchoate way attempting a distinction between active and passive prayer and their respective effects: the natural "consolations" of active prayer and the "supernatural" effects of passive or "infused" prayer?[50] But lacking the conceptual tools to make this distinction, they were reluctant to identify the other manifestations of the Spirit unequivocally as the initial evidence of Spirit-baptism, even though some of these spiritual experiences could well be similar to Teresa's "spiritual delight" arising from passive prayer. Teresa's distinction, therefore, could provide Pentecostals with the needed theological vocabulary to better nuance their understanding of Spirit-baptism. Besides confirming glossolalia as a form of contemplative prayer, it differentiates between manifestations of the Spirit associated with contemplative prayer and manifestations of the Spirit, which, while signaling the presence of the Spirit, may just be one's natural response to the Spirit's presence.[51]

Glossolalia as the chief identity marker of Pentecostalism not only sets Pentecostals apart from evangelicals but also helps explain why contemplation is theologically more compatible with Pentecostal spirituality than evangelical spirituality. This point is corroborated by the Catholic charismatics' experience of Spirit-baptism. The Catholic charismatic renewal

---

[48]"What Is Baptism in the Holy Spirit?," *CBN*, accessed April 10, 2016, www1.cbn.com/spirituallife/what-is-baptism-in-the-holy-spirit.

[49]Moody Adams, "The Filling of the Holy Spirit," *1 Timothy 4:13*, accessed April 10, 2016, www.1timothy4-13.com/files/chr_vik/filling.html.

[50]Teresa often uses the term *supernatural* to refer to that which is given by God apart from one's efforts, that is, to that which is "infused" rather than "acquired" (Teresa of Ávila, *Interior Castle* 4.1.1, 2.4; *Way of Perfection* 25.4, 31.2, 31.6, etc.).

[51]E.g., the "holy laughter" and other physical manifestations that became the hallmark of the Toronto Blessing would appear to belong to what Teresa calls "consolations." They are what Jonathan Edwards calls "uncertain signs" of religious affections.

(CCR) is generally much more open to the Pentecostal understanding of glossolalia compared to the evangelical charismatics even though Catholic charismatics do not use the phrase *initial evidence*. This is because Catholic charismatics already possess a language derived from their sacramental and contemplative tradition that makes sense of their experience of glossolalia. They have no difficulty understanding glossolalia in sacramental terms and as a form of contemplative prayer. As the Catholic charismatic Simon Tugwell has astutely observed, "It would not be too far wrong to suggest that for them [Pentecostals] speaking in tongues is a sacrament in the fullest catholic sense of the word, in that it is a human act given to men to do, in which . . . we may unequivocally and without reserve identify an act of God himself."[52] They understand speaking and singing in tongues as passive modes of prayer.[53]

Catholic charismatics who are familiar with their own contemplative tradition are therefore able to appreciate the special place of glossolalia by assimilating it into their existing spiritual framework. The result is that their understanding concerning glossolalia comes very close to the classical Pentecostal doctrine of initial evidence, as seen, for instance, in the CCR Life in the Spirit Seminar (LISS). LISS was started by an early leader of the CCR in 1971, not long after the outbreak of the charismatic renewal in the Catholic Church in the United States. It consists of seven sessions aimed at deepening the spiritual life among Catholics. One of the sessions involves praying for the baptism of the Holy Spirit. Here, the LISS teaching is remarkably similar to the classical Pentecostal position:

> The baptism of the Holy Spirit is a gift of God which we can choose to receive *after* we become Christians (Acts 1:4-5, Luke 11:11-13), and the purpose of this gift is to *empower* every believer for being a witness of Christ to a hurting and unbelieving world (Acts 1:4-8, Luke 24:49). The usual outward evidence that we have received the baptism of the Holy Spirit is not that we "feel" anything but that we are able to begin praying in tongues by the Holy Spirit.[54]

---

[52]Simon Tugwell, "The Speech-Giving Spirit: A Dialogue with Tongues," in *New Heavens? New Earth?* (Springfield, IL: Templegate, 1976), 151.

[53]Léon Joseph Cardinal Suenens, *A New Pentecost?*, trans. Francis Martin (New York: Seabury, 1975), 101-4; Francis A. Sullivan *Charisms and Charismatic Renewal: A Biblical and Theological Study* (Ann Arbor, MI: Servant, 1982), 147.

[54]*Life in the Spirit Seminar* (Vatican City: ICCRO [International Catholic Charismatic Renewal Office], n.d.), 86.

LISS is still being used today in many Catholic parishes.[55] Besides LISS, some Catholic parishes also use the Alpha Course for their "New Evangelization."[56] The Alpha Course is produced by the Anglican charismatic church Holy Trinity in Brompton, London. It, too, contains a component where new believers (or nominal Catholics) are prayed for to be filled with the Holy Spirit.[57]

The initial-evidence doctrine may not be popular with many classical Pentecostal theologians today (not to mention evangelical-charismatics),[58] but it is very much alive in the CCR even if it does not go by that name. Catholics have no difficulty with the concept since they already possess the theological vocabulary with which to process their Pentecostal experience. For example, the Carmelite Ernest Larkin associates his own baptism in the Spirit with contemplation: "I felt the immense love of the Lord for me. No fireworks, nothing sensational, but a consoling experience. I have often thought that this was the grace of contemplation which Teresa calls 'spiritual delight' or *gustos*, the experiencing of God's love."[59]

Both experientially and theologically glossolalia bears the closest fit with contemplation; they belong to the same "language game." The early Pentecostals understood it instinctively by calling it the initial evidence of Spirit-baptism. Today, the situation is quite different. Sociological studies have shown that fewer modern Pentecostals speak in tongues and fewer still believe in the initial evidence doctrine.[60] Given the inadequate theology of

---

[55]A local LISS leader tells me that it is being conducted at least once a year in many parishes in Singapore and is used in many English-speaking countries. To date, 110 million Catholics have gone through the LISS course.

[56]For Catholics, the "New Evangelization" has less to do with evangelistic outreach to non-Christians than with reaching out to non-practicing Catholics. The phrase was coined by Pope John Paul II. See Ralph Martin, *John Paul II and the New Evangelization* (San Francisco: Ignatius, 1995).

[57]Although the Alpha Course states that speaking in tongues is "not necessarily a sign of being filled with the Spirit," the extent to which it goes to elaborate on the practice suggests that it holds a special place in relation to being filled with the Spirit. *Alpha Guide* (Singapore: Alpha Singapore, 2014), 57.

[58]According to a survey, the initial evidence is the number-one theological reason for Pentecostal scholars leaving their denominations. See Paul W. Lewis, "Why Have Pentecostal Scholars Left Classical Pentecostal Denominations?," *Asian Journal of Pentecostal Studies* 11, nos. 1-2 (2008): 76, www.apts.edu/aeimages//File/AJPS_PDF/08_-_1-2_Paul_W._Lewis.pdf.

[59]Ernest E. Larkin, "The Charismatic Renewal and Forms of Contemplation," Order of Carmelites website, 61-62, citing Teresa of Ávila, *Interior Castle* 4.2.24, accessed February 4, 2016, http://carmelnet.org/larkin/larkin015.pdf.

[60]Margaret M. Poloma, *Assemblies of God at the Crossroads: Charisma and Institutional Dilemma* (Knoxville: University of Tennessee Press, 1989), 40.

glossolalia among Pentecostals, this is hardly surprising, but it is also tragic because by rejecting the theology of glossolalia, they have deprived themselves of a resource from their own history to discover the richness of contemplative prayer.

CONCLUSION

If Pentecostal sacramentality and glossolalia open a natural avenue to contemplative prayer, we may conclude that the Pentecostal way of being Christian shares a deep affinity, theologically and spiritually, with the contemplative tradition. This cannot be said of evangelicalism. The latter has greater difficulty assimilating the ancient practice. There are movements within evangelicalism that come closer to the contemplative tradition, such as Keswick spirituality. But Keswick spirituality is problematic because the passive mode of prayer is divorced from the active mode, and as a result runs into the danger of quietism. This is why other evangelicals are rightly suspicious. As for contemplative prayer practiced by a broad spectrum of evangelicals (as Tom Schwanda has shown in his essay), it exists as isolated experiences of individuals. It was never normalized and made an integral part of an evangelical theology of prayer. This is perhaps the Achilles' heel of evangelical spirituality as far as contemplation is concerned. If contemplation is to become a veritable part of evangelical spiritual practice it would require an expansion of or perhaps even major structural changes to their existing theological framework. They have to realize, as the evangelical-turn-Catholic Thomas Howard did, that being evangelical is not enough.[61] But becoming more open to contemplation does not mean becoming less evangelical, as some conservative evangelicals fear,[62] or that the evangelical has to become an "evangelical Catholic";[63] rather, it means that he or she has

---

[61]Thomas Howard, *Evangelical Is Not Enough: Worship of God in Liturgy and Sacrament* (San Francisco: Ignatius, 1984).

[62]Conservative evangelicals who are deeply suspicious of contemplation not only are deficient in historical vision (as Tom Schwanda has pointed out in his essay) but have also confused historically conditioned habits of thought with Christian doctrine. Ingrained habits are hard to change!

[63]Cf. George Weigel, *Evangelical Catholicism: Deep Reform in the 21st-Century Church* (New York: Basic Books, 2013). Weigel's book is an attempt to recover the evangelical dimension of the Catholic faith for the Catholic Church's renewal. Weigel is quite clear, however, that the *Evangelical* in Catholicism is not derived from the evangelicals but from within Catholicism. Mutatis mutandis, I am making a similar claim for contemplative prayer in Pentecostalism.

to become a "catholic evangelical,"[64] that is, an evangelical with a catholic vision and a more comprehensive theological framework capable of incorporating contemplative prayer from their own history as well as non-evangelical sources.[65] By contrast, within Pentecostalism there is already a contemplative dimension in the form of glossolalia. For Pentecostals, then, contemplation is not about assimilating a foreign idea, acquiring a new habit, or changing their theological framework; it is about learning a new language in order to make explicit what is already implicit in Pentecostal faith and experience. The new language is actually the old language of the contemplative tradition. The theology of prayer as seen in Teresa of Ávila could help Pentecostals make better sense of their understanding of glossolalia and other spiritual experiences associated with the baptism of the Spirit. Spirit-baptism could be seen as the crossing of a threshold into passive prayer expressed initially in glossolalia, but also having other effects like silence and "joy unspeakable."

The contemplative tradition has much to teach both evangelicals and Pentecostals, but it teaches them different lessons in different ways. Perhaps the most important lesson that evangelicals could learn from that tradition is that it offers a way of integrating seemingly irreconcilable strands of evangelical spirituality. Within the theological framework of contemplation exemplified by Teresa of Ávila, there is a place for both ascetical spiritual disciplines, such as vocal prayer and discursive meditation, and passive Keswick-type spirituality. For Pentecostals, the contemplative tradition provides the linguistic tools to recover an essential part of their own spiritual heritage. From it, Pentecostals learn "to drink water from [their] own cistern, / flowing water from [their] own well" (Prov 5:15) and move deeper into the life of prayer.

---

[64]As seen, for instance, in Kevin J. Vanhoozer and Daniel J. Treier, *Theology and the Mirror of Scripture: A Mere Evangelical Account* (Downers Grove, IL: IVP Academic, 2015).

[65]Evan Howard too acknowledges this when he notes the "happy discovery . . . of spiritual disciplines from *nonevangelical* traditions." Howard, "Evangelical Spirituality," 181 (emphasis added).

A DISTINCTIVELY CHRISTIAN CONTEMPLATION

A Comparison with Other Religions

GLEN G. SCORGIE

INTRODUCTION

A devout Christian rises before dawn with a busy day ahead. She has cultivated the habit of spending time with the Lord first thing, before all manner
of duties and deadlines rush into her mind like (to use C. S. Lewis's vivid
image) wild animals.[1] After prayerfully reading the Scriptures, she quiets
herself. She pushes back the distractions that are already threatening to in-
trude and waits on the Lord. She communes with him, delights in him, and
in a posture of reverent receptivity listens for his guidance as the new
day dawns.

Meantime, an earnest Hindu man, wearing only a wraparound loincloth,
his forehead smeared with ochre, emerges from a dark grotto beneath the
floor of his temple grounds. He squints as his eyes adjust to the tropical
sunshine. His body is covered with perspiration from the sauna-like conditions of his subterranean sacred space. For some time, he has been seeking,
through repetition of a sacred mantra, to distance himself from all thought
and sensory perception in order to achieve a higher, more enlightened state
of consciousness. But now it is time for him to change into his street clothes
and get on with the rest of his day.

From the perspective of a religious studies expert, both this Christian and
this Hindu are practicing contemplation. For a person of faith, an important

---

[1]C. S. Lewis, *Mere Christianity* (New York: Simon & Schuster, 1996), 170.

question surfaces: Are these two forms of contemplation delivering essentially the same experience, or distinct and different ones?

This chapter is an invitation to think about Christian contemplation in relation to the contemplative practices and experiences of other religious (and even secular) traditions.

At the outset, some readers might detect irony in the very invitation to think about contemplation, since it is, by definition, something to be differentiated from the logical processing of thought. However, such an invitation to reason together about contemplation is in fact quintessentially Christian, for the Christian tradition generally regards our capacity for discursive reason as a gift to be stewarded rather than an obstacle to be overcome. It is equally Christian, of course, also to acknowledge that there are limits to the efficacy of this gift.

BENEFITS OF COMPARISON

It may be helpful to state upfront that my goal in offering such comparative assessment is not to establish the legitimacy of contemplation for Christians. Any legitimate apologetic for Christians practicing contemplation must necessarily be based on a careful examination of relevant scriptural teachings, and contemplative precedents found within Scripture itself. A supplementary ground for commending contemplation will be the personal edification attested by Christians who have devoted themselves to this discipline through the centuries. These are the legitimate foundations on which Christian contemplation should stand.

Recognize and accept reality. Nonetheless, there are other benefits that accrue from comparing Christian contemplation to the contemplative practices and experiences of adherents of other faiths. In the first place, it gives us an opportunity to come to terms with an important factual reality. Contemplation, in one form or another, has been and still is practiced (albeit to varying degrees) in all the world's religions, and even by some secularists today.

All religions have by definition certain similar features, certain common structural elements that allow us to recognize them as religions. They all have, for example, some apprehension of the transcendent, some diagnosis of what is wrong with humanity, and some proposal for addressing that problem in a saving, healing way. Moreover, each submits to particular authoritative texts or traditions, promotes a set of ethical ideals, gathers its adherents into structured forms of community, and envisions a particular future. In short, religions share a similar structure, regardless of how much they may differ in their individual features. Especially relevant to our reflections here is the fact that each religion promotes certain practices and disciplines as pathways to spiritual encounter and personal transformation.

It does not invalidate Christianity's claims to uniqueness to acknowledge this fact. As Christians, we do not need to reject a practice like contemplation simply because a similar practice may exist in another world religion. After all, Christians do not avoid meditative reading because Jews do so much of it. We do not cease gathering in community because Muslims and Buddhists happen also to congregate. We do not stop singing because music is part of other faith traditions as well as our own. Likewise, we do not have to turn our backs on contemplation simply because others practice forms of it as well.

One reason why religious traditions have similar features is that throughout history they have frequently borrowed from one another. How much of Buddhism, for example, reflects the earlier Hinduism from which it emerged so long ago in India? Who can possibly calculate the debt our own Christian faith owes to the Judaism from which it emerged? And how many Muslim beliefs, practices, and even architectural features echo Christian antecedents?

As just one case in point, the earliest Muslim Sufis were clearly influenced by their contemporary Christian contemplatives and appropriated many of the latter's disciplines. The term *Sufi* (literally, "wool") designates one who wears a woolen cloak, the distinguishing attire of eighth-century Christian ascetics. In times of religious transition, historian Philip Jenkins explains, "older forms can remain alive for many years, and even come to form part of the newly dominant faith." There is a venerable Sufi practice of constantly repeating the affirmation "there is no God but Allah" until it triggers a trance-like altered state of consciousness. This almost certainly reflects imitation of earlier, similar usage by Christian ascetics of the Jesus Prayer, or Prayer of the Heart. And typically Sufis manifest a special devotion to Jesus as the prophet of the heart par excellence.[2]

---

[2]Philip Jenkins, *The Lost History of Christianity* (San Francisco: HarperOne), 197-201; cf. Dudley Woodberry, "Sufism," in *Dictionary of Christian Spirituality*, ed. Glen Scorgie (Grand Rapids:

But similarities in contemplative practice exist even where borrowing has not occurred. In many such instances, similarities exist because the architects of the different religions share a common humanity.

Every religion is a complex expression of the beliefs, ideals, and practices of a particular group of human beings. While each religion originates from a powerful perceived encounter with the transcendent, its ensuing development is decisively shaped through the creative efforts of its adherents. Thus there is a profoundly human side to every world religion. Each bears the indelible marks—the fingerprints—of its earthly co-creators. And each religion has crafted ways to accommodate the breadth of human experience, emotions, and needs. No one, therefore, should be unsettled to learn that Christianity is not the only religion to sanction and encourage contemplation. It is no more surprising than the realization that adherents of other religions know joy and pain, eat food, and sleep regularly. Contemplative practices are present within religions across the board, because contemplation is a response to needs and longings we all share.

As image bearers of God, we are all wired similarly. We share deeply felt psychological needs and spiritual longings that draw us all toward what contemplation offers. Recognizing elements of commonality in religious practices does not undermine the Christian faith. The uniqueness of Christianity does not depend on its utter uniqueness in every aspect. It lies, rather, as C. S. Lewis eloquently explained, in the manner in which it completes and fulfills the aspirations to which all the other ancient mythologies and contemporary world religions attest.[3]

Understand and appreciate our own tradition more deeply. In addition to helping us come to a nonanxious appreciation of contemplation's ubiquity among the world's religions, studying it in comparative perspective also helps us apprehend our own contemplative tradition more perceptively. Far from minimizing our differences, comparative study has a way of casting the distinct features of each tradition, including our own, in bolder relief. Studying other religions, and grasping their distinct ways

---

Zondervan, 2011) (hereafter *DCS*), 775-76; and Louis Komjathy, ed., *Contemplative Literature: A Sourcebook on Meditation and Contemplative Prayer* (Albany, NY: State University of New York Press, 2016), chap. 9.

[3] C. S. Lewis, "Myth Became Fact," in *God in the Dock*, ed. Walter Hooper (Grand Rapids: Eerdmans, 1970), 63-67.

of doing life, gives us the perspectival advantage of a little distance. It helps us look back on our own tradition with greater insight. Otherwise we can remain too close to our own faith to understand and appreciate it fully. Occasionally the practitioners of other religions may even remind us of legitimate aspects of our own tradition about which we have grown forgetful.

It is important to remember these benefits of studying contemplation in comparative religious perspective. Honestly facing the similarities among the religions and their practices—including our own—fosters integrity. Perceiving the distinct features of our own faith and its contemplative practices can be illuminating and constructive. Embracing both realities—the similarities as well as the differences—enhances genuine discernment.

Identify what is distinctive about Christian contemplation. In addition to these two benefits of studying contemplation in interreligious perspective, there is a third. Many Christians who affirm the uniqueness of Jesus and of his saving work are troubled by the thought that the contemplative practices of other religions may deliver essentially the same spiritual experience as their own. It is true that the testimonies of contemplatives in different faith traditions may sound somewhat similar at times. If the contemplative experience is identical, then it follows logically that all of these paths have the potential—perhaps an equal potential—to lead practitioners into real encounter with the one we Christians know as the triune God. It is commonly inferred from precisely such an analysis that while our doctrines may divide us, our shared spiritual experiences—our shared contemplative experiences specifically—unite us at a deep level across interreligious lines.

But is it true that the contemplative experiences of different religions and religionists are identical to our own? The premise of this chapter is that in fact they are not.

No doubt many forms of contemplation are similar, sometimes strikingly so, particularly with respect to the specific practices believers engage in and the physiological and sensory responses such practices evoke. But what about the full-orbed spiritual experience to which all of this leads? Carefully comparing contemplative experiences can help us frame an informed answer to this important question.

DEFINING CONTEMPLATION

Contemplative practices are the things people do to facilitate contemplation. Contemplative experiences are the subjective outcomes or interior consequences of the initiatives they have taken. The first is a means and the second is a goal. Any attempt to compare contemplative practices and experiences will surely be an exercise in futility unless we are first clear about what we mean by the term *contemplation* itself.

The first thing we need to get our heads around is that the term means one thing in circles that practice the scientific study of religion, and other things in more in-house Christian conversations shaped by the history of Christian spirituality. I will summarize the three main meanings that circulate today.

A broad umbrella category. Contemplation per se has until recently not enjoyed a particularly high profile in the scientific study of religion. Consider, for example, the multivolume *Encyclopedia of Religion*, edited in the 1980s by renowned scholar Mircea Eliade, and arguably the standard work in the scientific study of religion. It does not contain a single entry on contemplation. Readers seeking for such are directed instead to one on meditation, or, alternatively, to ones on attention, prayer, and silence. Here the *Encyclopedia of Religion* reflects a tendency in earlier comparative religious studies not to clearly differentiate contemplation from meditation.

The Christian mystic Thomas Merton and the Zen Buddhist teacher Thích Nhất Hạnh developed a rather high-profile friendship in the mid-twentieth century. It was grounded in their shared appreciation for contemplative practices and experiences. In his heartfelt introduction to Merton's little classic *Contemplative Prayer* (1969), Thích Nhất Hạnh appears to treat contemplation, meditation, and the prayer of the heart as undifferentiated synonyms.[4]

We can detect, however, a subsequent evolution in the meaning of the term *contemplation*. The *HarperCollins Dictionary of Religion*, produced in the late 1990s as a joint endeavor with the American Academy of Religion, is an example. While including a substantive entry on meditation, it still lacks an entry on contemplation. But notice the thumbnail definition of meditation it provides: "A *process of contemplation* usually undertaken in a

---

[4]Thích Nhất Hạnh, introduction to *Contemplative Prayer*, by Thomas Merton (New York: Image, 1996), xiii.

structured manner" (emphasis added). Here contemplation has morphed into an umbrella term beneath which meditation is now subsumed as a subcategory. And indeed this has become the normative way of differentiating the two terms in the academic discipline of the study of religion.[5]

Today contemplative studies are finally emerging as a discrete discipline within the scientific study of religion. A massive anthology of essays on key contemplative sources from across the span of global religions was recently published. In both its title, *Contemplative Literature: A Comparative Sourcebook on Meditation and Contemplative Prayer* (2015), and in its contents, this book subsumes meditation beneath the larger, umbrella category of contemplation.

The emerging academic discipline of contemplative studies examines a remarkable diversity of practices drawn from a wide spectrum of religious and secular traditions. In seeking to provide definitional parameters for his declared subject of contemplation, *Contemplative Literature* editor Louis Komjathy puts forward this tentative but heuristic assessment: "Possible connective strands or family resemblances [characterizing contemplation] include attentiveness, awareness, interiority, presence, silence, transformation, and a deepened sense of meaning and purpose."[6] One of the reasons contemplation was chosen as the overarching label for this cluster of motifs is that meditation is too frequently equated with exclusively Buddhist techniques. Komjathy goes on to explain how the phenomenon of contemplation can actually be subdivided into about twenty different types. These types are carefully distinguished according to the practices they advocate, the goals to which they aspire, and the experiences they evoke.

Especially in this present age of frenzied activity and cognitive overload, this broadly defined contemplative portfolio offers an intriguing set of techniques to calm, recenter, and renew the harried soul. It offers multiple pathways to deeper connections to that which is "not merely me," and through this the possibility of significant personal transformation. Beyond its psychologically therapeutic appeal, contemplation is also thought to hold promise of connectivity to the transcendent, and other positive spiritual outcomes. Consequently,

---

[5]Jonathan Smith, ed., *HarperCollins Dictionary of Religion* (New York: HarperCollins, 1999), 692.

[6]This phrase is repeated in Komjathy, *Contemplative Literature*, 4, 6, 711, and 714.

contemplation defined in the aforementioned way is au courant across a broad spectrum of religious traditions and more innovative movements.

A godly disposition. There is a second sense in which the word *contemplation* is used today, and it is one that circulates in Christian contexts. Particularly in more popular Christian literature, it can be used to describe a sustained disposition or habituated orientation—what we might call a contemplative life.

Take, for example, Richard Foster's presentation of the contemplative stream in his influential *Streams of Living Water* (1998). He includes within this stream numerous figures, from the desert fathers to the European Pietists to Scottish Presbyterian John Baillie. The basis for such inclusiveness is that Foster regards contemplation as something more encompassing and longitudinal than an isolated discipline or episodic act. He equates it with an inward disposition and an entire way of life. For him, the contemplative designates a prayer-filled life in which the presence of God is faithfully and assiduously cultivated. In such a contemplative life, Foster explains, the "gaze of the soul" remains oriented toward God, even in the midst of everyday duties and activities.[7]

Such a gaze is characterized preeminently by love—a reciprocating response to the one who first loved us and loves us still. A contemplative Christian is one who makes loving God their chief aspiration in life, and discovers in so doing that their heart is progressively more attuned to God's heart. It is not unusual for contemplatives, when describing their experience, to employ metaphors of purifying fire and enveloping love. Often it is a bittersweet experience in which consciousness of deep emptiness coexists, paradoxically, with ecstasy and delight. Keep in mind that Richard Foster is still a Protestant with an instinctive tilt toward the whole people of God. Not surprisingly, therefore, he wants all Christians, even the most ordinary among us, to practice the loving attentiveness to God that the so-called contemplative pathway entails.

A similar vision informs Eugene Peterson's widely read book *The Contemplative Pastor* (1989). In this instance, the adjective *contemplative* designates a quieter, deeper, slower, less ambitious style of pastoral leadership than the

---

[7]Richard Foster, *Streams of Living Water: Celebrating the Great Traditions of Christian Faith* (San Francisco: HarperSanFrancisco, 1998), 32.

stereotypical norm. It requires slowing down and attending to what is genuinely important and spiritually significant. More than anything else it represents a pervasive disposition, one that is less fixated on making an impact, one that witnesses to the truth without abrasively pushing for it.[8]

A specific practice. As I have already noted, a clear prior definition of contemplation is crucial to making meaningful comparisons between contemplative traditions. Here is yet a third meaning of *contemplation* and the one on which I will focus in the rest of this chapter. It is the meaning that Christians have historically attached to it.

In contrast to the aforementioned works in the study of religion, the *Encyclopedic Dictionary of Religion* (1979), edited for a Roman Catholic publishing house, includes an entry on contemplation, and two cognate ones on the contemplative life and contemplative orders. Tellingly, so does the definitive *New Dictionary of Catholic Spirituality* (1993). It seems fair to infer from instances like these that Christians displayed the earlier interest in contemplation and also more readily differentiated it from various meditative disciplines.

Contemplation was part of the Christian vocabulary from early on. Variations of its Latin equivalent (*contemplatio*) surface at least thirty times in the Vulgate translation of the Bible, wherein its semantic range encompasses seeing, considering, and experiencing.

Even more formative was the emergence of a four-stage model of lectio divina—the spiritual reading of Scripture—in the twelfth or thirteenth century. This model, affirmed by Guigo de Ponte (also known as Guigo II), led practitioners first to read, then to meditate, then to pray, and finally to contemplate.[9] Not only was contemplation thereby validated as a legitimate discipline for Christians, but it was also inextricably embedded in a larger cluster of associated endeavors. Significantly, contemplation rested on a foundation of rational considerations and meditative reflection on them, all within the locus of a conscious, prayerful relationship to God. Such

---

[8]Such a contemplative orientation is best represented by the grammatical middle voice, rather than either its active or the entirely passive alternatives. See Eugene Peterson, *The Contemplative Pastor* (Carol Stream, IL: CTI, 1989), chap. 9.

[9]Guigo de Ponte, *On Contemplation*, in *Carthusian Spirituality: The Writing of Hugh of Balma and Guigo de Ponte*, trans. Dennis D. Martin, Classics of Western Spirituality (Mahwah, NJ: Paulist Press, 1997), 3.3: 218-20.

contemplation is not divorced from the life of the mind, or from interactive communion with God, but intimately associated with, and friendly to, these closely related aspects of the Christian life. It simply constitutes a capstone on all these, as it gathers all the preceding into a culminating response of affection, wonder, and delight.

Upon further examination, we discover that in instances where Christian writers distinguish meditation from contemplation, contemplation's defining feature is rest or pause from mental concentration. One might venture to suggest that contemplation in the Christian tradition is a matter of applying the principle of Sabbath to the labors of the intellect. Both this analogy to Sabbath and contemplation's persistent proximity to meditation in classic Christian spiritual writing suggest a rhythmic cadence and harmonious reciprocity between the states of intellectual focus and intellectual rest that the terms *meditation* and *contemplation* respectively represent. It is reasonable to infer that contemplation in its Christian sense is not intrinsically hostile to the life of the mind.

Christian contemplation's central motif is vision or gazing rather than thinking or reasoning something out. In its essence it involves an inward beholding and an unhurried delight. It requires being quietly and attentively present, and among its practitioners it often evokes experiences of heightened awareness. It can trigger a deep sense of belonging and unitive inclusion. It is known to evoke dispositions of profound gratitude.

I am proposing a formal understanding of Christian contemplation as a practice of attentive beholding—a kind of gazing on the object of our delight that assumes and builds on certain rational convictions about that object but goes beyond them in terms of the experience it generates. In terms of its impact, contemplation tends to be formational, inasmuch as it alters in its own unhurried way the default settings of the psyche, and brings the contemplating self into a more consistent and integrated harmony with its own convictions. Typically, the experiential outcomes of such contemplation include inner peace and centered settling. Not uncommonly, as I have already noted, it evokes a consciousness of belonging to a larger union.[10]

---

[10]The contours of Christian contemplation are carefully nuanced throughout Tom Schwanda, *Soul Recreation: The Contemplative-Mystical Piety of Puritanism* (Eugene, OR: Pickwick, 2012); see, for example, 75-79.

Hopefully we are able now to understand that at least three definitions of contemplation are presently in play in conversations about it. In the academic study of religion, contemplation typically designates an overarching category of centering practices that includes, but is not restricted to, meditation. Within the Christian tradition, and intramural Christian conversations, however, contemplation (or its adjectival form, *contemplative*) sometimes designates a God-attentive manner of life and ministry. It can also designate a more narrowly defined ancient practice that patiently moves beyond prior and preparatory cognitive reflection to quietly transform its practitioners and unite them more deeply with God.

The first sense in which the word *contemplation* is used, the one that now dominates in the scientific study of religion, is too large and amorphous to permit meaningful comparisons in such a brief chapter. The greatest interest of discerning Christians is surely in the second sense, which is contemplation as a sustained disposition—as a defining characteristic of a godly person. Nevertheless, the specific discipline of Christian contemplation is an essential instrumental means to this ultimate goal, since the cumulative residue of such focused contemplative moments will naturally permeate and shape a Christian's entire disposition over time. It is contemplation in this latter sense that we will now compare to its functional equivalents in other religions.

THE ABRAHAMIC RELIGIONS

It is hazardous to venture generalizations about the world's religions. The first reason is the fabulous internal diversity and complexity of each. The second is the evolving nature of these religions, such that their current states do not always correspond exactly to their historic profiles. I will proceed cautiously, taking these caveats to heart. The great world religions divide rather naturally between East and West, and I will consider them accordingly.

Similarities. The contemplative practices of the Abrahamic Western religions are similar. I am not suggesting for a moment that they are identical or interchangeable. I am simply acknowledging that greater similarities exist between Christian contemplation and the contemplative practices of Judaism and Islam than between Christian contemplation and its Hindu and Buddhist counterparts.

This is fairly predictable, since the Western religions presuppose the existence of a personal and personally responsive God, while the Eastern religions do not. The lived experiences of Jewish, Christian, and Muslim believers, therefore, are assumed to unfold before God.

Moreover, these religious communities are, as Muhammad famously declared, people of the book. Each considers its sacred text an inspired conduit of the voice of God and therefore worthy of devoted attention. This has also reinforced the idea that divine communication is apprehended first of all through cognitive reflection—in a manner that must engage the mind. The mind is not an enemy of enlightenment, but a sanctified instrument to attain it. The role of contemplation in the Western religions, while important, tends not to usurp the role of the intellect but to respect it and make its peace with it.

Contemplation, while present, has not been as dominant and pervasive in the Western religions as it has been in the Eastern ones. One reason is that the three monotheistic religions of the West—Judaism, Christianity, and Islam— share an assumption that the earth is a good creation of God and therefore a proper sphere for human exploration, development, and care. This shared view of the world has had implications for the Western religions inasmuch as it has validated engagement with the world as an important, legitimate aspect of living all of life before God. The Western religions have therefore tilted toward the so-called active life with a resultant limitation of the scope of the contemplative. These shared assumptions have led the Western religions to somewhat similar contemplative practices and experiences.

It should not surprise us to discover some parallels among these religions in the physiological responses that their contemplative practices evoke, including the patterns of brain stimulation that scientists are increasingly able to track. As it turns out, the same sectors of the human brain "light up" when people of different faiths engage in contemplative disciplines. Nor should it surprise us to discover that our respective practices may evoke similar experiences of, say, settled calm, ecstatic love, or radical surrender.

But it is well worth remembering that no spiritual experience consists of its physiological, neurological, or emotional correlates alone. It is wise to reject such materialistic reductionism. For one thing, religious experiences are not just embedded within belief systems, but profoundly shaped by them.

The experiences themselves are defined by the cluster of assumptions and values within which they occur. Because of their unique convictions and collective experiences, for example, Jews often wrestle with Yahweh and lament before him. Muslims submit themselves to Allah, whose power and glory so greatly exceed their own. Christians have similar experiences themselves, but the uniqueness of the Christian contemplative experience flows from the Christian's adoring focus on the face of Jesus Christ, who lightens our darkness and draws us into the presence and heart of God.

The main point is that every religious experience remains embodied within, and conditioned by, the life view of the contemplative practitioner. Christian contemplative experience occurs in the context of certain convictions about God and God's ways, and these undergirding assumptions ensure that the Christian contemplative experience itself will inevitably be different from its Jewish and Muslim counterparts. Of course, the more contemplative Christians focus their restful interior gaze on Jesus Christ, and intentionally keep company with him, the truer this will be.

Differences. The Western religions all affirm the existence of one real and glorious God, who happily can, to some extent at least, be truly known. It is the duty and privilege of believers to make this one true God the object of their unhurried adoration and delight, and to understand that such a worshipful, contemplative gaze is also the key to their own transformation. For these religions, then, the practice of contemplation is preeminently contemplation of the one true God—as this God is understood through the lens of a particular religion's beliefs about God and according to the disposition cultivated by that particular religion.

These latter caveats are important reminders that, despite all the aforementioned commonalities among the Western religions, the experiences generated by contemplation are not identical across the board. Even when the forms are similar (say, acts of kneeling or prostration or cultivating stillness), their perceptions of God as the object of their contemplative delight are necessarily different (e.g., the difference between the unitary nature of Allah and the complexity of the triune God matters), and those differences will ensure that the experiences themselves are not the same either.

Moreover, the different Western religions foster different contemplative dispositions. For example, unlike the Qur'an, which is primarily oracular, the Hebrew Bible and the New Testament consist largely of progressive narrative, of the rehearsal of divine acts in human history. Jewish and Christian spiritual traditions are therefore relatively more intentional in their cultivation of narrative memory and the spiritual discipline of remembering.

Jewish, Christian, and Muslim believers also respond differently to the revealed will and actions of God. For the Jews, a certain intracovenantal wrestling predominates, with the element of struggle all the more acute since the theodicy trauma of the Holocaust. For Muslims, the dominant response to God is submission—a posture of obedience enshrined in the very name of their religion—and this inevitably alters the ethos of Muslim contemplation as well. For Christians, contemplation of God is characterized chiefly by love—a self-forgetful, self-giving delight in the object of one's adoring gaze. This is not to say that a disposition of love cannot characterize Jewish and Muslim contemplation as well—on occasion it certainly can and does. I am simply differentiating the responses that are most characteristic of these respective traditions.

In which of these three Western religions does contemplation find the most congenial fit? In spite of the rich scriptural examples of contemplation enshrined in the book of Psalms, it is probably not contemporary Judaism. Most Jewish scholars acknowledge that Judaism today is not very strongly inclined toward contemplation. Perhaps this is due in part to residual anxiety over sheer survival in a hostile world, as well as a wounded ambivalence toward a God who has allowed what he has. In any event, the minority of Jews who are inclined toward contemplation are more likely now to draw resources from Eastern spirituality than their own in-house traditions of Kabbalah and the like. In such instances Eastern religious practices are given a veneer of familiar Jewish terminology.[11]

Given the Muslim practice of praying five times a day, one might reasonably assume that Islam has the best built-in structure of all the Western religions for cultivating contemplation. However, there are no strict controls over what goes through a Muslim worshiper's mind while praying, and there are also legitimate questions about the heuristic potential of a disposition of submission to foster meaningful contemplative experience.

---

[11]Komjathy, *Contemplative Literature*, 222.

Christianity certainly has a rich heritage of contemplative experience and practice on which to draw. Its most authentic expressions appear to be what has been described as a "mixed life"[12] in which contemplation informs and structures active service in the world. This is certainly the pattern that predominates among many giants of the faith, from Augustine to Gregory the Great in the early centuries to John Wesley and A. W. Tozer in the modern period. One thinks of the latter's practice of worshiping prostrate on the sandy south Chicago shoreline of Lake Michigan in the early dawn, even being kicked by a policeman who assumed he had lain there drunk all night. And yet this same man can also be found in his longtime role as a magazine editor, focused intently on meeting his latest deadline, his green-shaded visor low over his eyes, and then, at the very last minute, running down to the post office to get the finished copy off for overnight delivery to his publishing house in New York. The pages of Christian history—from Bernard of Clairvaux to Hildegard of Bingen—are filled with such exemplars.

THE EASTERN RELIGIONS

Hinduism. My comparative work pivots now toward the great religions of the East—religions that developed for the most part independently of concurrent religious developments in the West. Here my attention will focus briefly on contemplative practices in the Hindu and Buddhist traditions.

Hinduism is the oldest and most diverse of the major religious traditions of Asia. Buddhism emerged in the sixth century BCE initially as a reform movement within the diverse Hindu conglomerate, and carried over into its own development a number of the features of its parent Hinduism. Nevertheless, there are enough differences between their respective approaches to contemplation that we will treat them separately.

Hinduism assumes a view of the world that is very different from its classic Christian counterpart. The quest for nirvana—that is, the Hindu's heavenly destiny—requires escape from the confinements of the ordinary, time-place world accessible to our senses. Similarly, our consciousness of, and ability to enter into, this other, superior realm requires the transcendence of reason and the evoking of an altered state of consciousness. The recommended

---

[12]Arthur Holder, review of *Gregory the Great*, by George E. Demacopoulos (2015), in *Spiritus* 16, no. 2 (2016): 280.

pathways to such deliverance are necessarily diverse because human persons are themselves considerably diverse. But what they share in common is the conviction that rational reflection is more an impediment than an aid to such deeper, spiritual understanding. The quest for spiritual enlightenment demands the cessation of ruminating, rational reflection. This is so essential that it becomes a primary focus of Hindu spiritual discipline.

It should come as no surprise that contemplation—or something a lot like it—has become central to Hindu religious experience. It is, indeed, epistemologically essential to enlightenment. This also helps us understand the level of physiological sophistication achieved within Hinduism when it comes to contemplative disciplines. Hindus use mantras in ways that put the mind on automatic pilot, so to speak—freeing it up for higher-order apprehensions of reality. And, of course, Hindu spirituality is replete with testimonials to the experience of awareness of the unity of all things, and of the submergence of one's own finite identity into the larger, undifferentiated all.

Like the primal religious substrate from which it emerged, Hinduism remains extravagantly polytheistic, and devotion is directed toward a multiplicity of deities, among whom three in particular dominate. In the current environment of global religious cross-fertilization, Hindu beliefs and practices have been mediated to the West most effectively through groups like the highly visible Hare Krishna (devotees of the deity Krishna), through physical disciplines and exercises of yoga, and through so-called Transcendental Meditation. Their appeal in the West lies chiefly in their apparent willingness to celebrate a pluralistic tolerance of all paths to God, and their relatively sophisticated approach to becoming quiet, calm, and centered in the midst of an excessively busy, frantic, and ultimately superficial way of life.

Buddhism. Buddhism began as a reform movement within Hinduism in India in the sixth century BCE. It sought to purge Hinduism from corrupt and superstitious accretions. Even Hinduism's venerable belief in real, personal deities (countless numbers of them, actually) was considered a superstition to be rejected by the Buddhist faithful.

The moment that defined Buddhism, and triggered its trajectory away from the Hindu mainstream, was Prince Siddhartha's experience of enlightenment while meditating beneath the iconic Bodhi tree. While the original Buddha's spiritual discipline at the time is most commonly described as meditation, it was in fact a spiritual activity more akin to what we have been labeling contemplation.

Buddhists understand the world to be one characterized supremely by suffering, and a suffering created by the thwarting of desire. The pathway to freedom is one of negating desire in favor of a cheerful neutrality and indifference to outcomes. One must come to a point of acceptance of the ultimate emptiness and silence of the spiritual realm, and make one's peace with the bleakness this realization evokes. Rather than despair, however, one can embrace the emergent realization of the unity of all things, and open up one's heart in compassion toward the suffering experienced by other sensate creatures within the larger whole.

Like Hinduism, Buddhism views contemplation as the essential pathway to enlightenment. As such, it enjoys the status of an epistemological and soteriological necessity. Little wonder, then, that Buddhist practices of contemplation also have a sophistication seldom matched by Christian equivalents. One can think, for example, of an ancient Buddhist text attributed to the Buddha himself, the *Anapanasati Sutta* (that is, *Discourse on the Mindfulness of Breathing*). In it the Buddha goes into great detail to explain how a focus on breathing can purify the mind of hindrances to equanimity and related dispositions.[13]

Like Hinduism, Buddhism tends to coalesce around defining experiences and practices, and is therefore not so tightly structured and regulated as an organized religion. It has a broad diversity of expressions. In certain regions, its dominant forms reflect the residual assumptions of antecedent primal religions (i.e., folk Buddhism), while in other areas it has taken on more intellectual and philosophical forms. Of these, perhaps Zen Buddhism, with roots primarily in Japan, has been most attractive to Westerners. It is known for its very rigorous contemplative practices, such as the use of mind-bending koans (e.g., the sound of one hand clapping), to "liberate" the mind from entrenched habits of ratiocination.

In somewhat paradoxical fashion, Buddhism also promotes mindfulness—an intensification of our ability to notice, and to be attentive to, what is quietly going on in the present moment. Small, otherwise neglected things can become revealing windows into a deeper reality all around us.

---

[13]Sarah Shaw, "Southern Buddhist Meditation," in Komjathy, *Comparative Literature*, 265-95.

The goal of deeper attunement to what is real has become very compelling for many exhausted, disillusioned seekers caught up in the rat race of the West's materialistic economy. It requires a posture of attentive listening, and comes across as gentler and humbler than the aggressive change agents that modern cultures and economies laud.

The Neoplatonic strain in Christian spirituality. Parts of the Christian tradition have been infected with similar attitudes toward the life of the mind. Some early Christians inhaled the Platonic oxygen of their host culture, which led them to view God much like Plato did—as the all-encompassing One or the undifferentiated All. They also inferred from this philosophical outlook that the journey back to God necessitated detachment from the material world.[14]

One of the earliest promoters of such ideas was the fourth-century Cappadocian father Gregory of Nyssa, author of the famous spiritual work *Life of Moses*. Gregory treats the biblical account of Moses' life as an allegory of the Christian life itself, and paints the dark storm cloud into which Moses enters as he ascends Mount Sinai as the "dazzling darkness" of the seeking Christian's intellect.[15]

The trajectory of Christian spirituality was later shaped by a similar vision promulgated by a sixth-century Platonist writer posing as New Testament convert Dionysius of Athens (Acts 17:34). According to this writer, identified since as Pseudo-Dionysius, God is ineffable and ultimately unknowable. God is not only beyond all things material but also beyond all human conceptualization. All language and analogies fail us in our quest to return to God. In the end we must meet God in the dense, dark cloud of unknowing.[16]

This Dionysian vision of radical discontinuity between the infinite God and God's human creatures bound by time and space, and the limits of their cognitive capacities, influenced numerous streams of Christian spirituality, particularly the more mystical ones, in both the Latin West and the Greek East. *The Cloud of Unknowing*, by an anonymous fourteenth-century English writer, is a prominent example. Such a cloud, argues the author, can only be

---

[14]Glenn Myers, "Platonism and Neoplatonism," *DCS* 676-78.
[15]Carole Dale Spencer, "Gregory of Nyssa," *DCS* 486-87.
[16]Kin-Yip Louie, "Pseudo-Dionysius the Areopagite," *DCS* 698. Cf. *Pseudo-Dionysius: The Complete Works*, trans. Colm Luibheid, Classics of Western Spirituality (Mahwah, NJ: Paulist Press, 1987).

pierced by "darts of love" hurled earthward by God toward us. Somehow, mysteriously, and despite the failure of our intellectual powers, we are thereby able to enter into an experience of the hidden God's loving presence.[17]

Such ideas are typically harbored within the so-called apophatic tradition, or *via negativa* (that is, the way of negation), within Christian spirituality.[18] Accordingly, this is the Christian spiritual route that bears the most affinities to Eastern religious practices of contemplation.[19] The shining insight of this tradition is that the reality and fullness of the God whom Christians worship inevitably exceeds the limits of our human cognitive capacities. And this in turn fosters among believers a fitting disposition of humility and patient waiting on God. Nonetheless, there are no legitimate equivalents to be found within the apophatic tradition of Christian spirituality to the negative epistemological premises of the Eastern religions. Christians must discerningly reject all forms of ostensibly Christian spirituality that affirm pantheistic notions of union with God, or seek to suppress the life of the mind for the sake of a deeper actualization of such union.

NONRELIGIOUS SPIRITUALITIES

It is more and more common for people to self-identify as spiritual but not religious. What people generally mean by this distinction is that they are desirous of experiences of the transcendent and eager to embrace the potentially positive and even transformational effects of such experiences. At the same time, however, they are reticent to buy into the belief systems of organized religions, participate in those social communities, or fulfill the moral and ritual expectations of those religions for their members. As a descriptor of this brand of spirituality, *nonreligious* designates a characteristic indifference to what historic religions have to offer, including, in some instances, even belief in a supreme personal Being who created the world and is actively engaged in its unfolding history.

Instead, the practitioners of nonreligious spirituality tend to develop personally customized clusters of beliefs and practices to enrich and sustain

---

[17]Todd Johnson, "Cloud of Unknowing, The," *DCS* 361. Cf. *The Cloud of Unknowing*, trans. James Walsh, Classics of Western Spirituality (New York: Paulist Press, 1981).

[18]Bruce Demarest, "Apophatic and Kataphatic Ways," *DCS* 271-72.

[19]See, for example, Thomas Matus, *Yoga and the Jesus Prayer Tradition* (New York: Paulist, 1984); and Thomas Merton, *Contemplative Prayer* (New York: Image, 1996).

their lives. They may even selectively appropriate various offerings of the great religions, based on their perceived therapeutic benefits, especially the benefits of release from anxiety and stress, and a stronger inner sense of centeredness and meaning. It is not uncommon for such spiritually oriented secularists to appropriate associated religious terminology in an eclectic way as well.[20]

The contemplative practices that are especially popular among this group are those that offer a healing cure for the psychological stress of modern life and the vacuity of consumerist lifestyles. Sometimes the most profound contemplative moments that such nonreligious persons experience are sui generis ones that occur out in nature and break into a person's consciousness sideways and unexpectedly. Many people, including environmentalists like John Muir and scientists like Albert Einstein, have testified to moments of profound spiritual impact as they beheld the exquisite beauty and intricacy of nature, or felt awe before the mind-boggling dimensions of the starry night. Typically, testimonies to such experiences convey a profound sense of belonging to a much larger and unifying whole. Christian theology tends to account for such experiences in terms of general revelation or common grace, but such acts of convenient theological classification should not diminish our estimate of the profundity of such experiences. They can be revitalizing, transforming, and consoling for those who experience them, even though God in any theistic sense remains unacknowledged. But are they Christian experiences? If we remember the basic formula that sensation plus interpretation equals experience, they are not.

CONCLUSION

I have very briefly—and, admittedly, quite superficially—compared Christian contemplation to contemplative practices and experiences of other religions. We have discovered certain similarities across the board, but in the process we also acquired some idea of what remains distinctive about Christian contemplation. At the outset I noted that a number of definitions of contemplation are presently in play in conversations about contemplation. I chose to focus on the one with the strongest Christian pedigree, namely,

---

[20]Charles Taylor, *A Secular Age* (Cambridge, MA: Belknap Press of Harvard University Press, 2007), chap. 14.

contemplation as the culminating phase of a thoughtful, prayerful engagement with God's truth and presence.

The ubiquity of contemplative practices among the world's religions, and among the modern irreligious as well, suggests that there is a felt need for contemplation embedded in the human psyche itself. If anything, the clamorous distractions of contemporary life are putting our mental and emotional health even more at risk, and causing our spiritual sensibilities to atrophy. The crisis is now acute as the pace and noise of modern society intensify. It seems clear that Christianity cannot afford to be indifferent or unresponsive to these soul-threatening developments.

All of the world's religions, and secular spirituality too, offer contemplative techniques for dealing with cognitive distractions, calming the body and mind, and bringing a measure of relief from anxiety and stress. Such outcomes, as we know, are vital to holistic well-being. The contemplative practices of the different world religions also purport to connect practitioners to the transcendent in transformative ways. We understand how contemplation can positively alter the default settings of our psyches in ways that merely acquiring knowledge cannot match.

As Christians, we have our own rich history of contemplation, although in recent years, and in some quarters, this heritage has been downplayed. Consequently, many spiritually sensitive seekers are now looking elsewhere for satisfaction of their needs for centered calm and wholeness, and for encounter with the transcendent.

It is important to realize that Christianity has more than functional equivalents to what other religions offer in the areas of contemplative practice and experience. Its offerings are distinct and superior.

My brief survey of contemplation within the Western religions brought to light the fact that the contemplative experiences evoked by these different traditions are not the same. This is because Judaism, Christianity, and Islam function within different convictional frameworks. It is true that the contemplative experiences of each of these three Western religions presuppose a relational context and a personal presence. However, this divine presence, this Other, is known to the contemplative Christian as the triune God—mysteriously present to us in the undivided unity of an embracing Father, a redeeming Son, and a communing Holy Spirit. And the disposition that this contemplative act evokes is one characterized preeminently by adoration and delight, secure attachment, and self-forgetful love. For the Christian, then, the generic sense of unification that contemplation can sometimes trigger acquires uniquely Christian contours and substance.

Moreover, contemplation is essential to our formation and transformation. By a spiritual law operating in all religions, we become like what we adore. We all unconsciously imitate and gradually approximate the object we most highly value and most deeply desire. As Christians, our perception of God—one that, among other things, elevates Jesus to the status of worship-worthy deity—determines the trajectory of our own moral transformation.[21]

My survey of contemplation within the Eastern religions further underscored how important it is that Christian contemplation remain situated in an irreducibly relational context and before a personal, interacting presence. These convictions are in direct opposition to the dominant assumptions of the Eastern faith traditions. But even a brief consideration of the Eastern practices of contemplation exposes another fundamental difference—our perception of contemplation's relationship to the normal operations of our God-given reason.

At the risk of oversimplification, a key distinction between Christian contemplation and its Eastern alternatives lies in their respective goals. The chief goal of Eastern varieties of contemplation is epistemological—to achieve, through the suspension and suppression of reason, a higher plane of consciousness and enlightenment. We should also note that such enlightenment, in its completed state, is deliverance, so that contemplation becomes a soteriological necessity as well. As an essential instrument of epistemology and soteriology, contemplation naturally occupies a central place in the overarching structures of the Eastern religions. Not surprisingly, therefore, the sophistication and diversity of the contemplative techniques that have been developed in these religions are largely unparalleled in the Western religions.

The chief goals of Christian contemplation, by contrast, are relational and transformational. Grounded in revelation, and hopeful about the human

---

[21]This classic insight has been recently and ably presented by James K. A. Smith in *You Are What You Love* (Grand Rapids: Brazos, 2016) and earlier works like *Desiring the Kingdom* (Grand Rapids: Baker Academic, 2009) and *Imagining the Kingdom* (Grand Rapids: Baker Academic, 2013).

capacity to apprehend divine revelation, Christian contemplation is not concerned to achieve an altered state of consciousness in order to apprehend the higher truths of the transcendent realm. Instead, what Christian spirituality feels acutely is the need for cognitive rest in order to quiet mental preoccupations, and thereby to pave the way for a more profound apprehension of God's presence and embrace, and a deeper and more transforming appropriation of the truth of God into one's soul.

For Christians generally, meditation is an important precursor and companion to contemplation, and contemplation depends on the fruits of cognitive reflection. Contemplation is never a substitute for meditation, but an advanced step upward from it and all the while persistently dependent on it. Contemplation is chiefly an instrument of internalization and formation. It presupposes revelation. It is not in itself a level of spiritual attainment or a goal. And it involves no intentional suppression of the life of the mind.

Some Christians (typically a minority) of each generation will be drawn to the contemplative life—in which they devote themselves almost full-time to contemplation and related disciplines. Most of us, however, will still find our vocation within the larger and more familiar sphere of the so-called active life. What we should seek is a more contemplative tone to our ways of life.

Sooner or later, there will come a day for each us when, to use a familiar idiom, all will be said and done. The significant thing is that our journeys toward that day were designed by the Creator to be punctuated by moments of pause that anticipate this final cessation. We regularly pause, take a breath, and live into the experience of all having been said and done. Even our brow-furrowing intellectual workouts.

And what is left? The very best, actually. The adoring gaze. Presence. Joy. And so the reciprocating, active-contemplative rhythm of the Christian spiritual life will beat on, as it was intended,

> Till we cast our crowns before thee,
> lost in wonder, love and praise.[22]

---

[22]Charles Wesley, "Love Divine, All Love's Excelling" (1747).

CONCLUSION

Recovering Contemplation

JOHN H. COE AND KYLE C. STROBEL

THROUGHOUT THIS VOLUME WE HAVE SEEN accounts of contemplation and contemplative prayer that show both the breadth of the topic as well as the untapped resources that this theme can provide for evangelical spirituality today. If one were to consider simply the figures represented throughout the text, we would find a list of some of the most important theological, pastoral, and spiritual writers in the Protestant tradition, from John Calvin to Richard Baxter, from Jonathan Edwards to John Wesley, from Luther to Bonhoeffer, from Sarah Jones and Sarah Edwards to our own present-day Sarah Coakley. To conclude, therefore, we want to cast a vision for what it might look like to do what these Protestant figures did so well, namely, articulate a spiritual theology that was steeped in both theological and biblical sophistication along with real experimental depth. These figures were not talking about realities that were foreign to their own existence, but were speaking directly from their experience (and often struggle) with God in their day-to-day lives. This naturally leads us to ask: How might we do this in this present age? Here, in brief, we point to ways that we can continue to develop this aspect of evangelical spirituality.

First, this volume provides a unified voice, even if individual voices disagree on what it will entail, concerning the need to think theologically and biblically about the nature of the contemplative life of the Christian. This means that we do not simply accept a spiritual practice or a mode of prayer because it strikes our common-sense notions of human flourishing, but because we understand spiritual practices within the broad movement of God's gracious actions to his people and directions in Scripture.

Second, picking up on Richard Lovelace's notion of the "sanctification gap," there is a strong voice in this volume that points us toward the Protestant spiritual tradition as a place to mine for depth of spiritual analysis. Too often evangelicals do not consider their mothers and fathers in the faith, and there is a current in this volume to encourage us to "honor your father and your mother" (Deut 5:16). We are far from the first to consider questions concerning the Christian life, and our tradition provides us with conversation partners who do not share our modern assumptions. These voices are not without error, of course, but they are fellow believers of the faith who, in the Spirit, have sought out biblical, theological, and experiential faithfulness to God.

Third, as put well by James Wilhoit in his consideration of centering prayer, there is a theoretical and experiential package deal that we have to take seriously when it comes to Christian practice. In other words, it is not helpful to break off spiritual practices from their theological framework, because theory and practice are necessarily intertwined. This means that evangelicals must not simply adopt practices naively without considering what sort of theological axioms a given practice assumes. Instead, while it is helpful to attend to the tradition broadly, we have to read and appropriate through our own distinctive lens. While this is true for contemplation, it will be even more so for accounts of contemplative prayer. Such accounts have to rest on evangelical understandings of grace, justification by faith, and the objective nature of Christ's work, but those realities should not undermine a profoundly subjective description of a Christian's experience of prayer. When the objective features of Christian doctrine blind pastoral judgments about the lived reality of the Christian life, then we fail to take seriously both Word and Spirit.

Fourth, from within this call for an evangelical form of contemplation and prayer, the resounding emphasis has been on the personal and relational features of evangelical Christian practice. The contemplative dimension of the Christian life, as noted by Steve Porter, is necessarily a relational participation in God's agapeic love. This means that we have to take seriously the nature of the subjective and experiential realities of the Christian life and, according to biblical wisdom, come to speak meaningfully about our lived experience of God for the sake of the church. The focus, importantly, is not on the generation of a subjective state; rather, the focus is on the objective work of God to give himself in love to the believer. The believer's openness to this reality, as a response to God's work, is the contemplative calling of sanctification.

Fifth, there is a universal call in this volume to attend to aspects of Scripture that have been (broadly speaking) ignored by evangelicals. If one were to consider key doctrines and imagery that tend to be located around contemplation in the tradition, they are areas of neglect by evangelical thinkers and practitioners in our current theological climate, such as the beatific vision, ascent, Sabbath, light, and faith as a kind of spiritual sight. Even love, which is ubiquitous in discussions of the Christian life and faithfulness, is not often addressed concerning the inner dynamics of the human person, or the nature of knowing the love of God that "surpasses knowledge" (Eph 3:19). These are features of Christian doctrine and practice that our Protestant forebears refused to neglect, not only in their pastoral theology, but from within all of their theological work.

Finally, and we think most clearly, this volume testifies to the fact that contemplation and the contemplative life is fundamental to the maturing Christian life. We have argued that it is wrong to think that contemplation is a philosophy or religious act foreign to the Christian faith, or that it is only for those whose personality inclines them to this life. Rather, believers are called into the presence of God as those sanctified by the Spirit to abide in the Son: whether we know it or are consciously aware of this reality, it is going on. The Spirit is always bearing witness to our Spirit that we are sons of God (sons from within Christ's Sonship), from which all our cries of "Abba! Father!" issue forth (Rom 8:15-17). The contemplative life is this life in the Spirit, and along with Paul we want to learn to walk in the Spirit and fully participate in relearning how to be with God who is always with us— how to contemplate God—in all things (Gal 5:25). This means that all of life, and not simply what we think of as our goodness, is caught up in this activity. The presence of God awakens the depth of the human soul, in all of its brokenness, to know God's love poured forth precisely at those points of brokenness. This means that our experience of God's purgative work on the soul is not a sign of God's absence, but of his loving presence. The darkness we experience, and the reality of our souls' lament, is not a sign that God has abandoned his people, but that our experience is moored to Christ's, whose life we are being conformed to.

The goal of this volume has not been to answer all of these issues, or even to raise all of the questions that need answering. Rather, this volume serves to restart a conversation that has deep roots in our own evangelical tradition. There has been a dearth of pastoral and spiritual insights concerning evangelical contemplation and prayer because it was falsely assumed that these conversations were outside the bounds of our church context. Unsurprisingly, the failure to attend deeply to our forebears has led many in the evangelical church to more worldly forms of spirituality and self-help models of personal growth that are antithetical to the gospel. This volume sets up a different way to have this conversation, one we hope will fuel more profound insights into a lived description of Christian maturity in Christ.

What we see throughout this volume is not a call by evangelicals to push one technique over another, or to see any one spiritual practice as the solve-all discipline for Christian faithfulness. Rather, the focus of these essays has been on a proper articulation of God's salvation and the Christian's embrace of God in his saving work. Far from being a subversive attempt for New Age or Eastern spirituality to undermine biblical Christianity, this volume has been a call to recover a truly biblical spirituality along the same contours as our evangelical forebears. Importantly, this will look differently than a less-is-always-better approach of Biblicism, but evangelicals have always seen that approach as unbiblical in its articulation of the Christian life and doctrine. Scripture points Christians to real wisdom and discernment in the spiritual life, and the church must continually wrestle with the lived reality of that calling. Today, this means much discernment concerning what is often passed on as Christian spirituality, but equally, it means that we come to our Christian heritage remembering that all is ours in Christ. This is not a call to accept uncritically, but to embrace the height, length, depth, and breadth of the love of God known in Christ Jesus by the Spirit.

CONTRIBUTORS

Hans Boersma (Utrecht University, ThD) is the J. I. Packer Professor of Theology at Regent College.

Ryan Brandt (Southern Baptist Theological Seminary, PhD) is assistant professor of Christian history and theology at Grand Canyon Theological Seminary and also serves as the managing editor of the *Journal of Biblical and Theological Studies.*

Simon Chan (University of Cambridge, PhD) was the former Earnest Lau Professor of Systematic Theology and now in his retirement is a part-time faculty member at Trinity Theological College in Singapore.

Diane Chandler (Regent University, PhD) serves as an associate professor at the Regent University School of Divinity.

Ashley Cocksworth (University of Cambridge, Trinity College, PhD) is a senior lecturer in theology and practice at the University of Roehampton, UK.

John H. Coe (University of California, Irvine, PhD) is the director of the Institute for Spiritual Formation at Talbot School of Theology and professor of spiritual theology and philosophy at Rosemead Graduate School of Psychology at Biola University.

Evan B. Howard (Graduate Theological Union, PhD) is the founder and director of Spirituality Shoppe, an Evangelical Center for the Study of Christian Spirituality. He is an adjunct professor of philosophy and religion at Colorado Mesa University and other institutions.

Greg Peters (St. Michaels College, University of Toronto, PhD) is associate professor of medieval and spiritual theology in the Torrey Honors Institute of Biola University.

Steven L. Porter (University of Southern California, PhD) is professor of theology and philosophy at Talbot School of Theology and Rosemead School of Psychology (Biola University). He also serves as the managing editor of the *Journal of Spiritual Formation and Soul Care.*

Tom Schwanda (Durham University, PhD) is associate professor of Christian formation and ministry at Wheaton College.

Glen G. Scorgie (University of St. Andrews, PhD) is professor of theology at Bethel Seminary.

Kyle C. Strobel (University of Aberdeen, PhD) is associate professor of spiritual theology at Talbot School of Theology, Biola University.

James Wilhoit (Northwestern University, PhD) is professor of core studies and Scripture Press Chair of Christian Formation and Ministry at Wheaton College.

GENERAL INDEX

active, 59, 76, 79, 93, 100, 121, 242
affections, 63-64, 69, 168, 268
Aquinas, 56, 63, 88, 189, 210
ascent, 72, 86, 88, 92, 101, 168, 172, 178, 221
    mental 22, 27, 30
ascetic, 29-30, 41-42, 100, 111, 113, 242, 253, 258, 261
attentiveness, 100-102, 227, 233, 268
Augustine, 71, 88, 122
beatific vision, 101, 167, 170, 176, 180, 193, 197-200, 206-7, 213, 216
Bernard, 66-71, 102, 183
Calvin, 78, 86-88, 84, 105, 146
creator/creation, 61, 73, 84, 105, 123, 143, 167, 214, 249
Dante, 68, 71-72
delight, 64, 102, 105, 107, 109, 112, 123, 189, 253
desire 60, 69, 84, 92-93, 109-10, 113, 120-21, 123-24, 154, 178, 226
distractions, 41-42, 45-46, 53, 227-28
Edwards, 1, 5, 8, 12, 98-99, 101, 104-8, 112, 166-68, 187, 207, 212-13, 283
effort, 23, 28-30, 43, 46, 89, 93, 101, 155
Evagrius, 38-42, 233
experience 41, 43, 63, 72, 100, 105, 107-8, 120, 144, 148, 178, 198, 202
gift, 44, 88-89, 102, 124
grace, 44, 63, 69, 71-72, 81-84, 88-89, 94, 102, 107, 123, 142, 174, 190
Gregory of Nyssa, 121, 186, 192, 199, 221
Holy Spirit, 8, 25, 27, 44, 52, 68, 78, 81-82, 87, 100, 102, 114, 128, 130, 141-43, 145-47, 152, 154, 164, 167-68, 172, 174, 196, 199, 201, 226-27, 246-47, 253-54
    as agent/conduit of contemplation, 31, 33, 54, 82, 134, 143, 165, 169, 177, 179, 181, 230
immaterial/invisible, 43, 46, 61-62, 72
Jesus Christ, 8, 74, 73, 78, 81-83, 87, 106, 118-19, 123-24, 127-28, 133, 142, 144-45, 150, 152,

155-57, 163, 168, 170-71, 174, 186-88, 195, 204-8, 230, 233, 246, 249, 263
    as beloved/end of contemplation, 101-3, 107, 113, 115, 117, 179
justification, 75, 183, 201
lectio divina, 194-96
love, 68-70, 100, 103, 110, 116-17, 120-25, 143-44, 150, 152, 168, 179, 189-90, 208, 215
maturity 42, 46, 50, 53
medieval, 57, 59-60, 120
meditation, 30, 40, 41, 100, 107, 110, 126, 189, 237, 242, 268
mindfulness, 231
mystical, 62, 75, 106, 120
Nicene, 11, 20, 24-25, 27
opening, 30-33, 100, 240
Origenic, 20, 39-40, 82
passions, 41-46, 53, 67, 129-30, 132
Paul, 81, 103, 112, 118, 128, 143-44, 150, 152-60, 172, 190, 208
purity/purification, 64, 70, 79, 121, 125, 207
Richard of St. Victor, 60
revelation, 128, 142, 169, 180, 190, 206, 221, 208, 214, 243
    basis for contemplation, 11, 23, 27-28, 30, 46, 63, 123, 168
rhythm, 40, 80-81, 93, 135
sanctification, 141,147, 178, 183
Scripture, 40, 41, 47-50, 52, 74, 76, 85, 100, 102, 107, 117, 126, 145-46, 227, 237
self-knowledge, 66-67, 84
solitude, 106, 124, 134, 230
soul, 20, 22, 25, 33, 61, 65, 71, 121, 197, 285
    as participant in contemplation, 88, 101, 109-10, 125, 181, 192, 266
third heaven, 60, 103, 112
thoughtless, 45, 50, 180, 228
unity, 79, 82, 103, 119-21, 123, 146, 148, 163, 169, 172, 188, 205, 230
virtue, 44, 64, 67, 77, 121, 123, 148, 151, 209
wordless, 37, 41, 46, 47-49, 180

SCRIPTURE INDEX

OLD TESTAMENT

Genesis
1:31, *73*
28, *58*
28–29, *57*
28:12, *57*
28:16, *58*
29, *58*
29:11, *58*
29:16, *58*
29:26, *58*

Exodus
2:24, *218*
3:1, *218, 220*
3:2, *218*
3:4, *218*
3:6, *218*
3:14, *205*
13:21, *218*
19:11, *218*
19:16, *218*
19:18, *218*
19:21, *218*
20:1–23:33, *218*
20:21, *121*
24:1, *219*
24:9, *220*
24:10, *219*
24:18, *219*
25–31, *219*
33:2, *219*
33:7, *220*
33:9, *205, 219*
33:11, *219, 222*
33:14, *219*
33:16, *223*

33:18, *197, 219, 222*
33:19, *220*
33:20, *220*
33:23, *220*
34:6, *220*
35–40, *219*
40:34, *205, 223*
40:38, *223*

Leviticus
25:4, *92*

Deuteronomy
5:16, *284*
21:23, *127*
34:10, *103*

Judges
13:22, *175*

1 Kings
8:10, *205*
8:12, *190*
19:11, *49*
19:12, *103*

Job
11:7, *47*
31:1, *232*
38:1, *191*
42:3, *191*

Psalms
1:2, *30*
4:4, *48*
8, *231*
8:4, *231*
16:11, *116, 147*

19:1, *86*
22:14, *126*
27:4, *102, 120, 170, 189, 199*
34:8, *34, 193*
36, *176*
36:9, *176*
37:4, *34*
37:7, *34, 48, 103*
42:1, *34, 103*
46:10, *47*
50:2, *187*
62:1, *47*
62:5, *47*
63:1, *103*
73:25, *109*
73:28, *109*
86:11, *117*
88, *47*
94:17, *47*
101:3, *232*
119:11, *30*
119:16, *30*
121, *181*
121:1, *181*
131, *48, 233*
131:1, *48, 202*
131:2, *48*
131:3, *48*
139:1, *120*
139:6, *190*
139:17, *190*
145:3, *190*

Proverbs
2:2, *233*
4:21, *233*
4:23, *233*

5:15, *258*
9:10, *179*

Isaiah
26:3, *151*
40:13, *47*
40:28, *47, 190*
53:5, *127, 129*
53:7, *47*
60:9, *187*
63:10, *152*

Jeremiah
1:5, *120*
31:31, *34*

Lamentations
3:26, *48*

Ezekiel
1:28, *216*
2, *60*
28:12, *187*
31:8, *187*
31:9, *187*

Amos
5:13, *48*

Habakkuk
2:18, *48*
2:20, *48*

Zephaniah
1:7, *48*

Zechariah
2:6, *48*
2:13, *48*

New Testament

Matthew
3:17, *176*
5–7, *150*
5:8, *207*
6, *155, 159*
6:1, *155, 156*
6:2, *155, 156*
6:4, *155*
6:5, *155, 156*
6:6, *155, 156*
6:9, *79, 156*
6:16, *155, 156*
6:18, *155*
6:25, *150*
6:26, *150*
6:28, *150*
6:32, *150*
7:7, *183*
7:22, *145*
8:1, *129*
9:18, *129*
10:38, *127*
11:27, *187*
13:44, *218*
14:23, *157*
16:24, *127*
20:29, *129*
22:36, *60*
23:25, *145*

Mark
2:3, *129*
7:31, *129*
8:33, *158*
8:34, *127, 128*
14:35, *49*

Luke
1:48, *231*
2:19, *104, 196*
6:12, *49*
8:26, *129*
9:23, *127*
10, *59*
10:27, *51*
10:38, *59*
10:39, *104*
10:42, *104*

11:2, *79*
11:11, *255*
14:27, *127*
22:42, *163*
22:44, *163*
23:48, *164*
24:49, *255*

John
1:4, *205*
1:9, *205*
1:14, *205, 249*
1:18, *161, 175*
3:16, *2, 205*
4:23, *73*
5:37, *161*
6:35, *195*
6:46, *175, 178, 180*
6:50, *205*
8:12, *205*
9:39, *145*
10:30, *204*
12:45, *204*
13–17, *203*
13:20, *204*
14–17, *103, 146, 187*
14:2, *204*
14:6, *204, 205*
14:7, *204, 222*
14:9, *173, 176, 204, 213, 222*
14:16, *144, 254*
14:18, *144*
14:19, *144*
14:20, *188*
14:21, *144*
14:22, *144*
14:23, *103, 144, 187*
14:27, *150*
15, *102*
15:1, *120*
15:4, *147, 148, 174*
15:7, *147, 148*
15:9, *147, 148*
15:11, *147*
16:12, *146*
16:27, *182*
17:17, *146*
17:20, *34*
17:21, *103, 187*

17:24, *103, 187*
17:26, *171, 175, 182*
19:8, *47*
19:30, *181*

Acts
1:4, *255*
2:42, *156*
2:45, *156*
7:54, *104*
7:55, *197*
10:9, *50*
17:16-23, *118*
17:28, *119*
17:34, *276*

Romans
1:18, *28*
1:20, *62*
3:12, *28*
5:5, *6, 143, 178*
5:10, *128*
5:18, *28*
6:13, *159*
8, *81, 82, 87, 174*
8:1, *179*
8:6, *150, 201*
8:9, *201, 254*
8:14, *32*
8:15, *28, 36, 285*
8:16, *145, 146*
8:26, *6, 32, 50, 54, 81, 174, 182*
8:32, *128*
8:34, *157*
11:33, *47, 187, 190*
11:36, *175*
12:1, *159*

1 Corinthians
1:11, *154*
1:17, *128*
1:18, *127*
1:30, *183*
2:2, *128*
2:5, *154*
2:10, *211*
2:13, *153*
2:14, *28*
2:16, *47*
3:1, *50, 153*

3:3, *153*
3:16, *254*
3:21, *4*
7:34, *152*
8:3, *147*
11:23, *129*
13:1, *208*
13:8, *192, 193*
13:9, *208*
13:12, *10, 160, 170, 175, 200, 208, 209, 210, 217, 220, 222*
13:13, *209*

2 Corinthians
3:18, *104, 177, 198, 222*
4:6, *177*
4:18, *183*
5:14, *143*
5:17, *143*
8:9, *163*
11:14, *53*
12:1, *59, 103*
12:2, *50, 112*

Galatians
2:20, *103, 189*
3:1, *164*
3:3, *154*
4:4, *171*
4:6, *143, 145, 146*
4:9, *147*
5, *8, 154*
5:16, *32, 154*
5:17, *154*
5:19, *46*
5:22, *151*
5:25, *8, 144, 155, 285*
6:14, *128*
37, *103*

Ephesians
1:4, *175*
1:17, *33, 34, 35, 176*
1:18, *34, 164*
1:20, *157*
2:1, *28*
2:5, *35*
2:16, *128*
2:18, *168, 169*

2:19, *187*
3:14, *7, 33*
3:16, *28, 32, 33, 152*
3:17, *33, 36, 104, 147,*
   189
3:18, *33, 152, 190*
3:19, *7, 33, 35, 52, 164,*
   182, 285
4:14, *50*
4:17, *171*
4:17–5:4, *46*
4:30, *152*
5:18, *35, 152*
6:17, *146*

Philippians
2:8, *129*
2:12, *33, 35*
3:13, *183*
3:14, *181*
4:4, *233*
4:7, *150*
4:8, *6, 232*
4:9, *156, 159, 160*

Colossians
1:15, *158*
1:17, *158*
1:19, *29, 152*
1:20, *128*
1:27, *30*
1:28, *32*
2:2, *30*
2:3, *159*
2:6, *104, 157, 189*

2:8, *29, 30, 158*
2:9, *29, 152*
2:10, *30, 159*
2:11, *30*
2:16, *30*
2:20, *29*
3, *6, 151, 157, 158, 170*
3:1, *157, 164, 172, 184*
3:2, *232*
3:3, *120, 172, 175, 184*
3:5, *158, 159*
3:12, *158*
3:15, *150*
3:18, *29*

1 Thessalonians
4:11, *47*
5:17, *9*
5:19, *152*

1 Timothy
2:1, *49*
2:2, *47*
2:8, *46, 49*
4:13, *254*
5:5, *51*
6:16, *190*

2 Timothy
3:16, *28*
4:16, *164*

Titus
3:15, *28*

Hebrews
1:1, *28*
1:2, *206*
1:3, *146*
2:17, *171*
3:1, *233*
4:3, *94*
4:9, *87*
4:12, *28, 146, 182*
4:13, *176*
4:16, *171*
5:11, *153*
5:12, *50*
6:19, *171, 181*
7:11, *182*
7:19, *171*
7:25, *171, 174*
7:26, *182*
8:1, *171*
8:5, *171*
9:24, *174*
10:22, *46*
12:2, *104, 130*
13:21, *87*

James
3:1, *253*

1 Peter
1:8, *164*
1:23, *146*
2:2, *146*
2:9, *176*
4:7, *233*
5:8, *53*

2 Peter
1:3, *198*
1:4, *175, 198*
1:19, *232*

1 John
2:5, *188*
2:28, *209*
2:29, *209*
3:2, *143, 167, 177, 198,*
   209, 211, 212
3:5, *209*
3:8, *209*
3:9, *209*
3:20, *179*
4:7, *209*
4:10, *146*
4:12, *149*
4:15, *174*
4:16, *149*
4:17, *149*
4:18, *179, 230*
4:19, *147*
5:1, *209*

Jude
21, *139, 152*

Revelation
6–16, *49*
8:1, *48, 49*
19:3, *130*
21:3, *143, 160*

Finding the Textbook You Need

The IVP Academic Textbook Selector
is an online tool for instantly finding the IVP books
suitable for over 250 courses across 24 disciplines.

_____

ivpacademic.com

_____